POSITIVELY FIFTH STREET

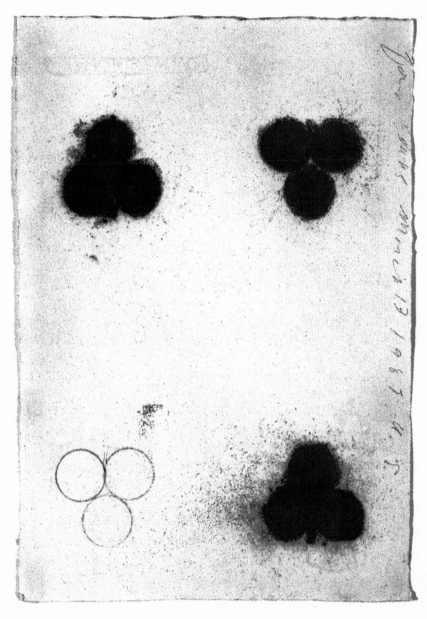

Four Clubs by Donald Sultan, March 13, 1989

POSITIVELY FIFTH STREET

MURDERERS,

CHEETAHS, AND BINION'S

WORLD SERIES OF POKER

JAMES McMANUS

FARRAR, STRAUS, GIROUX

NEW YORK

Farrar, Straus and Giroux
19 Union Square West, New York 10003

Grateful acknowledgment is made to the following for permission to use illustrations and quotations: frontispiece drawing used courtesy Donald Sultan; poster p. 2 courtesy Jed Whitney and *Las Vegas Review Journal*; drawing p. 68 courtesy A. Alvarez; playing cards p. 159 courtesy Gemco Playing Card Co. / Kardwell International; illustration p. 114 courtesy Daphne Koller; photograph p. 36 courtesy Howard Schwartz; photographs p. 183, 224, 270, and 312 courtesy Tom Sexton and Poker Masterpieces; photograph p. 206 courtesy B&G Publishers; photographs p. 147, 338, 354, and 368 courtesy Jeff Scheid and *Las Vegas Review Journal*. Excerpts from Mary Ellen Glass's interview with Benny Binion used courtesy University of Nevada Oral History Program. Excerpts of works by Peter Costa, Andy Glazer, and Nolan Dalla all used courtesy the authors; by Norm Clarke and John L. Smith, courtesy the author and *Las Vegas Review Journal*; by Susan Wheeler, courtesy the author and Four Way Books; by T.J. Cloutier, Tom McEvoy, and Dana Smith, courtesy of Cardsmith. Excerpts from "Rock Music" from *Subhuman Redneck Poems* by Les Murray, copyright © 1997 by Les Murray, and from "Symposium" from *Poems: 1968–1998* by Paul Muldoon, copyright © 2001 by Paul Muldoon, reprinted by permission of Farrar, Straus and Giroux, LLC.

Library of Congress Cataloging-in-Publication Data
McManus, James.
    Positively 5th street : murderers, Cheetahs, and Binion's world series of poker / James McManus.— 1st ed.
        p. cm.
    Includes bibliographical references (p.   ) and index.
    ISBN 0-374-23648-8 (hc : alk. paper)
    1. World Series of Poker.   2. Poker—Competitions—United States.
    I. Title: Positively fifth street: murderers, Cheetahs, and Binion's world series of poker.   II. Title.
GV1254 .M37 2003
794.41'2—dc21

                                                          2002033882

Designed by Debbie Glasserman

www.fsgbooks.com

1   3   5   7   9   10   8   6   4   2

in memory of my son, James, 1979–2001

CONTENTS

POSITIVELY FIFTH STREET

Sandy **MURPHY**   Rick **TABISH**   John **MOMOT**   Louis **PALAZZO**   & Ted **BINION**

Everyone
Is Suspect...

Everything
Is For Sale...

And It's All
Too Sleazy...

L.V.
Confidential

ULTIMATE SIN CITY TALE OF GREED AND LUST

THE END

Sex is a Nazi. The students all knew
this at your school. To it, everyone's subhuman
for parts of their lives. Some are all their lives.
You'll be one of those if these things worry you.
— LES MURRAY, "Rock Music"

Come, you spirits
That tend on mortal thoughts, unsex me here . . .
— LADY MACBETH

A nubile blonde squats on her boyfriend's bare chest and he's too stoned to do much about it. Nipple clamps? No sir, not this time. Even one would just be, like, way generous. Seizing him by the neck with both hands, she raises her shins from the carpet and presses her full dead weight onto his rib cage and solar plexus, forcing more air from his lungs. How's *that* feel? As she rocks back and forth, they lock eyes. "You like that?" she asks, flirty as ever. "How come?" Her name is Sandra Murphy. When she wears clothes, her taste runs to Gucci, Victoria's Secret, Versace. Her latest ride is the SL 500, in black. She used to work at a high-end sports car emporium in Long Beach, so she knows what the good stuff is. After that gig she moved to Las Vegas and danced topless professionally, but she hasn't had to work in three years—not since she danced for the guy she is currently laying her hands on. "My old man," she calls him sometimes, or "my husband," especially since she moved in. And she would sort of like to get married. Settle down, kids, that whole deal. Not right now, though. *Because you, you've got time*, as Liz Phair advises in "Polyester Bride," one of Sandy's all-time favorite songs. Time to get rich, see the world, party hearty. And lately she's been having the time of her used-to-be-not-so-great life. Million-dollar mansion, cute boyfriend, bionic sex, Benz, plus she's keeping her looks, above all. That's the key. In 1989 she was runner-up for the title of Miss Bellflower, a south-central suburb of Los Angeles. That was nine years ago, when Sandy was seventeen, but she maintains her dancer's physique by working out five days a week, and she still keeps the sash in her closet. Most men, her boyfriend included, cannot get enough of her, especially the way she looks now. She is lithe, wet, determined, on top.

The boyfriend, Ted Binion, is heaving for air. He used to run the Horseshoe Casino with his father and brother, but those days are long gone. The Nevada State Gaming Commission threw its Black Book at Ted a few months ago, banning him from even setting foot in his family's venerable gaming house. Plus his heroin habit has been shutting him down sexually, closing him off from the world, getting him into real fixes. He's promised himself, promised Sandy, promised just about everyone (at least three or four times) that he's going to kick, stick to booze, but he isn't so sure that he can anymore. What he is goddamn sure of is that he's in serious pain. In fact, he could die any moment here. Wrenched into a bone-on-metal knot against the small of his back, his wrists are fastened together with the rhinestone-studded handcuffs he and Sandy picked up a few months ago at a boutique in Caesars Palace, down on the Strip. Clamps, thumbcuffs, clothespins, wet strips of rawhide—this stuff has been part of their routine since they first got together, a day he's exhausted from cursing. It was part of what *got* them together, but whose fault was that? They'd always loved boosting their pain-pleasure thresholds with pot, XTC, Ketel martinis, tequila, sometimes bringing one or two of Sandy's girlfriends into the picture. This time Sandy got the drop on him, and she's used it to cross a big line. Ted doesn't have too much fight left, however, so there isn't much else he can do about it. Fifty-five years old, he's been smoking cigarettes, using street drugs, and drinking extravagantly since he was a teenager. Right now—just after nine on the morning of September 17, 1998—he has three balloons' worth of tar heroin and eighty-two Xanax in his stomach and large intestine, some of it already coursing through his arteries, triggering the soporific enzymes he was hoping this time wouldn't take. He's always had a weakness for what he calls Sandy's pretty titties, and he's getting an eyeful right now, whether he wants to or not. In spite of the Xanax, the heroin, and the fact that she's choking him—maybe these things have all canceled each other, he thinks, like waves out of phase—there's really no denying the low, distant stir of an erection. It's a million miles away now, thank God, already receding at the speed of light squared . . .

Because Sandy's *new* boyfriend, Rick Tabish, kneels on the carpet behind Binion's head, facing Sandy. Standing up, Rick is tall, dark, and, to Sandy's mind, handsome. Six two, two thirty, with springy hair, beady brown eyes. Plenty strong. A star linebacker in high school and college back in Montana, he is now thirty-three, getting soft through the middle, hairline receding above his temples, developing confidence issues. For non–early bloomers, thirty-three can become the age of miracles—the time to start a family, launch a new venture, make partner, publish your first novel, even found your own worldwide religion. For the last couple of years, though, Rick's been afraid that his best days are a decade behind him, and he desperately needs to make sure that he proves himself wrong. Because what the fuck else is he doing here? People around Las Vegas know him as Ted Binion's friend. They met manning side-by-side urinals at Piero's, and since then they've partied at Delmonico's, the Voodoo Lounge, and plenty of strip clubs together, both with and without Sandy Murphy. When Ted needed a place to stash six tons of silver bullion, he hired Rick's company, MRT Transport, to dig and construct a secret underground vault on Ted's ranch in Pahrump. They used an MRT truck to haul the bars of silver from the Horseshoe's vault out to the new one, along with a few million bucks' worth of rare coins, paper currency, and $5,000 Horseshoe chips. Rick and Ted, in fact, are the only two people who know how to get at that vault. The ranch is now managed by Rick's latest partner, Boyd Mattsen, and its front gate is guarded by peacocks. The peacocks were Teddy's idea.

The story gets better and better, then worse. Much, much worse. Less than ten minutes ago, for example, Rick and Sandy tried to have sex alongside—even, for a regrettable moment or two, on top of—Ted's handcuffed torso. If junkie Ted couldn't fuck her, then Rick would take charge, and Ted would have to watch them, then die. That was their logic. Or, more accurately, their syllogism, if either of them knew what that word meant.

Ted knew. When he wasn't out (or back home) raising hell, he read books and magazines as though his life depended on it. Civil War, western history, biographies of Sherman and Grant, Carl Sandburg's biography of Lincoln. He loved local and national politics, public television, the History and Discovery channels. He even loved reading the dictionary. So exactly how had a smart guy like him gotten himself in this fix?

Ninety minutes earlier, Rick and Sandy forced him to choke down nearly half a liter of tar heroin after lacing it with a hundred and seven 50 mg Xanax tablets. They'd handcuffed him at gunpoint and told him to lie on the floor, on his back. After cursing them out, even snickering at their gall, he complied. Still wearing shorts and a navel-baring T-shirt, Sandy straddled Ted's chest and yanked up his shirt, something she'd done countless times—only now, instead of tweaking his nipples, she was pinching his nostrils together, leaving him no choice but to open his mouth. Careful not to scratch the esophagus, Rick used a turkey baster to squirt the gunky beige concoction past Ted's teeth, down his throat. The stuff reminded Sandy of melting brown pearls, like some stupid mini-sculpture you'd find in New York or LA. In the meantime, gagging and desperate, Ted was offering her $5 million to get off him, and she could tell from the sound of his voice that he meant it. He'd pay her. They could kill Rick right now in self-defense, then get married, have a baby—a girl baby, maybe, named Tiffany—and never even have to talk about this crazy Rick bullshit again. All she had to do was take the 9-mm pistol they both knew was hidden in the bench of her white baby grand piano and blow Rick away. (Ted and some cops had taught her to shoot at that range, and later she'd practiced on bottles and cacti in the desert.) Ted was begging her, calling her "baby." That hurt.

Sandy's outward response was to smirk, glance at Rick, shake her head. Even so, she was tempted. As Ted kept on pleading, her jangly nerves made her cackle and pick up a cardboard Halloween goblin. The goblin, with R.I.P. stenciled across the front in white-lightning letters, was left over from last year's trick-or-treat decorations, and she thought it might add a nice touch; that's why she'd tossed it onto the sofa last night in the first place. "You're already dead," she said now, jouncing the goblin in front of both men. Even Rick, who had beaten and tortured people before to get money, was taken aback by the ghoulish dementia of this weird cardboard *Totentanz*. Yikes!

While Sandy puppeteered the death dance on his half-naked chest, Ted was reduced to proposing to set Rick up in a series of ad hoc construction projects, overpaying him lavishly. "Whatever you want, man. Enough to, you know, change your life."

"Change my *life*!?" Rick snorted, "Change *my* life?!" while Sandy jeered, "Rest in peace, motherfucker."

"I'm about to start laying the pipe to your *wife*," Rick added more coolly, making the rhyme without meaning to. He undid his belt. "*Keep* laying the pipe to her, Teddy, is what I should say." And Teddy had swallowed enough of this gunk, Rick decided as he watched Sandy inch off her T-shirt. Three and a half creamy doses. If that didn't do it, then fuck him.

But the plan to sexually taunt their handcuffed friend while he slowly gave in to the drugs never quite got off the ground. Even after Sandy's elaborate striptease, Rick couldn't keep his erection "because of the vibe around here." No faggot, no warlord, Rick still had no spur (in the cowboy or Shakespearean sense) to prick the sides of his intent, but only his vaulting ambition—his ambition, punnily enough, to loot Teddy's vault, shove his prick into his woman. But his half-erect penis had accidentally grazed Ted's warm hip, zapping both men with a nastier shock than they'd get from leather soles on a carpet—this as Sandy pushed open one of Ted's eyelids, just to make sure he at least caught a glimpse of their triumph. How's about *them* apples, Teddy?

You jealous? (Teddy Ruxton Bear is what she called him sometimes. Not this morning.) But prick then zapped hip, just before those heart-attack knocks on the glass . . .

This was Tom Loveday, Ted and Sandy's gardener, rapping on the window that looked back out toward the pool. Loveday had arrived at five before nine for his regular Wednesday morning stint on their grounds *that Sandy had totally spaced on.* Loveday was trimming the hedges along the back of the house when he noticed that Ted's dogs, Princess and Pig, were oddly lethargic; instead of bounding up to meet him as usual, they stayed hunkered on the patio, whimpering. Loveday had already sensed something was off because the drapes of Ted's den were pulled closed for the first time in the twelve years he'd worked here. Shielding his eyes from the glare, he tried to peer into the den while rapping a knuckle against the warm glass. He couldn't be sure, but he thought he heard two muffled curses.

So now, using the thumb and index finger of his left hand, it is Rick who holds Ted's nostrils together, using his right palm to clamp the mouth shut, his knees as a vise for the head, while Sandy compresses the lungs and chokes off the windpipe. Even in his opiated and oxygen-deprived delirium, Ted flops and arches his back, bucking so furiously that Sandy slips off him. Climbing back on, she's a little freaked out that, despite what Rick promised, doing Ted has become kind of unpleasant. Rick, for his part, would love to just beat Ted to death with the butt of one of his pistols, but he knows that the marks would defeat their own purpose. This begs the question, of course, of how the threat of a gunshot or two had persuaded Binion to submit to the cuffs, not to mention his shivering embarrassment at the discovery and *use* of one of his sex toys. Should've let them shoot me, Ted realizes now. Would've had a better chance of making it through this and watching them *pay*. He also understands that because it was only yesterday that he himself scored the heroin and filled the Xanax prescription, a coroner may well declare his death an accidental OD or, worse, a suicide. The previous evening Ted had instructed his estate lawyer, James Brown: "Take Sandy out of the will if she doesn't kill me tonight. If I'm dead, you'll know what happened." Yet there may not have been enough time to execute the order; even though he'd given

Brown the word, didn't testamentary amendments need a third-party witness to be legally binding? Plus Brown might've thought he was kidding! Ted changed his will all the time, and Brown often gave him a couple of days to cool off before bringing him papers to sign. Ted's net worth is between $50 and $70 million, and with Oscar Goodman representing her, Sandy might wind up with all of it; she was already getting the house and $300,000 in cash. What Ted wanted now was for every last dime to go to Bonnie, his nineteen-year-old daughter, who'd left home three weeks ago to begin her first year of college in Texas. But he didn't need to die for her to get it.

Digging his bare heels into the carpet, Ted bucks and thrashes with all he's got left, causing Rick and Sandy to step up their efforts. "Change *your* life!" growls Rick under his breath, viciously twisting Ted's nose. When the meat of his thumb gets smeared with wet mucus, it pisses him off even more. "That's right, you decrepit old fuck!" Sandy hangs on with her knees like she's breaking a stallion, rocking down into her grip on Ted's throat. Capillaries in his eyelids have ruptured, his face and neck brightening from pink-tan to purple. And still she holds on, keeps her balance. Rick grunts and curses through his teeth, remembering not to make noise but forgetting again when his forehead bangs hard into Sandy's. "You—*fuck*!" To keep from crying out herself, Sandy grinds her molars together and blinks back the sting, but the squeak and whine of her exertions go a half octave higher.

Thirty-five more airless seconds—the time it takes a boat to go under completely, for the last waves and bubbles to clear—before Ted loses consciousness, though his thigh and neck muscles continue to spasm. Misreading these as further resistance, his tormentors keep rocking forward. Sandy leans a bit to her left, and Rick to *his* left, so their heads won't collide anymore.

A long minute later: no heartbeat, no spasms. Something else, though. Something so bad Sandy yelps. Breathing through their mouths, she and Rick have little choice but to listen as Ted's bowel gurgles and splutters, the appalling sounds audible above the buzz of Loveday's hedge clippers out beyond the swimming pool. Even so, Rick keeps the pressure on Ted's nose and mouth, just in case the fucker's playing possum. Sandy hopes Rick will stop now, let go, but says nothing. They glance into each other's eyes, then away. Rick believes Sandy is crying. Both of them are happy, at least, to hear no more knocks on the window.

They take off the handcuffs. One to an ankle, they drag the body across the room and arrange it faceup on a sleeping mat. They intend to make it appear as though Ted had been watching TV as he turned out the lights on himself. Classic rock videos? Porn? Unable to find what they want, Rick turns off the set. They arrange Ted's black Levi's, his loafers, an almost full pack of Vantage cigarettes, three lighters, the remote control, and the empty Xanax bottle—all within easy arm's reach of the mat. But now they discover *the trail,* a dark, wet, brown dotted line across the moth-colored carpet. At first Tabish thought it was gunk that had spilled from the baster, but no. Murphy understood right away.

Another thing creeping them out is that Ted isn't moving. At all. A volcano two minutes ago, now nothing. Extinct. The stillness and silence make them leery of even glancing in his direction, yet how can they not? Tabish has personally never seen the cocksucker looking so dignified. To Murphy, Ted seems—what is the word for it?

Regal.

"Your boyfriend is leaking," notes Tabish.

Murphy laughs, catching herself. "Not funny," she says.

It takes them a good twenty minutes to expunge the dark trail—no soap, just a couple of rags and warm water—but they won't be able to tell how thorough they were until that area of carpeting dries. Murphy composes herself, calls the housekeeper, Mary Montoya-Gascoigne. Adopting her lady-of-the-house persona, she tells her maid not to come to work today because "Ted isn't feeling well." Trying to think even further ahead, like a lawyer, she asks herself: Isn't that technically accurate?

Out in the garage they empty Ted's safe of jewelry and cash, his collections of coins and paper currency. Everything. But something's not right, Tabish thinks. *What's wrong with this picture?* Then: *Whoa, baby, I've got it.* He fishes around in the jingling booty and plucks out a Mercury dime. Grinning in spite of himself, he places it heads up, dead center, on the safe's middle shelf, a token of his gleeful contempt.

To round up the rest of the loot more efficiently, Murphy snatches a couple of pillowcases from the linen closet next to the dining room. She tosses one over to Tabish, and they ransack the rest of the 8,000-square-foot house, searching low and high for bundles of currency, jewelry, vials of loose diamonds, tubes filled with old silver dollars that Murphy knows Ted kept hidden at home, though she didn't always know exactly where. Teddy never trusted banks, hated bankers. "Weasels," he called them. What he trusted were gold coins and bars of silver, though he usually kept a quarter of a million or so in hundred-dollar bills stashed in the outboard motor of the fishing boat parked in the garage, and she dashes back out there to jimmy it.

Bingo.

Eventually she and Tabish take a shower together, try making a version of love. Doesn't work. This makes twice in one day, a first in their eight months together. I just hope, Murphy thinks before cutting off the thought with the edge of her palm. Way too horrible. But if these didn't count as extenuating circumstances, Tabish wonders aloud, then what does?

Once Loveday departs, Murphy drives Tabish to the MRT lot over on Sixth Street, where he'll commandeer the earthmoving equipment he needs to dig up the vault in Pahrump.

"Adios," he says, kissing her. "Love you."

"Love you too." Her forehead still throbs. She's exhausted. "Bye-bye."

"We did it."

"Yeah," she says, delicately smoothing the bump on *his* forehead, "we did."

This is how I imagine Ted Binion's murder and its immediate aftermath. The scenario gradually came together as I pored over accounts of his death on the web sites of the *Los Angeles Times* and the *Las Vegas Review-Journal* and *Sun*, and followed the legal proceedings on Court TV. I interviewed neither Sandy Murphy nor Rick Tabish, but since they repeatedly denied through attorneys that any such thing had occurred and law enforcement officials believed them, I figured my version (which continues to change as new facts come to light) wasn't any less accurate for my not having talked to the killers. The fact is, they bragged to their friends about doing it, and their friends talked to detectives and, later, to prosecutors. The goblin, the heroin and Xanax, the peacocks, the rhinestones, the curious gardener, the Mercury dime are all facts. I've kept my interpolations as faithful as possible to the newspaper and courtroom revelations about the three people involved. Everything else in this book is a matter of public record.

Undisputed eyewitness accounts, for example, revealed that just before 3 p.m. on September 17, Murphy showed up at the office of Ted's executive assistant, Cathy Rose. Interrupting a Horseshoe business meeting, Murphy made a production of handing Rose a check for the grand sum of $100. The check had been made out to Ted from a couple to whom he'd loaned $300. Murphy then made a point of informing Rose that she'd been up all night with Ted and was going to get a bite to eat now that he'd finally fallen asleep. Why interrupt me, Rose recalls wondering, over this piddling check? To tell me you're going to lunch?

Tabish's phone records show that at 3:47 p.m. he called Murphy's cell phone from his. She was back at what was now *her* Palomino Lane mansion, as bequeathed to her in Ted's will. Tabish and Murphy's conversation lasted three minutes. At 3:53, she punched 911, caught her breath, and began screeching into the receiver that her husband had stopped breathing.

Four minutes later, when firemen and paramedics arrived, they found Ted Binion's body lying faceup on the floor of his den. Rigor mortis had set in along his jaw, and his pupils were dilated. Doll's eyes, they call this condition. He had no vital signs whatsoever. A half-buttoned long-sleeve shirt was pulled up diagonally across his bruised ribs. Autopsy photos also made clear that he had a partial erection under his white Calvin Klein Y-front briefs, and that his backside was horribly fouled.

On his end table four feet away were a glass ashtray, tortoiseshell reading glasses, and a hand-lettered invitation to the Las Vegas premiere of *Mob Law*, a scathing documentary about the career of Oscar Goodman, Ted's friend and former attorney. At the other end of the sofa, on a low wooden bench, lay a Victoria's Secret catalogue addressed to Sandra Murphy, 2438 Palomino Lane, Las Vegas NV 89103, alongside a handwritten note on a white nine-by-twelve envelope: "Teddy, I went to the gym. I couldn't sleep this morning. Love you, Sandy." A diptych of their perfect confederacy.

Make that a triptych. Not only because of Tabish's implicit presence between them, but also because in the bathroom a few feet away detectives found paraphernalia for smoking heroin, including scorched Reynolds Wrap and a hunting knife with black tar heroin smeared on both sides of the blade.

Sandy Murphy was hysterical. "She came running into the room and just about fell on the body," one paramedic reported. She was far enough gone to be packed up and wheeled from the mansion on a stretcher, then taken by ambulance to the emergency room of Valley Hospital. A nurse trained to observe such patients testified that Murphy blubbered and shrieked melodramatically, that her behavior appeared "almost theatrical." She pulled a sheet over her head and kept blurting "boo-hoo-hoo, boo-hoo-hoo-hoo-hoo" in unconvincing fashion, though she calmed down enough to coolly inform a detective that Ted had returned to using heroin back in March after forfeiting his gaming license. She described Ted as suicidal, claiming he had recently stuck a gun into his mouth, had been planning to enter a drug rehabilitation center, and had obtained the fatal prescription for Xanax from Enrique Lacayo. "My neighbor's a doctor," she told the detective between heaving sobs. "And my neighbor used to give him that shit before, when we were . . . and I told him if you ever give him that stuff again . . . and he gave him some more last night." Referring to Ted now, she said, "He told me this was the last time, and he wasn't gonna ever do it again." She also insisted to the detective that, if foul play was involved, even though she didn't think it *was*, then Becky and Nick Behnen were the likeliest suspects. "She said Binion hated his sister and 'most of the rest of his family,' " the detective wrote in his interview notes. "She stated that the Behnen family, and especially Becky, are 'treacherous' and 'lowlifes.' "

Back in Ted's driveway, LVPD Sgt. Jim Young informed reporters that no evidence of foul play had been discovered. No signs of a breakin or struggle, no trauma to the body, no suicide note. The LVPD had arrested Mr. Binion more than once for possession of heroin, and these arrests had led directly to the permanent revocation of his gaming license in March 1998, so Murphy's version of events added up. Sgt. Young continued: "Preliminary results indicate he may have made an ingestion error in regards to medication." Interviews with family members also led detectives to conclude that Ted probably hadn't planned to kill himself. "While it's suspicious," Young added, "it's not suspicious to the point where we are talking about criminal activity."

The *Review-Journal* reported the next morning that Ted was an admitted heroin addict; that his older sister, Barbara, had died of a drug overdose in 1983; and that his father, Benny, had a reputation as a "hard partyer and big-time poker player." Ted's friend Herbert "Fat Herbie" Blitzstein had been the victim of an organized-crime hit in 1997, and police subsequently received tips that Ted might also become a target of violence. Months later, in fact, someone fired several shots at Ted's home and car, and one of the suspects was twenty-year-old Benny Binion Behnen, who could have been responding to threats his uncle had made against his mother. The *Review-Journal* also declared that Ted had been "an acquaintance of P. J. Ribaste, who has ties to organized crime interests in Kansas City."

Augie Gurrola, a member of the Gaming Commission that had passed down the "death sentence" on Ted back in March, expressed his condolences to the Binion family but couldn't help taking one final shot at Ted's lifestyle: "Somehow, sooner or later, it will wear you down. I think for some reason, whatever it was, he always seemed to be going up the wrong street." The celebrated mob mouthpiece Oscar Goodman was interviewed, too. " 'He was one of the best guys I ever met,' Goodman said before scurrying into his car and fleeing a flock of news crews." An *R-J* reporter noted that ownership of the Horseshoe had recently been turned over to Ted's sister Becky Behnen following "a lengthy and heated legal dispute that severed many of the Binion family ties," once again corroborating Murphy's version of things. Ted's older brother, Jack, was out of town and couldn't be reached for comment, but Becky Behnen issued a statement: "My brother's untimely death is just so sad and tragic. Through all of his trials and tribulations, Ted was a caring man, even though as brother and sister we had our sibling differences, as any family will have. But through it all, I loved my brother and I admired his keen intellect, his sense of humor, and the many little things that he would do to help a lot of friends without anyone's knowledge." She concluded: "After I bought the Horseshoe, Ted really looked like he was finally ready to accept some dramatic changes in his life, and so this sudden loss really has an even greater impact on our family."

Neighbors and friends were besieged for reactions. One appeared on the front page of the next morning's *R-J*, along with a photo of a dark-haired, muscular young man standing in Ted's driveway. " 'I never had any bad dealings with the man—what a tragedy,' said a shaken Rick Tabish, who was a friend of Binion's. 'I know he was trying really hard to change his life.' "

To Christ the King Roman Catholic Church for the funeral. Seven hundred people showed up for the service, led by the Reverend Bill Kenny, who had known Ted since they were boys. One reporter described the crowd of mourners as "an odd mixture" of "high-stakes gamblers, politicians, civic leaders, wise guys, casino executives and ranch hands, even a topless dancer or two."

Jim Morrison's apocalyptic, Seconal-laced requiem "The End" opened the ceremony, unlikely music for a Catholic service only if you didn't know Ted. It had been a close call, but Bonnie Binion had selected it that morning after sifting through CDs and albums by Dylan, Hendrix, the Stones, Neil Young, Prince, and Pearl Jam, her dad's other favorites. Morrison, of course, was notorious for abusing alcohol, audiences, women, and barbiturates, and for having OD'd in the bathtub of a Left Bank apartment at the age of twenty-seven.

This is the end, my only friend, the end . . .

By the time Francis Ford Coppola employed it in 1979 as the soundtrack to the ritual slaughter of a water buffalo, Col. Kurtz, and the rest of his renegade enclave in the last scene of *Apocalypse Now*, the song had become the anthem not only of nihilistic, suicidal funks but of the bloody-minded depravity of the war in Vietnam and all that was wrong with Amerika. Bone-deep machete slashes crosscut with napalm and war paint: The End. A lit major and UCLA graduate before joining the Doors, Morrison in death had morphed somehow into the hyperseductive voice of Joseph Conrad's heart of darkness. Both Ted and the Lizard King were twenty-four when "The End" was released, and Ted was thirty-six when the movie came out. When he died at fifty-five, the song was a part of his cell structure. Now it was making his outlaw debauchery more glamorous and poetic for his mourners. Whether his brown-haired, bespectacled, fragile-seeming daughter was aware of these associations isn't clear, but certainly her father would have been. No doubt he loved the song, too, but he must have shuddered in his coffin at how much visceral credence it lent to the notion that he'd killed himself, or let himself go, as surely as Morrison had. Even though Hendrix had OD'd as well, at least his acid-flecked R&B cover of "Hey Joe" would have been closer to how Ted was feeling in spirit. *I'm goin' down to shoot my old lady, you know I caught her messin' 'round with another man, and that ain't too cool.* Either that or Hendrix's cover of "All Along the Watchtower," or something off the Stones' *Let It Bleed* . . .

On top of the casket were Ted's favorite brown cowboy boots and white hat, along with his spurs and a lariat. (No handcuffs, of course, rhinestone-studded or otherwise. No lighters or tinfoil.) Floral arrangements featured the Binion family's signature horseshoe fashioned from daisies dyed gold and adorned with a royal flush in clubs. Born in Texas and raised in Nevada and Montana, owner and host of the Horseshoe Casino, Ted was a cowboy and a cardplayer, as well as an old-school rock-and-roll badass and unapologetic enjoyer of dangerous women. His favorite sports were fishing and no-limit Texas hold'em, which during the past twenty-eight years Binion's World Series of Poker had made the most popular version of the game on the planet.

Kill, kill, kill, kill, kill, kill . . .

Surveying the diverse crowd in the pews before him, Rev. Kenny proclaimed: "This shows that Ted was a most affable person and that he was a friend to so many people of all different backgrounds." Kenny admitted that his friend had had a wild streak since he was a teenager, and got some hearty laughter while recounting how Ted had once thrown blue ink on a porous cinder-block wall at school and been forced by the priests to clean it off with a toothbrush. Yet for all its ribald frankness, Kenny's eulogy skipped any mention of Cheetahs, the topless cabaret over on Industrial Road where Ted had met Murphy three and a half years earlier. Some subjects were still out of bounds.

In the front row with Bonnie was her mother, Doris Binion, an ethereal strawberry blonde to whom Ted had been married for twenty-six years. Not far away were his siblings Becky and Jack, who hadn't spoken to each other in almost two years; nor did they speak at the funeral. After their father, Benny, died in 1989, Ted and Jack ran the Horseshoe together until Becky bought them out in '97, and the brothers weren't happy about it. Jack now ran a string of casinos in Illinois, Indiana, and Mississippi, and *Forbes* had started listing him as one of the five hundred wealthiest Americans. He'd long been the shrewd financier while his little brother, Ted, played the rake.

Behind the Binion family sat Las Vegas mayor Jan Laverty Jones, who was running for governor, and the man who wanted to succeed her as mayor, Oscar Goodman. Also on hand to pay his respects was the Strip's supermogul Steve Wynn, a protégé and friend of Ted's father, and dapper, curly-haired Bobby Baldwin, the former world poker champion who had since become president of Wynn's new Bellagio resort. Off to their left, cane in hand, sat two-time world champion Doyle Brunson, author of *Super/System: A Course in Power Poker.* That 1978 bible, passages of which countless players have memorized, is dedicated "to the Binion family for their contribution to Poker." The 350-pound Brunson soon took his turn at the podium to say, "Ted Binion had the whole package: the personality, the looks, the talent, the guts, and the money. He had some problems, but he was one of a kind." Other eulogists spoke of Ted's generosity, intelligence, love of western history, of his gambling spirit and desire to change his life lately.

Rick Tabish was not in attendance. Sandy Murphy and her stepmother, also named Sandy Murphy, arrived about ten minutes after the service began, having spent the previous night at the old Desert Inn. The leggy, dyed-blond former stripper wore a beige Gucci pantsuit and black-on-black Dior sunglasses behind which she audibly wept throughout much of the service. She actually ran sobbing from the church a few minutes before the Mass ended. Oscar Goodman and his partner, David Chesnoff, who now represented her, followed the young woman outside, forming a two-lawyer phalanx to escort her past the photographers.

By the time Ted's coffin was entombed beside his parents in a crypt at the Eden Vale Mausoleum, Clark County coroner Ron Flud had ruled the cause of death "undetermined," while Chief Medical Examiner Lary Simms had declared it the result of an accidental overdose. Neither official, however, was willing to rule out suicide. Flud's toxicology report confirmed lethal levels of Xanax and morphine (a by-product of heroin) in Ted's bloodstream. During the autopsy, Simms drew forty milliliters of gray-brown fluid from the stomach. Ted's fear of needles was well known around Vegas. Even the police were aware that he always got high by "chasing the dragon"—dabbing expensive tar heroin onto the shiny side of tinfoil, holding a lighter beneath the dull side, and inhaling the white smoke that curled off it, something like the tail of a dragon. The question became: How had liquefied heroin, mixed with Xanax no less, found its way into his digestive tract?

In spite of the bad blood between them, Becky Behnen persuaded her dead brother's estate to hire a detective to investigate Murphy and Tabish. Estate lawyers also moved aggressively to bar Murphy from entering Ted's house or inheriting any of his property. Oscar Goodman soon withdrew as Murphy's attorney, citing his decision to run for mayor. Represented now by William Knudsen, Murphy told Gaming Control Board agents that members of the Behnen family had made threats against Ted's life. It was also revealed in probate court that five weeks before Ted died, Murphy had secretly filed a palimony suit demanding $2 million for "services provided" while living with him. Her attorney at the time was Oscar Goodman.

Six months later—on March 5, 1999—as the mayoral campaign heated up, the coroner reclassified Ted's death as a homicide. On

June 8, Goodman defeated nuts-and-bolts city councilman Arnie Adamsen in a 64–36 percent landslide. Less than a week afterward, the new mayor's last client was indicted on charges of first-degree murder, along with Richard Bennett Tabish. Arrested together in Murphy's townhouse at 7 a.m., the couple denied they had been lovers before Binion's death, insisting that even now they were "only good friends." Murphy was placed under house arrest, Tabish held without bond. Rare coins missing from Ted's safe turned up in Montana in the possession of Dennis Rebhein, the brother of Tabish's wife, Mary Jo. Other coins had been bartered to settle the retainers of Chesnoff and Goodman.

During preliminary hearings in August, New York City pathologist Michael Baden testified that Ted Binion didn't die of a heroin overdose but was, in fact, manually suffocated. The chief forensic expert for the congressional committee that investigated the deaths of John Kennedy and Martin Luther King (and in fifteen thousand other murder cases), Dr. Baden had discovered significant errors in Flud's toxicology report. Instead of indicating the amount of Xanax in Ted's blood in milligrams per milliliter, for example, it was listed in nanograms, which is a million times less. Someone had typed "ng" instead of "mg." Ted therefore seemed to have a therapeutic level of the drug in his bloodstream, an amount easily tolerated by most adults. Examining the autopsy photographs, Baden detected petechial hemorrhages inside the victim's lower eyelids. Such hemorrhages form when capillaries have ruptured under pressure, suggesting his throat had been violently compressed. Baden also noted significant bruising around the victim's mouth, as well as small, neat, circular marks that looked like button imprints on the upper chest, and a large bruise on the front of the ribs. Bruises on the wrists were the type most often associated with handcuffs. The defense attorney cross-examining Baden suggested that these bruises could have been caused by a watchband, though the victim was never known to wear more than one watch at a time. Baden pointed out that having practiced forensic pathology for forty years in New York City, he'd seen a lot of handcuff abrasions. That's what these were.

Baden called this method of suffocation *burking*, a stealthy and brutal technique named for William Burke (1792–1829), a determined Scots-Irishman who held his victims' noses while his partner squatted on their chests. Burke had to kill without leaving marks in order to be able to sell the bodies, for ten guineas apiece, to the Royal College of Surgeons. Eventually one of the surgery students recognized a cadaver he was dissecting as his putatively healthy uncle. Found guilty of fifteen murders by a jury of his peers, Burke was hanged in Edinburgh before a passionate throng of witnesses. His body was then donated to the medical school for dissection.

Jury selection in the burking trial of Murphy and Tabish began on March 27, 2000, in the Clark County courtroom of Judge Joseph Bonaventure. Four days later opening statements were presented by prosecutors and defense attorneys just as, one block up Second Avenue in downtown Las Vegas, the thirty-first annual Binion's World Series of Poker was getting under way at the Horseshoe.

♣ ♥

DEAD MONEY

♦ ♠

I'm about to give you all my money . . .
—ARETHA FRANKLIN

Homer! If I had known there were loose women in Las Vegas, I would never have let you go!
—MARGE SIMPSON

While teaching my spring-semester classes at the School of the Art Institute of Chicago, I continued to follow the trial on TV and the web sites of the two Vegas dailies. After six weeks of testimony had been heard, nearly everyone I talked to understood that Murphy and Tabish were guilty, but most folks still doubted that either or both would be convicted of murder. No eyewitnesses, no smoking weapon, too many other plausible suspects, expensive attorneys defending an attractive young couple in love. Some people were also surprised that, so far, neither defendant had turned state's evidence against the other. And no one could forget about O.J.

On May 10, the blustery Wednesday the case finally went to the jury, I caught a flight out to Las Vegas. Finished with school for the summer, I'd also wangled an assignment from Lewis Lapham at *Harper's* to cover the progress of female players at the World Series of Poker, as well as the mushrooming impact of advice books and com-

Jennifer Arra

puter programs—the ways in which information-age technology was neutralizing seat-of-the-pants experience at the poker table, helping nerds, chicks, and foreigners to match up more evenly with leather-assed Texas road gamblers. The other part of my assignment was to keep an eye on the Binion trial as the verdict came in.

As a novelist trying his hand at nonfiction, how could I beat stuff like this? Nerve, sex, aggression, big money, deception, and, above all, no-limit risk taking were integral to both the celebrated poker tournament and what was being called, at least in Las Vegas, the Trial of the Century. The strongest no-limit players don't even need a good hand to take down pots heaped with hot-pink $10,000 chips; a well-timed, intimidating raise, in response to some glimmer of doubt in the bettor's eye or a twinge along the side of his neck, does the trick. Murphy and Tabish used street drugs, pharmaceuticals, handcuffs, and stealth to murder Ted Binion and abscond with his fortune, and their intimidating, big-budget defense team was capable of making sure they got clean away with it.

As usual, Lewis's instructions were generous but succinct: "Have fun and write a good story." But I knew he was counting on me, as a novelist and a poker player, to come up with new angles on what had become a slice of Americana, tinged now by the grisly execution of its host. My ulterior plan was to use the $4,000 check Lewis cut me (half for expenses, half as an advance on the article) to try to play my way into the championship event, which costs $10,000 to enter. I would then weave my own poker action, however short-lived, into the braid of my coverage of the trial and the tournament.

The scheme's only drawback was that, as a father of four with a jumbo mortgage and other unfortunate habits, I could "hardly afford to gamble away" (my wife Jennifer's phrase) this kind of money. Jennifer knew that even in regular poker tournaments nineteen of twenty entrants lose their entire buy-in. Her husband would be what the pros call "dead money," one of the suckers who fatten the prize pool but have almost no chance of sharing in the spoils. Scores of these wannabes ponying up $10,000 apiece are the reason the Binions can offer such lucrative payouts each year, including $1 million to the winner. Was that how I wanted to spend my hard-earned four grand, before

I'd even earned it to boot? You bet your sweet Polish-Sicilian posterior it was. In a heartbeat.

At home in our redbrick, three-bedroom, one-and-a-half-bath suburban ranch, I religiously turn lights on then off as I move in the dark from one part of the house to another. Jennifer clips coupons, and we often have spirited debates about whether to cough up $3.99 for a pay-per-view movie. Our daughter Beatrice is twenty-one months old, Grace only six months. Until the final three weeks of her pregnancy with Bea, Jennifer worked full-time as director of faculty services at SAIC, but she now works two days at home, one day in her office downtown, and has taken a 30 percent cut in salary. I have two adult children, Bridget and James, from my first marriage. Paying Bridget's rent, COBRA premium, and other expenses until she finishes her education costs us $1,300 a month; James-related expenses average about $5,000 a year. We're also $71,407 into our home equity line, which is more than my salary as a writing teacher. Yet seldom do I hesitate to sit down to a game of poker in which thousand-dollar losses and wins are routine.

I apparently still need to take risks while proving my competitive acumen. "Like an addict," Jennifer claims, even though she's a not-bad poker player herself, or "a teenager," deploying two of our household's most pejorative epithets. I'm also "possessed." Of what? "An addictive personality," that's what, by which she does not mean that other people find my person addicting. At least my wife doesn't, of late.

Okay. I admit that I'm juiced and flush when I win and that my penis feels like an acorn when I lose, plus my bankroll is paper-cut thin for a spell, but I'm hardly *addicted*. And I'm not gonna stop playing poker any sooner than I'd stop writing poems, a habit that's much more expensive. The most I have earned for a poem is $100, and that poem took eight months to write. Usually I earn much, much less. Yet I'm treated to no sermons about *that* risky, acumen-proving habit, even though it costs our household whatever my time is worth per hour—fifty bucks, surely—minus the 3.6 cents I make in honoraria. And don't forget postage and stationery.

But so what's more important, Jennifer wants to know, my competitive impulses or our children's college education? "Huh, Braino? Tell me." As though it has to be one or the other! She's convinced that gambling is "self-indulgent," even "kind of sick, in a way" because (1) it risks money I have no right to risk, and (2) I want something for nothing. She makes these claims, mind you, even though my poker bankroll is funded by writing essays and book reviews, as well as by *winning at poker.* Book advances and paychecks for teaching are deposited directly into our household account, from which skimming is never an option. (I don't even know our account number, nor any of our various PINs.) And *of course* I want something for nothing. Players and nonplayers alike get aced out of cherished, indispensable things all the time and get zip in return, so it seems only reasonable to want to balance the equation a little.

My competitive impulses used to be satisfied playing baseball, golf, hockey, tennis, and basketball, and by rooting for the Bears, Bulls, Blackhawks, Yankees, White Sox, and whoever was playing the Cubs. I often spent twelve hours a week watching Bulls games alone, then several more gloating over their exploits on ESPN, local TV, and in the sports pages of two or three newspapers. Why? Because that's what red-blooded men do when there isn't a war to be fought: we bask in other men's televised glory, trying to deflect some onto ourselves by showing off how much we know about our surrogate warriors' eptitude and virility. *You see him split that double team, man? No way Money don't finish even if weakside help arrives. Four-to-one says they take it in five.* Now, macho one-upsmanship strikes many people as trivial and pathetic, and no doubt they're right, but it's also a fact that without this competitive ardor, humans would be long extinct. One reason we're not is that the sociobiological legacy of our days as hunter-gatherers causes levels of testosterone, the primary hormone of both male and female desire, to rise by as much as a third when the local team does well. He shoots, he *scores!* And later that night, so do we. Edward O. Wilson calls these urges "Pleistocene exigencies," reminding us that humans have hunted and gathered for over 99 percent of our history. Most of the hunting these days is performed on TV by our surrogate warriors, but their fellow tribe members still react the same way. We can't help it. A winning team not only raises morale and gooses productivity, it literally helps populate the tribe that supports it. And vice versa. When Brazil defeated Italy for the 1994 World Cup, researchers testing saliva in spit cups found that "eleven of the twelve Brazilian men had increased testosterone levels after the game, and all nine Italian men had decreased levels." One Italian fan had injured his throat while futilely cheering, so there was blood in his saliva sample. "Saliva Girl," he winsomely explained to the researcher, "it is my heart that is bleeding." Nine months after France won the Cup in '98, the French birth rate jumped 55 percent and remained elevated for weeks. Even in brainy, sedentary, individualist games like chess, the loser's postmatch testosterone level tends to drop off the table. A recent study commissioned by the Academy of American Poets found that when a writer gets her first villanelle accepted by *The New Yorker*, her lover is 5.926 times as likely to score in the next eighty minutes, slightly less when her lover is the editor.

Beatrice and Grace, as it happens, were both conceived during the Bulls' second threepeat. Granted other exigencies were involved, the fact is that when Jordan, Pippen, and Jackson—those consummate surrogate warriors—got run out of town by Jerrys Reinsdorf and Krause in 1998, I suddenly had, at age forty-seven, an extra twenty hours a week to work off competitive fury and boost my plummeting testosterone level. Poker did both. I still ride a bike and swim laps when snowfree roads or pools are available, but I've pretty much retired from ball sports. Middle age, shinsplints, a torn meniscus, and a much more deliberate temperament have reduced me to a spectator— to "hiker-biker guy," as Jennifer identifies Good Jim. Yet Bad Jim still needs to keep score. To keep scoring. The thrill of victory and the agony of defeat and all that. Who's the *man*?

So the main thing I love about poker is that it's gotten me back in the action. And I doubt it's a coincidence that the rhythms of baseball, my best sport thirty and forty years ago, readily transfer to the poker table. Both games are contested nine- or ten-handed but place a huge premium on individual success. (Baseball teams win championships, but it's the homerun kings and strikeout artists who make the long money.) The tactics of both games are dominated by probability. Baseball managers deploy pinch hitters, shifts, lefty-righty matchups, alter rotations and batting orders; poker players factor in pot odds, randomize bluffs, fold when their hand is a statistical underdog, raise when they're getting the best of it.

Between sixty and eighty million Americans play poker, making baseball the *second* great American game: second to make its appearance, second in the number of participants. And many more millions play elsewhere. While baseball and poker are probably the only two games to settle their championships in an annual World Series, they're certainly the only two in which players wear billed caps, sateen jackets, and sunglasses. In both contests position, aggression, and stealing are critical, but patience is what turns out to be the most necessary virtue. Baseball and poker players spend most of their time waiting, getting into position, and strategizing, but once every nine chances or so (on both offense and defense) they really do have to come through. And more than in most competitions, luck becomes pivotal. A batter makes more impressive contact with a four-seam fastball when he flies out to the centerfield warning track than when he bloops a bases-clearing double to the opposite field, yet the duck-snort is what gets the job done—just as duck-snorts like A-7 suited routinely crack pocket kings. "Hit 'em where they ain't," the key to run production in baseball, is less a coach's imperative than a plea for good fortune, reinforced more dependably by rally caps than slugging percentages, just as bad luck in poker often seems reversible by changing hats, cursing dealers, fingering heirlooms or talismans. I think, for example, of the black wool White Sox cap I got married to Jennifer in as my poker cap, though I have several others. And sometimes, for luck, I wear my Bellagio baseball cap backwards.

That cap, by the way, with its yellow-gold "B" fancily embroidered on the brim, was purchased at the Las Vegas Bellagio, though I wear it to summon the luck of the original, where the Rockefeller Foundation has a villa for artists and scientists. In October 1997, Beatrice was conceived there near a window overlooking the Lecco arm of Lake Como.

We named her after her great-great-aunt Bea, a childless Sicilian widow who helped to raise Jennifer after her parents split up. Dante's muse figured in, too, so sometimes her name ends with *Tree Che*.

But Pleistocene exigencies have reared their ugly heads more than once, let me tell you. Allow me to also admit that maintaining equilibrium between Good Jim and Bad Jim has never been easy, for me or for Jennifer. The prospect of me in Las Vegas for ten days packing a quarter-inch wad of Benjamins therefore wouldn't have thrilled her under any circumstances, but since she'd given birth to Grace only seven weeks before I got the assignment from Lewis, Jennifer thought my "gambling" plan was more than a little bit reckless. "Isn't it, Jimmy?" Well, sort of. I granted her that $4,000 for gambling didn't really fit into our budget but also insisted that poker wasn't gambling, and who said I was going to lose? Plus a responsible journalist needed actual table experience to capture the rhythms and texture of the hair-raising brand of no-limit Texas hold'em that decides the world championship, right? Krakauer on Everest, I mentioned. McPhee in Alaska. Bill Buford rioting in Sardinia. Susan Orlean slogging through the Fakahatchee Strand . . .

"Don't forget García Márquez," my wife interrupted, apparently in support of my thesis, "who presumably had to get kidnapped to write *News of a Kidnapping*. Just like Hemingway had to get gored to write *Death in the Afternoon*. Or John Hersey had to get vaporized . . ."

Fine.

We went back and forth for a couple of weeks in this manner, but she finally signed off on my plan. Bottom line? I needed her to have faith in me. She needed me to be faithful.

She also knew how badly I'd wanted to play in the World Series, ever since my alcoholic Uncle Thomas told me about it back in the seventies, and especially since I'd read *The Biggest Game in Town*, A. Alvarez's account of the 1981 event. What Jennifer didn't know (because I didn't admit it) was how intrigued I'd become by Ted Binion, the tournament's prodigal host and a man with whom I was afraid I had too much in common. Both of us were middle-aged married guys with a weakness for gambling, alcohol, recreational drugs, nubile women. Raised Irish Catholic in the middle of the last century, we'd been treated to the same gospels, suffered the same fish sticks and tartar sauce on Friday evenings, dug the same music, and probably lusted for girls who wore the same combinations of kneesocks and pleated plaid skirts—or nothing at all, as the ad said. Two key differences were that Ted had a heroin habit and an eight-figure inheritance with which to indulge it. A third was that as soon as *his* first wife left him, Ted invited a stripper to move into his house, whereas I had been lucky enough to find Jennifer. (Watching Bill Kurtis flirt with her, I was helping to answer her telephone during the Dread Scott Tyler "flag on the floor" incident at our previously quiet little art school.) Like Sandy Murphy, Jennifer Arra may look fatally fetching in Victoria's Secret, but it's not the only reason I married her.

That's Good Jim talking, of course. Bad Jim's more likely to blurt things like this at the woman who saved his life: "Who finished the goddamn tequila?" Or: "You should have an unlimited underwear budget." Or: "I think I'm gonna fire my agent!" Or: "I think I need to fire my editor!" Or, somewhat contradictory to the blurt about lingerie: "Every time a plane takes off from O'Hare for Las Vegas without me, another little piece of my heart dies."

Now that I'm on such a flight again, and now that I'm perfectly sober, I'm starting to feel a bit anxious. Having finished my peanuts and silver-slipcased *déjeuner*, I reach down next to my feet for my notebook and one of my strategy manuals. The fact is, I'm scared.

I've been playing poker for thirty-nine years now, everything from penny-ante family games in the Bronx to strip poker during high school in the Chicago suburbs to $80-$160 hold'em in Vegas and LA casinos. I was taught to play by my uncle and grandfather, both named Tom Madden, then got schooled in caddy shacks by guys with names like Doc and Tennessee. I also played in college with some fairly bright mathematicians. My current home game in a Greektown law office involves day traders, attorneys, a circuit court judge, a professional Frisbee player, a CTA systems analyst, and a pizza delivery man. Three of the regulars have entered WSOP satellites and preliminary tournaments; all but a couple can play. While I've stolen my fair share of pots in this game, we're only playing $4-$8 or $8-$16. Five hundred dollars is about the most you can lose or win for the night, a relative pittance when most of the players have six-figure incomes. Even a $16 reraise fails to make knees or hands tremble, though it can make a good player fold. The championship event of the World Series, however, draws the top two or three hundred professionals in the world, along with dozens of masterful amateurs, most of whom have decades of tournament experience. I'm good but not that good. Not nearly. I've held my own playing medium-stakes games against the pros in the Bellagio's poker room, but I still have no reason to doubt T.J. Cloutier, the former Montreal Allouettes tight end who is now one of poker's best players. "The World Series is a conglomeration of local champions," he says. "There's Joe Blow from Iowa who's the champion from his game at home; hundreds of local champions like him come to Vegas to play the World Series. But it's like the difference in going from playing high school football to college football: It's a big step up."

Be that as it may, Joe Blow from Chicago will be damned if he's going to cover the entire event from the sidelines, not when he's got over $4,000 in his pocket. Hilariously steep odds say I'll only embarrass myself by paying $1,000 each to enter four winner-take-all satellites (one-table feeder events designed to fiscally democratize the main competition), and that I'll have no chance at all against the no-limit maestros who dominate the actual tournament. But like most poker players these days, I'd give a digit and maybe a testicle for a chance to sit down in the Big One.

To reduce the long odds that I'll only make my penis feel small (but still big enough to piss four grand down the toilet), I've spent the last five months playing no-limit hold'em against computer programs and studying strategy manuals. The Gambler's Book Club in Las Vegas stocks 133 poker titles, but I didn't have time to read all of them. When I explained my plan over the phone to the manager, Peter Ruchman, he put three books at the top of my list: *Super/System*, Cloutier's *Championship No-Limit and Pot-Limit Hold'em*, and David Sklansky's *Theory of Poker*. I already owned the first one; the second two Peter FedExed to me. The next day I had all three of them open on my lap as I pondered whether to call bets of sixty thousand virtual dollars.

Since the programs reshuffle and deal in a flash, your digital opponents decide what to do in split seconds, and you can automatically "zip" to the next hand the instant you fold, it's possible to play hundreds of hands per hour, instead of the twenty or so when vying for real money in a brick-and-mortar casino. In one snowbound season of research and practice, I probably made a decade's worth of no-limit decisions. By playing hundreds of thousands of hands (and winning thirteen virtual tournaments), I sharpened my card sense and bankroll-management skills, and developed what I hope is a decent feel for no-limit wagering tactics. Yet I don't wanna kid myself. Computerized action gives you zero opportunities to read faces or body language for "tells" about the strength of your opponents' hands, and may even undermine the mental and physical stamina required for live-action poker. Then there's the shaky-knees factor, virtually absent when playing for free on a screen. My opponents at Binion's will be well-funded hombres and artists, and the McManus household income at risk will be real, with better than 10-to-1 odds that I'll lose every cent of it before the championship even starts or I've written word one of the article.

Bad Jim, of course, cannot wait.

Three hours west-southwest of O'Hare come dark, snowcapped mountains rising below me in perfect diagonal light. I lucked into a window seat on the north side of the plane, so I'm taking a time-out from my notes just to gape. But thirty seconds later we're over parched desert again, with the occasional dead river or butte wrinkling the preternatural flatness, a lone white semi (I think) inching west through gradations of umber. And then, just to prove where my head is at, a cluster of huge green irrigated circles reminds me of $25 chips on the blasted, irregular beige.

Detaching my face from the window, I stick my nose back in my blue three-ring binder, where it belongs. Interleaving typescript with newspaper clippings, stray Post-its, xeroxed pages of poker advice, web site printouts about female poker stars and homicidal strippers makes it easier to flip back and forth between the loose threads of the story. In no-limit hold'em, I note for the three hundredth time, you don't play small pairs or suited connectors. *Don't call—fold or raise!* Sandy Murphy's father is a repo man in south-central LA. After his first wife took off in 1982, he married a woman with the same first name as his ten-month-old daughter. Was "The End" the last song on *LA Woman* or on the Doors' first, eponymous album? Jim Morrison's girlfriend claimed he died of a heart attack, that no drugs at all were involved . . .

Next time I look out, there's the canyon: iron-red sandstone etched a half mile down into itself. Viewed from thirty thousand feet, the jagged diorama extends well beyond the horizon. Even through my progressive bifocals, I can make out the white-water crinkles of the chalky gray-green Colorado zagging west toward Lake Mead and Las Vegas.

Of the half dozen computer programs I've researched, Masque's World Series of Poker is the only one depicting your actual trip to the Horseshoe. The first thing you see is an ATA 727 cruising through a starry night sky. After you land at McCarran Airport, a Horseshoe driver greets you in the luggage-claim area, ushers you into a limousine. "You" are a lean, brown-haired guy wearing sneakers, jeans, Dodger-blue T-shirt, and baseball cap. (Players who log in with a woman's name get a slim, shapely female alter ego.) Once you register, your bags are sent up to your room, and it's time to play poker. Clicking your beltpack displays room number, return airline ticket, bankroll of $5,000. You'll need to double that in a satellite to be able to enter the championship event. The buy-in for each nine-handed satellite is $1,125, and one winner takes all. You therefore have four chances to win against 8–1 odds each time that you won't. With average poker skills, it's a coin flip. After a bit of practice, however, I seldom failed to win my way in.

Getting to the tournament area requires passing a gold, horseshoe-shaped display of what the screen calls "$1,000,000 in cold cash." This is modeled on the one hundred ten-thousand-dollar bills that used to be displayed in the actual Horseshoe. The wacky verisimilitude continues as you enter the championship. After a cartoon Jack Binion welcomes the players, a bearded Jack McClelland inaugurates the action with "Shuffle up and deal!" The tournament takes four "days" to winnow the field of 216 players (reflecting the year, 1990, that the program was written) down to one winner. Then as now, he or she will be showered with ten thousand hundred-dollar bills, to go with a monogrammed gold bracelet in a Neiman Marcus box. Second place pays $600,000, on down to $16,000 for finishing twenty-seventh.

Winnings may be spent at a travel agency, buying poker books, redeeming your grandfather's gold railroad watch that you pawned, or in the naughty cabaret two doors down from the casino. There, for $25, you can take in the well-endowed Wanda the Juggler, followed by Samba the Magician, who makes a scantily clad maiden levitate, twice, before your very eyes. Now that you and the rest of the audience have been sufficiently warmed up, the tuxedoed MC introduces "the finale": six leggy chorus girls in nothing but spangled headdresses and a bead on each nipple, cancanning away for your pleasure. Still horny? Book a $100 day trip out to Lake Mead, where you're virtually certain to happen across a platinum blonde sunbathing topless. Click anywhere on her body and read: "Don't you wish!" Click on her again and get summarily dumped in the lake, lose your beltpack, and be forced to hitchhike home, minus your entire bankroll.

The virtual Horseshoe, just like the real one, is a twenty-two-story affair. The top floor features a steakhouse with glittering views of the Vegas night skyline. Downstairs, your room has a desk, dresser, TV, king-sized bed. On top of the desk is your poker log, which allows you to ponder your track record: number of satellites entered, results, average net when you do make the Big One, lifetime winnings (or losses). If your accumulated bankroll exceeds $5,000, you may bring back the surplus the following "year." If you're lucky and skillful enough to net over $200,000, you are immediately dispatched home, and the most you can bring back to Las Vegas is $100,000. "No rational gambler," the program lectures, though it could easily be Jennifer talking, "would risk more than that in a single trip."

To enhance your odds of getting that far into the black, the gift shop has a selection of primers: *Winning Poker* by David Sklansky, *Poker Essays* and *Gambling Theory* by Mason Malmuth, *Seven-Card Stud* by Sklansky and Malmuth, and, of course, *Super/System*. Excerpts can be scrutinized, then put into practice on the virtual tables. Malmuth is a former Census Bureau statistician, and he knows poker odds inside out. He also knows tournament strategy. He explains, for example, that when prize money is distributed on a percentage basis (as it is in every WSOP tournament), the value of your chips isn't constant: "The more chips you have, the less each individual chip is worth, and the less chips you have, the more each individual chip is worth." This as opposed to the home games I'm used to, wherein green chips are worth exactly twenty-five bucks all night long. Similarly, Malmuth reminds you that during the early rounds of a four-day tournament, "a large stack is still only a small proportion of the total number of chips, while late in a tournament a significant amount can be present in one large stack." Obvious? Counterintuitive? Either way, Malmuth makes the strategic implications quite clear, emphasizing that survival to the later stages of a tournament is much more important than contesting a lot of pots early.

The program's gift shop provides other good counsel, to go with its lifelike temptations. When you click on the bottle of tequila, a reminder pops up: "You need to keep a clear head!" Cigarettes? "Bad for your health!" No handcuffs or heroin for sale here, or even a Victoria's Secret catalogue, but *Playboy* sure is. Try picking one up—after visiting the cabaret, for example, or hitchhiking back from Lake Mead—and the screen will admonish: "You came to play poker!" All words that Bad Jim needs to live by.

> Virgil Earp they gunned down in the middle of Fifth
> Street outside the Oriental Saloon. It was shortly before
> midnight three days after Christmas and the pair of
> double-barrel shotguns discharged over a distance of 60
> feet blew apart his left arm, reducing $5\frac{1}{2}$ inches of
> humerus bone to slart between the shoulder and elbow.
> Against the advice of doctors he kept the arm and
> survived, crippled for life.
>
> —BRUCE OLDS, *Bucking the Tiger*

> Satellites are out tonight.
>
> —LAURIE ANDERSON

My actual room at the Horseshoe, 1016, has no log book—yet—but is twice the size of a room in Manhattan or San Francisco, at a fifth of the price: $45. The decor I would call Hotel Functional circa 1973, with mauve-aqua-lavender drapes, aqua-mauve-lavender abstract floral print over each of the beds, like-minded velvet headboards, white enamel furniture. Since I want to sleep in the darkest and quietest corner of the room, I open my suitcase on the bed closest to the window. All I need to unpack now are toiletries, vitamins, pens, and a notebook; my clothes will come out as I need to wear them, then be transferred to a laundry bag. The writing surface attached to the dresser is a minimalist prank, but the round, roomy table by the window should work perfectly well as a desk.

The window overlooks the white latticed archway above Fremont Street. Dubbed The Fremont Street Experience, it's hardly a tribute to Hendrix. The arch is designed to mottle the afternoon sun; at night

Ted, Benny, and Jack Binion

it functions as video screen and vast neon billboard, with miles of circuitry projecting concerts and light shows and advertising. Now that
Benny Binion is dead, this is downtown Las Vegas's dolorous, last-gasp
attempt to keep up with the billion-dollar extravaganzas five miles
south on the Strip. Nearly all of the city's 33 million annual tourists
prefer the Strip's pixilated facsimiles of Paris and Bellagio, Gotham
and Luxor, Renaissance Venice and Imperial Rome. This last, Caesars
Palace, is where Sandy and Ted liked to shop.

Nothing that racy up here, although just to my right we have the
Girls of Glitter Gulch, whose facade features neon and video cowgirls
winking and pouting in various states of undress. To my left is the six-
story Clark County Courthouse on the corner of Second Street and
Carson, so I'll never have to walk more than a block to cover either
part of my story. Blinking red and white beyond its flat roof are the
jets in and out of McCarran—bearing off losers, ferrying in reinforce-
ments. I can also see the new Eiffel Tower, Bellagio's water-and-light
show, the glittering black Luxor pyramid. Beyond all that are the
South Virgin Mountains, maybe thirty miles off in the moonlight.

Rummaging in my suitcase for a shirt, I discover *Compulsive Gambling: The Hidden Epidemic* tucked away near the bottom. I bring home
flyers like these from Chicago riverboat casinos to mine for material,
and Jennifer has taken to booby-trapping my pockets and briefcase
with them, as a "joke." To amplify her moral this time, she's underlined key words in red: "The longer the disease continues untreated,
the greater the probability of <u>arrest and imprisonment</u>. The disease
can <u>wreck family, career, even life</u> . . ." I appreciate her sense of humor
on the subject, but I'm also aware that she's 49.94 percent serious. At
home I respond to her pop-up reminders by taping snippets from articles about the dangers of aphids, say, in the finger of one of her gardening gloves, or a piece about mammography in the lace of a bra cup,
making sure that the spiniest creases face in. (Glossy magazine stock
makes for the wickedest corners, I've found. Or, rather, *she's* found.)
It's not that I think my wife has become an uptight penny-pinching
wet-blanket Puritan teetotaller since our daughters were born, as she's
accused me a few times of thinking. Because Sicilians can never be Pu-
ritans. As I brush my teeth and gargle, however, I resolve to find

printed material to fold up as payback—a crisp new hundred-dollar bill, for example, with Ben Franklin's amplified portrait creased into stickleback origami. I also know just where to hide it.

I'm further inspired, I guess, by the fact that Hunter S. Thompson stayed two floors below me while covering the Mint 400 motorcycle race for *Sports Illustrated* back in '71. (The Horseshoe annexed the Mint Hotel sixteen years later.) The 250 words *SI* assigned him quickly became 2,500 having zero to do with the race. When his editor "aggressively rejected" it, Thompson persuaded Jann Wenner at *Rolling Stone* to commission an even longer piece, which became *Fear and Loathing in Las Vegas*. One of Ralph Steadman's psychotically lyrical illustrations showed a Mint Hotel maid discovering the naked author bent over a toilet bowl puking up meals, vital organs, intestines. My plan is to avoid any vomiting, at least while the maid's in the room. Another difference is that Thompson checked into Room 850 having already run through his entire $300 expense account scoring "extremely dangerous drugs." Even at my age this sounds like some fun, though it isn't the angle I'm after on this trip. (Maybe Lewis will spring for Ritalin and XTC *next* time.) Instead of the trunkload of psychedelics, booze, and pharmaceuticals Thompson deployed as both subject and fuel for his piece, I'll be sticking to vitamins and mineral water, Zocor and laps in the pool. Because I have plenty of fear about what's in store for me downstairs at the satellite tables but not a single iota of loathing, for now. Whatever the opposite of gonzo is, that will be me.

The Horseshoe, of course, is gonzo enough on its own. Lewd, gaudy, infamous—people get whacked around here when things don't go right at the tables. Killers have hosted and won its World Series; so have hipsters and cowboys, Vietnamese boat people and Irish carpet manufacturers. Yet somehow the place remains the homey, even venerable anchor of downtown Las Vegas, the original high-stakes emporium and the last family-owned casino in America. The feel of this joint isn't transplantable to the Strip. It has never tried to be a pirate's castle, the lair of albino tigers, or a Venetian *sestiere*, but only what it is: a no-frills gambling hall with the intimacy of an old-time saloon. In the coffee shop downstairs, a slab of prime rib with potatoes, vegetables, and salad costs $7.77 and is served up by affable middle-aged women with twangs, hips, and permanents. The casino operation is long past its prime, just like the rest of Glitter Gulch, but only for forty-seven weeks a year. Late May through early April it caters mostly to working-class locals, but right now it's home to the poshest, most lucrative gaming competition in the world. Thirty to fifty million dollars will change hands in the card rooms downstairs before the World Series ends May 18, and the Horseshoe will take a fair cut.

Press credentials (and the free meals and computer access they confer) are available on the mezzanine, but first I want to see Ted's old safe. Taking a page from her father, Becky Behnen has positioned it not far from the door of her casino, provocatively open and empty at the end of a long row of slot machines. Six feet high, with foot-thick lead-lined doors, it's a bulky relic from the days when funds didn't travel on light waves—all the more suitable, then, for millennial Vegas, where C-notes, drink tokens, ingots, and twelve-gram clay chips still are the coin of the realm. Beside it a black-and-white photo shows Becky's brother and father in happier times. Ted looks toothy and hale, Benny more grizzled and chubby. The caption explains: *"The safe was built and was at one time used in the Northern Casino in Goldfield, Nev. Over the years it has been owned by Tex Richard, Doby Doc and Wyatt Earp. It was last owned by Ted Binion. At the time the safe came into Ted Binion's possession, it had not been opened for over 50 years. The contents of this safe are presumed to have been stolen by the person or persons responsible for the murder of Ted Binion in September, 1998."*

I don't know Tex Richard, but Doby Doc was a cowboy, junk collector, and road gambler who became one of Benny's original Horseshoe partners. Wyatt Earp, of course, was a saloon owner, faro dealer, and sheriff in Dodge City, Kansas, and Tombstone, Arizona. He not only miraculously survived the shoot-out at the O.K. Corral, along with his brother Virgil, but lived to the age of eighty-one, confounding every known actuarial table for gunslinging sheriffs.

Doing Earp four years better, Benny Binion confounded the tables for racketeers and enforcers. He was born Lester Ben Binion in Pilot Grove, Texas, sixty miles north of Dallas, in 1904. His grandparents had migrated there from Chicago, and both of his parents grew up Catholic and po'. Benny spent his youth punching cattle, trading horses, running numbers, sitting on the fringes of card games in Dallas, finally making his bones in the twenties and thirties. Starting with $56 he'd saved, he and his younger brother launched their own numbers "policy," a kind of neighborhood lottery, netting $800 their first week in business. His brother died in a plane crash a few years later, but Benny carried on. From numbers he branched into dice, running no-limit craps games in the shadow of the Dallas courthouse. Regulars at his illegal casino included H. L. Hunt, Clint Murchison, and Howard Hughes, all of whom played for vast stakes, but Benny had already learned a few tricks that guaranteed profitability. Among the surest of these were daubing or loading or fading—making his dice slightly tacky, or heavy, or large on one side—in ways that disadvantaged the shooter even more than the mathematical percentages, also known as the edge. Benny and his young family prospered.

Cards were another story. "I was never a real good poker player," he told a biographer, contrasting himself with several friends who made a living at the game. "They know the cards, and know the percentages, and somebody can have a hand, and all this money in . . . they got to know how many cards is gone, and how many chances he's got to make it, and this, that, and the other. I can't do that. I don't know that end of it." What he did know was how to create a secure, seductive environment for games of skill and chance, and to take a fair cut for his trouble. Since the games were illegal in Texas, he and his fellow racketeers had to police both themselves and their clients, and without courts or prisons their principal means of enforcement was violence. Their weapons of choice included baseball bats, shotguns, homemade bombs, and brass knuckles. By nearly every report, Benny was a warmhearted, generous family man who happened to savor his reputation as a cold-blooded killer. "There's no way in the world I'd harm anybody for any amount of money," he declared near the end of his life, this after certain statutes of limitations, and not a few of his enemies, had expired. "But if anybody goes to talkin' about doin' me bodily harm, or my family bodily harm, I'm very capable, thank God, of really takin' care of 'em in a *most* artistic way. And I'm still very capable. I don't have to hire nobody to do none of my dirty work. That sounds a little bit like braggin', but if they don't think that I can do it, well, just let 'em come on."

Benny's aura of violence still permeates the game his family has helped make respectable: no-limit Texas hold'em, the game we're all out here to play. We know about Benny's main bodyguard, for example, from reading Cloutier's Tales from T.J. column in this week's *Card Player*. "Ken Haroldson, who killed that judge, Judge Woods, down in San Antonio—he played in that game. There was R. D. Matthews, who used to be Benny Binion's bodyguard—he always packed a gun, but his big thing was getting 'em with a baseball bat." An intimidating presence himself, Cloutier (pronounced CLU-tee-ay) is one of the last of the renegade road gamblers—men like Johnny Moss, Amarillo Slim Preston, Titanic Thompson, and Blondie Forbes, who invented Texas hold'em and played it extralegally across the Southwest before transplanting it into the Horseshoe, and who still have an air of remorselessness. About another regular opponent, a man who was later gunned down with his wife, Cloutier writes: "George loved to play poker, but he was a stone killer. . . . Around Texas, they said that George had been accused of killing about 30 or 40 people, but he was never actually convicted of murder." If I somehow make it into the tournament, I'll be competing against Cloutier and Preston et al., as well as a few hundred more proper ladies and gentlemen.

As the boss gambler in Texas during the Second World War, Benny Binion was targeted for hits by his competition and prosecuted by the government on a regular basis. The cumulative heat became so intense that he decided to get out of town. "My sheriff got beat in the election," was how he explained it. In 1946 he piled his wife, Teddy Jane, and their five young children—Barbara, Jack, Ted, Brenda, and Becky—and $2 million in cash into his maroon Cadillac and drove to Las Vegas, where most of his games were now legal.

The fledgling desert resort the Binions arrived in had been invented out of whole cloth by two people. Bugsy Siegel, the man who built the Flamingo Hotel just south of town, was a Brooklyn hit man with a penchant for flashy dames, garish nightclubs, and gardening. Bugsy's roses continued to flourish in the garden of the Flamingo three decades after he took a bullet in the eye (think Mo Green in *The Godfather*), the roses blooming larger and more deeply scarlet each year. His phenomenal secret nutrient? Not Miracle-Gro. Not manure. Las Vegas lore has the bodies of Filthy Frankie Giannatasio, Big Howie Dennis, and Mad Dog Neville all buried in Bugsy's strangely fertile soil. One plaque even claims that if you stand in the garden at midnight beneath a full moon, you can hear three muffled voices. *Bugsy*, they mutter. *How do you like the roses, Bugsy?*

Siegel's more ascetic boss, Meyer Lansky, was a Polish immigrant who'd made a vast fortune bootlegging liquor from Cuba and Canada during Prohibition (think Hyman Roth in *The Godfather II*). Lansky's working assumption was that Wall Street firms, banks, industrial giants, labor unions, and political parties were themselves de facto gangs from which nominal gangsters like himself had plenty to learn. Learn he did. The term "Lansky operation" was coined soon thereafter by FBI agents to define a cunning blend of criminal and legitimate business practices. Nor was Lansky above the deployment of mortifying photos of J. Edgar Hoover in lingerie to neutralize the FBI's ability, or will, to investigate him. But his most far-reaching entrepreneurial act was to fund Siegel's vision of Las Vegas, seeing its location in the middle of the Mojave Desert as a critical asset. Once tourists had eaten and drunk all they could, only two choices remained: sex and gambling.

When the rival Chicago Syndicate took over Dallas in the late forties, Lansky helped his protégé Benny Binion move his operations out west. Benny first became a partner in the Las Vegas Club, but his freewheeling habits and the size of the bets he took on caused a split in the merger. And Benny had other big problems. Back in Dallas, numbers boss Herbert "the Cat" Noble's wife was incinerated by a car bomb meant for the Cat. So certain was Noble that Benny had authorized the hit that he fitted an airplane with bomb racks and managed to procure two incendiary devices and a map with Binion's new home on West Bonanza Road circled in pencil. The sortie was thwarted by Texas police, but word of the bomb racks and map made its way out to Benny. In 1951, the year Benny took over the El Dorado casino on Fremont Street and renamed it Binion's Horseshoe, Noble (whose nickname referred to the number of lives he seemed blessed with) was decapitated by a pipe bomb planted next to his mailbox.

A few years later, Benny pleaded guilty—but to tax evasion charges, not murder. With his black chauffeur, Gold Dollar, he drove back to Dallas with a satchel full of cash to persuade the judge not to impose a jail sentence. Benny had every reason to believe the $100,000 bribe would do the job—and it probably would have if Dallas police hadn't already coerced the judge into sentencing Binion to four and a half years in the federal penitentiary at Leavenworth. "I could've beat this damn case if I hadn't got tricked into pleadin' guilty," Benny claimed. "I got tricked all the way around by the government." He served forty-two months, during which he rediscovered his Catholicism and learned to make jailhouse chili, vocations of perhaps equally dubious utility. In the meantime his old friend Joe Brown helped Teddy Jane and her two teenage sons run the Horseshoe.

Benny emerged unrepentant. "I'm not a damn bit sorry I went to the penitentiary. I'm absolutely glad of it. When I came out of the penitentiary, my youngest daughter [Becky] was walkin' funny, and my family couldn't see it. So I kept a-hollerin'. I got out in March, kept a-hollerin', 'This girl don't walk right.' So I just kept on, kept on. Finally, in October, my wife took her and had her x-rayed, and she had a cyst inside of her thighbone, right up close to that socket, that was all ready—'most ready to burst. If it'd've bursted, it'd shattered that bone and ruined her leg. They'd had to cut her leg off, right at the hip. Well, to have me recognizin' this thing makes me absolutely *glad* I went to the penitentiary. So they say everything happens for the best. Maybe it does. This did, anyhow. And I have no regrets, about the money, or nothin'."

Benny had plenty of critics, of course, which he dismissed as categorically as he did the legal system's ability to chasten him: "I just don't think that these people walkin' around all rared back and writin' and raisin' up hell about this, that, and the other, to me, they just don't mean nothin'. I just don't pay no attention to them because I know they're gonna go away. Don't mean nothin'. They'll lose their job or they'll get sick, or they'll have a stroke, or just any damn thing happen, or they'll get to doin' somethin' else. They can't stay on you forever."

To help get his casino back on the map, Benny took to wearing a white ten-gallon Stetson cocked to the side like a gunfighter's, custom-stitched alligator boots, and western-cut suits with three-dollar gold pieces for buttons. He also brought Doby Doc Caudill down from Elko, Nevada, as a partner. Caudill's sartorial taste ran to diamond stickpins adorning bib overalls, set off by a pearl-handled revolver tucked into an ornately tooled holster. Their less colorful partner was Eddie Levinson, who sported Brooks Brothers suits as he watched over the skim for Meyer Lansky.

When cheaters or burglars were caught in the Horseshoe, security guards didn't call the police; they administered their own brand of frontier justice, from which at least seven of the accused never managed to recover. To safeguard his delicate legal and political privileges, Benny paid off senators, governors, judges, and beat cops, boasting in 1978 of having delivered the vote of Senator Howard Cannon on the Panama Canal Zone Treaty to President Carter. According to Benny, he received in exchange a federal judgeship for his friend Harry Claiborne. Eight years later, Claiborne became the first U.S. District Court judge since the Civil War to be impeached and convicted of a felony—namely, failing to pay taxes on an $85,000 bribe from the owner of the Mustang Ranch brothel. He serves now as Ted Binion's estate lawyer.

It was during this period that Texas narcotics kingpin Jimmy Chagra began laundering tens of millions of dollars in drug profits at the Horseshoe. Chagra had ties to both the Patriarca family in New England and to the Chicago Syndicate, then run by Tony Accardo. (Accardo's children's nanny, Madeleine, attended Loyola University with me in the fall of '69, Bad Jim's most mobbed-up semester, Good Jim's most revolutionary.) With Chagra on trial in Texas for heroin trafficking, Jack, Ted, and Benny convened in Booth 1 of the Horseshoe coffee shop with Oscar Goodman, the hyperaggressive young Philadelphia attorney representing the accused. The upshot of that meeting was a $50,000 contract for Charles Harrelson (actor Woody's father) to assassinate U.S. District Court judge John Wood—or so the lore has it. Nicknamed Maximum John because of the stiffness of his sentences, Wood was presiding over Chagra's trial in San Antonio.

The working assumption in the coffee shop must have been that neither a satchel stuffed with hundred-dollar bills for Maximum John nor
an eloquent closing by Oscar would yield the desired results. Admissi-
ble evidence that a hit had been authorized? None. Harrelson was registered at the Horseshoe that week, however, and the FBI case file
called WOODMUR concludes: "it was the Binion family that introduced [censored] to [censored] in the Wood shooting. It is believed
that their introduction took place at the Horseshoe Casino" in May
1979, during the final event of the World Series of Poker (won that
year by Hal Fowler). On May 29, Judge Wood was fatally shot in the
back with a hunting rifle as he left his Alamo Heights apartment for
the courthouse in San Antonio. As Hooper, the feisty ichthyologist in
Jaws, might have concluded: "This was no hunting accident." Chagra's
case was nonetheless declared a mistrial, the defendant went free, and
young Oscar Goodman's reputation was made in the bargain. The
money went on being laundered.

By this point Jack Binion was in charge of the general casino operations, while Ted ran, or "hosted," the gaming floor, especially during
the Series. "Jack is the boss," their father reported. "Ted's next boss."
The basic division of labor had Jack around during regular business
hours, while Ted ran the show after dark. Ted oversaw the pit bosses,
settled big-money disputes, approved crazy bets. One high roller, fed
up after three days of heavy losses at the blackjack table, accused his
dealer of cheating and began making threats. Ted strolled over and
heard the man out, then told him, "Have your bodyguard deal." The
man calmed down a bit after that, though his losing streak continued.
Case closed.

Benny had come to prefer the kitchens as his bailiwick. His motto
was, "Good food cheap, good whiskey cheap, and a good gamble." He
also insisted on cleanliness. "My kitchens get dirty," he threatened
with weirdly draconian logic, "I'll call the health department. They'll
straighten 'em up pretty quick." All beef served at Horseshoe restaurants, from the ground chuck in burgers and chili to the prime rib up
in the steak house, came from his 400,000-acre ranch in Montana.
Quality nonbeef selections also appeared on the menu. Cloutier recalls
that Benny "always had some oddball item in the players' buffet line—

buffalo steak, rattlesnake, bear meat, this and that—and the main courses were never repeated during the Series. This was true all the time that Benny was alive." Poker players loved him for it, and loved his two sons, but no one doubted who was in charge. "Them boys mind me like they was six years old," Benny bragged.

Christened Lonnie Theodore, as his father had been christened Lester Ben, the younger of "them boys" was always called Ted after his mother, Teddy Jane. Following the same reverse-gender system, Barbara and Brenda and Becky got soundalike versions of their father's name. Ted eventually grew up into Benny's hat and shoe size and big, moon-faced features, but not into his commanding personality. As to being "next boss" behind Jack, it probably wasn't the first time Ted had suffered the perils of birth order.

Ted was more rakishly handsome than his brother—brighter eyes, toothier, scalp yielding more hair, which he let grow longer and wilder than Jack did his. Inclined to dark business suits, Jack was a brilliant executive—World Series revenue multiplied almost a hundredfold during his tenure—while Ted preferred dressing down while mixing it up with hard-living high rollers. Ted also drank more, inhaled more drugs, partied harder. A lot of folks formed the impression that the untamed and savvy traits blended so formidably in the senior Binion got separated out in his sons. Ted, in fact, was less like his father or brother than he was like his big sister, Barbara. Reckless with street drugs since she was a teenager, she'd married Clay Fechser too young; once she and Clay separated, she moved with their three sons to her father's ranch in Montana. Unable to stop using heroin, though, she stole back to Vegas whenever she could. Cloutier used to eat breakfast with Benny in the old Sombrero Room, and it gradually became clear to him that Barbara "was the apple of his eye." One morning Benny made a somber announcement: "Fellas, I just let it be known in the whole town that if I hear of one man selling one thing of dope to Barbara, he's a dead man." His threat didn't work. Barbara's addiction went uncured, and she finally committed suicide in 1977 at the age of thirty-nine.

Wounded but unchastened, Benny soldiered on. To compete with the Rat Pack, Folies Bergère, Elvis Presley, and all the extravagant architecture down on the Strip, he had put together something more true to his roots: a seven-foot-tall golden horseshoe with his collection of one hundred $10,000 bills affixed behind Plexiglas. Working-class tourists flocked in, drawn by the opportunity to be photographed next to the money. "That million dollars advertises us a lot, you know," Benny reckoned, sounding more like a down-home J. Walter Thompson than a Lansky lieutenant. "Them people that has their picture made there, I just wonder, there's no tellin' how valuable that is advertisementwise, because even if they show it to two people each, that might come in here—in the summertime we take six hundred pictures a day, so that's quite a lot of people." The Horseshoe vault still houses thousands of negatives, including one of the Manson family posing in front of the moola, demonic little Charles front and center.

Benny's first and more epochal move advertisementwise had been launching the World Series of Poker in 1970. The idea had been germinating ever since Nick "the Greek" Dandalos came to town in 1949 wanting to play "the biggest game this world has to offer." Having broken every high roller back east (including Arnold Rothstein, who'd fixed baseball's World Series in 1919, thus jinxing my Black Sox for the next eight decades and counting), Dandalos had won in the neighborhood of $60 million, though he lost most of it back on the Thoroughbreds at Joe Kennedy's track in Hialeah, Florida. He had earned a degree from a British university, and his reading in the humanities may have helped him fathom that he'd best stick to cards. Told that Benny Binion was the man to see about no-limit action, Dandalos proposed that the Horseshoe's impresario match him against "any man around" in a head-to-head, winner-take-all poker marathon.

Benny conferred with his friend Jimmy Snyder, who also used "the Greek" as his moniker. Snyder had contended for years that poker was America's natural game. Still played mostly in back rooms and kitchens, however, it remained an underground national pastime. All it needed to become more visible, Snyder imagined, was the institutional organization of baseball; and to get that, it needed a forum. Snyder also surmised that the best poker players were Texans, partly because of the vastness of their landscape and how little else it afforded by way of amusement. (More recently, British journalist David Spanier argued that poker's wide-open betting patterns went more naturally with the "aura of adventure" in the American west, very much including the Lone Star State, while more tightly regimented games like gin rummy were better suited, as it were, to densely populated eastern cities.) In any case, Snyder argued that the best man to stand up to Dandalos would hail from that ornery state.

Convinced by Snyder's logic, Benny phoned his friend Johnny Moss, the best poker player he knew. Moss's formal education had ended, like Benny's, in second grade, but no one could beat Moss at poker—or Benny at entrepreneurship. Legend has it that Moss was already in a pretty good game in Odessa when his friend finally reached him. He'd been playing for three days straight without sleep, but he still got on the first plane to Vegas, took a taxi to Benny's place on a crisp Sunday afternoon in January, and immediately sat down to play.

Since Dandalos was fifty-seven years old and Moss forty-two, stamina was going to be a factor. So was publicity. Benny positioned their table near the entrance to his casino, where it was soon hemmed in by respectful audiences of two or three hundred. From time to time wealthy aspirants were permitted to "change in" to the game for a minimum of $10,000, but none lasted more than a day or two. Early on, the Greek pulled dramatically ahead, threatening to wipe out Moss's more limited bankroll. Apparently the Greek seldom slept, since he spent nearly all of their break time at the craps table. Once, when Moss came back downstairs from a nap, Dandalos joshed him, "What are you going to do, Johnny, sleep your life away?"

They played for five months, breaking for sleep only once every four or five days, this as fresh dealers rotated in every twenty minutes to keep the action brisk and precise. Meanwhile, the flock of railbirds continued to grow. Noting how much they were wagering elsewhere in his casino, Benny accurately proclaimed his new main attraction "the biggest game in town." During one break, he and Dandalos got to chaperone Albert Einstein along Fremont Street, introducing him as "Little Al from Princeton—controls a lot of the action around Jersey."

In one famous hand of five-card stud, the faceup cards were 8-6-4-J for the Greek and 6-9-2-3 for Moss. With over $100,000 already in the pot, the Greek bet $50,000. Moss, who had a nine in the hole, moved all his available chips in, reraising. The Greek had only $140,000 left of what had recently been an eight-figure bankroll. "I guess I have to call you," he said, pushing the last of his chips toward the pot, "because I think I've got a jack in the hole." Moss told him, "Greek, if you've got a jack down there, you're liable to win a helluva pot." Dandalos indeed had the jack. By recklessly chasing Moss's pair of nines during the final two betting rounds—hoping for, even counting on, then *getting* the miracle jack—Dandalos had just won a half million dollars.

"But that's all right," Moss said years later, observing that the Greek's risk-reward ratio didn't bode well for him. "I broke him in the end." The Greek finally succumbed with a handshake and the famous line, "Mr. Moss, I have to let you go." Legend has it that the Texan took between $2 and $3 million from the game. Adjusted for inflation, this would be like winning $100 million today.

Lest all these dollar signs appear a bit crass, it's important to understand that money is the language of poker, its means of keeping score, just as points are the language of ball sports, fire and produce the language of cuisine, and words—as Lancey Howard (played by Edward G. Robinson) notes in *The Cincinnati Kid*—the language of thought. And nowhere does money speak more eloquently, with greater or more precise impact, or as part of a longer tradition, than at Binion's World Series of Poker.

Yet the tournament started out small. In the spring of 1970, Benny simply invited six of his high-rolling cronies to compete among themselves, then vote for the best all-around player. Moss was sixty-three now, yet he thoroughly outplayed all five younger rivals, who voted him the champion. He received a small trophy and whatever he'd earned at the table.

The current freeze-out structure, in which everyone sits down with exactly $10,000 and plays until one person has all the chips, was established the following year. Moss won in this format, too, netting $30,000 for defeating six opponents, all of them fellow professionals. (The other $30,000 was divided between two runners-up.) The next year's winner, Amarillo Slim Preston, won $80,000 for beating twice as many opponents. Much more the raconteur than Mr. Moss, the tall, rail-thin Preston put together a quickie best-seller called *Maverick Poker* and went on the talk-show circuit. His four appearances on Johnny Carson's *Tonight Show* were a smash, boosting exponentially the public's interest in tournament poker. Slim's looks and garrulousness captivated the vast TV audience, and he went on to do three stints on *60 Minutes* and seven more appearances on *Tonight*; he also addressed the National Press Club and the United States Senate. Slim became such a hot guest, in fact, that Tom Snyder gave him and Benny an entire *Tomorrow Show*, during which they put on what Slim called "an hour's commercial for the Horseshoe."

"Benny," asked Snyder at one point, "why is it that those places out there on the Strip in Vegas have a five-hundred-dollar limit and you've got no limit?"

"Well, they got great big hotels and little biddy bankrolls," he told Snyder. "I got a little biddy hotel and a great big bankroll."

"But aren't you afraid someone will break the bank?"

"Well, not really. I got a darned good head start on 'em."

The Horseshoe was now on the map.

"This poker game here gets us a lot of attention," Benny told University of Nevada oral historian Mary Ellen Glass in 1973. And he wasn't exaggerating. Seven thousand stories about Binion's World Series had appeared that year alone in newspapers and magazines. Yet Benny was just getting started. "We had seven players last year, and this year we had thirteen. I look to have better than twenty next year. It's even liable to get up to be fifty, might get up to be more than that . . ." He paused, gazing beyond his interviewer for a moment. "It will eventually."

By the time Doyle Brunson became the second repeat champion in '77, eighty-five players had entered, with first prize mushrooming to $340,000. Jack and Ted ran the tournament now, with Eric Drache, Jim Albrecht, and Jack McClelland as their principal lieutenants. Their boldest move was to introduce satellites, less expensive mini-tournaments designed to democratize entry into the Big One by giving players with as little as $220 a chance to win a $10,000 seat; before then, only the top poker pros and a few millionaire amateurs had been able to afford it. By 1986 the number of entries, and total prize money, had multiplied by an order of magnitude.

First prize rose to $700,000 by '88, the second year Johnny Chan won. This time the Orient Express narrowly defeated Erik Seidel, a tall, pensive New Yorker who had outplayed the entire field until the very last hand; in that hand, however, Chan made a straight on the flop and trapped Seidel into going all-in with a pair of queens. Unfortunately for Seidel, this was the only hand featured in *Rounders*, the Matt Damon–Edward Norton vehicle that ends with the Damon character heading to Binion's from downtown Manhattan with $30,000 in his pocket.

Since 1991 first prize for the World Series championship has been an even $1 million, with entries and total prize money steadily climbing. Almost from its inception, the dollars awarded at the WSOP have dwarfed the purses of Wimbledon, the Masters, and the Kentucky Derby, not to mention baseball's World Series. There are now twenty-three preliminary events, the smallest of which yields more lucrative spoils than the largest event at most other tournaments. The 1999 championship drew 393 entries, with second place paying a record $768,625. As far as prestige is concerned, a recent poll of fifteen touring pros asked them to rank the fifty most important tournaments worldwide: the championship event at Binion's received every first-place vote, giving it a perfect aggregate score of 15. Twenty of the next thirty best scores, in fact, were preliminary WSOP events. Golf and tennis have four majors apiece, boxing a shifting variety, horse racing three. Poker still has only one.

When Benny Binion died on Christmas Day, 1989, Slim Preston proposed an epitaph for his friend: "He was either the gentlest bad guy or the baddest good guy you'd ever seen." T.J. Cloutier recalled Benny's generosity this way: "If you caught him on a good day—say that you went broke and he knew you and knew that you gambled at his joint—Benny was the type of guy you could go to and get a couple of thousand without putting up any security. He'd just flip it to you and say, 'Pay it when you can, son.' "

The steepest buy-in at the tournament Benny invented remains $10,000, almost cheap when you consider that the same amount was required of interlopers to the 1949 Moss-Dandalos epic. These days the majority of players gain entry by winning satellites or super-satellites. Last year, as a matter of fact, Irishman Noel Furlong parlayed success in a $220 super-satellite into $1 million and the gold championship bracelet. Satellites are also thought by many players to be the most legitimate route into the final, since they reward poker skill instead of deep pockets, though the two often work hand in hand. They also give people like me the only chance we might ever have to play with the big boys and girls.

The $3,000 no-limit hold'em event starts tomorrow at noon, so that's when I'll play my first satellite—while the best three or four hundred no-limit players in the world are otherwise engaged. It's now 10:22 PST, but my body clock says it's tomorrow. My Wednesday began in Chicago at 7 a.m. After teaching my last class, I turned in my grades, took the Blue Line out to O'Hare, and got on a four-hour flight. But as much as I'd love to, I can't go to bed yet, mainly because I need to habituate myself to late hours on Pacific time. I should also take a few notes on the action, if only because I'll feel more comfortable playing when I've at least got that stage of my article off the ground. The $1,015 satellites (with $15 making up the house juice) are contested ten-handed, which will make me a 9–1 underdog, assuming I'm evenly matched with my adversaries, and of course I will not be. But a night's sleep and diluted competition will give me the best, or least bad, chance of winning.

Another harsh fact: I only have enough money for three one-table satellites and a couple of $220 supers with two or three rebuys apiece. As Tom McEvoy argues persuasively in *Tournament Poker,* "three is the over and under on satellites." Any more than three, in other words, is probably neither cost-effective nor psychologically healthy. McEvoy bases a lot of his advice on having won the Big One in '83, the first time a satellite winner went on to take the championship; the second-place finisher, Rod Peate, had also gained entry that way. The winner of dozens of tournaments since then, McEvoy is also coauthor of all three of Cloutier's books, so he clearly knows whereof he speaks. Any more than 30 percent of the buy-in is too much to risk on the satellites, besides being a fair indication that you're not on your game at the moment. Cut your losses, McEvoy advises. With $4,500 in toto, I really won't have any choice.

Picking up my credentials in a tiny office on the mezzanine reminds me of how Hunter Thompson picked up his for the motorcycle race back in '71, when the drip of LSD through his cranium caused him to see the press liaison folks as a pit of fanged reptiles. After threatening them with a marlin spike, Thompson gave his name as Dr. Gonzo and was promptly issued a pass. Thus armed, he skipped the big race altogether, heading back up to 860 to imbibe more intoxicants, the better to understand the TV news coverage from Southeast Asia—"explosions of twisted wreckage, men fleeing in terror, Pentagon generals babbling insane lies," as he saw it. Reporting in a more peaceful epoch, I shake hands with Emily Fitzsimmons, a beautiful, dark-haired nonreptile, then give her my actual name. And it works.

The *Guardian*, *Le Monde*, and the *Times* of London and New York and Los Angeles are all here. So is the Discovery Channel, says Emily. Their documentary video of the '99 event was one of their most highly rated broadcasts ever, so they're producing an even longer report on this year's final table. ESPN will continue to present nightly features on the results, with live radio and Internet coverage.

Before checking out the main poker room, I detour to the cafeteria for my first meal since lunch on the plane. Turkey, mash, carrots, green salad, iced tea. No rattlesnake this evening, apparently; no grizzly, either. No problem. My battle plan for the week is to swim every morning, avoid alcohol, smoke no more than one cigarette per day, go easy on red meat and viper. At home I drink far too much red wine, tequila, and vodka, so I have to cut down for both poker and health reasons. I've also been advised to take aspirin and 50 mg of Zocor every morning with my oatmeal and orange juice, and 50 mg of Trazodone for insomnia. In light of all this, I recently bought a second life insurance policy, making me worth almost a million the moment I expire, another sense in which I'm dead money.

The crowded main tournament room has thirty-five kidney-shaped tables, each surrounded by ten or eleven chairs, every last one of them occupied. During the rest of the year, this is the Bingo Room. The size of a grammar school gym, the room has a ceiling fitted with cameras and monitors but not quite enough ventilation for the number of players who smoke. Three times brighter than the casino downstairs, this room is quieter, more serious. Posters along two of the walls list results from the seventeen previous events, including breakdowns of prize money and color photographs of the winners. Very little else in the way of adornment; no music except for the droning announcements of poker activity and locustlike clacking of chips.

Shangri-la.

Most of the satellites tonight have $300 buy-ins to generate a seat in tomorrow's $3,000 event, but a couple of tables along the near rail are reserved for $1,015 action. The only player I recognize here is Jack Keller, the 1984 world champion. A famously arrogant (and successful) road gambler, Keller also finished ninth in '87 and eighth in '92, and six years ago was inducted into the Poker Hall of Fame. Still only fifty-seven, the former Air Force pilot no longer plays many tournaments, concentrating instead on high-stakes live action in Mississippi, though I've heard he makes it out to Las Vegas for the last few events of every World Series. Fingering chips with his long pale fingers, white hair brushed back in a sideburnless pompadour above hooded, forbidding brown eyes, he's the sort of fellow about whom it feels reasonable to assume there's a switchblade taped inside his boot.

Among the crowd of folks only watching right now, I finally spot Linda Johnson, *Card Player*'s plump, red-haired editor. Most of what I know about female players I know from reading her magazine, along with her e-mails and other material she sent me. She's also promised to introduce me to three or four of the best once I got here, as well as to her writers Andy Glazer and Nolan Dalla, whose columns I've studied with pleasure. Introducing myself to Linda now, I'm also meeting in person one of only three female WSOP bracelet owners. Linda got hers for winning the 1997 razz championship. Razz is a form of seven-card stud in which the lowest hand takes the pot, and Linda's new book, *Championship Stud*, cowritten with McEvoy and Dr. Max Stern, is the definitive work on that game.

As we stand here discussing former champions, Linda points out that Jack Keller's daughter, Kathy Kolberg, is playing one of the $300 satellites three tables in from us. Briefly married at seventeen, Kolberg now has a son, Brad, that age. She usually works as a proposition player in a southern California casino. (Props are paid a small salary by card rooms to fill out their tables.) She also happens to be one of the most attractive women on the tournament circuit. Even as she sits at a table smoking extrathin cigarettes, you can tell that she's rangy and lean, with straight old-gold tresses to the middle of her back. But the main reason I'm interested in talking to her is I've been told (not by Linda) that she used to be Rick Tabish's girlfriend. I'd like to know whether it's true.

Another gossipworthy aspect of Kolberg's life is easier to verify. Raised as a Latter Day Saint by her mother and stepfather, Kathy was told that her biological father was a rogue poker player—"and sort of a hustler," as Kolberg told an interviewer—who died when she was an infant. Jack Keller became, in a sense, Exhibit A in the two-count Mormon indictment of gambling and sex out of wedlock. In spite or because of this, Kathy felt ineluctably drawn to poker as she became a young woman, even as she excelled academically and, like just about everyone else in those days, made love before she got married.

In 1983 she received a four-year scholarship to the University of Montana, but as a seventeen-year-old single mother she still needed to wait tables four nights a week. When the bar she worked at suddenly needed a poker dealer in its back room, Kolberg volunteered. She excelled in this discipline, too. Dealing countless hands and observing what good players did with them, she began to develop a sense of her father's old game. And she loved it.

During the spring semester of her first year at the university, she happened to hear Paul Harvey on the radio interviewing the newest world champion of poker—"Gentleman Jack Keller," as Harvey referred to him. Kolberg put two and two together, called the *Las Vegas Sun*, and persuaded someone to send her a half dozen photographs of the winner. And damn if his face didn't bear a strong resemblance to the pictures she had of her father. With no address to go on, she called

Binion's Horseshoe but was informed that no one named Jack Keller was registered. (He was staying, as usual, as an unregistered guest of the Binions.) Kolberg kept pressing the woman on the switchboard and was eventually connected to the poker room. After sweet-talking a couple of off-duty dealers, whose language she knew from her own job, she finally managed to get Mr. Keller on the line. Through the clatter of chips and table talk, she heard his reedy voice skeptically inquire, "Hello?"

"This is Kathy," she said. "I think I'm your daughter."

After a lengthy silence, the man cleared his throat. "I think you are, too."

He sent her two plane tickets to Vegas, where she met his wife, Gloria, and her younger half brothers, Jack and Scott. She also introduced her father to his grandson. If Jack hadn't won the World Series, of course, this gathering might never have taken place.

Kolberg went on to earn a B.A. with honors in psychology, then entered Montana's graduate program in sociology, choosing criminal justice as her major concentration. To support herself and Brad, she was dealing—as well as playing—more poker around Missoula. She played at the Stockman's Bar (the establishment that inspired the "Liquor Up Front, Poker in the Rear" placards now displayed in barrooms throughout the world) as well as at the Silver Tip, the Claim Jumper, and the notorious Ox, whose *other* back room featured topless dancers. While working toward her master's degree, Kolberg also trained and was licensed as a polygraph examiner, eventually landing part-time jobs with prosecutors, defense attorneys, and probation officers.

It was during this period that she supposedly met and began dating Rick Tabish. Tabish had played linebacker at Montana State down in Bozeman. He was now back home, using his Missoula family's connections to gain a foothold in the booming construction business. The dark-haired former jock also had outlaw cachet, having already been arrested four times. He had even served five months in prison for using a FedEx mailer to smuggle cocaine up from Phoenix.

Two of Kolberg's friends have told me that Rick and Kathy dated and lived together for about eighteen months, and that Kolberg broke off the relationship when Tabish started seeing Mary Jo Rebhein, the daughter of one of the wealthiest families in Montana. After going to work for her father, Tabish married Rebhein in June 1990.

By 1995, with Tabish well out of her life, Kolberg was earning more as a poker player, both in cash games and small tournaments, than she was in criminal justice. Further inspired by her father's induction that year into the Poker Hall of Fame, she entered the Hall of Fame tournament at Binion's. In her first poker foray outside Montana, Kolberg made the money in three preliminary events, then shocked herself and more than a few other people by finishing second in the no-limit hold'em event. She was hooked.

A female player this talented is a natural interview subject for the poker dimension of my article. I'd also love to ask her about Tabish's interest in lie detector tests. Was he taking one from her when they first locked eyes, for example, in the ultimate outlaw cute-meet? Not that I'd phrase it that way, but the reason I'd like to inquire is that last April, Tabish hired Robert Furu, a private polygraph examiner in Bozeman, to ask him whether he had "participated in the death of Ted Binion in any way." According to Tabish, his answer was no, and the results were deemed by Furu to be "nondeceptive." So I'd love to get a sense of how familiar Tabish was with the parameters, or "foolability," of the various exams and examiners. If Kolberg volunteers anything else about their relationship, so much the better.

I wait until she gets up from her satellite before going over to introduce myself—too quickly, I realize, since everyone needs time to cool off after getting knocked out. My next mistake is bringing up Tabish. Kolberg shakes her head with contempt, making it blazingly clear she doesn't want to talk about, or be associated in any way with, "that asshole." I immediately change the subject to her father and their poker connection, but it may be too late. She gives me to believe that she isn't real happy with Dad at the moment, and that it has to do with his current young girlfriend, who drinks and encourages Jack to; nor is she happy with me. No Chatty Kathy to begin with, Kolberg is pretty unthrilled with every subject I've brought up so far. She will say she's never read poker advice books, relying on her experience as a dealer and player. "Plus instinct," she says, flashing me the ghost of a smile. Up close, there's a sadness in the cast of her almond-shaped hazel eyes that puts me in mind of a Kurt Weill tango crooned by Patricia O'Callaghan. Mesmerized, up way past my bedtime, I blurt yet another dumb question: How curious was Rick about her polygraph expertise?

"Look," she says, staring at me as though I'm severely retarded, "I've gotta go now."

"Of course. But can I talk to you any time later—"

Interview over. With firmness of purpose and a fine, erect posture, Kolberg departs toward the elevators, golden hair swaying minutely.

So how do I feel, having blown our Q&A so spectacularly? I suppose I feel pretty much the way I always do when a beautiful woman walks away from me angry. I feel . . . sociobiosophical, is how. Because an impressive variety of genetic theories have been tested by tracking identical twins raised in different environments, but Jack Keller's daughter, raised as she was in a radically different environment than he would have provided, may be the best evidence we're likely to get that poker acumen is borne along in the helices of our DNA. (Doyle Brunson's son, Todd, also plays poker professionally.)

The beauty of no-limit hold'em, in fact, parallels that of all human mating procedures. Biologically, we bet that our hole cards (read: DNA) will combine with the cards on the board (our prospective mate's DNA) to produce the strongest hand or fittest amalgam—that is, the one with the best chance of surviving the contest of life by launching the most, and most fit, genes into the next generation. Translation? I'd love to play poker with Kolberg, if only to get her to talk about Gentleman Jack and Slick Rick. Certainly the pleasures of poker are at least partly genetic, because all pleasure is. And all play. Among mammals, humans have the longest period of immaturity or preadulthood; and during our extended childhoods, play is the key to our ability to learn complex tasks: how to feed ourselves, read, calculate, write, find a mate. The leisurely timetable of development encoded in the sequences of our DNA allows this to happen, or else it evolved *to* allow it. Either way, our imaginative flexibility as adults springs from stimulating experiences we had under stable conditions free from serious danger when we were children. From playing. That's why we *still* love to play. In which case . . .

Disturbing my overwrought revery, a harried blond floorperson with a clipboard and microphone is trying to fill the next satellite. "One more seat, players," she says. Her name tag, I now see, says CAROL. "Chance to win a seat in the Big One!" I can also see that nine hopefuls already have chips stacked in front of them, along with their Walkmans and water bottles, ashtrays and fans.

As my hero Fyodor Mikhailovich confessed to his second bride, Anna Grigoryevna, who'd conquered his heart while taking down *The Gambler* in shorthand, "Once I hear the clatter of the chips, I almost go into convulsions." Hear, hear. Down I sit, forking over $1,015. Tired schmired. And *screw* Kathy Kolberg! Because once I get my own stack of six pink five-hundred-dollar chips, eight black one-hundreds, and eight green quarters and the dealer starts shuffling, I've never felt any more ready.

How is this game played, exactly? Or, as the proverbial son asked his father: "How long does it take to learn to play poker?" Father: "All your life, son." You can change these to daughter and father, son and stepmother (or, in my case, to nephew/grandson and uncle, grandmother, and grandfather), but whoever is asking and answering, the first thing you'll need to know is the

RANKING OF POKER HANDS

Straight flush: five consecutive cards of the same suit. The highest possible hand is an ace-high straight flush, called a *royal*.

Four of a kind: four cards of the same rank.

Full house: three cards of one rank and two of another, such as three fives and two queens, called *fives full of queens*.

Flush: five cards of the same suit.

Straight: five consecutive cards of mixed suits. (In a straight, an ace can be used as either a high or low card.)

Three of a kind: three cards of the same rank.

Two pairs: two cards of the same rank and two other cards of another rank.

Pair: two cards of the same rank. (If two players both have the same pair or three-of-a-kind, the highest other card in their hand, called a *kicker*, determines the winner.)

No pair, in which the highest ranking cards take the pot. (A-Q-9-7-2 beats A-J-10-8-6, for example.)

This hierarchy is determined by the mathematical scarcity of all five-card hands makable from a 52-card deck; the more rare the hand, the higher its rank. Once the hierarchy has been established, we can say that Texas hold'em involves nine (but sometimes as few as two or as many as ten) players receiving two facedown cards each (called *hole cards*), followed by three faceup community cards dealt simultaneously in the middle of the table (*the flop*), a fourth community card (*the turn*, or *fourth street*), then a fifth and final community card (*the river*, or *fifth street*). Two rotating antes called *blinds* initiate a round of betting before the flop, with three rounds of bets after that. (Read slowly through here. Go back and reread if you miss something.) The player to the left of the dealer *posts* (puts into the pot) the *small blind*, and the player to *his* left posts the *big blind*. Starting at $25 and $50, respectively, the blinds in this satellite double every twenty minutes, so we'll have ourselves a winner in an hour or two, not a week. And, since we're playing no-limit, the process of elimination is further accelerated. A player may bet anything from $50 (the size of the big blind) up to all his chips at any point in the sequence, though a raise must at least match the size of the previous bet. No-limit action seldom reaches a showdown on fifth street; if it does, however, then the best five-card poker hand wins. Most often, an intimidatingly massive wager before or just after the flop gets no *callers* (players willing to match the bet), and the bettor receives the whole pot.

Read this next paragraph even more slowly. Because things get much trickier when factoring in your *position*. Acting last from the dealer's position (since the dealer doesn't play in casinos, this position is denoted by the *button*, a white pucklike marker that rotates clockwise around the table hand by hand) or just to the right are the strongest positions, since you see everyone else's action before having to decide yourself whether to call, raise, or fold. You can therefore get away with playing slightly weaker hole cards (a jack and a queen of different suits, for example) in late position. Whereas only big pairs, ace-king, or suited connecting face cards (the king and queen of diamonds, for example) are likely to make money when played from an early position. As early shades clockwise into middle then later and later position, the subtlest valences of wagering assert themselves and less savvy players (like me) tend to get soundly outmaneuvered.

Even though no-limit hold'em didn't become widely popular until the mid-1980s, most players now consider it the purest version of the game, and it continues to be the form that determines the World Series champion. Although I grew up playing five-card draw and seven-card stud, these days I much prefer hold'em, mainly because it doesn't penalize poor short-term memory. Players with photographic recall have a whopping advantage in stud games, wherein as many as twenty-four faceup cards that have been folded decisively circumscribe the hands still in play. (If six clubs have been folded, for example, you don't want to draw to a club flush. Clubs are now "dead," as stud players would say.) I have enough trouble remembering my own pocket cards without having to keep track of two dozen cards that were folded three minutes ago. Hold'em is also faster (fewer cards dealt yield more hands per hour) and more subtly competitive, mainly because five sevenths of your hand consists of community cards, which your opponents will also be playing. (See Poker Terminology on p. 389 for any further clarification.)

My satellite rivals are mostly middle-aged guys of all stripes: the anxious, the collected, the pocky, the sleek; ex-beatniks, ex-jocks, and ex-hippies. So I feel right at home on all counts, except one. At least four of them are able, with the fingers of one hand, to cut a stack of a dozen chips into two stacks of six and then riffle them neatly back together. You don't learn to riffle like that while playing against a computer.

One of us is gonna stroll off with everyone else's thousand bucks, yet the table has a friendly, if not quite munificent, vibe. When someone gets edged at the showdown—a king kicker over a jack, for example—the response is, "Good hand." We also make chip change and tip cocktail waitresses for one another. None of this fools me, however.

A long-haired Vietnamese dude in round mirrored shades has taken the lead, winning three of the first eleven pots. Doing less well is the toothless varmint in Seat 1, immediately to the left of the dealer; a victim of poker's worst-case scenario, he's come in second now twice in a row and is down to a short stack of greens. He doesn't look happy, of course. He also appears to have blown off his last few appointments at the haberdasher, dentist, gymnasium, spa, and salon. How can one know this? Because his scraggly gray beard starts high on his cheekbones and covers his Adam's apple, with scalp hair of similar aspect, the entire gnarled package tentatively winched together by a powder blue UNLV cap. Yee-haw. Yours truly sports poker face, professional haircut, neatly trimmed goatee, progressive titanium shades, and pale gray Bellagio cap but still hasn't entered one pot. Him too scared.

The one thing I'm happy about is the opportunity to wear my sunglasses indoors for the length of the tournament. As everyone knows, image is crucial at the poker table. Opponents gauge the strength of your hand by reading dozens of signals, and appearance is certainly one of them. Entire chapters of advice books, in fact, are devoted to "table presence." Cloutier and McEvoy say: "You want to instill a little fear in your opponents, because when they are afraid of you, you sometimes can get free cards." Your opponents will check, in other words, instead of betting into you; thus, if *you* choose to check as well, the next community card is seen "free." Cloutier and McEvoy also recommend "confusing your opponents about the type of player you really are"—pretending, for example, to be confident about your hand when you're scared, or vice versa. Doyle Brunson once proclaimed he could vanquish most opponents without even looking at his own cards, since he picks up enough clues from his opponents' mannerisms and tendencies to separate them from their money.

Even though in my regular glasses I'm several degrees less intimidating, I just may look smarter in clear lenses, if endowed with a bit less machismo, at least according to the code of movie and rock stars. (I have Keith Richards' recessive chin but lack his swashbuckling brio. On my good days, I've been told that I resemble Eric Clapton or Gary Oldman; on bad days—don't ask.) But in sunglasses, man, it's a whole other story. My albeit progressive-bifocal shades suggest not feeble nearsightedness but its opposite—penetrating 20/20 vision to go with impenetrable coolth. Wearing them indoors without a legitimate reason (blindness, jazz mastery) annuls the entire effect, since you look like you're trying too hard, prolly because you's *ascared*. But what better excuse can there be than competing for the heavyweight championship against no-limit experts who can tell at a glance whether your irises are expanding with pleasure or contracting with fear? And what better screens to conceal yourself behind while scrutinizing *their* facial tics, heaving chests, trembling fingers? Now if only this dealer—JOHN, says his nameplate—would shoot me a card above nine . . .

Not a chance. Four-seven . . . trey-seven . . . queen-five. Muck, muck, muck.

Four of my opponents have also put up $200 each for a last-longer pool; the final person eliminated among them gets $800. Everyone at the table was invited to enter the pool, but confidence and bankroll issues made me choose not to participate. Neither did the guy in Seat 10, a jock in his early twenties with a freshly stitched wound running from behind his left ear to the collar of his navy Lacoste shirt. Surgery or knife fight, I figured, then found myself weighing a call against him based on which I thought it was: if surgery, fold; if knife fight, reraise. (I folded.) At another point, staring balefully at a flop of low spades, he asked of no one in particular, "Straight flush beats four of a kind, right?" After twenty-five minutes he ended up going all-in, and when his pocket nines went down to three sevens, the kid just shook his cropped head and stood up. The CINDY tattoo on his calf looked fresh, too.

Even having played poker for thirty-nine years, I'm still so nervous that I don't always follow the betting sequence. Twice the dealer has had to say, "Your action, sir," meaning it's my turn to check, bet, or fold. Despite the fact that computer poker goes thirty to fifty times faster, the action here is plenty swift for me. I've got so many extra factors to consider, and so much at stake, that, if anything, the play is too fast. Nor can I put the Stones, Townes Van Zandt, or Lee Morgan on the stereo; I can't talk to Jennifer or my kids (or my friends on the telephone), or stroll to the powder room every time I feel a slight twinge. And I certainly can't sit here with strategy manuals open in my lap, thumbing an index or two for advice about playing A-J. (No rule prohibits it, other than the desire not to look like a shlub.) The main thing I need here is *feel*, and for this books and computers can't help much.

Right now from middle position I'm playing A-J, both red but of two different suits, having called a $200 preflop raise. The raiser is a muscular Arab in salt-stained tortoiseshell Wayfarers with an unlit cigar in his teeth—not Masque's "Player #4" or "Gentle Ben" on Wilson Turbo. I believe that his name is Amir. Much more important to know is: What is he thinking that I'm thinking that he's thinking? Is his visceral aplomb all an act? The only thing I'm sure of is that he *wants my money* more than Gentle Ben or Player #4 ever could. If I can't look into his eyes, at least I can observe how hard his lungs and face muscles are working. If I've tuned him in right, I can feel it. But two other guys have called, too.

The flop now comes ace, five, king—all of spades. With a spade flush a distinct possibility, there's a $300 bet and a call just behind me. That no one has raised makes my pot odds about 10–1, with my chance to make a full house (the only hand I can make that would beat a flush) a lot worse than one in eleven. But I call—*what the hell*, runs my crazed-chicken logic—and fourth street comes up jack of spades, giving me aces and jacks. I now have four outs (cards that will probably make me a winner): the remaining two aces and two jacks. That is, of the forty-six cards that could be turned over next, forty-two cannot help me, assuming a flush has been made. It would only take one measly spade.

After Amir bets $300, the slender Pakistani guy next to him raises $800 and . . . and the next thing I know the dealer is staring at me. So is Amir. So is the guy who just raised him.

I push my cards into the muck, and Amir calls the extra $800. Folding a four-outer makes me groan with irrational pride, but when the dealer burns the top card (slides it facedown) and turns over the jack of clubs, I no longer have a good feeling. The Pakistani turns out to be holding the 9–10 of spades, and he rakes in what must be a $3,000 pot.

I need to take a piss about now, but I hold it, sit tight, and the poker gods deem fit to reward me for folding when the odds were against me. In a slow-motion flash, fifteen hands go by in which I can do no wrong. I win *six* good-sized pots, three in a row toward the end. Holding J-J, I raise the blinds to $800, get no callers; my set of queens beats a set of tens; and my king-high straight holds up against a queen-high for a $9,800 pot.

By midnight I have $19,500, almost half the chips on the table, with only two opponents between me and a seat in the Big One. The Pakistani (his name, I have learned in the meantime, is Hasan Habib) has roughly $11,000, and a big, bearded guy named Tom Jacobs is riffling $9,500. Wanting to "spread the wealth," Jacobs calls time-out to propose what he calls "a straight $2,000 save." This means we'd play on till one of us has all the chips, but each of us would now guarantee the other two 20 percent each of the $10,000 prize, with the winner keeping $6,000.

Habib is not slow to agree, and it's clear that he hopes I will, too. When I remind them that I have half the chips, Jacobs reminds *me*: "That can flip in one hand." This is a man, I also have learned, who was runner-up in the '92 championship, so I have to take seriously whatever comes out of his mouth. If I'm hearing him right, he's proposed that I accept in a Zen sort of way that the horseshoe up my ass is gonna fall out any hand now, stimulating though it has been.

Well, Tom, correct me if I'm wrong, but fuck you. My polite counteroffer is $2,500 for me, $1,500 for them. No dice, of course, but at least neither guy seems insulted. We settle on $2,200 for me if one of them wins, $1,700 each for them if it's me.

With the blinds at $500 and $1,000, Jacobs moves all of his chips in on the third postdeal hand. Habib calls the bet, turning over 7-7 before pushing his entire stack forward. (In heads-up action, when one player goes all-in both must expose their hole cards since no more betting is possible.) Jacobs flips over an unsuited A-10, making Habib a slight favorite. Having folded my puny Q-4, I get to watch their do-or-die "race" from the sideline. The flop comes J-J-3, followed by a trey, then a deuce. Habib pumps his fist: his jacks and sevens have held up over Jacobs's jacks and treys. Jacobs gets out of his chair, taking his late-inning ouster quite well, I would say. He shakes Habib's hand then moves toward the rail, waiting to see who'll be paying him.

I'm thrilled to be down to a single opponent. The only problem is that it's Hasan Habib, who finished second—I've learned from a railbird—last month at Jack Binion's World Poker Open no-limit hold'em event down in Tunica. And Hasan has me slightly outchipped.

We fence from long distance for a half dozen hands, neither of us willing to call even modest preflop bets. I've pulled maybe a few hundred dollars ahead—a meaningless lead at this stage—when I discover a pair of black queens peering back up between my thumbs. Betting first, I have three alternatives. I can try to trap Hasan by merely calling his big blind. I can put in a modest raise, satisfied to collect the $1,500 in blinds. Or I can move all-in, goading him, in hopes that he calls me but doesn't have aces or kings. I decide to try door number three.

Hasan calls. With this much money at stake, I assume that he has a strong hand, though I'm still pretty sure mine is stronger. Once both our stacks have been pushed toward the center and I've shown him my queens, Hasan puts the frighteners on me by turning over a king and . . . a ten, both of diamonds. This is good, sort of. Only one of the three remaining kings or a flurry of tens or diamonds can save him.

But now comes the flop. I can't look—yet it turns out I can, even though I wish that I hadn't. It's a seven, a jack, and a nine, and the seven and nine are both diamonds. This gives Hasan twelve outs twice, since he has all twelve on both fourth street and fifth street: the nine other diamonds in the deck, the two other kings (the fourth having been counted among the diamonds), and the queen of hearts for a straight. John thumps the table with his fist, burns a card, turns over . . . a jack. A *red* jack. But of *hearts*! Another thump, another burn—Jesus Christ, get it over already! When the last card turned up is the harmless six of spades, John calls out, "Winner on Table 64!"

Hasan shrugs. We look at each other. More than a little flabbergasted, I sit back and try to relax. Hasan stands up and reaches across the table, shaking my hand. "Had to call you there, buddy."

"At least you had the overcard, and then the big draws . . ."

"You made a good bet."

Carol shakes my hand, takes my name, then leads me back to her desk in the corner. Tom and Hasan tag along. Both of them say that they already have seats in the Big One, which explains their unagonized faces. If either of them had caught me, he would have received the ten grand in cash. All I will get is a voucher for my seat, so I'll have to pay *them* from my pocket.

Carol types my name and address into the computer, which prints a receipt for $10,001, the last dollar being the token entry fee. *Event 25*, it says. *World Championship, 5/15/2000.* I've already been assigned to Seat 6 of Table 53.

Tom says, "Congratulations, my man."

"I got lucky."

"No one wins $10,000 without getting lucky."

Hasan pats my shoulder. "You made a good deal there, buddy."

"I did?"

"Absolutely," says Tom.

"You did," says Hasan. "You played awesome."

Paying them $1,700 apiece and tipping John $60 pretty much cleans me out. I even have the sense that I've *lost* as I head toward the men's room. For one thing, I've got barely enough cash left to play even one super-satellite, let alone any side games or preliminary tournaments. Until high noon on Monday, that is, four and a half long days hence.

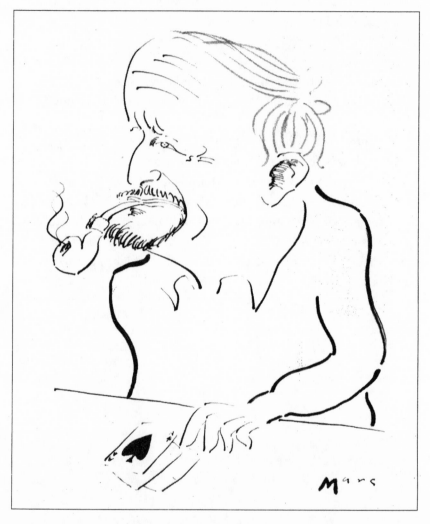

Drawing of A. Alvarez by Marc Boxer

♣ ♥

BLACK MAGIC

♦ ♠

I was sent here for a reason I have not yet been able to fathom.
—HENRY MILLER, *Tropic of Cancer*

Her blacks crackle and drag.
—SYLVIA PLATH, "Edge"

After breakfast Thursday morning I take a cab down to Neiman Marcus to check out the salon where Sandy Murphy conjured Ted's death for her manicurist. Seven days before she burked him, Murphy showed up here for an afternoon of pampering, all charged on Ted's MasterCard. She actually bragged to the woman doing her nails, Deana Perry, that she was about to inherit her "husband's" mansion plus $3 million in cash because he was going to overdose on heroin "within the next three weeks." And besides, her new lover, "Richard," already had the combinations to all her husband's safes, so even if her husband *didn't* die, Richard was still in position to make off with his money. What isn't clear is whether this was brazen stupidity, a clumsy effort to establish "for the record" that Ted was prone to a heroin overdose, or a kind of weird-sister prediction. *Anon! Fair is foul and foul is fair. Hover through the fog and filthy air. Stir in some toads, a dead sailor's thumb, grease from a man on the gallows. And while you're at it, sweetie, push back my cuticles.* As soon as Perry saw on the news that Ted *had* OD'd, she got in touch with the LVPD. The detective who interviewed Perry wanted to be certain he was clear about what she was telling him: "It's my understanding when [Sandra Murphy] said these things to you, you didn't take it as engaging in risky behavior . . . but that you took that to mean something more sinister or threatening. Is that true?"

"She was gonna kill him," Perry replied.

Asked to describe Murphy's attitude while telling such things to a stranger, Perry said: "She was joking about it the entire time [she was at the salon], and she was very adamant that this guy was going to die of a drug overdose, of a heroin overdose . . . and $3 million would get her to the next guy." Called to the witness stand by the prosecution last Monday, Perry also testified that Murphy had asked her opinion about whether a public appearance with her new boyfriend at the Andre Agassi children's benefit a few days after Ted's funeral would be in bad taste. If so, she would wait until the grand opening of Steve Wynn's Bellagio three weeks later.

What I want to get a look at is the place where Murphy uttered these witchy pronouncements. I'd also like to interview Perry, or anyone who worked at the salon in '98. Had Murphy come across as a scheming soap actress, a motormouth necromancer, or a nut job plain and simple? Was she stoned or intoxicated? How well had you known her before that? I also hope my touch is more deft than during my interrogation of Kolberg.

When I ask a woman behind a perfume counter for directions to the beauty salon, she tells me it closed.

"And when does it open?" I brilliantly inquire.

"No, no. They closed that department. You know, shut it down." She makes a sad face. "This was way back, okay, a few months ago. Sorry."

"We're talking about the place you'd get a manicure."

"Right. Like, last year?"

I thank her and smile but decide, as I head for the escalator, to explore the possibility that she misunderstood me somehow, or didn't have her facts right. She was selling perfume, after all, not manning the information booth. This is a pretty big store, plus I just spent eighteen bucks for the cab. And why would Neiman Marcus shut down a perfectly good beauty salon, just because one of its clients—

I stop. It may be sour grapes, but I suddenly can't imagine how Sandy Murphy's nail parlor might be relevant to my article. Deana Perry says what she says under oath, Court TV and the newspapers duly report it, that's that. Whatever information I need is now in the public domain. What do *Harper's* readers care about pedicures, bikini waxes, or which Eurozines grace the waiting room coffee table? I also have a better idea. A long fluorescent tube, in fact, seems to literally blink on above my head amid all these mirrors and mannequins.

The next employee I approach confirms that the beauty salon closed in December, then directs me around the corner to the jewelry department. It's along the main aisle on my right, in its own little parlor, with extraposh furniture and attendants and more subdued lighting, except for inside the display cases. I glance through the more garish stuff till I come across a plain silver band inlaid with three small square diamonds. *Voilà.*

A young Asian saleswoman—chic plastic glasses, blue-gray silk suit—unlocks the case and presents me with the ring I have pointed to, singing its praises while I squint at the thing in the light. It's a honey. Ninety-five percent pure platinum, hypoallergenic, "custom designed" by Rudolf Erdel. In the midst of her spiel, the young woman suddenly says, "blah blah blah," waving off her salesmanship with a delicate hand, as though she doesn't want to tax a romantic like me with too many niggling details. But who said Good Jim's a romantic? The fact is, he'd love to hear more.

"And the diamonds are how many carats?"

"Looks lock point six or point seven," she says with her cowgirlish twang—the first Asian woman I've heard with an accent like this. "Ah can check?"

While she goes to confer with a more senior person, I rotate the ring on my pinkie. Jennifer likes platinum because that's what her Aunt Beatrice wore. She also likes—how did she put it?—the way the stuff "glimmers against your skin." And now I can see what she meant. This ring has been brushed to catch light the way tennis pros can catch a stray ball on the face of their strings, as though fielding it with a lacrosse stick. I'm also impressed by the way all three diamonds are flush with the surface of the band, like little track halogen bulbs, only square. Square and *weensy*. But at least there are three of them, the number all Catholics and Dante fans relish, the number of children Jennifer and I would have if—if we had one more child. We've also been together since 1989, so maybe the diamonds could represent our three decades; not that it's been thirty years, but with one year in the eighties and one in this latest one, assuming this *is* a new decade . . .

"Past, present, future," the saleswoman tells me, as though I've been audibly mumbling. "The classic anniversary ring."

That would work, too. Our eleventh first-date anniversary was back in March, but our eighth wedding anniversary is coming up on July 9. I could stash it till then behind the CDs in my office.

The ring, I am told, has zero point seven five carats and costs twenty-six hundred bucks even. No sales tax. Another quick scan of the display case reveals nothing that even comes close. But the only way I can truly afford this is with the $10,000 I won, even though strictly speaking I haven't won anything yet. I'm probably not going to, either, since well over 90 percent of seat holders won't make the money. So I'm actually *down* $4,415 as of this morning, with 18– or 19–1 odds against winning dime one of it back. The fluorescent tube only went on because I *feel* like I just won ten large; I have a receipt, after all, for that gaudy amount in my pocket. But if I don't make the final four tables next week, charging this ring would simply put Jennifer and me $2,600 deeper in debt.

Well, then, so be it. My fee from *Harper's* will eventually cover it anyway, though I won't get a check till I turn in the piece in September. Yet isn't my wife worth a ding in our budget? You bet. (She wouldn't, but I would.) Aside from a watch and a couple of pairs of earrings, I've never bought her anything like this. When we eloped to Alaska we didn't have wedding rings; I never bought her an engagement ring, either. The idea that rings weren't "us" was probably more mine than hers, but she went along with her usual humor and grace. Money was a factor, of course, in deciding what was us in '92. We'd just rented a small house in the ridiculously expensive New Trier school district so my first two children could finish at the high school. The move gave Jennifer a harder commute to work, a longer drive to visit her family, and much higher rent coming out of our budget. The only upside for her was some yard space for Yoko, her thirteen-year-old flat-coated retriever, and the chance to start a vegetable garden, small compensation for marrying a middle-aged gambler with two rowdy teenagers and resolved not to have any more. But Jennifer never complained about this, and—long story short—I changed my position on kids. I've also picked up a few clues that she at least wouldn't *mind* wearing a ring from her husband and, now, the father of her children. The biggest clue, I guess, was her teary response to the jewelry she inherited when Aunt Beatrice died. That's also how I know they shared the same ring size, a six.

"I'll take it."

"Excellent choice, sir. She's gonna *adore* it."

"I hope so."

Once again I have broken our thirteenth commandment: Thou shalt wait for thy check before spending thy money. And I've yet to write even one coherent paragraph for Lewis. The other thing is, they don't have a size six in stock; will need, in fact, at least five business days to special-order one. Typical. At the same time, it's a perfect opportunity for me to pass, to just fold this dicey hand and wait till I'm solvent before splurging on jewelry. If I hustle, I might even finish the article in time for our anniversary, for which I could pick up the ring at the Neiman's in Chicago. Yet how better celebrate winning the satellite and make up for the time I've been gone than to arrive home next week with a glimmery present in hand?

I decide to have them ship the damn thing to our house. I'll be home by next Friday, and if it happens to beat me there, I'll simply tell Jennifer not to open the package—though how's *that* gonna sound? And when would I tell her? "Not open what?" she would ask. A better plan is to address it to myself. Our Visa statement won't arrive until June, so that wouldn't tip her off, either.

I can't wait to see her face when she opens it; I'll be watching her eyes, her green eyes, and that patch on her throat where she blushes. I pictured myself walking out of the store with a little satin box and carrying it home on the plane, but at least now I won't have a chance to lose it, or have it boosted from my room, before it gets paid for.

I hand over our plastic, fill out the shipping and insurance forms, then head back through the heavy glass doors and into the glare of a hundred and two dry degrees. The truth is, it isn't half bad out, as long as you don't move too quickly. A raggedy contrail is the only piece of lint on the luminescent sapphire sky. And now here's a cab, right on schedule. I hold the door for a linen-clad brunette climbing out, declining to look at her legs, then take her warm place on the ratty upholstery. Mission aborted and mission accomplished, I figure.

The buoyant placard on top of my television says, "Come On Up, The Water's Fine." So I have. Put on swim trunks and sandals, grabbed T.J., hit the top button in the elevator, emerged into harrowing dazzle.

Mein Gott! Nearly blinded, I stagger and tiptoe across the roofless, glassed-in hot plate that apparently is meant to function as a pool deck. Once my eyes start to adjust, I can see that however fine the water may be there isn't very much of it, especially compared to the Olympian acreage of lap lanes and balanced pH of resorts on the Strip. The Bellagio by itself has seven swank pools artfully arranged among ducal colonnades and horticultural majesty, while Mandalay Bay has palm trees and a wave machine for a sandy beach teeming with supermodels—or so I have heard. This pool is nothing fancy, maybe fifteen by thirty feet in the corner of a bare concrete slab, but I do have the place to myself. Not even a lifeguard up here, just a girl back near the elevators dispensing brown, fluffy towels while watching TV. If I get a cramp and drown, she can fish me out, call the coroner, then get back to *Passions*. No problem.

Along with workmanlike pool chairs and plastic tables, the deck has a 360-degree view of the Strip, downtown Vegas, and the muddy blue mountain ranges bracketing the valley. Not bad. The more I look around, in fact, the more it reminds me of the open-air vistas from the eighty-sixth floor of the Empire State Building, since having only two other structures this tall makes it feel a lot higher than twenty-four stories. To the south, just beyond the Stratosphere Tower, I believe I can see Neiman Marcus, and right below me is the powder blue courthouse. To the east, north, and west is the Las Vegas Valley: parched, prickly, alkaline, flat as any stretch of Corn Belt I've had the displeasure of driving through. God only knows why some homesick conquistador decided to call it The Meadows. And somewhere out there to the west, just beyond the Clark County line, is Pahrump.

The pool itself is clean, well maintained, rimmed at the waterline with purple-blue-green Spanish tiles. I dive in. Fierce noontime sun has made the water too warm, but I've never liked cold water anyway. To make the laps longer, I start doing them diagonally. Since I didn't bring sunscreen, I won't be able to do all that many, but a swim is exactly what I need to limber up, promote a few ion exchanges. Tomorrow I'll make sure to smear on some SPF 297.

In the meantime, my lazy backstroke allows me to squint up every other lap at the same giant temperature-clock that appears in the opening sentence of *The Biggest Game in Town*. The Horseshoe didn't have a pool back in 1981, because this entire 300-room tower still belonged to the Mint. With the Horseshoe and the Mint both booked solid, Al Alvarez had to stay across the street at Steve Wynn's Golden Nugget, poolless as well in those days. A lifelong swimmer used to regular exercise, Alvarez resorted to a vigorous walk around Glitter Gulch, but the merciless heat soon obliterated his moist English constitution. "I returned sweating," he wrote, "feet swollen, mouth parched, as though I had just spent a bad half hour in a prison recreation yard." Stewing in his own juices, on deadline, he decides that he has little choice but to sneak into the pool on the roof of the Mint. And it works. His trespass is never discovered, and he's able to revel each morning in the "fresh air, physical release, and space: I felt like a prisoner reprieved." Fortunately, the Binions bought the pool soon thereafter, replacing the "M" above the digital clock with a horseshoe, so my laps this afternoon are legitimate. Otherwise I would've had to follow the master's creative example.

The book he produced is a brief (181 uncrowded pages) yet comprehensive account of the '81 championship. Few books on any game have been received with as much enthusiasm over so long a period. Poets, journalists, casual poker players, and world-class professionals all tend to gush over its lapidary prose, sage hold'em insight, and droll use of cowboy patois as they pass around hard-to-find copies. "Journalism that reads like literature" was its author's lofty ambition; with a narrative involving poker characters instead of a treatise on strategy, he fulfilled it. Now seventy-one, Alvarez writes in his memoir, *Where Did It All Go Right?*: "It is one of the ironies of my life that although I helped change the way poetry was read in Britain during the fifties and sixties by speaking up for American poets like Lowell, Berryman and Plath, and introducing the poets of Eastern Europe to British readers, the only place where I am truly famous is Las Vegas, Nevada. And that is only for three weeks a year, while the World Series of Poker is in progress." He also admits, rather sadly, that *Biggest Game*, among twenty-three others, is "the only book I have ever enjoyed writing."

An accomplished poet and critic, Alvarez also edited the notorious 1962 anthology *The New Poetry*, which not only featured "extremist" Americans like Berryman but had the chutzpah to leave out more genteel British stalwarts. Yet his bravest book was probably *The Savage God*, a 1971 meditation on suicide that grew out of his own failed attempt and his friendship with Sylvia Plath. No one was closer to Plath and Ted Hughes during the final two years of their marriage. Hughes bunked at Alvarez's studio after separating from Plath, while Al and Sylvia developed such intimate rapport that it almost turned bleakly, perhaps vengefully, sexual after Hughes took up with Assia Wevill. Plath, for her part, seems to have desperately wanted that solace from Alvarez. Recently in love with another woman, however, and approaching the second anniversary of his suicide attempt, he decided he "was neither willing nor tough enough to shoulder her despair."

On his way to a dinner party, Alvarez, at Plath's invitation, did visit her new flat on Christmas Eve, 1962. (A blue plaque above the door announced, auspiciously enough, that William Butler Yeats had once lived there.) When she came downstairs to let him in, he was startled.

> The bright young American housewife with her determined smile and crisp clothes had vanished along with the pancake make-up, the schoolmistressy bun and fake cheerfulness. Her face was wax-pale and drained; her hair hung loose down to her waist and left a faint, sharp animal smell on the air when she walked ahead of me up the stairs. She looked like a priestess emp-

tied out by the rites of her cult. And perhaps this is what she had become. She had broken through to whatever it was that made her want to write, the poems were coming every day, sometimes as many as three a day, unbidden, unstoppable, and she was off in a closed, private world where no one was going to follow her.

While she drank wine and read her new poems, he recalls, "I listened and nodded and made the right noises—until I looked at my watch and said, 'I've got to go.' She said, 'Don't, please don't' and began to weep—great uncontrollable sobs that made her hiccup and shake her head. I stroked her hair and patted her back as though she were an abandoned child"—not a lover; not a potential suicide, either. He left at eight o'clock, knowing he "had let her down in some final and unforgivable way. And I knew she knew. I never again saw her alive." In his memoir three decades later, he seems to reconsider: "I have never kidded myself that changing from friend to lover would have made a jot of difference to her in the end."

He had made a big difference before that. As poetry editor of *The Observer*, he published several of her searing last poems, providing her work with its first sizable audience. He would also write some of the most penetrating responses to her short life and verse. "In these last poems," he said in the *Guardian* the Sunday following her death, "she was systematically probing that narrow, violent area between the viable and the impossible, between experience which can be transmuted into poetry and that which is overwhelming." In *The Savage God*, he called these poems "naked and brutal," not unlike "assault and battery," then laid out the risk such a practice incurs: "art is not necessarily therapeutic: [the artist] is not automatically relieved of the fantasies by expressing them. Instead, by some perverse logic of creation, the act of formal expression may simply make the dredged-up material more readily available to him." Returning specifically to Plath, he went further:

"Lady Lazarus" ends with a resurrection and a threat, and even in "Daddy" she manages to finally turn her back on the grinning, beckoning figure: "Daddy, daddy, you bastard, I'm through." Hence, perhaps, the energy of these poems, their weird jollity in the teeth of everything, their recklessness. But now, as though poetry really were a form of black magic, the figure she had invoked so often, only to dismiss triumphantly, had risen before her, dank, final and not to be denied.

Ted Hughes had ascribed occult powers to himself and his wife, writing that her "psychic gifts . . . were strong enough to make her frequently wish to be rid of them." More dubious about things supernatural, Alvarez called Plath's uncanny poems "a triumph of mind over ectoplasm." In her marriage and psyche, however, she faced overwhelming defeat.

Absent her famous last journal (which Hughes plausibly claims he destroyed for the sake of their children), Alvarez sharply illuminates one of the abiding enigmas—and battlegrounds—of twentieth-century poetry. Whose "fault" was Plath's suicide? What can her fans and detractors "read into" it? (And what, we also might ask, if she and Al *had* become lovers?) Alvarez doesn't say, but he does provide chilling evidence—a deaf neighbor, a "Please call Dr.—" note beside her body—that Plath meant to be discovered and revived. "She had always been a bit of a gambler," he writes, arguing that her "psychic courage" enhanced "the authority of her poetry." He concludes that while her two young children slept in the bedroom upstairs, Plath rolled the dice by laying her head in the oven and turning on the gas, "and she lost."

Clearly this was a writer who brought more to the table than familiarity with double belly-busters and reverse implied pot odds when *The New Yorker* sent him to cover the World Series in Vegas. After noting the boisterous, jostling throng at the Horseshoe craps tables, he begins a report on the cool nonchalance with which poker players, even before the tournament gets under way, venture astonishing volumes of cash. He is also blown away, almost literally, by springtime in southern Nevada, which lashes him with furious winds and "a night temperature hotter than the hottest English summer." Once he gets access to this pool, however, the town's blend of decadence and warmhearted hospitality comes alive for him. He sees that the friendship the Binions maintain with many of their guests is what distinguishes their casino from the "grisly, Hollywood-style palaces" along the Strip. "The professional poker players I spoke to were unanimous only in their attitude toward the Binion family: not just admiration but—an even rarer feeling in that edgy and exclusive world—affection." His profile of Benny, the seventy-eight-year-old paterfamilias, covers his racketeering and doesn't soft-pedal the two murder charges brought against him. "One was dismissed as 'self-defense,' " he writes, letting those bemused quotation marks do the talking, "and for the other he was given a suspended sentence." Benny's legend is adroitly combined with the history of the tournament he invented, and equipped with a crystalline summary of the rules and valences of no-limit hold'em. Choice quotes from experts add nuance to the o'n'ry rapaciousness of big-bet poker. "Limit poker is a science," in the words of Crandall Addington, a Texas oilman of majestic hold'em facility and sartorial splendor, "but no-limit is an art. In limit, you are shooting at a target. In no-limit, the target comes alive and shoots back at you."

Alvarez fuses the lingo of these high-rolling cowboys with his own more cerebral inflections. One player reminds him of "a fleshy West Coast version of Saul Bellow," while the man's daughter is "a California Matisse odalisque." To limn Bugsy Siegel's taste in architecture, Alvarez invokes Mario Puzo—and Andrew Marvell. By his own lights, the real Vegas is a place "begotten by an East Coast hit man turned warlord upon the alkali-and-mesquite wastes."

On the subject of eros and poker, Alvarez rehearses the dismal fate of a fellow Londoner. While playing at Caesars Palace, the man becomes enamored of a prostitute and in short order loses his business, his marriage, and his poker skills, becoming a player with "no chance" because he is "unable to disentangle his gambling from his sex life. This is not a muddle that the professional players ever allow themselves." Such muddles were the province, we gather, of Alvarez himself in his younger days. At fifty-one, however, he finds it almost disappointing not to be tempted by the pair of dewy prostitutes who come on to him in an elevator. "Ah make you feel young again, man," one promises, yet the author remains unaroused. "But later," he writes, "when I settled down to the evening's hold'em session at the Nugget and picked up my first cards, my eyes felt fresh, my heart was beating sweetly, all my senses were alert. As the hooker would have said, I felt young again. Perhaps the Freudians are right, after all, when they talk of gambling as sublimation. In the words of another addict, 'Sex is good, but poker lasts longer.' "

Another favorite subject is an author himself: Doyle Brunson, the World Series champion in '76 and '77, who then published *Super/System*. Cowritten with five other maestros, each of whom covers a separate variety of the game, this was the granddaddy of primers, and at $100 per copy by far the most expensive. Alvarez decrees that "the prose will not win any prizes—except for its unwavering determination to split every infinitive. But as a postgraduate guide to the intricacies of high-level, high-stakes poker the work has no equal." Brunson himself covers no-limit hold'em, introducing readers to, among hundreds of tactical breakthroughs, the value of small pairs and suited connectors, with detailed advice on how to rake in big pots while holding them as hole cards. "The grammar may be shaky in places, the punctuation baroque, but the voice is distinct and the message is clear: aggression, constant aggression." *Biggest Game* also makes tangible the expensive irony of giving such solid advice. "But now they've read the book," Brunson laments, "they recognize what I'm doing, they think I'm bluffing, and call me. It's hampered my style. I used to be able to wreck a game without holding any cards at all, because I never got called. Now I need the cards."

The much wider upshot—of both *Biggest Game* and *Super/System*—is that, instead of a few of Benny's pals outsmarting each other for a couple of days, the five-week-long Series now fields thousands of serious players inspired by Alvarez and schooled by Brunson and his numerous heirs. Publishing poker advice remains fraught with pitfalls—unlike, say, a surgeon teaching colleagues and students a better way to cauterize a capillary. When medical know-how is shared everyone benefits, and the pioneer doesn't lose money; nor is it ever his *job* to fool patients or fellow M.D.'s. But when poker pros deconstruct moves cultivated over decades, the pots they no longer take down (having given up their edge to readers now poised like Ray-Banned condors across the table) can vastly outweigh whatever royalties their primers bring in. As Brunson told Alvarez back in '81: "If I had it to do again, I wouldn't write that book." He hasn't won the World Series since.

At the melancholy heart of *Biggest Game* is a young Jewish player named Mickey Appleman. Alvarez calls him "the odd man out of the tournament—a New York intellectual among the cowboys, clever eyes peering out from under a Harpo Marx mop of blond curls." With master's degrees in education, statistics, and business, Appleman instead became a social worker in Harlem, this while spending years in analysis. But he pleasantly surprises the author of *The Savage God* when he claims: "Gambling was never an addiction. On the contrary, it helped me more than analysis. I suffered from depression—I was so entwined with my inner world I never had a chance to enjoy myself. For me, activity was the answer. I took up gambling *after* I finished with psychoanalysis, and the depressions never returned." As the interviewer warms to his fellow near-casualty of melancholia, Appleman continues: "Poker for big money is a high-risk sport, like driving a racing car. . . . I'm a romantic, and for me gambling is a romance." Citing W. H. Auden on the romance of risk, Alvarez says, "Poker was Appleman's way out of worry into alertness and objectivity. When he said 'Gambling is a romance,' he was not referring to the smoke-filled rooms, the sullen tribal faces, or the stilted backchat that passes for conversation; he meant the art of the game at its highest level and the romance of personal liberty."

Biggest Game climaxes with the championship event, in which seventy players competed for shares of a $700,000 purse. Infusing their hand-to-hand combat with at least as much drama as an NBA Finals telecast, Alvarez demonstrates once and for all that an understated prose account of poker action can be orders of magnitude more exciting than watching in person. His book has no weaknesses, really, though it does involve a missed opportunity. Stuey Ungar, who repeated as champion that year, was a coke-addled enfant terrible whose wavelength happened to be out of phase with that of the London man of letters. Compared with the soul baring Alvarez summons from other contenders, the champ's closed-off psyche amounts to fingernails down a blackboard, and the culprit gets much shorter shrift in the book than he otherwise might have received.

What's puzzling is that Ungar's modus operandi could have been characterized in the same terms Alvarez deployed to elucidate Sylvia

Plath's. Brutally precise while assaulting big pots, Ungar's near-suicidal black magic with chips mesmerized countless opponents into folding superior hands to him, much as Plath's verbal magic has mesmerized three generations of readers. Part of our bewitchment has to do with her suicide, and not for nothing did awestruck opponents dub Ungar "The Kamikaze Kid" after trying to read him.

Lorca, Robert Bly, and, more recently, Edward Hirsch have called the leaping, scarifying, anarchically creative spirit *duende*, from the Spanish for "lord of the house," and Hirsch specifically refers to Plath "storming upward through the air" in the *Ariel* poems. "The furies were certainly loose and stalking," he writes in *The Demon and the Angel*, "when Plath wrote her ferocious last poems in England. The notoriety of Plath's suicide has obscured how dedicated she was to her poetic craft, how persistently she worked to shape experiences, even as she probed the depths—braving taboo subjects, courting a wildness that defies control. . . . It's as if the duende was struggling out of her body to become a spirit of pure air." Hirsch also clarifies the musical dimension of poetic acts, as well as the death-hauntedness of many great artists. Describing the *Kind of Blue* studio sessions, for example, he quotes pianist Bill Evans comparing the lunar former addict Miles Davis to Japanese brush painters: "These artists must practice a particular discipline, that of allowing the idea to express itself in communion with their hands in such a direct way that deliberation cannot interfere. The resulting pictures lack the complex composition and textures of ordinary painting, but it is said that those who see will find something captured that escapes explanation." In a similar context, Nolan Dalla, who is completing a biography of Ungar, compares him to Bobby Fischer, another spellbinding persona whose artistry "escapes explanation." A player whose brains, paranoia, and other demons drove him in 1970 to the pinnacle of chess, Fischer soon vanished down the maw of pathology; Ungar and Plath each traced a similar, though steeper, trajectory.

Mental illness remains disgracefully misunderstood in our culture, yet it seems fair to say that the headlong talents of Fischer and Ungar and Plath (or van Gogh, Davis, Berryman, Lowell, Billie Holiday, Janis Joplin, et al.) stem from parallel habits of mind, which themselves spring from brain chemistry. In the back of their forehead, more specifically in the anterior cingulate of their frontal cortex, some humans have more vulnerable dopamine systems, "psyches" (as we used to call them) more easily hijacked by rewards like sex, dope, money, or laurels. Mastering the inherent unpredictability of any game or art form can trigger overpowering "pleasure," and this dopamine rush gets deeply embedded in the memory of some of the most talented practitioners. Normal brains work this way, too, but they tend to operate within narrower "mood swings," with smaller jolts (or squirts) of strange insight. "The same neural circuitry involved in the highs and lows of abusing drugs," says Harvard neuroscientist Hans Breiter, "is activated by winning or losing money, anticipating a good meal or seeking beautiful faces to look at." The difference is that while geniuses work hard at their vocation, as neurobiologist Steven Pinker reminds us in *How the Mind Works*, they "may also have been dealt a genetic hand with four aces." Their muse may be chess, hold'em, trumpet, or verse, but impossible, even deranged leaps of insight seem to be a common denominator dividing ordinary artists from the biggest of the big boys and girls.

Ungar could not have been easy for a reporter to get next to; few self-destructive, semiliterate, monomaniacal gamblers and coke addicts are. Alvarez was naturally more taken with the grace and generosity of Perry Green, the Orthodox Jewish furrier from Anchorage who outlasted every Texas and Vegas professional to finish heads-up against the Kid (who was Jewish himself, though extravagantly not Orthodox). Green really never had a prayer, though. On the last hand he made a strong move by betting all his chips on an open-ended draw, hoping for one of eight unseen cards to provide him with a straight, or to "steal" the pot from Ungar right there. Ungar held only the ace and queen of hearts (not even a pair) but somehow, after staring down his opponent for eight or ten seconds, divined that Green was bluffing and called him. When Green's straight failed to materialize and a queen "spiked" on fifth street, Ungar leapt up, shouting "Hey!" Was this poetry? Card sense? Black magic? Ungar could not have cared less what we call it. He'd only been playing hold'em a little over a year, but he'd just notched his second world title.

At what passes for a press conference afterwards, Alvarez can't hide his disappointment in, even contempt for, the back-to-back champion's inarticulate comments. "Someone stuck a microphone in front of Ungar, but all he could manage was 'Great!' " Having compared him to both a female ape and a corpse, Alvarez zooms in on his twitching and fidgeting, his giggling and muttering—"sumtin' like that," in a typically unflattering quote. Nothing along the lines of *unstoppable*, *broken through*, or *weird jollity*, all of which would have hit the nail right on the head. Who can blame Alvarez, though? He had just spent three weeks with the thoughtful and loquacious likes of Addington, Brunson, and Appleman, and his luminous portraits of them and the Binions are the main reasons *Biggest Game* remains a classic of reportage, to say nothing of its preeminence in the literature of poker. Still, it is Ungar who emerged as the game's most incendiary artist. During his short, mostly unhappy life, the Kid entered thirty no-limit tournaments with buy-ins above $5,000 and finished first an astounding nine times, often vanquishing fields of over three hundred challengers. Even legends like Brunson, Preston, and Johnny Chan win less than 10 percent of their starts (Tiger Woods not much less seldom), while for most players first is a once-in-a-lifetime affair, if they're lucky. When Ungar won his third world title in '97 (including the $1 million prize and solid gold bracelet) and then died a few months later—age forty-three, deep in debt, after overdoing booze and cocaine for most of his life—he became, in a real sense, a priest emptied out by the rites of his no-limit cult.

What's also clear in hindsight is that his preternatural dominance emanated from a feverish, Plath-like abandon at the poker table. Likewise, his self-medication can be usefully understood as a slow-motion suicide, if not an intentional one, just as it seems fair to say that both Ungar and Plath died accidentally on purpose. As Plath had in late '62, Ungar appeared "deathly pale" while winning those back-to-back titles, like a doomed, long-haired waif among ruddy old cowboys and fur traders. Yet in a series of no-limit, do-or-die showdowns, he *systematically probed that narrow, violent area between the viable and the impossible*, only in poker, not verse. Off-putting personal habits aside—"a faint, sharp animal smell" hardly seems out of the question—Ungar's perverse, creative logic surely epitomized the art of the game at its highest level, even though his MO wasn't necessarily therapeutic. Therein lay his genius.

No reporter could have known in May of '81 how and when Ungar would perish, and the pages Alvarez devotes to the wunderkind are elegantly composed, telling us more about poker than several thick tomes of advice and statistics. The book they appear in is central to the lore of our national game, just as its author's keen take on Sylvia Plath's works and days has enriched American letters. Reading a fully sympathetic Alvarez on the Kid in his prime would have been even more of a pleasure.

Seven years later, Alvarez's poker *compadre* Anthony Holden took a thirteen-month sabbatical from literary London to play the pro tournament circuit, bookended by a pair of World Series championships. *Big Deal*, Holden's account of his frenetic high-stakes odyssey through Britain, Malta, Morocco, and across the United States, makes for spirited, often hilarious reading. Like Alvarez before him, Holden was already a seasoned person of letters, having written respectable biographies of Shakespeare and Laurence Olivier and translated Aeschylus and *Don Giovanni*, all this while ascending to the unofficial No. 1 rank among British pokerists.

On the very first hand of the '88 world championship, Holden finds himself in a showdown with—who else?—Stuey Ungar, whom he describes as "a diminutive stick-insect of thirty-four-going-on-twelve . . . his wrists so emaciated that his championship bracelets all but pinned them to the table." Holden acquits himself impressively, relieving the emaciated insect of $1,850 that hand. The author even survives the first day of the tournament (as Ungar does not), going to bed with $8,000. Yet the best he can manage in two tries is ninetieth out of 167. Chastened, he goes back to writing full-time, restricting his poker to the regular Tuesday night game with, among others, his mentor Al Alvarez.

While Alvarez had played low-stakes side games in '81, he entered no World Series tournaments. He now says—continuing his protégé's insect motif—he was simply too "bug-eyed with wonder" during his first assignment to function effectively with both notepad and chips. In '94, however, he ventured into the Big One as a competitor. Before putting up the $10,000 buy-in, he'd practiced on a computer program and played in small London tournaments, steeling his no-limit game while trying to stay realistic. "Although I often reached the final table and occasionally won an event, I knew that in Vegas they marched to a different tune. I would be like a good club tennis player with a wild-card entry to Wimbledon: the game played by the top players has no relation to the game played by the likes of me; it just looks the same." Unfortunately, he was right. He lasts less than four hours, losing a third of his chips when he "slow-plays" a straight—greedily checking in hopes of building an even larger pot—and gets counter-bushwhacked on fifth street by Barbara Samuelson's higher straight. *The target comes alive and shoots back.* (Samuelson uses these chips to help her place tenth, at that time the highest finish ever by a woman.) Alvarez surrenders his final $6,000 when his pocket queens get ironed out by the ace-king he "knew" his opponent was holding, especially after a king appears as one of the community cards. "I had been preparing for this day for fifteen months," he sheepishly confesses, "and when it came I blew it. I had made the classic mistake of a newcomer to the big league: I played what the pros call 'tight-weak'—afraid to bet without the stone cold nuts and easily scared out. But at this level players can smell your fear, and they run all over you."

My fear, I'm afraid, may also be quite aromatic.

♣ ♥

URGE OVERKILL

♦ ♠

A murder is committed. Why? To get another man's
wife or wealth, or to get the necessities of life.
—AUGUSTINE

Make me wonder who's in charge.
—LUCINDA WILLIAMS, "Essence"

After lunch, I head a block south to the courthouse. The satellite
trucks of local TV stations and national networks take up most of the
curb space along Second Street and Carson. On the lawn beyond
them, trial junkies and media personnel are mingling outside Court
TV's air-conditioned interview tent with brides in lace veils, grooms in
tuxes, and people with traffic citations or beefs about property taxes.
One pimply dude sports a sleeveless black Mopar shirt that says DRIVE
IT LIKE YOU STOLE IT, extra clean for his big day in court.

Jurors have had the Binion case for twenty-five hours now. The
nine women and three men are identified only by number, of course,
but we know they include a pharmacist, a registered nurse, a storage
facility owner, a wildlife biologist, three or four housewives, a retired
aerospace engineer, a lab technician, and a medical assistant; their average age is between forty-five and fifty. It's a group that seems
eminently capable of "getting" complex hypotheses—autopsy minutiae

Sandy in ankle device, with Rick

reconstrued to indicate burking, for example. We also know they've selected the aerospace guy as their foreperson. Last night he sent a letter to Judge Bonaventure asking him to clarify a point of law related to an extortion plot in which Tabish, but not Murphy, is charged. "If a person(s) have been found guilty of 'false imprisonment' AND guilty of 'extortion,' does that elevate the charge to kidnapping?"

Bonaventure wrote back: "The answer to your question is, 'No.' "

"They don't want to find him guilty of kidnapping, which carries a life sentence" was the spin imparted this morning by Tabish's lawyer. Murphy's, I'm guessing, may now be a half step closer to letting her testify against Tabish in exchange for a Get Out of Jail Free card, which would fit her MO to a T.

The case against Murphy—against both of them—is pretty substantial, if not quite a tomahawk slam. At four in the morning of September 18, twelve hours after Murphy dialed 911, Tabish and two other men were caught removing 48,000 pounds of silver and other valuables from Ted's underground vault in Pahrump. When Sheriff Wade Lieseke showed up, he discovered that Tabish had loaded the entire cache onto one of his MRT gravel trucks, once again leaving a taunt: this time it was a single silver dollar in the center of the vault. He told Lieseke that he had "specific instructions" from Binion, in the event of his death, "to dig up the silver and get money for it, and then put it in trust for his daughter." The sheriff arrested him anyway. He also arrested David Mattsen, the man Ted had hired to manage the ranch, and Kurt Gratzer, a childhood friend of Tabish and former U.S. Army Ranger.

Tabish's $100,000 bond was posted by one Sandra Murphy, though the two denied to police and reporters being anything but "close friends." After a police spokesman said, "Even if there's a romantic relationship between the two, it doesn't elevate this to a homicide," Becky Behnen persuaded her brother's estate to hire a private detective, Tom Dillard, to investigate Murphy and Tabish.

Tracking phone records and credit-card receipts, Dillard came up with beyond-a-doubt evidence that the pair had been lovers for at least two months before Binion died. Ted's MasterCard statement showed that Murphy had charged a black velvet Armani shirt and a Wilke Rodriguez shirt of similar aspect, plus Gucci jeans, hiking boots, and more, all in Tabish's size. Half a dozen people reported that Tabish or Murphy had bragged to them about the affair. One eyewitness (a cabana boy named, of all things, Dante Cabanas) put them together in a Beverly Hills hotel the weekend before Ted was murdered.

Two days before he died, Ted instructed his secretary, Cathy Rose, to cut off Murphy's credit line of $5,000 a month, motive enough for a shopaholic like Sandy to kill him. Yet the ballsy con artist was still able to use Ted's MasterCard the day *after* he died to get a $3,000 cash advance. She also arranged to have Sprint mail the Palomino Lane phone bills to her in care of one of Tabish's businesses.

Two days before Ted's funeral, Murphy arrived with bags of silver coins at the law offices of Oscar Goodman. She told him that Ted had bequeathed her the home and its contents, and that she wanted Goodman to accept the coins as a retainer, apparently anticipating that estate lawyers, if not the police, would come after her. While Goodman was having the coins inventoried, however, Murphy took them back to make her own inventory. Her numismatic eye may not have been the sharpest one around, but she suddenly didn't trust Oscar's.

The sand-covered coins and Murphy's seven-page handwritten inventory soon turned up in Missoula in the hands of Dennis Rebhein. Rebhein agreed to testify under a grant of immunity that Tabish gave him the coins as collateral for a $25,000 loan, and that Tabish admitted, "If I was caught with the silver, it wouldn't look good." But how would it look to Rebhein's sister, Mary Jo Tabish? She and Rick had been married eight years, most of which Rick had spent either in Las Vegas or in prison. Yet they'd been together often enough to produce two children: Amanda, five, and Kyle, two, probably the only two reasons that Mary Jo has continued to "stand by" their father throughout the investigation and trial.

Since the prosecution contends that Ted died between 9 a.m. and noon, the defense called two MRT employees who testified that their boss was at All Star Ready Mix, a North Las Vegas concrete company, from 7:30 to 11:30 the morning of September 17. But another Tabish business associate, Jason Frazer, testified that Rick asked him to persuade at least one employee, Jim Mitchell, to testify falsely. Prosecutors introduced a handwritten note from Tabish to Frazer offering to pay an attorney to help Mitchell solve some unrelated legal troubles if Mitchell would provide an affidavit that he saw Tabish at All Star on the morning in question. "My life is on the line," the note concluded, "and we need to fight fire with fire."

Phone records proved that Tabish and Binion ranch manager David Mattsen were continually in touch in the hours before and after Ted's death. Dillard also found canceled MRT payroll checks made out to Mattsen, one per week since Ted Binion died. In exchange for immunity, Mattsen testified that Tabish told him he planned to move the silver to Chicago. (Dillard's investigation had already linked Tabish to organized crime figures there.) Mattsen also testified that Tabish bragged that he and Murphy used handcuffs to restrain Binion, then drugged him and had sex in front of him. Dillard discovered that the handcuffs were manufactured in Los Angeles, and that the only Las Vegas outlet was a high-end women's clothing shop in Caesars Palace, which sold them attached to a black leather belt for $700, for which Dillard produced Ted's receipt. Other witnesses testified that Tabish had bragged he was "laying the pipe to Ted Binion's woman." He boasted to Kurt Gratzer that Murphy was "one of the pigs" he was fucking. "She is in his back pocket," Gratzer said Tabish told him, "and she'll do whatever he wants her to do."

Shortly after dawn on February 19, 1999, detectives with search warrants knocked on the doors of Tabish's Las Vegas apartment and business addresses, of his home in Missoula, and of Murphy's apartment in Henderson, a few miles southeast of the Strip, toward Lake Mead. That door was opened by a sleepy-eyed Murphy and Tabish.

"I knew you guys were coming!" Murphy was reported to blurt. "I had a dream this morning that I woke up and you guys were in our apartment."

"I would think that is the best evidence one could get of a relationship," said Chief Deputy District Attorney David Roger. "A man and a woman together in the same apartment at seven in the morning. We find that very intriguing."

Maybe so, said Oscar Goodman, but not even close to evidence that Ted Binion had been murdered. "From what I understand, what was

taken as a result of the searches is all very explainable and all very innocent." He acknowledged that Murphy and Tabish were extremely
close friends, but pointed out that caring for one another is not a
crime. "There is no question that they are looking to each other for
support to get through the intensity of the investigation."

Attorneys for Ted's estate deposed Murphy in district court, part of
their effort to retrieve the coins, currency, and silver missing from
Ted's house and vault. Before the hearing began, though, Goodman
tried to forge an agreement. He had already sought across-the-board
immunity for Murphy, but the district attorney rebuffed him. He now
proposed that his client would answer questions regarding the missing
property, but only if estate lawyers agreed not to share her answers
with officials investigating Ted's death. (At this point, the cause of
death was still "undetermined.") Richard Wright, representing the estate, objected to these restrictions, promising to notify authorities of
all evidence related to Ted's death; any new information, he promised,
would also be incorporated into the civil lawsuit the estate planned to
file against those it deemed responsible, though Wright refused to
specify who they might be. Thus, on the advice of her future mayor,
Murphy asserted her constitutional right against self-incrimination
over two hundred times. (Tabish did the same ninety-eight times.)
"The fifth amendment is for the innocent!" Oscar crowed to reporters
afterward.

Standing close by on the courthouse steps, Becky Behnen coun-
tered that she'd spoken to Ted regularly during the last months of his
life and had seen no signs at all that he wanted to die. "I definitely
know it wasn't suicide," she said. Asked by a reporter what prompted
her suspicions of Murphy, she replied, "Woman's intuition."

Old-buddy connections had pertained just as readily. Both parties,
their attorneys, and district court judge Michael Cherry all knew one
another quite well. Cherry had once represented Nick and Becky
Behnen. Ted's close friend Richard Wright had acted as Murphy's attorney on the day Ted's body was discovered, though Wright had since
declared that he thought she and Tabish had killed Ted. Murphy's current defense team of Goodman and Chesnoff had once represented

Harry Claiborne, the impeached district judge now speaking for Ted's estate.

Lamenting Ted's death and its aftermath, columnist John L. Smith wrote in the *Review-Journal*: "Like a lot of people who are stupid rich, Binion had all the friends money could buy, and his money is at the heart of this story." Smith called the scene in district court "reminiscent of a time, not so many years ago, when casual observers could stroll into the coffee shop at Binion's Horseshoe and watch attorneys and judges dine daily with Horseshoe patriarch Benny Binion. Those same attorneys and judges later represented and stood in judgment of Binion family members who faced felony charges. . . . This eerie brand of legal incest is a tradition around these parts. From the look of things, the tradition continues."

Less than a week later, Oscar Goodman excused himself from Murphy's case and announced his candidacy for mayor, although one of his campaign deputies, William Cassidy, stayed on Murphy's team as a paid investigator. After Goodman's landslide victory, Cassidy was hired as a political operative in the mayor's office but was granted an immediate leave of absence to continue working for Murphy's defense. Sources within the defense team told *Sun* reporter Jeff German that Cassidy "was attempting to protect Goodman from any embarrassment in the case." In the meantime, Oscar's fees had been paid by Bill Fuller, a retired silver-mine executive. The eighty-one-year-old Irish citizen testified that he "loaned" Murphy $125,000 to pay her former attorney; the collateral she put up is best left to Bad Jim's imagination. While under house arrest, Murphy was living, at Fuller's expense, in the ultraposh Regency Towers on the grounds of the Las Vegas Country Club; he also leased her a new Mercedes and paid for frequent meals at gourmet restaurants, as well as for a publicist and a pollster (namely William Cassidy, who also took polls for the mayor). Yet Murphy still managed to have herself declared indigent by the court, which granted her twenty thousand taxpayer dollars to cover her legal expenses.

Even though Murphy and her previous attorneys had denied for nineteen months that she and Tabish were lovers before Binion died,

John Momot, her latest, used his opening statement to ask the jury rhetorically: "What do you think, there's some secret about a relationship here? There's no secret about it. It existed between Sandy and Rick. So what? . . . He's talking to her, and she's trying to maintain a relationship with Ted. And then after a while, he's the caretaker of Sandy. That's what happens with Rick. And then affection develops. Is that so inhuman to understand that that can happen? Is that against the law?"

Tabish's lawyer, Louis Palazzo, waxed even more obtuse, protesting that his client "should be charged with being felony stupid, not murder." As flying buttresses to this line of argument, Palazzo associate Tom Pitaro used "juxtaposition" in court as a verb and accented the first syllable of "negate." Both young attorneys were proud to be known as protégés of the city's new mayor, who'd steered them toward the case upon his own withdrawal. Palazzo's felonious way with words was verified once and for all when he claimed: "This case is garbage and it belongs in the toilet."

The silver-tongued defense team attributed Ted Binion's demise to his drug use, which had escalated during 1998 because of the battle among his siblings for control of the Horseshoe; it had nothing to do, they asserted, with his relationship with Murphy. Binion was "a paranoid drug addict" with a family history of suicide, a "control freak" whose frequent beatings of Murphy left her with little choice but to seek solace from the couple's new friend. "If you don't take care of your woman, someone else will," Momot told jurors. "That's what happens when you love drugs more than your woman." Ted Binion OD'd on his own tar heroin and Xanax. This, after all, was what the coroner had determined before "the Binion money machine" coerced the state into prosecuting his client, "a nice young girl who didn't bargain for death in the desert." The money machine's motivation? To preserve the family's dwindling reputation as well as Ted's $70 million fortune. The cruelest irony, said Momot, was that Sandy Murphy was the only person who really loved Mr. Binion, the one who cleaned up after him when he soiled himself while bingeing on vodka and smack. He also chided the state's attorney, David Roger, for not prosecuting Peter Sheridan, the man who sold Binion the heroin. He emphasized that Sheridan had delivered twelve balloons of heroin, instead of his usual four, the night before Binion died, and that Dr. Lacayo had written Binion a prescription for Xanax that same afternoon. (The prescription called for 120 Xanax, but Sheridan asked Ted to give him 30 as partial payment for the heroin, so only 90 pills were left in the bottle.) "Sandy Murphy didn't get the heroin," Momot insisted accurately enough. "Sandy Murphy didn't get the Xanax prescription."

Palazzo argued that Tabish was digging up the silver at Binion's explicit request. It was "ludicrous" to believe that his client would bring earthmoving equipment to the busiest street in Pahrump and not expect to be noticed; Tabish had even notified Sheriff Lieseke ahead of time that he was going to dig up the silver in order to give it to Bonnie.

"Ted Binion was murdered," David Roger told jurors. "He was murdered for lust; he was murdered for greed. He was murdered by someone he trusted and her new companion." Both Sandy Murphy and Rick Tabish had motive, Roger argued, to kill the casino executive. Murphy stood to inherit his mansion and $300,000 in cash. Tabish's company was bankrupt and he was $1.6 million in debt to the IRS, with no way to repay it but by robbing his wealthy friend. "It was Ted Binion's silver that he was going to get to solve all his problems," said Roger. Murphy and Tabish had even been vicious enough to commit "a signature crime," taunting Ted's family by leaving a single silver dollar in the vault, one Mercury dime "left precisely in the middle of the safe." Roger did not mention sexual taunting in front of the jury because he had only hearsay evidence of that. But he knew. And the knowledge gave him extra incentive to win a conviction.

Under a grant of immunity, Kurt Gratzer testified that Tabish had asked him to kill Ted Binion with one of the handguns he kept stashed around the mansion. Tabish also proposed helicoptering into an adjacent field—"GI Joe stuff," according to Gratzer—and dropping Ted with a .378 Weatherby Magnum hunting rifle while he grilled steaks and veggies on his patio. Another scheme Tabish floated was forcing Xanax and heroin down Ted's throat with a turkey baster; he even told Gratzer to find out what constituted a lethal dose by calling a pharmacist friend of theirs in Missoula. As payment, Tabish promised Gratzer a '98 Trans Am, presumably with flaming decals and a whale tail, plus a share of a life insurance policy of which Murphy was the beneficiary.

Roger next introduced Michael Baden. The sixty-eight-year-old pathologist had been director of forensic sciences for the New York State Police and worked on the O.J. Simpson and JonBenet Ramsay cases as well as the congressional reinvestigation of the John Kennedy and Martin Luther King assassinations. Baden laid out the state's theory—that Murphy and Tabish forced Ted to ingest potentially lethal amounts of heroin and Xanax, then suffocated him. Ted had always smoked heroin, not swallowed or injected it, and Baden testified that inhaling it could not possibly produce the two ounces of gray-brown fluid that the coroner found in Ted's stomach. The discolorations around his mouth, the bruises on his chest, the ruptured blood vessels under his eyelids were all the result of being imperfectly burked. Courtroom reporters called Baden a "favorite of the jury," noting his "fatherly" tone as he testified. The aggressive treatment he received from a Milwaukee attorney brought in to cross-examine him "did not appear to sit well with the jury."

The defense called state senator Ray Rawson, a Las Vegas Republican who was also a dentist. Contrary to Baden's conclusion, Rawson's review of the autopsy records found no evidence that Binion had been suffocated. The redness around Binion's mouth and nose, for example, could have been the result of attempts to resuscitate him, or of "a bad day shaving." Under cross-examination, Rawson admitted he had never physically examined a person who had been suffocated and was not as qualified as Baden to draw conclusions about causes of death. Dr. Jack Snyder, a young pathologist from Philadelphia, testified that the drugs in Binion's system were "a recipe for disaster," that he was a victim of "a classic heroin-plus death." Under cross-examination, Snyder admitted he had performed about 500 autopsies, compared with the 25,000 Baden had performed over forty years. Snyder then suggested that Baden's experience with heroin deaths was "outdated."

"He's forty years behind the times?" David Wall, the assistant state's attorney, wondered skeptically.

"Yes, that's exactly right," Snyder said, eliciting groans in the court-room.

Pathologist Cyril Wecht argued that Binion died of a self-administered overdose of heroin and Xanax, either accidentally or on purpose. In either case, he hadn't been murdered. The discolorations around his mouth and nose could have been the result of shaving, just as the marks on his chest could have been caused by attempts to revive him.

"This isn't about murder," John Momot urged the jury to conclude. "It's about heroin." He pointed out that Ted's body had not been dis-interred, forcing Baden to base his testimony on the coroner's original photographs, and few would dispute that this is one of the most vul-nerable chinks in the prosecution's case. Baden's burking theory is also at odds with the medical examiner, who testified that Binion had died of a drug overdose (not suffocation) after he was forced to ingest heroin and Xanax. Such discrepancies, of course, are routinely found by juries to be grounds for a reasonable doubt. Other possible grounds include the absence of a murder weapon or eyewitness: no handcuffs, no turkey baster, no awkward fourth wheel at the three-way. Nor had Kurt Gratzer been terribly credible or sympathetic as a witness. On the stand, he'd come off as "a dangerous wacko," staring menacingly at the judge, contradicting himself, and standing at military parade rest during breaks in his testimony. Two days later he was taken into cus-tody on a charge of domestic battery. Since jurors have not been se-questered, one or more of them could easily have watched, read, or heard about Gratzer's arrest.

Prosecutors Roger and Wall have declined to appear on television or grant newspaper interviews until a verdict is reached. John Momot, however, continues his regular spots on Court TV, Las Vegas One, and *Rivera Live* to attack the prosecution's case. (During one segment, after acknowledging that he wasn't familiar with the evidence, Geraldo still gushed to Momot, "I like your client's chances!") Mayoral aide Bill Cassidy has been all over local TV blasting the prosecution, de-tective Tom Dillard in particular. Speaking privately to a close friend of Dillard's, Cassidy went a bit further: "You go tell that motherfucker that he should back off of me if he wants to enjoy all of the money that he's made. I'm the gorilla on his back that will kill him." ("He's eccentric," the mayor admitted to the *Sun* about his pollster and confidant. "He's mysterious.") Speaking to jurors about Dillard's investigation, Palazzo was his usual articulate, levelheaded self: "This is—it's just like—it's like being in Nazi Germany, okay?"

Heading back to the Horseshoe, I run into Peter Alson, a Brooklyn writer (*Confessions of an Ivy League Bookie*) and poker player. Like me, Peter's in town to cover the trial and World Series while trying to play his way into the Big One. A wiry, bespectacled guy about my size but twenty years younger (and leaner), he seems genuinely pleased that I had such good luck in my satellite. So far, he hasn't fared well in the satellites, but he still has four days to amend that. As we compare other notes, it turns out that Peter believes, as I do, that the state didn't ask for the death penalty mainly because it would have been harder to get a conviction against an attractive young woman, especially when most of the evidence is circumstantial.

Peter had a chance to observe Murphy up close while covering the preliminary hearings last year for *Playboy*. His bemused, witty article, "Love and Death in the Desert," described her as "such a complex mixture of narcissism, manipulation and naïveté that one sometimes got the feeling that hers was a personality formed by watching daytime television and *Lifestyles of the Rich and Famous*. Her preoccupation with her appearance impelled her, on the first day of the hearing, to spraypaint her house-arrest ankle monitor beige to match her outfit." Peter also reported that Murphy's family brought ten different outfits to the prison, each with a matching belt and shoes. Now Peter's telling me he heard that before dropping her case, Oscar told Murphy that if only she had mourned Ted appropriately and kept a low profile, maybe even left town, she and Tabish would have been "big favorites" to be found not guilty. Since they hadn't, though, all bets were off.

"So the fifth amendment's really for perps about whose innocence her mouthpiece will not accept wagers."

"Something like that," Peter says. "Because they're off running for mayor."

This jibes with Peter Ruchman's opinion, expressed in the current *Gamblers Book Club Newsletter*, that Murphy "has treated her entire arrest and terms of confinement as a private joke shared by an overly curious public." Ruchman also quotes the prosecution: "It is as though she doesn't comprehend the fact that she is facing multiple life sentences."

Even so, Murphy's lithe stripper's bod has been camouflaged with sober suits and modest white blouses throughout most of the trial, presumably on the urgent advice of John Momot. Diagonal bags under her eyes and a patchy complexion make her look even less glamorous, as does the decision to allow her mousy roots to grow out. For several recent court dates, both she and Becky Behnen have, by coincidence, worn their shoulder-length brown hair primly pulled back into almost identical ponytails.

When Momot called Murphy's stepmother as a witness, it was her puckish daughter who first got out of her chair and moved toward the stand, before grinning and sitting back down. "Just kidding," she chuckled. Once on the stand, the senior Ms. Murphy testified that Binion physically abused her daughter several times during the three-year relationship. She had flown to Las Vegas to confront him about a beating in which Sandy received a black eye, a fat lip, and other bruises. "I asked him why he did it," she testified with some feeling, "and told him never to do it again." She also said she repeatedly begged her daughter to leave him, but that Sandy always refused, claiming she loved him too much. Then, when she saw her daughter sobbing on television the night of Binion's death, Ms. Murphy recalled that Sandy had reacted in a similar way when told that her grandparents had died. Sandy's boo-hoo hysteria in the emergency room, in other words, had not been a bluff.

Upstairs in the tournament room, while Alson heads off to play a one-table satellite, I decide to take in a bit of the $5,000 seven-card stud final table. Eight veteran stud artists remain in the hunt: David Chiu, Ken "Skyhawk" Flaton, Mel Judah, Scotty Nguyen, Bob Feduniak, Tony Cousineau, Jack McClelland, and Larry Flynt. There's $450,000 at stake on the table, yet the most interesting story here may involve

Flynt and McClelland's history away from it. After spending fifteen years as the coordinator and MC of the World Series, the dapper McClelland was fired last summer by Becky. He is widely loved by poker players for his humor, efficiency, and poker skill, and I'm told he received a long standing O when the final table was introduced at four o'clock. Flynt, of course, is the publisher of *Hustler*, backwoods Kentucky's answer to Chicago's Hugh Hefner. After being the first to "show pink" in a men's magazine, Flynt was paralyzed from the waist down by an assassin's bullet during a 1978 obscenity trial in Georgia. In *The People vs. Larry Flynt*, Milos Forman cast hit man Charles Harrelson's sons Brett and Woody as the Flynt brothers, Jimmy and Larry. The genuine Larry now sits at the final table in a gold-plated wheelchair upholstered in purple, this to go with his purple silk shirt. None of the Horseshoe heavies, I've noticed, appear to begrudge Flynt the pair of bodyguards standing by in matching white shirts and black ties, each of them obviously packing big heat beneath his black suit jacket.

Why would Horseshoe security begrudge helping hands in protecting a target of Flynt's notoriety? Because twelve years ago he was banned from these premises for life by Jacks Binion and McClelland for cheating at the World Series. According to Cloutier, Flynt "tried to buy off the table. He had a big bet with Doyle [Brunson], something like $1 million–to–$10,000, that Larry couldn't win the tournament. When it got down to three or four tables, Larry tried to buy off some of the players and actually did buy off some of them by getting them to throw off their chips to him. But Jack Binion had gotten wind of it and he had Dewey Tomko watching the table for him from the side. He saw what was going on, and Larry Flynt was never allowed to come back and play in the WSOP." Now that Becky is running the show, however, Flynt has returned to the Horseshoe's good graces, perhaps on the principle that the enemy of my brother is my friend— the obverse of which being why Jack McClelland got fired. Or so I have heard.

Impatient to get back in action myself, I ride down the escalator to sign up for tonight's super-satellite. The buy-in is $220, with unlimited $200 rebuys allowed during the first ninety minutes. "All-in orgies," they're called by some people, since the opportunity to replenish your stack can lead to some foolhardy wagers. While this doesn't make for great poker, it does have an upside: it gooses the sum spent on buy-ins and rebuys which, divided by $10,000, determines the number of seats awarded for the championship event. Two hundred players making one rebuy each, for example, would produce four seats as prizes; coming in fifth would pay zero. Sensible players budget $420 or $620 per super, but a few folks have made as many as ten rebuys in their effort to win a $10,000 seat. A bad bet. For the same amount they could have played *two* $1,015 satellites and had only 9–1 odds against them each time, instead of 196–4 (or 49–1) for one shot. Another way to look at it: $1,015 buys you a 10 percent shot, and $220 buys 2 percent, roughly a hundred bucks a point either way, but with 1.5 percent juice in one format versus 10 percent in the other, and putting aside the rather large question of which format requires more skill. To be even money to win a $10,000 seat in either format, you'd need to invest $10,000, which could simply buy you in Monday morning.

All-in myself in the first twenty minutes after flopping a set of queens, I get caught on the turn by a flush. I rebuy and build up my stack, mainly by raking a pretty nice pot with a flush of my own. Fifty minutes later I find a K-K and knock out two players when a third cowboy spikes on the river. By 12:45 I'm sitting at the final table in sixth chip position. The last five survivors tonight will get seats, plus $400 apiece; if you already have a seat, you get twenty $500 tournament chips, easily redeemable for cash, I am told, as other players wait to sign up on Monday. The player with the biggest stack when we stop also qualifies for the Tournament of Champions, to be held at the Orleans in July. Sixth place will pay the same as what the guy frozen out first, three and a half hours ago, will receive.

Down to eight players, I idiotically call a smaller stack's all-in bet with a suited A-8, deservedly losing to a pair of pocket tens. Two hands later I lose with A-K, calling a big preflop raise with a third of my stack (instead of reraising all-in, or just folding), then folding when my opponent goes all-in on the 5-4-7 flop. Weak!

With the blinds at $1,000 and $2,000, I'm down to $3,700, which more or less forces me to raise all-in with K-7 from the big blind. A stubbly guy in a Cincinnati Reds cap sitting behind a huge stack of chips decides to call me, flipping over . . . Q-7. That's all? That's fantastic! Only three cards can beat me right now; all the rest put me back in the hunt. But on fifth street the queen of clubs hits, and I'm frozen out three off the money.

Furiously re-re-recounting the last $78.37 of my bankroll, I ask for my messages before stalking back up to my room. I'll need $25 for cab fare to the airport and at least twice that much for tips between now and May 18. Every free meal in the cafeteria and bottle of water at the poker table will require a one-dollar thank-you.

I have to lie down for a minute. On top of the sheets. With my clothes on. For a minute or two. And just breathe.

After successfully impersonating a poker player for almost four hours, in less than twenty minutes I made a moronic loose call with A-8, played A-K tight-weak, then that *queen*, and it just cost me $10,400. Even lying still, even taking deep, trembly breaths, it feels like my testicles have been lopped off, marinated with high-octane leaded, lit up as *flambés rognons blancs*, then stuffed down my throat with a skewer.

Impatience is what doomed Rick and Sandy, of course. They were in such a fucking hurry to be rid of old Ted that they pretty much guaranteed their burke-job would be detected and prosecuted. If they'd waited for Ted to self-destruct, or let Sandy press forward with the palimony suit, they might be sitting pretty right now.

Lying in wait is what good poker players do best. More than any other character flaw, overeagerness is what does in the rest of us. As your stack dwindles and the antes and blinds keep doubling, you become less and less capable of waiting for sensible hole cards—just as, before going all-in with a capital crime, any decent player would have summoned the discipline to sit on the sidelines awhile. But the financial pressure on Tabish forced him to accelerate the timeline, pressing the action with what Cloutier calls a "trouble hand." Small aces, K-Q, or K-J don't look half bad before the flop, but the bigger the pot, the less likely they are to hold up. Why is that? Because all that money wouldn't be in the pot in the first place if you weren't up against a pretty strong hand, you loose, dumb, tight-weak motherfucker!

Having made the loose call of burking their affluent friend, Murphy and Tabish overplayed their weak hand by appearing as a couple in public and living too high off the hog. Yet despite all these blunders, they still have a real shot of getting clean away with it, not to mention a lode of Ted's fortune. Whereas I'll be heading home with two or three bucks in my pocket, plus this little item:

> Dr. Suck Won Kim, a psychiatrist at the University of Minnesota Medical School, is seeking compulsive gamblers willing to participate in a study of the possible impact of a drug called naltrexone on the urge center of the brain, which he says is overactive in addictive people.

This perfectly square clip of newsprint, lacking anything so square as a note or even a return address on the envelope, arrived in my message box with a 606 postmark, my first piece of mail as a resident of Las Vegas. The typeface, it seems, is from the *Chicago Tribune*.

PLEASE INFORM DR. SUCK WON, I print in big blocky red-marker letters on the back of a handy Horseshoe postcard, THAT HE CAN TAKE HIS NALTREXO before running out of space. The front of the card is a sepia print of a stagecoach hitched to a galloping team of six horses. In the narrow white margin surrounding the stage-coach, I use a black Horseshoe ballpoint to write: "But thanks for letting me venture this gamble. Whatever comes of it, you ruuuuule as per uuuuuusual. I'll get a prescription for naltrexone as soon as" before running out of space yet again. My first letter home from Las Vegas.

Jennifer is leaving tomorrow morning—just a few hours from now—on her annual trip to St. Louis to visit her mother. Which means the first real road trip for our girls will be minus their "Dat," as Bea has been calling me. (When I do something that especially pleases her, she pats my arm and says, "Good girl, Dat.") The fact that I'm *off gambling in Las Vegas* forced my mother-in-law, June Arra, to fly up to

Chicago today to help Jennifer drive back down through Illinois with the girls. Grace, Bea, and Jennifer could have flown on their own, but since June has a two-door Thunderbird with no car seats they wouldn't be able to go anywhere once they arrived in St. Louis, so the four of them are driving down tomorrow in our station wagon. That's Generous June for you, though. She sent us to Paris last summer with her frequent-flier miles, and she's paid for just about every Gap fleece top, red sneaker, and floral onesie the girls have ever worn. Her "Show Me State" license plates even declare BEA GRC, in case you want to know where she's coming from.

Another urge I had to overcome today was telling Jennifer about the ring. When I talked to her this afternoon, she seemed to be taking the crazy St. Louis logistics in stride, unless that was simply her poker voice—or, more likely, wishful hearing on my part. But I felt so guilty about missing the road trip that I clumsily hinted that Mom might be in for a little surprise once Dat arrived home, half hoping she'd "make" me reveal it right then. Instead of rising to the bait, though, she told me I sounded "awful distracted." And of course she was right. However much guilt I was feeling about my domestic responsibilities, whether to bet, call, or checkraise after flopping three queens has been the only sort of thing I've been able to concentrate on, and she heard that.

I swallow my Zocor and Trazodone with the dregs of stale mineral water, brush my teeth, gargle while I take off my clothes, urinate, spit, get in bed. Ten thousand four hundred dollars. I study Cloutier for a while but can't fall asleep until three or three-thirty. Fold or raise, raise or fold. Never chase. Ten thousand four hundred bucks.

Sometime later I dream that I'm lying facedown on a pool table. The slate beneath the felt has been padded somehow, because it feels like I'm on a massage table. Therapeutic massage, not the other kind. "Just like our mattress at home," I announce, in case anyone doubts my fidelity to Jennifer. "She gives great massage of *both* kinds," I reveal sotto voce, "in addition to a little known third variety."

It turns out the pool table is being used (inevitably, I suppose) as a poker table. The championship event started less than two hours ago, but we're already down to the last seven players: myself and the six football cheerleaders from Benet Academy, my alma mater in Lisle, Illinois. One maroon-pleated girl stands behind each of the pockets, shifting her weight from one ankleted foot to the other. Laurie Neff, my old favorite, is still wearing braces; I can see them plain as day, even though her chips tower sideways in front of my nose. The flop has come 5-4-7. Being in the prone position makes it hard to see my hole cards, but I understand that Laurie and Sherry Baumgartner each can see them—they're not even trying to disguise the fact that they're peeking. I also understand that if one of the next two cards isn't a six or a queen, I will lose this vast pot and be busted from the tournament, the last one to ever be played.

When the dealer turns over a card I can't see, Laurie whoops. Hands on her hips, she skips to her right across the green, chalk-scored field and launches into a cartwheel affording a slow-motion close-up of pale azure cotton, but all I really care about is what the final card, fifth street, will bring.

John von Neumann with Robert Oppenheimer at Los Alamos

THE POKER OF SCIENCE

If some one man in a tribe, more sagacious than others,
invented a new snare or weapon, or other means of attack or
defence, the plainest self-interest, without the assistance of
much reasoning power, would prompt the other members to
imitate him; and all would thus profit.

—CHARLES DARWIN

We can still be hunters in the million-year dreamtime.

—EDWARD O. WILSON

God may play dice with the universe, despite Einstein's last hope, but *serious* gamblers, scorning metaphysical crapshoots and the casino's house edge, prefer no-limit Texas hold'em. Light-years removed from the alcohol-soaked nickel-dime-quarter games of kitchen and dorm room, where the most you can lose is your beer money and who walks away with it depends less on skill than on luck, no-limit tournament action is always a ruthlessly disciplined fight to the death. The beverage of choice at these tables is mineral water, and the aces primly quaffing it have worked long and hard to make luck as tiny a factor as possible. How did they learn to do this? In as many ways as there are aces.

These days an education, even a refresher course, in big-bet poker can easily cost as much as four years at Stanford or Princeton. Even the textbooks are pricey. *Super/System* now goes for $50, *Theory of Poker* for $29.95, *Championship No-Limit and Pot-Limit Hold'em* for

$39.95, the latter two published in paperback—and at twenty times the price they're a bargain. (It goes without saying that all three spell out how to steal blinds and antes and pots.) Yet even if we read every last word of wisdom in print, few of us can afford to log enough hours at the no-limit table to attain even minimal skills.

One way to supplement book learning is to enter, as Alvarez did, a series of lower-stakes tournaments. If I lived in LA or Vegas or London, that would have been my plan as well. Stuck in the poker backwater of Chicago, however, my budget for airfares and lodging would have dwarfed what I'd spend on the tournament buy-ins. The most cost-efficient way to practice seemed to be on a computer screen, playing against either stand-alone programs or logged on to Internet sites.

NASA and the airlines spend billions on cockpit simulators because the risks of training pilots on actual shuttles and jetliners would be vastly more expensive and dangerous. So, too, with poker. This isn't to say that virtual hold'em is no different from the real thing, simply that the card sense and tactics required onscreen amount to a reasonable facsimile. The pot odds you need to correctly draw to a flush, for example, are identical to the odds you would need in a big-money tournament with actual chips, cards, and dealers. Tactics gleaned from primers can also be practiced ad nauseam on the computer screen gratis, until they're embedded in your neurotransmitters, where you hope they'll still fire when you're staring, cross-eyed and sweaty, down both barrels of a $200,000 all-in reraise.

No computer game besides chess, and very few other research facsimiles, so closely approximates the real-life model. Virtual baseball and basketball only nebulously resemble the actual games, plus it's easy for most people to simply go outside and play them. No one ever learned to hit a four-seam fastball staring at a screen or reading a howto book; and even with Ted Williams as my batting instructor, I could never touch Pedro Martinez. Ditto for Allen Iverson schooling my crossover dribble, or Calvin Klein's beauty secrets applied to my countenance. Yet once Doyle Brunson clues me in on how to enter pots cheaply with suited connectors, I'm perfectly capable of filling a straight or a flush and taking down a big pot from Texas Dolly himself, or from anyone. This is why Brunson's $50 primer sells like Irish coffee in the frozen ninth circle of Hell, though still not fast enough to cover what he's lost (or not won) at the tables. But that Brunson became his own Judas isn't really his students' concern. We should toast him—then call his wild bluffs.

Other leather-assed road gamblers, many of whom honed their chops before computers were even invented (and still refuse to publish them), naturally tend to scoff. "Seldom do the sheep slaughter the butcher" is Amarillo Slim's Lecterish way of putting it. But not all the old masters are contemptuous. Mickey Appleman is one who admits that the learning curve steeply accelerated during the nineties "because there are so many talented players today who have read many books and incorporated the knowledge of authors who have put in decades of poker play."

To supplement the floodtide of primers, software designers like Bob Wilson have written games designed to give you the feel of a live-action tournament. His Turbo programs dispense with the gimmicks on Masque: no plane rides or chauffeurs, no cartoon Jack McClelland or brusque topless blondes. Wilson's preprogrammed antagonists do sport ironically pokeresque nicknames—Gentle Ben, Bonnie Parker, Honest Abby, Seymour Cards—but what makes them worthwhile is the stiff competition they offer. Dial up their level to "tough" and they'll dropkick your ass good and proper. Beginners can set it on "average" or "above average," but even these require virtually the same betting decisions you'd make in a $10,000 tournament. What takes four days to settle at Binion's goes by in an hour at home—assuming you weren't eliminated in the first seven hands, in which case you start over. Bonnie Parker and Co. checkraise you, bluff, make adjustments for position and number of players in the pot, and alter their strategy based on your previous action. You can design (and name) other opponents, making them less or more aggressive, extracognizant of pot odds and whether you've bet or checked on the flop; you can even bestow upon them the ability to sense when you're on tilt—when you've "come unglued," as Peter Alson puts it—after losing a couple of pots. Very few flesh-and-blood players consistently cover all these bases at once.

You can also ask the Wilson program for advice, not a wise move in the middle of a live-action hand. When the board pairs on fourth street, making a full house a distinct possibility (but by no means a lock), should you reraise or fold with your flush? What are the exact odds of filling a straight with one card to come? The best way to learn, of course, is to come up with an answer on your own, then check it against Mr. Wilson's. You can also request to be warned when attempting inadvisable plays. Click on "stats" and the program evaluates your overall play, pinpointing weaknesses and offering tips for improvement. You can also hone skills interactively. The "stack the deck" option makes the program deal you calling or raising hands exclusively, so you waste less time folding the obvious garbage. (Cloutier calls foldworthy hole cards "toilet paper," but whether we call them garbage or Charmin, we should all take advantage of Louis Palazzo's household wisdom by flushing those Q-10's and suited K-9's down the toilet.) With Cloutier, Brunson, and Sklansky open in your lap, you can play A-Q offsuit from the small blind, for example, against 250 different random hands in a row and see how you do. No waiting while opponents spend three minutes studying their options, for the dealer to push the pot and reshuffle; you simply "zip" to the next hand of the exercise. It would take decades of live action, in which the number of hands per hour averages less than twenty, to get this much experience with a crucial no-limit predicament. You can also run high-speed simulations in which the computer plays a specific hand five thousand times for you against a random sequence of hands, then lets you know to the penny how much you would have won or lost with it.

At eighty bucks per CD-ROM, the cost of such programs is an infinitesimal fraction of the bankroll required to play uninformed big-bet poker for even a couple of minutes. Perhaps the best proof of their usefulness turned up in December 1999, when Sonja Camenzind outlasted a field of 220 in a no-limit hold'em tournament in Amsterdam, winning 55,202 guilders. It was the first tournament Camenzind had entered in her life, her only no-limit experience having come on Wilson Turbo. (I emphasized this fact to Lewis while pitching him the story, of course.) At least a third of the players I've talked to at Binion's now claim—or admit—they use Wilson programs to practice, and my guess is that the percentage is about to go up. The winner of this year's

$1,500 limit Omaha event, Ivo Donev, had been playing poker for less than two years, having spent the previous twenty as a chess pro. But he devoted eight months to soaking up Sklansky and practicing on Bob Wilson's programs, and he's just earned himself $85,800 and a World Series bracelet.

No doubt the best way to learn is still to play high-stakes poker every night against experts. But until you move to a serious poker town and boost your bankroll well into five-figure territory—"high society," as Matt Damon calls it in *Rounders*—you can put on your Bellagio visor and bifocal shades and keep a few primers open in your lap as you challenge some digital surrogates. Just don't checkraise Ben unless you're holding the nuts. He's not gentle.

Hold'em, as it happens, is also deployed by state-of-the-art researchers in game theory and artificial intelligence. Both Daphne Koller at Stanford and Darse Billings at the University of Alberta use the game as a model for computerized systems of incomplete information. Billings is a professional player who went back to grad school to study his vocation more formally. The program he works on, under the direction of Jonathan Schaeffer, is called Loki, after the Norse god of mischief and chaos. No see-through Spielbergian android with skinny fingers and sensitive features, Loki is the real AI deal, a rigorous domain for testing ideas in opponent modeling—for developing strategies, for example, to exploit the weaknesses of often much stronger adversaries. Like jujitsu and asymmetrical warfare, poker is about transferring leverage and wiping out bad guys efficiently.

Loki wins money in low-limit Internet games but still has a long way to go before it can realistically challenge a living, breathing no-limit expert. Strategically, it follows *The Theory of Poker*. Able to consider billions of possible hands in a flash, it gives a probabilistic estimate of what hand it's up against, then plays its own hand correctly according to Sklansky. Loki's advantage over most commercial programs is its ability to make tactical adjustments based on an opponent's previous moves. It bluffs with optimal frequency, learns from its mistakes, never tilts. To heighten the verisimilitude, it even tells prescribed jokes, quotes comedian Steven Wright, and responds to conversation on the Internet server, where it ranks in the top 5 percent of all limit hold'em players in ring games—playing nine-handed, that is, against regular cowgirls and dudes.

Heads-up against a live expert, however, Loki gets handed its lunch. Even though it's good with numbers, it can't make subtle logical leaps—can't have "insights." When a live expert raises with toilet paper, it may be either a mistake or a "move" designed to pay off twenty-five hands down the road. Loki can't tell; nor, without being told to, can it *make* moves like this. Despite its devilish Viking heritage, it wields no black magic to speak of.

Another problem is that poker is relatively meaningless without money, but no person or institution has yet volunteered to put up Loki's World Series bankroll. (Imagine those funding debates in the subcommittees of Alberta's provincial legislature.) Even once hitches like that get worked out, Billings concedes that Loki still needs to better account for opponents' unpredictability and generate some of its own; it needs to learn to think for itself. Right now it never slow-plays a strong hand, always betting aggressively. Good players are quick to pick up on this pattern and refuse to give Loki much action. "Computers are very dumb," admits Billings.

As early as 1979, Doyle Brunson predicted: "A computer could play fair-to-middling poker. But no computer could ever stand face-to-face with a table full of people it had never met before, and make quality, high-profit decisions based on psychology." What computers lack twenty-one years later, and what human players have always had in spades, is the capacity to learn strategic flexibility—to "playfully" randomize tactics. Pros call such tricks *changing gears*, suddenly playing much looser or more conservatively to keep their opponents off balance. They have learned since childhood how to do this by feel, making shrewd leaps of faith about what move will work best in a particular situation *as it comes up*, often flying directly in the face of the odds. Loki can't pick up facial tells, though neither does it give them away. But not only can humans read faces, we can generalize perspicaciously from previous oddball behavior. *Jen, I have noticed, will reraise preflop with a small ace or medium pair; therefore, with queens, I will call her and look at a flop.* We can also make out cryptic as well as obvious patterns, and take into account things like triple-reverse psych-outs. *Since Annie may assume that I think she's semi-bluff-raising on a flush draw, then maybe I'll play my trip sevens here straight by the book* . . . This last category may be where most of us get into trouble, but it's also the reason computers are no match for the best of us. Like the thirty-seventh American president, a terrific poker player himself, we're simply too tricky a species.

Billings and others insist that computers are catching up fast. What their machines already have, of course, are vast and perfect memories. IBM's Deep Blue can analyze in less than a second 200 billion chess positions, and it used this brute computational force to overwhelm world champion Garry Kasparov. That was chess, though, a game of complete, undisguised information; poker is much less straightforward. Yet if Billings and Schaeffer and their colleagues can somehow combine perfect memory with creative flexibility, they'd have an invincible program. "Somehow" and "if" are big caveats, though. "When it comes to imperfect information," Billings wonders plaintively, "how do you get around that? How do you deal with information that is possibly in error, or is deliberately deceptive?" For the time being, at least, his machine can't account for human guts and duplicity. What high-stakes gunslingers like Annie Duke and Jen Harman would do heads-up against Loki, in other words, would make Barbarella's obliteration of Durand Durand's death-by-orgasm gadget feel like a tender French kiss.

Daphne Koller and her colleagues in Stanford's robotics program de-emphasize opponent modeling in favor of classical game theory, a branch of mathematics used to maximize gains and minimize losses. "Opponent modeling is . . . very important in chess," she points out. "Nevertheless, chess-playing computers don't do that, and they do very well despite that limitation." She calls her program Gala, short for "game language"—no mischief or chaos at Stanford, thank you very much. Koller's goal is "to solve the general problem of finding game-theoretically optimal strategies in large games of imperfect information," which doesn't sound like black magic, either. Instead, she and her team have developed an efficient search algorithm for determining the best possible play in each of the four basic hold'em situations: preflop, flop, fourth street, and fifth street. Even bluffing, often assumed to be the most innately human and least programmable of poker tactics, emerges naturally from game theory in her algorithm. The architecture of her system looks like this:

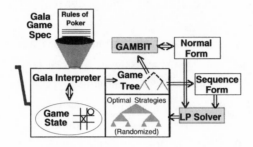

In a recent issue of *Artificial Intelligence*, Koller claimed that Gala is exponentially faster than the standard algorithm in practice, not just in theory. Its imposing speediness allows for the solution of games, such as no-limit hold'em, that are orders of magnitude larger than previously possible. (A good example of a "smaller" game is limit hold'em, with its preordained bet sizes, at this point the only version of poker that Loki can solve.) What Gala provides is concise declarative language for representing games by their rules. *Sevens beat sixes. A flush beats a straight. Players act in a clockwise sequence.* Each path of its game tree is then subdivided into products, each of which

can be re-expressed as the product of the realization weights of all the players' sequences on that path, times the probability of all the chance moves on the path. That is, for a given tuple $(\mu_1, \ldots, \mu_N)$ of randomized strategies, $\Pr_\mu(\rho) = \beta(\rho) \cdot \prod_{k=1}^{N} \mu_k(\sigma_k(\rho))$, where $\beta(\rho)$ denotes the product of the chance probabilities on the path to ρ. Incorporating this expression into Definition 4.1, we obtain that:

$$H(\mu) = \sum_{\text{leaves } \rho} b(\rho) \cdot \beta(\rho) \cdot \prod_{k=1}^{N} \mu_k(\sigma_k(\rho)).$$

If x is a realization plan for player k corresponding to the strategy μ_k, then $\mu_k(\sigma_k)$ is precisely x_{σ_k}, so that $H(\mu)$ is, indeed, linear in the realization weight variables for each of the players.

Confusing to laymen? *Oh* yeah. Yet, like every algorithm, this one is simply a set of rules for finding an optimal strategy in the smallest number of steps. In the January 2000 *Harper's*, David Berlinski humanized algorithmic logic by calling it "a recipe," as well as "an ambidextrous artifact, residing at the heart of both human and artificial intelligence." Cutting through the intimidating equations, Berlinski's piece helped me see that algorithms "belong to the world of memory and meaning, desire and design," things that Marcella Hazan or a lover might employ as naturally as would a Silicon Valley wonk. It also made Koller's working assumption—that a deep mathematical understanding of a game's rules reveals the best tactics for beating it—shine through even more clearly. She also assumes that the more we know about one game, the better we understand all of them, including social, financial, and military contests. "For me," says Koller, not a poker player herself, "this is more of an exercise in pushing the boundaries of game theory." In Gala's largest possible application, she hopes, one could extrapolate from poker to "an automated game-theoretic analysis of complex real-world situations." Defending ourselves, for example, from cunning, no-limit assaults of all kinds.

That's the theory. What happens in practice is that most computers now beat most humans at most forms of poker, but the best human players will still bust a cap in the most advanced programs, especially at no-limit hold'em. The dimensions of the programmers' quandary come into focus if someone says, for example: "The rule against balks and the one that sets bases ninety feet apart tell baseball managers when to put on the steal sign." These *are* the rules, but they help very little when deciding whether to challenge Pudge Rodriguez's arm with two outs in a one-run game in the top of the seventh and the hitter behind in the count. For that you need insight, feel, a patient hitter, an eagle-eyed sign stealer at the other end of the bench to tell you whether a pitchout is coming, a runner with base-stealing instinct and a lightning first step, and some luck. You need managerial genius. To steal a pot from Annie Duke or Jen Harman, you need a comparable range of munitions.

That computers can't dominate no-limit hold'em goes to the heart of why the game is the natural choice for settling the World Series Big

One. It's simply the most complex, and therefore the most deeply satisfying, version of poker. The most human as well, I believe, based on the "recipes" and "desire" of its highly abstruse bluffing rhythms.

All poker takes nerve, smarts, luck, art, and practice, yet a grounding in pointy-headed academic doctrine apparently doesn't hurt, either. Game theory, probability, and artificial intelligence were the subjects of Chris "Jesus" Ferguson's dissertation at UCLA this past spring. On May 3, a few days after being awarded his Ph.D., Ferguson took home the $2,500 seven-card stud championship, winning $151,000. Serendipity? Probably not.

Choice nicknames appear to help, too.

The godfather of probability and game theory is the Renaissance Italian Girolamo Cardano (1501–1576). This well-named physician was also a palm reader, a student of occult dreams, an astrologer, an algebraist, and a gentleman notorious for his *mala fortuna*. He was prone to toppling sideways into fetid canals, being struck by falling masonry, attacked by mad dogs. His bad luck at cards landed him briefly in a Milanese debtors' prison, making the peculiar suitability of his name best appreciated by imagining a crash-prone stock-car driver baptized Ford Nascarelli. Signor Jerome Cardplayer was even stripped of his lectureship at the University of Pavia after his son was convicted of, and executed for, wife poisoning.

There was no getting over the loss of his job and his son, but his bad luck at cards did become less pronounced once Cardano invented a method for combining probabilities; this, in turn, helped him calculate the exact odds of drawing certain hands at primero, an early version of poker wildly popular in Renaissance Europe. (Had Cardano experienced better luck beforehand, of course, he would have had less incentive to come up with his radiant discovery.) He eventually set down his ideas in the treatise *Liber de Ludo Aleae* (Handbook of Games of Chance), although during his lifetime only he and a few of his friends were able to benefit from its radical new principles. For reasons not fully understood by historians of science, Cardano's manuscript remained unpublished for 145 years, costing potential readers untold ducats and lire. Finally brought out in seventeenth-century

Florence, the book provided page after page of advice on how to make logic and probability work in a gambler's favor. It also laid the groundwork for a new branch of science: statistics. Its most famous calculation, however, turned out to be this one: "The greatest advantage in gambling lies in not playing at all." Cardano thus anticipates the words, if not the spirit, of Amarillo Slim Preston on how to thrive in turn-of-the-millennium Vegas: "Get yourself a six-pack of young blondes, have yourself a good time, and don't do no gamblin'."

Another imaginative virtuoso, John von Neumann, reached different conclusions about wagering. Tutored in Budapest as a thirteen-year-old math prodigy by a fellow with the Pynchonian name of Laszlo Ratz, von Neumann eventually helped usher the planet into both the computer and nuclear ages, both of which sprang from the Manhattan Project. (When screamings come across the sky, pardners, that's where they usually come from.) Between stints in the lab at Los Alamos, von Neumann relaxed with his colleagues by playing stud poker, although as a scientist he never stopped paying attention. Peering down at his hole cards, he noticed that his brain continued to function as it had in the lab: solving mathematical problems, making educated guesses, devising optimal strategy and tactics based on incomplete information and human psychology. Above his broad, freckled forehead, more than one lightbulb went on.

Unlike most of his fellow scientists, von Neumann got along famously with military men, especially the poker players among them. One of his regular opponents was General Leslie R. Groves, the no-nonsense administrative head of the Manhattan Project. Von Neumann soon became a member of the inner circle advising General Groves on the choice of a target for the first military use of the atomic bomb. Farther up the chain of command, President Harry Truman played pot-limit five-card stud with journalists twelve hours a day in the North Atlantic aboard the cruiser USS *Augusta*. Truman was returning from the Potsdam Conference, where he, Churchill, and Stalin had reapportioned Europe, and now he was trying to decompress while finalizing the decision about which Japanese city to evaporate. Kyoto had been high on the list, but Secretary of War Henry Stimson, a poker player himself, persuaded Truman that its religious and cultural significance would be crucial to rebuilding that nation. We needed to make Japan our trading partner, Stimson argued, as well as a buffer against the Soviet Union. (He publicly explained his position in the February 1947 issue of *Harper's*.) Secretary of State James Byrnes vigorously opposed Truman on a number of issues, but the president, already leaning toward a detonation above Hiroshima, used the daylong poker sessions to reduce Byrnes's access to him. A UPI reporter onboard the *Augusta* wrote that Truman "was running a straight stud filibuster against his own Secretary of State."

Meanwhile, back out in the Pacific, Lieutenant Richard "Nick" Nixon was winning almost $8,000—a genuinely whopping haul in the forties—in shipboard poker games against his fellow naval officers. Once, while holding the ace of diamonds in the hole, he drew four cards to make a royal flush, a 650,000–1 shot. "I was naturally excited," he wrote in *RN*. "But I played it with a true poker face, and won a substantial pot." Tricky Nick "was as good a poker player as, if not better than, anyone we had ever seen," a fellow officer recalls. "I once saw him bluff a lieutenant commander out of $1,500 with a pair of deuces." Upon discharge, Nixon used this money to finance his first congressional campaign, which he won against Helen Gahagan Douglas. As Eisenhower's running mate in 1952, he stopped playing poker for political reasons, fearing voters might think it unsavory. One of his professors at Whittier College, however, was moved to declare with some foresight: "A man who couldn't hold a hand in a first-class poker game is not fit to be President of the United States."

Having settled the war in the Pacific, von Neumann and company turned their attention to the Cold War, and this time it was *personal*. Inspired by his poker and military experiences as well as his youth in occupied Budapest, the Soviet-loathing Hungarian proceeded to invent Game Theory as a model of how potentially deceitful countries or groups interact when they have opposing interests. In spite of its fun-sounding moniker, Game Theory is an unplayful branch of mathematics in which naked self-interest determines every decision: how much to spend on conventional forces vs. ICBMs, which city to nuke in retaliation for a blitz of West Berlin, whether to bomb Cuban missile sites or blockade the whole island. Fun stuff like that. The discipline's ruthless utility made it the perfect tool for understanding poker strategy, and vice versa. Zero-sum games of complete information, such as checkers and chess, failed to interest von Neumann, mainly because the correct move is always discernible by both players, leaving no room for deceit. He found poker more lifelike, its tactics gratifyingly similar to those deployed by generals and presidents. Indeed, this was probably what gave the six-tenths-of-a-gram plastic cards their uncanny weight in the first place—not unlike plutonium 239, the royal flush of cold warfare elements and the one we may still have to answer for.

What von Neumann and others were onto was that poker is distilled competition, a less deadly version of combat, and therefore a good way to practice for it. The best strategy involves probability, psychology, luck, and budgetary acumen but is never transparent; it depends on the counterstrategies deployed by the enemy. Expert players misrepresent their hands, simulate irrational behavior, use surprise to intimidate, and deploy other mind games to confuse their opponents. Think of Nixon's "Mad Bomber" persona during the war in Vietnam, or of Truman's avuncular presence with reporters during the final days of World War II. Like von Neumann and Cardano before them, they knew both probability and people. They were also willing to set their opponents all-in in the ultimate no-limit stare-down.

Each poker session is a miniature global economy laid out on a baize oval table. Taking part satisfies not only our atavistic desire to play but our more modern urge to keep score. Money is to poker what MIRVs and megatons used to be to deterrence. As Jack Binion told Alvarez back in the heyday of the Cold War: "In the free enterprise system, you have to assume that each guy is the best judge of what he does with his own money. . . . So if a guy wants to bet twenty or thirty thousand dollars in a poker game, that is his privilege. Society might consider it bad judgment, but if that is what he wants to do, you can't fault him for it. That's America." A skeptical Alvarez commented: "that, too, is Las Vegas—the only place on earth where they justify gambling as a form of patriotism."

The fact is that financial markets around the planet continue to authorize gambling for vastly higher stakes, and national economies founder or flourish with the net results. And what better metaphor for democratic free-market risk taking than poker? Like futures traders, national security analysts, or stem cell research teams, poker players make educated guesses under radically uncertain conditions. That a few of them end up with most of the chips is what makes the game terrifying, ugly, and beautiful. It's what makes it *work*. As Walter Matthau dryly observed, "The game exemplifies the worst aspects of capitalism that have made our country so great." Because in no sense is poker a socialist or totalitarian enterprise. Much like financial markets, the game is a scary arena in which money management, pluck, and intelligence combine to determine who will get hacked limb from limb. Wealth gets created, egos deflated, blood spilled. Not for nothing are poker tables shaped like the floor of the Colosseum—the better to concentrate the butchery, the better to observe it up close. Lions and tigers and bears, oh my! Thumbs-up or thumbs-down on the river.

No-limit hold'em has also been called a black art, requiring players to broadcast and decipher fake tells, master complex (mis)information and amoral psychology, all of it illuminated by bolts of hideous and beneficent fortune. Folding, the thoroughly passive gesture at the heart of strong play, can be understood in religious or spiritual terms—as humble acceptance, for example, of a metaphysical order beyond our comprehension, sometimes known as the shuffle. While to *not* fold then backdoor a flush on the river after your all-in opponent filled an inside straight on the turn requires voodoo theology and titanium nerves to get your mind around, not logic or math prowess. Thank Shango or Oloddumare as you rake in the pot, or perhaps your lucky stars. As my daughter Bridget has been known to explain rare phenomena: "Whatever what*ever*, okay?"

Despite poker's nonrational dimension, philosopher John Lukacs was moved to call it "the game closest to the Western conception of life, where life and thought are recognized as intimately combined, where free will prevails over philosophies of fate or of chance, where men are considered moral agents, and where—at least in the short run—the important thing is not what happens but what people think happens." With everyone's hole cards lying facedown on the table, the hand perceived to be strongest in effect *is*.

Poker is also a game in which freely willed decisions prevail over class, race, or fate; the cards your opponents believe you are holding make everything else quite irrelevant. Above all, the game requires each player to account for deceit by the others. "Owing largely to the bluff," writes A. D. Livingston, "poker has influenced our thinking on life, love, business, and even war." (Livingston also reminds us that game theory has always been given "a high security classification by the armed services.") Bullfighting, by contrast, better expresses Spain's traditional gaming spirit, as *fútbol* does for Brazil, and Go for Japan, just as Dostoyevsky proposed in *The Gambler* and elsewhere that roulette "is a preeminently Russian game." Dostoyevsky believed that go-for-broke, Ungar-esque betting, whatever the game, was more "poetic" than frostily measuring the odds "like a German."

Speaking less nationalistically, the American poet Stephen Dunn has observed: "Good high-stakes poker players are neither noble nor greedy. They've sized up their fellow players, know a good deal about probabilities and tendencies, and wish like poets that their most audacious moves be perceived as part of a series of credible gestures." Dunn also points out that "the great gamblers, and there are not many, don't need anything. They simply wish to prevail. And we know how dangerous people are who don't need anything." As Cool Hand Luke handsomely drawled, "Sometimes nothin's a pretty cool hand."

To feel this dangerous ourselves, even for a couple of minutes, can be severely intoxicating. It makes both erotic and emotional sense to say that we *love* it, and sometimes we love it too much. "When I'm rushing on my run / and I feel just like Jesus' son" is Lou Reed's blasphemous apotheosis of going too far. (He's singing about heroin, of course, but it makes the same difference. Ask anyone chasing the dragon.) Another menacing quality of the rush is to make us want more of it, and getting more makes us want *more*. At the poker table, this can be good. Feeling both endangered and dangerous, we tiptoe barefoot along the business end of a scalpel and never get sliced, and it quickly becomes possible to imagine that our state of grace *never* will pass. Players use the expressions "playing my rush" or "having a horseshoe up my ass" to describe surfing a wave of big hands and successful bluffs. They often report the experience to be more stimulating than amphetamines, barbiturates, alcohol, music, or sexual intercourse. Certainly synapses fire at the poker table, and serotonin drips faster— or slower. Electrons and corpuscles rush to the pleasure centers of the cerebral cortex, and others rush lower. We blush. Pink and orange chips and green money, foot-thick wads of it sometimes, flood our burgeoning coffers. To moderate our breathing becomes a pivotal challenge, but surely we're up to it. Right? We haven't renounced *all* control of ourselves. Far from it, in fact. Dunn defines intoxication as: "That sensation of 'fine excess' Keats wanted from poetry, the adjective gracing the noun, keeping it alert." Focus, grace, poetry, black magic, fucking, too-muchness—the feeling that *I am invincible*. Even if you kill me I'll come back from the dead, just like Jesus. And if Jesus made love, I'm his son.

There's a downside to excess, of course. Antisocial urges like hitting and lying and thievery need outlets in games, but even in games we need limits. Or do we? No-limit hold'em is rarely favored in home games, since it tends to make for less than convivial evenings. For one thing, it routinely forces your houseguests to risk all their chips; when they lose them, buy more, then go broke, their feelings get hurt. *Boo-hoo-hoo.* They tend to prefer more approachable varietals, with wild cards, split pots, limited bet sizes, and bans against checkraising, all of which tend to make luck the most dominant flavor—or aftertaste. Anyone can win at these games, since whoever is dealt the best hand takes the pot. The shuffler has all the power, in fact, though he doesn't have any control.

Serious players are at war with the shuffle. They tend to prefer no-limit or pot-limit hold'em because big-bet poker gives them the leverage to win pots *without* the best hand. The most talented among them don't even need a small pair to take down a pot; one large, well-timed raise, in response to some flicker of doubt in the bettor's eyes or a twinge along the side of his neck, does the trick. Latter-day maestros like Harman and Duke, Men "The Master" Nguyen, John Juanda, and Erik Seidel can deduce with mind-bending precision from your facial tics and body language, and from how you played earlier hands, what cards you hold now; they play *you* and the size of your stack as much as they play their own cards, ruthlessly taking advantage of whatever anxiety you betray about your hand. If you've raised them with anything short of the mortal nuts—those rare pocket cards that combine with the board to make an unbeatable hand—they can feel your level of confidence *drip . . . drip . . . drip* a quarter-notch below 100 percent; and the meek won't inherit this pot. Extortionate reraises are called "coming over the top" of the initial raiser, often abbreviated to, simply, "coming." To come at most stages of a no-limit tournament requires shoving in all of your chips. For one of you, then, should your opponent have the nerve to call your huge bet, it's all over. (The spirit of these wagers is perfectly captured in the address of a new poker web site: ultimatebet.com.) Since the raiser has already expressed the strength of her hand with some confidence, to insist that your own hand is "nuttier" takes major-league chutzpah. By precisely this hair-raising process, hundreds of players compete until one of them has all the chips.

Here's another way to think about it. After Michael Corleone gets back to Nevada from Washington, D.C., where he fraternally intimidated Frankie Five Angels into recanting his testimony before the Senate, he immediately begins plotting to kill both his big brother Fredo and their father's old friend Hyman Roth. Even the news of his wife's miscarriage (actually an abortion, of course, because Kay refuses to bear another male Corleone) fails to daunt Michael's single-minded bloodlust. Exasperated, Tom Hagen pleads, "C'mon, Michael. You won. Do you feel you have to wipe out everyone?" In what is regarded as the clinching evidence of Michael's absolute ruthlessness, he tells his adoptive brother, "No, Tom. Only my enemies."

A no-limit tournament player's answer to Tom would be, "Yes."

3/23/18

Had an amusing even-
ing watching the odd
dances.

3/24/18 (Palm Sunday).

All clocks were set ahead
one hour, as specified by
the Daylight Saving committee.
Went to St. Patrick's Church and
attended 9 o'clock Mass.
Received evergreen instead
of Palm.

Visited Fr. Mac Mahon, S.J., of
St. Aloysius Parish.

3/25/18

Visited the Botanic Gardens.

3/26/18

Regular routine

3/27/18

Went ashore. Pleasant evening

3/28/18

Regular routine

James L. McManus's World War I journal, 3/23/18:
"Had an amusing evening watching the odd dances."

♣ ♥

NOBODY SAID ANYTHING

♦ ♠

There's a woman on my lap and she's drinkin' champagne.
—BOB DYLAN, "Things Have Changed"

She's sparkly. Very sparkly.
—RAIN MAN

T minus sixty-three hours, forty-seven minutes, and counting. The last time Time trudged this recalcitrantly Mary Beth Marino had agreed to let me take her to Topp's Big Boy as soon as I turned sixteen and got my driver's license, companion milestones a good seven months off. The time before that I was in second grade, looking forward with evangelical ardor to my First Holy Communion; having reached the Age of Reason—six and a half, according to the Roman Catholic Church—I'd recently made my first confession ("disobeyed my parents four times, told a lie twice . . .") and was champing at the bit to receive the body and blood of Christ on my tongue, then get showered with presents and cash. The time before that was in utero.

Taped to the wall above my desk-table is a poster for *L.V. Confidential*, a movie I'm dying to see. One of the *Review-Journal*'s artists, Ched Whitney, has draped Murphy's sultry puss with Kim Basinger's munificent cleavage and wavy blond tresses from the original *L.A.*

Confidential poster. Instead of Russell Crowe, it's Rick Tabish leering down at the décolletage, while attorneys Momot and Palazzo hover behind him above the Strip. Wearing a Borsalino hat at a rakish angle, Ted's head floats disembodied in the lower-right foreground. "The Ultimate Sin City Tale of Greed and Lust," reads the caption. "Everyone Is Suspect . . . Everything Is For Sale . . . And It's All Too Sleazy."

I've spent most of Friday clipping fresh articles, writing up my poker and trial notes, rearranging Post-its on the wall, and rereading myself into bleary-eyed dyspepsia. But going to bed now, at 8:56, would royally screw up my 2 a.m. rhythm, which everyone tells me I'll need to maintain through the tournament. And besides, I want action! I've been burning since Wednesday to sit at a poker table and parlay my flimsy receipt into something more tangible, to let the roll I was on then continue, even though it's hard to imagine any roll—any of *my* rolls, at least—carrying over a two-day *interruptus* . . .

I take a quick shower and put on my brand-new maroon Binion's polo shirt. With no computer on hand and no bankroll to scratch my itch with downstairs, I've decided that maybe what I need is a research trip to Cheetahs. That's where Ted first met Sandy, so I'll be counting on Jennifer to appreciate the exigencies of my article. The defense might also contend that such an excursion doesn't rise to the level of an infidelity because topless cabarets are ad hoc special cases, natural features of the landscape the defendant perforce must traverse. Plus all he'll be doing is looking.

Like most women, Jennifer doesn't see outings to strip clubs in exactly these jurisprudential terms. How do I know this? Because her last words while kissing me good-bye were much more straightforward: "Be good now."

"Don't worry," I told her while kissing her back, even though my expression, I'm afraid, begged her pardon.

Cheetahs is among the dozen or so cabarets spread out among the auto shops, tool-and-die plants, and used-car lots in the industrial heart of Las Vegas, a mile or so west of the Strip. During the fifteen-dollar cab ride, Treasure Island, the Mirage, and Caesars Palace all showed me their backsides to help set the tone for my evening.

The big CHEETAHS TOPLESS CLUB sign, smudged as it is with pink lipstick kisses, puts Bad Jim in mind of both long-legged felines and cheaters. Down below, the parking lot of the postwar, prefab, one-story edifice overflows with Camaros and Trans Ams and pickups, with limos and taxis logjamming the entrance. I've read that these clubs are separated widely enough by perilous corridors that taxis are necessary to move from one to the other, since tourists attempting to walk between them routinely get mugged. Even the locals are at risk. A few months ago a young man was carjacked and beaten into a semivegetative state. Yet doesn't every cheater, wherever he comes from, richly deserve such a fate?

The mood in the packed, mirrored room is thumpingly louder, and at the same time more "lite," than the West Loop or Times Square joints of my youth. If memory serves, those dives were more like the Last-Chance Brothel of the Indigent Dead, places for Catholic schoolboys with fake IDs to hook up with Little Richard (or Keith Richards) lookalikes. This place feels more like an indoor Daytona Beach break bash, juiced up but low-key and balmy, absolutely teeming with almost-naked college girls who look pretty happy to be here. Like most men my age, I've learned to extrapolate from forearms and wrists, from ankles and kneecaps, from the gist of a buttock or breast through denim or linen or silk, to what the rest of a woman's body would look like. You don't have to do that in Cheetahs.

Angling and excusing my way stageward, I find a single empty chair two rows back. Four seconds later a pink-blond valkyrie in a cheetah-spotted outfit not much less skimpy than the dancers have on arrives unsolicited bearing a two-foot cylinder fitted with a hose and a nozzle, perfect accoutrements to all her taut, gleaming skin. The stripping onstage seems redundant.

"Open wide!" I am told, and I cannot help thinking of Ted. I've already taken my Prozac and Zocor and aspirin today, and this semi-involuntary seven-ounce blast of Sex on the Beach is only four dollars, plus tip. I can hardly afford not to try one.

Sinking back into dark, plush upholstery, I take out my Post-its and green Horseshoe pen, hoping to feel less promiscuous. *See? I'm a serious anthropojournalist, profoundly disinterested in any material I happen to come across here. But no, I'm not gay. I'm simply husbanding myself for Jennifer, to whom I've been happily married since 1992.* While all manner of breasts are on display—I note studiously—from the dinky to the bombastic, the most popular are what I've heard are called Barbies. (I actually heard this from Jennifer while we took in *Real Sex* of an evening.) Barbies in person are high and hard orbs featuring telltale silicone curvature—unnaturally convex across the top—to go with a pale two-inch scar along the bottom. As curves go, they tend to be anti-alluring, at least to both Bad Jim and Good Jim.

Stints on the main stage last the length of two songs, but should a front-row patron especially relish a performance, it can be interrupted for an up close and personalized "leg show." A dollar or, better, a fivespot may be inserted into the G-string while the patron's face is swaddled in musk, perspiration, and silicone. For another dollar, a patron gains permission to poke his nose within sniffing distance of an aggressively splayed, writhing crotch. Such displays, I decide, should be called "posing for holy cards."

Once her two songs are over, the dancer exits stage left. She may retire to the dressing room for a breather, but more often than not she conserves enough energy to strike while the iron is hot. Planting herself in the lap of her most generous stageside fan, she offers him a personal gambol. Such dances run the length of one song, typically by Pearl Jam, Chili Peppers, U2, Lenny Kravitz, all played at thundersome volume through concert-caliber woofers. For $20 the dancer cavorts along most axes of her patron's seated form, keeping a forearm or thigh (but never a palm or finger) in continuous propinquity with his johnson, all this while he keeps *his* palms and fingers superglued to the chair or the back of his neck—till it's time, that is, for him to dig back down into his pocket and pay for song two. And so on. Three separate dances are under way within seven feet of me, so it's hard not to be a voyeur. From what I can gather, getting lap-danced is like being strapped to a chair for three minutes of frontal shiatsu therapy from an all-but-butt-naked masseuse whose hands have been amputated. A Sex on the Beach for the road helps me imagine more vividly.

Hi! What's your name? one girl after another wants to know. If I show a scintilla of interest she'll perch on my knee, stroking my triceps or nipple as she asks where I'm from. *Chicago, huh? I've been to Chicago,* this while strategically repositioning herself along my upper left thigh. *You like a dance, Jim from Chicago?* Yes I-a-do, but I can't, I may not, so I'll pass.

Lengthier interviews, some granted more reluctantly than others, reveal that a dancer earns serious money only by persuading you to retire with her to the VIP Room, where the rules of engagement are decisively more Clintonian. Junior VIPs pay $100 for three dances in a "semiprivate" three-sided booth. Tipping the bouncer at the door ensures both extra semiprivacy and a more lenient interpretation of the no-hands ordinance, all part of a system designed to peel Benjamins from your gangster roll of two *in a hurry.* Better-bankrolled clients like Ted can buy hourlong blocks of songs, together with finger food and bottles of Dom Perignon, that perennial warhorse of the libidinal marketplace, and tip their lap artists accordingly. I've been given to understand that for a mere thousand dollars—the cost of a satellite!— a handjob might well be administered, and for twice that nothing less than fellatio could be in the cards. My investigation has also led me to conclude that if you turn out to be sufficiently forlorn and well capitalized, a dancer may even retire and move into your house.

Age.	Unimportant.
Head.	Small and round.
Eyes.	Green.
Complexion.	White.
Hair.	Yellow.
Features.	Mobile.
Neck.	$13\frac{3}{4}$".
Upper Arm.	11".
Forearm.	$9\frac{1}{2}$".
Wrist.	6".
Bust.	34".
Waist.	27".
Hips, etc.	35".
Thigh.	$21\frac{3}{4}$".
Calf.	13".

Ankle. $8\frac{1}{4}$".

Instep.   Unimportant.

Height. 5'4".

Weight. 123 lbs.

This deeply sarcastic tale of the tape describes Celia Kelly, a Dublin prostitute in *Murphy*, Samuel Beckett's first novel. Note Beckett's signature comma before the deadly "etc.," his wry "Unimportants." Celia is the sometime girlfriend of the novel's eponymous, neurotically passive young hero. (Murphy is fond, for example, of binding himself with scarves to a rocking chair, but those who scan the novel for its bondage-and-discipline passages will be sorely disappointed.) Scholars have alleged that Beckett's model for Celia was Lucia Joyce, the daughter of his more bawdy mentor, James. Lucia in fact fell in love with the gauntly handsome young writer, and Sam found her achingly beautiful, a talented comedienne, and emotionally simpatico; the only problem, it seemed, was that because of the clash between his harshly Victorian Irish Protestant upbringing and his postmodern counter-perversity, Sam was unable to be aroused by any women other than prostitutes. It took being stabbed in the lung by a Parisian pimp for Beckett to break this pattern (he married the woman who nursed him back to health) as well as release himself from smothered obeisance to James Joyce (he switched from third- to first-person narration and took a stab at playwriting, too). Profoundly schizophrenic and luckless with men, Lucia Joyce never regained her equilibrium, though she and Sam corresponded for decades. It is one of the century's great thwarted-love stories.

The most amazing thing, though, for our purpose, is that except for eye color and waistline, the author of *Murphy* could have been describing our Sandy. Still coltish and knock-kneed when she showed up at Cheetahs in the spring of '95, Murphy was typical of women who dance topless professionally: early twenties, facially plain but with leggy, athletic physiques and the classic breasts-waist-hips ratio of 3:2:3, guaranteed to set penises firming and currency circulating. Few special skills are required beyond an aptitude for shimmying to Stone Gossard across a stage then dry-humping a vertical brass pole or a seated customer. The best-looking, most entrepreneurial dancers make $10,000 a week, so there's never a shortage of pretenders. Clubs like Cheetahs stem the flood by requiring girls to pass muster, then formally register and pay $100 per shift. Murphy, by her own admission, decided these were stipulations that sash-winning babes like herself didn't need to comply with. She never asked permission to dance, never paid a shift fee. "I took it upon myself to do what I wanted, and I did it. Nobody said anything to me."

Back in Bellflower, Murphy had attended two high schools, failing to graduate from either, but she managed to parlay her other credentials into a job at a luxury auto dealership. A male friend from those days, Mario Rottino, recalled her as "an eye-catcher, a head-turner. She was popular with people. She hung with the athletes, and her boyfriend was the star running back. We would all go to the movies, drive around and raise hell, go swimming—typical stuff. She was not a bimbo. She was well put together, but she could carry on a conversation—she could talk." At school, however, she was given to tantrums and rants, routinely appearing in vice principal Allen Layne's office. "Her senior year was a disaster," Layne told a reporter. "Her grades were terrible. There was something going on in her life already at that point—I don't know what. She kept it to herself." Attracted to car buffs and hustlers, Murphy loved tooling around Orange County in their Vettes and M3s and Carreras. "I saw her two years after high school," said Rottino, "and she was driving a brand-new Corvette." A reporter for the *Sun* characterized Murphy's world as a place "where sex appeal and fast talking go further and produce quicker cash than a suit and a college education."

Her first arrest came in February 1994 for driving on a suspended license and impersonating someone else—namely Tiffany Luna—to a police officer. Her stepmother put up her bail but soon wrote the judge: "I am the mother of Sandra Murphy. I bailed her out of jail . . . and since that time I am not convinced that she will appear at all of her court appearances. For this reason I have asked [the bail bondsman] to place Sandra back into the custody of the court. I no longer wish to assume the $10,000 liability." A DUI arrest the next year got Sandy a forty-five-day jail sentence and required that a Breathalyzer lock be in-

stalled on her Lexus, but she skipped town for Vegas without comply-
ing with either stipulation. Her attorney in that case, Randall Hite,
represented several dancers and topless clubs in Orange County. Hite
reports that while he didn't know how Murphy supported herself, "a
lot of Southern California dancers go to Las Vegas a few days out of
the month to dance. Girls make a lot more in Vegas—thousands in a
weekend. Then they come back here and lead very normal lives."

Murphy stayed. Her "plan" was to triple her nest egg playing blackjack at Caesars, but it took her less than forty minutes to lose her entire $13,000. Her new roommate, Susan Carroll, had taken a job as a
cocktail waitress at Cheetahs. When she heard about Sandy's losses,
Carroll told her she could earn decent money selling the scantily flattering costumes worn by dancers at the club. Such ensembles consist
of a half yard of material, if that, but their design and tailoring can
spell the difference between a $300 and a $3,000 night.

Clark County mandates that women wear G-strings at any cabaret,
such as Cheetahs, where alcohol is served. (G stands for Grafenberg
spot, by the way, after the diligent German gynecologist, Ernest, who
first surveyed the petite yet geopolitically sensitive territory G-strings
must shield.) Clubs may feature "totally nude" dancing, but if they do,
they cannot get a liquor license. This ordinance, I've heard, has the
bonus of attracting to licensed joints better-looking women, who as a
group prefer not to show pink in the workplace. Middle-class men
seem to prefer it this way—Sex on the Beach with fine women but
without raw exposure to crotches. "Cleavage is not nudity," as the cultural critic Wayne Koestenbaum reminds us, from whatever vantage
we view it. "Cleavage is a promise: not sight, but on the verge of
sight." For my money, too, the vertiginous is much more seductive.

What makes a G-string legitimate? That's easy. The Supreme
Court has ruled several times on the question, most recently in 1995.
At issue was the St. Johns County, Florida, statute protecting an erotic
dancer's first-amendment freedom of artistic expression while requiring that her entire pubis and one third of her buttocks be covered.
Nothing ambiguous about "entire," of course, but a third of two buttocks is trickier. None of one, two thirds of the other? Exactly where
does one place the tape measure? Officials charged with mapping

these critical spheres now can follow our highest court's guidelines: "The area of the human body (sometimes referred to as the gluteus maximus) which lies between two imaginary lines running parallel to the ground when a person is standing, the first or top such line being one-half inch below the top of the vertical cleavage of the nates (i.e., the prominence formed by the muscles running from the back of the hip to the back of the leg) and the second or bottom line being one-half inch above the lowest point of the curvature of the fleshy protuberance (sometimes referred to as the gluteal fold), and between two imaginary lines, one on each side of the body (the 'outside lines'), which outside lines are perpendicular to the ground and to the horizontal lines described above and which perpendicular outside lines pass through the outermost point(s) at which each nate meets the outer side of each leg.

"Notwithstanding the above, buttocks shall not include the leg, the hamstring muscle below the gluteal fold, the tensor fascia lata muscle or any of the above described portion of the human body that is between either the left inside perpendicular line or the right inside perpendicular line and the right outside perpendicular line. For the purpose of the previous sentence the left inside perpendicular line shall be an imaginary line on the left side of the anus that is perpendicular to the ground and to the horizontal lines described above and that is one-third the distance of the anus to the left outside line, and the right inside perpendicular line shall be an imaginary line on the right side of the anus that is perpendicular to the ground and to the horizontal lines described above and that is one-third the distance from the anus to the right outside line."

Got that?

To become a successful designer of G-strings, Murphy would have to heed the above in both letter and spirit, then match the results with flattering tear-away outerwear, failing to err on the side of either the dowdy or the overly skimpy. The first ensemble she came up with not only met these criteria but was a racier knockoff of the Dallas Cowgirls' uniform: white short-shorts spangled with blue stars, form-hugging white bustier. And voilà! Betsy Ross meets Jerry Jones meets Jasper Johns meets Barbarella. Modeling her scanty bunting in a full-length mirror, Murphy reckoned she'd warrant more greenbacks lap-dancing at Cheetahs her damn self.

She was right. She struck it rich her first night, in fact, when some wealthy Texan friends of her roommate showed up. "We went in the VIP Room and danced for them and drank Dom Perignon, made lots of money," Sandy later testified. "They were handing us hundred-dollar bills. We made thousands, like over $3,000 in probably three hours." Apparently two thirds of her nates, hips, and gluteal folds, combined with her untrammeled freedom of artistic expression, were enough to accomplish the trick, while the remainder was kept on the verge.

Not for long.

The guitar solo of Ted's favorite Neil Young song is too self-indulgent to be used very often at Cheetahs. If the entire (ten-minute-one-second) version were played, a G-strung contortionist might wear her-self out, even risk chafing a customer. Yet "Cowgirl in the Sand" remains the consummate sound track for Ted's first encounter with Murphy.

Ted had been smoking heroin in his pickup out in the parking lot with his friend Sid Lewis, but once they jangled inside Ted began redi-recting his buzz with tequila. So he was already doubly wired when he glanced up and spotted a leggy, all-American cheerleader boogalooing onstage. Fuzz-toned bar chords thundering against his cranium, he swallowed. He blinked. More than a little, the dancer reminded him of how his wife, Doris, had looked at seventeen, when they met: pale blond hair, boyish hips, real ethereal. Comprehensively bewitched, he knocked back a third shot of Sauza Tres Generaciones, and down came the star-spangled shorts.

It's the woman in you that makes you wanna play this game . . .

The moment this cowgirl sashayed off the stage, Sid Lewis let it be known that he and his friend wanted company. When Murphy, still sweetly perspiring, came over and sat in the chair beside him, Ted bought her a margarita and told her she had "real pretty titties." She thanked him, clinked glasses, then asked him his name, how he was. The Binion name didn't seem to ring a bell with her, but that was okay with Ted. That was fine. While she danced him for three or four songs, he told her that his wife had just run off with her personal trainer, so right there they had heartache in common. As Murphy later testified in the Binions' divorce proceedings: "I was having a hard time with my boyfriend. We had just broken up. [Sid Lewis] says Ted wants some company, but he is, you know, his wife just ran off tonight. He was drunk and I was drunk. We just sat and visited, and then I went back to California to face my DUI charges. It wasn't like we met then had this great affair because we just—we really didn't like each other."

Murphy also claims she told Ted: "I can't believe I'm doing this. If my dad ever found out, it would embarrass my family and everybody else." Ted proceeded to hand her a wad of money—"almost like $1,700, and I gave it back to him. I said, 'I don't want your money.'" Lewis remembered it this way: "She got the money and threw it back in his face and said, 'I don't want your goddamn money!' So that's what impressed Ted because she didn't want his money, so he picked up his money, put it back in his pocket and said, 'Hmmm, well maybe this little gal is different.'" When Lewis suggested she was bluffing, Ted waved him off. "No one's that good an actress," he insisted.

As soon as she returned from her court date in Los Angeles, Murphy dialed the number Ted had written for her on a bar napkin. He invited her to a party that night at his home and sent a white Horseshoe stretch to pick her up. When she arrived at the 8,000-square-foot mansion at 2408 Palomino Lane, Murphy was impressed. Tall white wrought-iron gate, high-caliber landscaping, double-wide driveway, the works. Once inside, she was introduced to a woman who apparently was Ted's date for the evening, and that pissed off Sandy but good. She yanked Ted aside and informed him that *she* was his date, and that he goddamn well better not embarrass her like this ever again. Ted, once again, was impressed. His divorce lawyer later testified that within days of that party, Murphy moved in. "She just sort of planted herself in Ted's life and never, uh, never was out of it." Murphy's version is that Binion arrived on her doorstep, literally swept her off her feet, told her, "I don't ever want to not know where you are again," and loaded her stuff in a truck. In either case, Murphy moved into Binion's home on April 17, 1995. She immediately commandeered Doris's bedroom and refused to allow her back in, even to pick up family snapshots.

Ted gave Sandy limousine service and comping power at the Horseshoe, let her remodel the interior of his house, and lavished inch-thick wads of hundred-dollar bills on her along with high-limit credit cards, a $97,300 black Mercedes SL 500, posh trips to Asia and Europe. He used her to schmooze Nevada politicians and other bigshots at the Horseshoe, and proudly introduced her to friends like "Fat Herbie" Blitzstein, who had been Tony "The Ant" Spilotro's top lieutenant. (Spilotro is the Joe Pesci character in *Casino*, the hard-on whose stop-at-nothing viciousness finally gets him beaten with a Hillerich & Bradsby into splintery jelly then buried alive, if just barely.)

The only fly in Ted and Sandy's ointment at first was fifteen-year-old Bonnie Binion, who now lived with each of her parents six months a year. Bonnie later told investigators that soon after moving in, Murphy threatened to shoot both her and her father. "And she threatened to hit me a lot of times. She just wasn't that mentally stable. . . . I actually told my dad she would have to change her behavior and the way she dressed and acted. Because I wasn't going to have basically a whore living at our house." One night, perhaps for revenge, Bonnie and her boyfriend borrowed Sandy's SL, promising to be back in an hour. Bonnie also tried on, without asking, a $9,000 Versace pantsuit her father had bought for Sandy. "We had the top down and were going about 120 out by Mount Charleston. Then he rolled the car seven times. People had no idea how we still had heads." In the emergency room, Sandy began ripping the pantsuit off Bonnie and screaming at Ted that she needed a new car. "My dad liked to see us fight," Bonnie told one reporter. "He grew up with his sisters always fighting. I think he missed that." Ted replaced the SL right away and packed his daughter off to Miss Porter's finishing school in Connecticut, Jackie Bouvier's alma mater.

To encourage her man in his trials with his family and the Gaming Commission, Sandy bought Ted the new Des'ree CD. For weeks they blasted it in the car and at home, gleefully singing along. "You gotta be hard, you gotta be tough, you gotta be stro-o-o-onger . . ."

"At the very beginning she was happy," Tom Loveday testified. "I mean, she was twenty-three or so, and Ted's a wealthy man who shows up at the club in a limo and spends tons of money on her for lap dances. Then he takes her to this house, she sees this big house—that's what she was looking for, you know. She may have told herself that he loved her, and she may have told herself that she loved him, but it was about money."

Ted began employing her to collect debts from deadbeat high rollers. In November of '95 she went all the way to Taiwan to dun an industrialist who owed the Horseshoe almost $1 million, but she failed to persuade the man to pay up. Loveday's opinion was that "Sandy was just in over her head. She thought she knew what she was doing, but [Ted] just had her there because she was pretty."

The following April, while Murphy was supposed to be under house arrest after her DUI conviction, Ted managed to get a Montana sheriff to report to the court in California that she had served seventy-five days of house arrest on the Binion ranch. But police produced evidence that Murphy was being chauffeured around southern Nevada in Horseshoe limousines instead. Ted had to pay $15,000 for Sandy to attend Sober Living by the Sea, a cushy substance-abuse program in Newport Beach whose name was the very antithesis of their life in Las Vegas. The director reported: "With the exception of a few minor 'glitches,' Sandra followed all of the rules and regulations that were established during her last appearance before the court." In this he sounded a bit like Alvarez describing Benny Binion's "self-defense."

One of the ugliest reports from this period was that Ted, while bingeing on smack, beat up Sandy on a number of occasions. Friends saw Murphy with bruises on her face and a patch of bare scalp where hair had been pulled out. "She took a lot of crap from him," Loveday reported. "She would show me the bruises. She'd put makeup on to cover it, but you could see it. I would get Ted's side, then her side. She got beaten a lot. Ted had a temper. And Ted always had a gun beside him. Always."

During one episode, Murphy ran to his sister Becky's place three blocks away, where she called the police. "My boyfriend beat me up," she told the 911 operator. "I want to press charges." The police escorted her back to Ted's house, where she gathered her belongings. But as soon as Ted returned from looking for her, they made up. Sandy dropped the charges, admitting she had lied to the cops. "I had BS'd a little bit to them because they wouldn't respond, and I had to tell them what I had to tell them to get them to take me over to the house to get my stuff." She even blamed herself for the original altercation. "I was really being a bit of a bully and mouthy," she said. "Let's be realistic. I work out five days a week. Look at him. Look at me. Do you think he could ever really do any physical harm to me? I don't think so."

On another day, Ted's real estate agent heard Murphy say to Ted, "Every woman needs a beating once a month. Isn't that right, babe?"

Nodding, Ted chuckled, thinking perhaps of their handcuffs. "And you got yours already."

And what about Bonnie? Is there a worse one-two punch for a fifteen-year-old girl than to have her parents separate, then have dad's party-animal girlfriend move in to mom's bedroom? This is the scenario to which Ted had subjected his fragile, impressionable daughter.

"Sandy hung out with dancers," Loveday would testify. "Big-busted girls. Girls who don't mind showing it to strangers. They'd be walking around the house in tiny T-shirts with no bras. These girls got everything done—plastic surgery. I remember seeing her girlfriends in there with Band-Aids over their noses after having their noses done.

"Partying was big with them, and sex was the thing with them, big time, at first. But then after a while it petered out. Once he went back on heroin, he couldn't perform sexually and that pissed her off," Loveday said. "I think Sandy is basically a nice person. She was always very pleasant to me. She'd tell me to help myself to a drink if I was thirsty." She also invited him to smoke marijuana with her, saying, "Tom, I'm twenty-six and I need sex. Ted hasn't made love to me in a long time." Loveday declined both her offers.

A lot of this stuff I picked up reading "Snake Eyes," Stephen Rodrick's piece in *GQ*. Rodrick accompanies Benny Behnen to the

Olympic Garden, another of Uncle Ted's favorite joints. Benny buys Rodrick a lap dance and regales him with stories of Ted's prowess at partying. He and his eighteen-year-old nephew would cruise the Naked City in a limo, firing .45 automatics at the sky. One night, for jollies, Ted dropped a tear gas canister in the craps pit of a rival casino. If a woman wouldn't go home with him, he would take out his lighter and burn hundred-dollar bills in protest. "He was a cross between Larry Flynt and a bum," Benny tells Rodrick. "He'd leave home with $30,000 in his pocket, but he'd be wearing ratty denim, and he cut his own hair. He wouldn't go home until the money was gone."

Rodrick also spends time with Murphy and Tabish. This was in early May 1999; they hadn't been indicted yet, and they seem fairly proud of their glam notoriety. Although they share an apartment, and Sandy welcomes Rick home to a candlelit dinner wearing chiffon pajamas and black underwear, they vigorously maintain that their relationship is "purely platonic," oblivious to even the possibility that a reporter, let alone the district attorney, might not believe them. They treat Rodrick to dinner at Mandalay Bay, then move on for a nightcap at Club Paradise, the high-end topless cabaret across from the Hard Rock Hotel. Decked out in black leather breeches, Sandy's in the mood to get down. While she checks out the competition, Tabish buys Rodrick a lap dance and encourages him to admire Sandy's "nice ass," all the while complaining that the Binions and Behnens ignored Ted's heroin addiction. "We were the only people who tried to help him. His family did nothing for him. Now they're fucking us."

Two days later, Sandy and Rick take Rodrick with them to Mass, where the reporter can't help noticing that Sandy remains kneeling in her pew throughout the Communion ceremony. "I'm a strict Catholic," she explains afterward. "If I don't go to confession on Wednesday, I don't take Communion." In the next breath she's recalling how jealous Ted got when she danced with her "old pal" Dennis Rodman and allowed him to touch her. She and Rick eventually admit that some things, such as spending the night together in Beverly Hills the weekend before Ted overdosed, or getting caught with his silver and lying to the sheriff about it, may make them *look* guilty, but that is as far as it goes. "Do I look stupid?" Tabish asks Rodrick rhetorically, and the reporter bites his tongue. "Would I go up there with my trucks if I was actually stealing the silver? I'd have gone up there by myself and taken just the expensive coins and got out of there."

The article is lavishly illustrated with press photographs and family snapshots: Ted as a gap-toothed seven-year-old, in white chaps and cowboy hat, riding a pony at a rodeo, testifying at fifty before the Gaming Commission, and his hat and boots bedecking his casket. Another shows Nick, Becky, Ted, and Doris, all in their twenties, hugging one another and laughing in a chic, brick-walled nightclub. Nick and Ted are toothsome and bushy-haired, with Neil Young–caliber sideburns to go with their snazzy two-button suits. Smoking a filtered cigarette, Doris is a delicate honey-wheat blonde in a white crepe dress while Becky, in wavy auburn locks to her collarbone, grins impishly out from between her two guys. The four of them couldn't be happier.

Pictures like that may be worth a thousand words, but some individual words reveal more than any picture ever could. As a district attorney might say, they go directly to motive.

"I have new words for the dictionary," says the writing teacher who narrates Susanna Moore's horrifically sexy fourth novel, *In the Cut*. Her new words include:

> *to knock boots*, phr., to have sexual intercourse
> *track*, n., contract (as in "I got a track to kill him")
> *to do*, v., to fuck
> *to do*, v., to kill

As the rest of Moore's novel makes clear, violence and sex can get stirred into sublimely pleasurable and dangerous permutations, especially once New York detectives get involved. Even then, words change everything.

High-risk sexual behavior springs from the same psychic and sociobiological crannies that can generate poker success: intelligence, stop-at-nothing aggression, hunger for money or status, a willingness to take outsize chances. The jargons, as always, are telling. *To come*, v., to have an orgasm, to ejaculate; *to come*, v., to reraise, to put one's opponent all-in. *Dog*, n., an unbeautiful woman; an ill-bred, discourteous man; *to dog*, v., to chase pantingly; *dog*, n., a losing poker hand; a bad bet or unfavorable proposition. *Stud*, n., something that pierces or projects from a surface; *stud*, n., a stallion at stud; *stud*, n., a man thought to be very active sexually or regarded as a good sexual partner; *stud poker*, n., a game in which the first two cards are dealt facedown, the next four faceup. And so on. This all goes directly to the question: Why would a stud and a nondog be tempted to do one another?

All warm-blooded animals are prone to what biologists call extra-pair copulations. EPCs are the reason humans feel sexual jealousy; they may also be why we make art, do battle, play games, and "play games." Helen's EPC with Paris generated nothing less than the first world war, not to mention the world's greatest poem; the mere *possibility* of Penelope's EPC after a twenty-year separation from Odysseus, braided together with the sheer number of those engaged in by her husband, gave us what may well be the second greatest. (Greatness in poetry, of course, is the measure of narrative power times the number of centuries of readership and cultural influence divided by the resentment engendered by those who wish they had written it, or NP $(CR + CI)/r$.) The pattern has changed little since.

Most contemporary women, Jennifer certainly included, refuse to split hairs on one subject: a lap dance is a full-fledged EPC and that's that. They sense that no wife sitting at home can compete with a topless dancer for the husband's immediate carnal attention, no matter how attractive and sexy his wife is. And no matter how evolved, reconstructed, or *menschlich* the husband may be at home, at his job, on the surface. In the parlance of bookmakers, once a girl from Cheetahs plunks down in his lap, his wife is a serious dog.

But why would a civilized human risk his own, let alone his child's, well-being just to rub limbs with a bitch who so flagrantly does him for money? Most fathers probably wouldn't, but many of us feel sorely tempted. Is this because we're self-destructive ignoramuses? In terms of modern domestic bliss: yeah. Biologically, though, it's a much longer story. In *Why Is Sex Fun?*, Jared Diamond explains that simple evolutionary logic encourages males to "walk off the job immediately

after copulation, seek more females to impregnate, and leave the females to rear their offspring." Just watch the parents at a Little League
game when there's lightning in the distance. Most dads want to get in
another half inning to "make it an official game," while the moms are
beseeching the fifteen-year-old umpire to suspend it. Showing how
male parental care "would be a bad evolutionary gamble," Diamond
gives the example of Morocco's Emperor Ismail the Bloodthirsty, sire
of approximately 1,400 offspring, and points out that in seven months
even a sanguine nonemperor can easily "broadcast enough sperm to
fertilize every one of the world's approximately two billion reproduc-
tively mature women." Diamond, of course, is hardly recommending
such wanton polygyny; instead, he wants to help his reader "understand why your body feels the way it does, and why your beloved is be-
having the way he or she is. Perhaps, too, if you understand why you
feel driven to some self-destructive sexual behavior, that understanding may help you to gain distance from your instincts and to deal more
intelligently with them."

So it's not that men are pigs—men are males. The only way we can
survive genetically is by exchanging food and shelter for access to re-
productively mature females. And how do such females decide which
male to couple with? By attending to signals indicating his relative status in her tribe; the higher his status, the better he'll be able to provide
for her and their offspring. How does a high-status male determine
which females aren't already pregnant? By the ratio of her waist to her
hips. Which one's the best bet to carry and suckle his offspring? Simply check out her complexion and the upstandingness of her breasts.
Bottom line? The 3:2:3 ratio of a cute stripper's hips, waist, and
breasts, so frankly paraded onstage, is altogether irresistible to hetero-
sexual men, especially high-status middle-aged chubby hubbies desperate before they die to get as much of their personal DNA as
possible into the next generation *without getting anyone pregnant*.
When that's what men want, and when young women know it, things
can get terribly sticky.

A further complication is what Wendy Doniger in *The Bed Trick*,
her magisterial survey of erotic double-dealing, calls *la morte douce*: the
lethal aspect of sex. Female praying mantises, who eat their insemina-

tors alive, have nothing on women like Murphy; as far as she was concerned, getting sport-fucked by Tabish before they burked Ted made
perfect sense. Her accomplice's motive? According to Doniger, the
male adulterer's primary incentive is usually not the seduction of the
wife-consort but the destruction of her husband. In this light, Tabish
becomes just another wanna-be-alpha male doing away with higher-
status competition. Doniger reminds us that ancient texts such as the
Kamasutra tacitly condone adultery when its purpose is to harm the
woman's husband. The inspired adulterer reasons: "If I become intimate with this woman and kill her husband, I will get for myself his
great wealth and power, which ought to be mine." All males, deep
down, think this way, though few of us act on these impulses. Why?
Because La-Z-Boy time dandling our kids with the game on while
Mom beams across from the sofa is simply too scary to contemplate
losing; most of us also respect other men's need to preserve *their* domestic bliss. As a group, however, we traverse every point on the adultery continuum, from the lust in Jimmy Carter's heart and Bill
Clinton's lap to the parallel sexual universes of Jack Kennedy, François
Mitterrand, Saddam Hussein, and not a few athletes and rock stars and
actors. Even so, it's only at the farthest point out that we encounter
the likes of Rick Tabish. Because of its escalating spiral of betrayal, his
act can fairly be called adultery in the first degree. He went outside his
own marriage to have sex with a woman who was herself as good as
married to his friend. Tabish also betrayed his adulteress-in-arms,
since his primary goal was getting Binion's loot, not pleasing Murphy.
(Who was, after all, merely "one of the pigs I'm fucking.") Finally, he
taunted and murdered the friend he was cuckolding *while he was doing
it*, an act downright biblical in apocalyptic dastardliness.

As Moses instructed his followers after they defeated the Midian-
ites: "Now kill every male dependent, and kill every woman who has
had intercourse with a man, but spare for yourselves every woman
among them who has not had intercourse." Clausewitz was heeding
similar logic when he recommended: "Be audacious and cunning in
your plans, firm and persevering in their execution, determined to find
a glorious end, and fate will crown your youthful brow with a shining
glory, which is the ornament of princes, and engrave your image in the

hearts of your last descendants." Kill the men, fuck the women. Go, Ricky! But he wasn't so off-the-charts, really. As London psychoanalyst Robert Stoller has argued convincingly: "It is hostility—the desire, overt or hidden, to harm another person—that generates and enhances sexual excitement." *La morte douce* thus becomes the logical extension of "rough stuff" as prosaic as nips, pinches, thumbcuffs, and hip checks. "Human beings are not a very loving species," Stoller reminds us, "especially when they make love." And since nubile women excite affluent men and vice versa, imbalances of power will tilt along so many social and biological vectors at once that their sex tends to get out of hand.

"It would be lovely," Daphne Merkin writes in the *New York Times Magazine*, "if we all conducted our intimate lives on a mature and responsible level, if we lived in an amorous universe without power plays, role reversals or adult enactments of unmet infantile longings. But much as we would wish otherwise, the reality is that such a bill of sexual rights can't begin to hold its own against the lawless and untamable landscape of the erotic imagination." Sodom and Gomorrah, Calcutta and Bangkok, Kyoto and Berlin, New York and Los Angeles have all vied to be the premier metropolis of that landscape, but in A.D. 2000 its capital may well be Las Vegas. Certainly it's no accident that the Strip features mock-ups of so many other Sin Cities: imperial Rome, Paris, Venice, Luxor, Hollywood, Rio, New York, Monte Carlo, New Orleans . . . including thirteen of the fourteen largest hotels in the world. The largest, the MGM Grand, has 5,005 rooms and employs a small army of locals. Little more than a desert rest stop fifty years ago, Las Vegas is now home to 3 million people and remains our fastest-growing metropolitan area. It also attracts more annual pilgrims than any destination but Mecca. People travel to Mecca to have a religious experience, what Mircea Eliade calls "a hierophantic relationship to the numinous." And that's why we come to Las Vegas. Except for the sun and the occasional thermonuclear blast, this is the brightest source of light in our solar system. Its most famous drink, in fact, is the Atomic Cocktail—vodka, brandy, Champagne, splash of sherry. Gamblers enjoying them in the fifties were treated, by paying

slightly *more* for their rooms, to views of Johnny von Neumann's hy-
drogen bombs going off sixty-five miles north of town.

Slainte!

Sipping one final Sex on the Beach—from a glass—I notice that it's
12:45, and I need to make my 2 a.m. bed check. I'd stand up this instant, in fact, if it weren't for a woman named Anya, the latest and
maybe the prettiest dancer to arrive on my lap. Anya tells me she's
Vietnamese and Russian, in her case a comely alliance. Narrow eyes,
pale gold complexion, dark blond bangs and ponytail. Before sitting
down she allowed me to take in her lime green Day-Glo bikini, the
bottom piece wrapped with a gossamer hanky that failed to cloak
much of her buttocks. She is girded up elsewhere by only the de
rigueur belly ring setting off the de rigueur floral tattoo wending
crotchward. Apparently a purse would ruin the effect, since Anya
keeps a roll of twenty-dollar bills rubber-banded to the heel of one of
her de rigueur eight-inch-high Lucite mules. Sometimes she looks
terribly happy to be on my lap, answering questions while running her
gold and black fingernails across the front of my shirt and expertly
shifting her weight, and sometimes she looks very bored. This changes
every few seconds or so, back and forth, especially since I asked
whether she was around back when Murphy worked here.

"You a cop?" she asks now. When I assure her three times that I'm
not, she kisses my ear, whispers, "Shame." Apropos the wet snow in St.
Petersburg, she suddenly volunteers that Mike Tyson was in the club a
few nights ago. "He's here just about every night, but Monday is different. One of the girls, Flower, she *called* the cops. Claimed he shoved
her or something."

I scan the still burgeoning crowd, stupidly hoping to spot Iron
Mike. "Is Flower here tonight?"

"Maybe later. No no, I think she got fired . . ."

Pearl Jam's "Black" is the first song a redhead called Mia will dance
to onstage. Starting off in silver lamé, Mia looks a tad nervous, as
though it's the first time she's tried this. Cavorting with unlimber
knee, her dance seems to say, "Mia white girl." Watching her intently,

Anya tells me that Flower had gone *with her husband* to the police station that night and filed a complaint, which Anya decrees was "not sensible. I mean, girls all around them. Guys come up to ask for his autograph, he gives them two C-notes to go away, this high squeaky voice . . ." She seems pleased that I'm writing this down.

When the slow dolce overture of "Black" ends, rim shots and power chords rip through the jumbo speakers. I watch Mia shrug off her glittering frock and get down unshyly to business, a veteran taker-of-clothes-off.

"Have you ever danced for Tyson?" I shout.

Anya shrugs, shakes her head. "You know the weirdest thing?"

I do not.

"There were two Tysons sitting there, when she—"

"Could you say that again?"

"They were sitting right there," she says, pointing to a table near the corner of the stage, "when all this went down."

I must have misheard her. "Two Tysons?"

She holds up two fingers, presses her lips to my ear. They are smooth as fine powder, as dry. And insistent. "This other big muscle-bound guy *looks exactly like Mike.* He claimed he was Tyson's half-brother, like they had the same father and all . . ." I'm trying to picture a pair of Mike Tysons when Anya nips my earlobe. "So what do you say, Jim from Chicago?" she purrs. "Ready for that dance about now?"

"I'm sorry," I holler into her small pale gold ear, barely resisting the temptation to reciprocate. "Like I told you, I'm only here to try and—"

"I gotcha." She lets go my nipple and slides off my lap. "I'll be back to you, Jim. You be good now . . ."

Home safe and sound in Room 1016, I count what is left of my bankroll: a twenty, a five, and three singles. Sex on the Beach gets expensive, I guess, though cheaper than a quick EPC. Which is good. Somehow I wound up with Jennifer while Ted wound up with Sandy, the principal reason I'm alive and he's dead. Not to be melodramatic.

While removing my smoky duds, I check out the *L.V. Confidential* poster one more time. Tabish continues to gape, much as I do, at

Basinger-Murphy's perpendicular cleavage. Pure milky promise, as Koestenbaum would have it, all girded up in white silk. And such rondure! Such—what's the word? Such, such . . . Hopping sideways as my cuff snags a heel, I spin around, land on my ass.

Cursing, humiliated, I haul myself up and crawl under the covers. Plus I'm thrilled, I keep telling myself, to be breathing, alone, in a comfortable bed at the Horseshoe, not burked on the floor of my den by a whore and a linebacker. *Mama!* I don't even wanna imagine what that would be like, with his legs as a vise on my head and some squirty thing shoved down my throat . . .

I switch off the light and lie back, close my eyes. Open them. There. That's much better. The room or my head revolves not unpleasantly, singed, as it is now, with golden Vietnamese afterburn.

Murphy with Goodman and Chesnoff

CHICKS WITH DECKS

He came here straight from his battery at Sevastopol,
moved in with me, and plunged into a headlong spree.
Orgies, gypsies, cards all night long . . .
—TURGENEV, speaking of Tolstoy

Play to win, or don't bother. Check friendship at the
door. A "friendly" game is a misnomer. If what you
are looking for is recreation or entertainment, there is
the theater. If what you want is camaraderie, there is
the bar. If it is companionship you seek, there are any
number of likely whores.
—DOC HOLLIDAY, in Bruce Olds' *Bucking the Tiger*

Sifting through the papers for trial coverage, I actually find confir-
mation of Anya's crazy tale from last night. Mike Tyson was in Cheetahs on Monday, apparently in a bad mood over his deteriorating
relationship with his wife, Dr. Monica Turner. As one of the *Review-
Journal*'s sources explained: "He's making it known he's single now." A
dancer named Victoria Bianco told police that Tyson reached out and
shoved her with an open hand, "causing her to literally fly across the
room and land on the floor." She reported that just before striking her,
Tyson said, "Get away from me, skanky whore." According to club
manager Rich Buonatoni, the dancer, whose stage name was Flower,
approached Tyson to offer a lap dance and was rebuffed; but Tyson
merely waved her away with his hand, said Buonatoni, which made it
appear as though she'd been shoved. Another Cheetahs manager,
Lonny Roybal, concurred: "He raised his hand and said, 'Don't come
near me,' and then she came near him. He told her, 'Get the fuck away

from me,' so he wasn't very flattering about it, but he didn't hit her." Roybal pointed out that Flower had worked the last three hours of her shift before going with her husband to the police station to file a complaint. Flower, for her part, also claimed that Cheetahs director of marketing, Mike Beasley, slipped $700 into her purse and said, "Nothing happened, right?"

The *Sun* has an interview with Cliff Couser, "a dead ringer for Tyson" who was sitting close by when Flower approached Iron Mike. (And I had thought Anya was pulling my leg, or my chain, when all she was tugging was my earlobe, my nipple.) "I was there and I can tell you what she said happened didn't happen," Couser is quoted as saying. "She came up to him and tried to sit on his lap. She asked, 'Can I dance for you?' and he said he wasn't interested. She got up and said something about how cold he was, and then she walked away. Next thing we know the police were there. She was trying to get some money out of it." Couser also contends that he and Tyson have the same father. "We've just started talking," he told the *Sun*'s reporter. "Mike said he can hardly trust anybody and said, 'Can we just be like friends?' and I said, 'Yes,' of course."

The *Sun* also reports that Dennis Rodman and Prince Albert of Sweden paid visits to Cheetahs this week. The club's employees made further news with their first entry into the Las Vegas Corporate Challenge, a mini-olympiad organized for charity. According to Buonatoni: "We wanted to show everyone we're normal people." He admitted, however, that sometimes his teammates drew special attention. "Every time we played co-ed softball, our stands were packed." The spectacle I keep imagining, though, is the side-by-side Tysons not getting lap-danced, but simply expressing their friendship and brotherhood in lisping contralto-falsettos.

A story I've heard around the Horseshoe this week also rings true— that back in '93 Ted ordered twenty thousand white $1 chips and twenty-five thousand dark brown $5,000 chips from a company in Arizona. The first part of the order was unremarkable, but the second part seemed off. Why would a casino suddenly need $125 million worth of extra-high-denomination chips? When the chip maker called the Horseshoe to double-check the order, Ted confirmed the numbers, so the company put the chips into production. (In a run of this size, chips cost the client only eighty cents apiece, though each one is fully redeemable for $1—or $5,000—in cash.) In the middle of the run, a different Horseshoe executive called and told them to stop production of the chocolate-colored $5,000 chips. Fifteen thousand were already finished, however, so it was agreed that these would be shipped. And since none of them were ever logged in to the casino's vault, it seems reasonable to assume that Ted, in effect, had minted himself $75 million in legal tender.

When Teddy Jane Binion died in 1994, Ted was the most devastated of her four surviving children. Not only her namesake and the one who looked the most like her, Ted had been the closest to her emotionally. He began smoking heroin again, as often as five times a day, and quickly got himself busted making a small purchase. A righteous prosecutor decided to make an example of him by upping the charge to trafficking, which further weakened Ted's legal position as the siblings battled for control of their mother's estate. In September of that year the Nevada Gaming Control Board suspended Ted's gaming license. Banned from entering the Horseshoe for the next sixteen months, he was fined $250,000 and barred from receiving money from the casino.

The feud over Benny and Teddy Jane's legacy climaxed in January 1996 when Becky filed suit against Jack to remove him as president of the Horseshoe Company, alleging mismanagement. The four heirs had earlier signed a licensing agreement giving Jack the right to use the family name on his new casinos in Mississippi and Louisiana; in exchange, Jack would pay each of them $1.7 million. Becky's lawsuit claimed that Jack was diverting money and other resources from the flagship casino to his new operations down south. Jack's ameliorative counteroffer was to make Becky co-president, though he would still control 43 percent of the holding company; even less soothing was his lawyers' contention in court that Becky and Nick Behnen didn't understand the gaming business and were destroying the company. In the meantime Control Board chairman Bill Bible had launched an investigation into whether Ted's signature on the licensing agreement

violated his compliance with the suspension. Ted's lawyers claimed the
licensing deal had been agreed to years before he was suspended; and
besides, Becky and Brenda may have received $1.7 million, but Ted
claimed, "I didn't get one quarter. [Jack] just wanted clearance to use
the name." He also shaved every hair on his body to try to defeat the
drug testing called for by the board.

Bible and the other gaming commissioners lost patience. In March
1998, citing his drug use, mob connections, and failure to comply with
their suspension, they imposed the industry's death sentence on Ted,
inserting his picture into the dreaded Black Book. Established in the
days of Estes Kefauver and J. Edgar Hoover, the Black Book is simply
a three-ring looseleaf binder holding mimeographed records and mug
shots of the thirty-eight "Excluded Persons" barred for life from
Nevada casinos. Ted's only consolation, perhaps, was that he found
himself in fast company, including that of Sam Giancana, Marshall
Caifano, Meyer Lansky, and Frank Sinatra. He had upped the Irish
quotient a bit.

Shot in the heart several times now, Ted saw his problems with
Sandy and heroin begin spiraling out of control. His parents were
dead, his wife had left him, his only child was away at school, his siblings either dead or estranged, his livelihood taken away. "Ted running
a casino, that was his lifeblood," Sid Lewis believed. "There was nobody that could hold a candle to him in that business, no one who had
guts like him—except Benny. High rollers would come in from all over
the world, and Ted would never back down—you know, 'Book it, book
it.' A million-dollar bet? 'Book it.' Just like his dad." Gambling historian Peter Ruchman saw him this way: "Ted possessed all of his father
Benny's bravado and none of his insight and good sense." Ruchman
points out that Ted and Rick Tabish were both raised in privileged environments by powerful fathers, and that Tabish "had more in common
with Ted than they both realized." Each man vacillated between self-
destructive acts of low self-esteem and a sense of invulnerability. "A
long-term drug user who never hid the fact that he lived hard, drank alcohol in large quantities, hung with mobsters, and often used topless
bars to conduct business," Ruchman wrote, "Ted felt his status as the

son of Vegas icon Benny Binion would forever shield him from the problems his lifestyle might have brought to others less connected."

Ted never gave up his fight to resurrect himself as host of the Horseshoe, even when his twenty-year-old nephew began taking over his duties. The day before Ted was murdered, he invited Mayor Jan Jones to swing by Palomino Lane to pick up a $40,000 contribution to her gubernatorial campaign. Hardly suicidal, Ted was betting on the possibility that if Jones became governor, she would help get his gaming license reinstated, but he was also feeling nostalgic. He and Jones had been friends for almost thirty years, and before she left his house Ted pulled some old photographs from a box and showed them to her. He seemed especially proud of one of himself at age twelve marching in a parade along Fremont Street. "He was upbeat," Jones recalled. "It's a nice last memory."

A corollary. Bob Stupak, the man who built the Stratosphere Tower (the tallest building in Las Vegas), somehow got his hands on a few racks of Horseshoe chocolate chips. Stupak is the sort of operator who bets $1 million on a single football game at the sports books of competing casinos, and who in 1989 anticipated Oscar Goodman's chutzpah by running for mayor, but lost. When he attempted to redeem $250,000 worth of chocolate in August of '99, Becky's cashiers turned him down. Stupak protested that he'd won the chips playing blackjack, but no Horseshoe pit boss could remember a score of this magnitude. Becky also insisted that hundred-chip racks of chocolate had been stolen, and that it was her fiduciary responsibility to protect her casino from gross fraud. Responding with drearily majestic cynicism, Stupak brought an antigambling minister into the fray by donating one chocolate chip to his congregation, banking on the pressure and negative attention the crusading minister would bring to bear against the Horseshoe. Stupak also sued Becky, of course, but the kicker was that Jack Binion took *his* side in court, submitting an amicus brief saying Stupak had won all his chips fair and square. Jack had run the Horseshoe with Ted and their father since the late sixties, and neither brother ever took seriously little sister Becky's managerial prowess, especially after Ted was forced out. Two months before Ted was murdered, however, the brothers tried to settle the feud by purchasing Brenda's shares and selling the entire bloc to Becky. The deal called for her to make payments to Jack of $1 million per month, with a final $20 million balloon coming due on July 1, 2000. Rumor also has it that Jack and Ted used ten chocolate chips to put out a contract on Becky, payback for ousting them from power, and Becky has said she believes it.

The Horseshoe remains the last family-owned casino in America, but what a clan these Binions and Behnens are. Despite or because of all their bad blood, they remain the first family of poker, and no student of the game can escape their pervasive influence. Becky runs the World Series now, with twenty-two-year-old Benny as the heir apparent. If she misses the July 1, 2000, deadline, I've heard that control of the Horseshoe will revert to her brother again. It is likely, however, that he would close the place down. The explosive development of Euroresorts on the Strip has turned downtown Vegas into a commercial graveyard, which is why he branched out nationally in the first place. I'm told there's a real chance that the 2000 World Series will be the last one put on at the Horseshoe.

In the meantime, it's still by far the most prestigious and lucrative five weeks in poker. The Super Bowl of Poker in Los Angeles, the United States Poker Championship at the Taj in Atlantic City, and the inaugural PokerMi££ion scheduled for next November on the Isle of Man all closely mimic the format invented by Benny and refined by his children and their deputies. But it is the cunningly named Jack Binion World Poker Open, held for the first time last month at the Horseshoe in Tunica, Mississippi, that has become the most threatening pretender.

Unlikely as it may sound at this point, the history of poker begins long before any Binion arrived in Las Vegas. When the Chinese invented paper around 200 B.C., in fact, the first uses they found for it were as writing material, money, and playing cards. All three applications spread along trade routes, especially to places where divination and gambling with straws, beads, and pebbles (called *lots*, as in *lottery*) were already common. Since card games could be made more complex than the casting of lots, they tended to appeal to more literate cultures.

Once priests, scribes, and warriors took up cards, they were further disseminated, along with the means to produce them, via conquest. In *Guns, Germs, and Steel*, Jared Diamond describes the transfer of Chinese papermaking methods to the Islamic world, "made possible when an Arab army defeated a Chinese army at the battle of the Talas River in Central Asia in A.D. 751, found some papermakers among the prisoners of war, and brought them to Samarkand to set up paper manufacture." The earliest cards in the Islamic world were oblong, with decks later divided into as many as ten suits. Christian crusaders and Venetian merchants eventually brought cards back to Europe, where Spaniards and Italians began playing with forty-card decks, and Germans made do for a while with thirty-six. By the early fourteenth century, as Florence's exiled ambassador Dante Alighieri worked on his *Commedia* near Venice, Persians had developed a deck of fifty-two cards arranged in four suits, each with ten numerical ranks and three hand-painted court cards. The suits were Coins, Cups, Swords, and Polo Sticks, emblematic of the officers providing a sultan's court with money, food and drink, military protection, and sporting entertainment. As these and similar decks made their way to Italy, polo sticks became scepters or cudgels, which eventually turned into our clubs. Usually safer than physical combat, wagering on the turn of a card was deemed a socially acceptable way to spend leisure time. Portraying the moral code of this epoch in his *Inferno*, Dante found no need to punish any cardplayer or gambler in Hell, whereas charging interest, blaspheming, practicing homosexuality, and even dying unbaptized were grounds for eternal damnation.

Renaissance Venetians kept separate apartments, called *casini*, just to play faro and consort with *cortigiane oneste*, those well-educated "honest courtesans" feted as symbols of Venice's splendor and liberal values. At least one such courtesan, Veronica Franco, became famous as a poet, ambassador, and philanthropist, and as one of the first European women to compete on equal terms with male courtiers. While card games continued to be the province mainly of male aristocrats, women and farmers and tradesmen gradually figured out ways to get in on the stimulating new pastime.

The cards themselves have always represented the strata into which societies arrange themselves. A report from 1377, for example, has many Swiss decks with the sun at the top of the hierarchy, followed in descending order by the king, queen, knight, lady, valet, and maid. In another popular deck, the order was snarling lions, haughty kings and their ravishing ladies, soldiers in breastplates and helmets, then bare-breasted dancing girls. On Florentine decks of this era, most of the women were naked.

By 1470, French card makers in Rouen had settled on the four suits we're familiar with today. The church was represented by hearts, the state by spades, merchants by diamonds, farmers by clubs (which resembled more and more the clover they harvested). Earlier cards had been expensively hand-painted for the actual king and his court, but widespread demand among common folk soon led to mass production of uniform decks using woodcuts and stencils. Rouennais designers fashioned their court cards after historical figures. The king of spades was drawn to resemble David, King of the Hebrews, his sword modeled after the weapon he took from Goliath upon slaying the giant with a leather slingshot, which was shown lower down on his card. The club king depicted a stylized Charlemagne, the king of diamonds Julius Caesar, the heart king Alexander the Great. The four kings thus represent the Jewish world, the Holy Roman Empire, Rome, and

	HEARTS (Church)	SPADES (State)	DIAMONDS (Merchants)	CLUBS (Farmers)
Ace or 1	A	A	A	A
King	Alexander	David	Caesar	Charlemagne
Queen	Rachel	Athena	Argine	Judith
Jack	La Hire	Hector	Ogier	Judas Maccabbees
Dancing Girl	10	10	10	10
Valet	9	9	9	9
Maid	8	8	8	8
	GREECE	ISRAEL	ROME	HOLY ROMAN EMPIRE

Greece, the four main wellsprings of Western civilization. The queens and jacks align much less neatly in this new Judeo-Christian scheme of things, and the bare-breasted dancing girls have been chastened on most decks to featureless Arabic tens. The ace was now uniformly the highest ranked card of each suit.

By the nineteenth century, as standard playing cards became double-ended, designers had to jettison the heraldry on the lower halves of the court cards. David's slingshot disappeared, making his kingship more generic. Two images that survive are the orb of Christendom cupped in the left hand of the club king, and the three-belled flower, emblematic of the Holy Trinity, held by his queen.

The modern poker deck continues to provide clear expression of erotic, theological, and military politics. Like towering alpha spires, sex-neutral aces dominate the tabletop cosmos. Kings, just below them, outrank their consorts, who in turn outrank the young male soldiers who protect them, who outrank the dancing girls, valets, maids, sevens, sixes, etc. In addition to gender-based status markers, we can follow a seniority-based progression up the social ladder—the idea being that white-bearded kings used to be clean-jawed soldiers, or that queens have spent time promenading with uncovered bosom. Even the more abstract numbered cards can signify social arrangements. Some historians argue that the ace, or one, for example, made its counter-numerical switch from lowest to highest rank during the American and French revolutions, when it suddenly became possible for the merest commoner to become emperor, prime minister, or president. These days the ace represents whatever intangible force (such as God, Allah, aleph, I, the Arabic number one, or what physicists call a singularity) can overcome the most august human being. Edward O. Wilson has shown that in complex societies, culture and religion have always combined to determine status. "Power belonged to kings by divine right, but high priests often ruled over kings by virtue of the higher ranks of the gods." Magic and totemism occur almost universally in human societies, for deep biological reasons. Rituals such as cardplaying, says Wilson, "celebrate the creation myths, propitiate the gods, and resanctify the tribal moral codes." The kings, queens, soldiers, and dancing girls represented on the faces of our decks permutate and combine into untold variations on the theme of what our genes make us do. When we play cards and abide by the rules, surrendering without comment or resistance a massive pot to the tiny old woman holding jacks to our tens, we participate in and "resanctify" these tendencies and hierarchies; but that three tens overcome queens and jacks is a fact that we wouldn't dispute. We also accept that a deuce is the smallest a thing can get, smaller than even a one; that in tandem, however, deuces overmatch any ace, any face card; but that even three deuces must lose to a straight or a flush—unless, of course, another pair materializes, in which case we have a full house. Straight flushes at the top, then quads, fulls, flushes, straights, sets, two pairs, pairs, and highest card: poker's recombinant hierarchy, based as it is on social order and mathematical scarcity, feels right in our market-based marrow.

Other metaphors have attached to the fifty-two cards. The queen of hearts naturally represents love, while her counterpart in spades is the more overtly sexual "bitch." The ace of spades is as black and as bad as things get—or as good, in the sense that Rhett Butler, Adam Cartwright, John Shaft, or Achilles is good. The ace of spades also is *real*, the most real, in that our willingness to "call a spade a spade" shows us to be forthright, clear-eyed, realistic. We're "aces" when we couldn't be better, "at sixes and sevens" when baffled. At a bawdier level, a hold'em starting hand of 3-8 is called "Raquel Welch," 2-9 is "Twiggy," and Q-Q is "four tits" or, more recently, "Siegfried and Roy." Soberer logic determines that 4-5 is "Jesse James" because of his favorite sidearm, that 7-6 is "Union Oil," A-A "American Airlines." Because he flopped three straight-flushes with the hand in one year, "T.J. Cloutier" became the nickname for the nine and jack of clubs (but not for any other 9-J, nor for the 10-J, as is often assumed because of the alphabetic resonance with his name). On the back of *Super/System* it says that 6-9 is "Joe Bernstein," from which I infer Mr. Bernstein is either quite tall or has a predilection for two-way, yin-yang oral sex. It also makes sense to call 10-2 "Doyle Brunson" because those were his hole cards on the final hand when he won the world championship in both '76 and '77. Even more astonishing, his 10-2 combined with the board to make tens full of deuces both years.

Sandy Murphy, the dancing girl who moves into the horizontal castle on Palomino Lane but never gets crowned, is best represented, I think, by a single card. The queen of spades suits her, of course, but the ten of clubs is even more apropos: black three-belled flowers, emblematic of an unholy trinity, adorning the bare-breasted lap dancer, One Zero. She was also Ted's "10," in the Bo Derek sense, for a while—was a 10, in fact, for all of her customers, at least for a couple, three minutes—until she became Tabish's 10, or his fuck pig. Tabish is her mustacheless jack of clubs, the trusty knave who pips the dancing girl then persuades her to help him kill the king in order to ransack the castle and its treasury. Ted Binion, then, since he brought this menacing pair of suited connectors into his court to begin with, can be none other than the sad-eyed king of hearts, burked by subordinates joined in a smothering flush. He shows his regret for these foolhardy choices of consort and friend by yanking his sword from its scabbard and stabbing himself in the head.

The earliest versions of poker seem to have derived from the Persian game *as nas*, or the French version, known as *as naz*. Which game developed first isn't clear, but both can be translated as the ejaculation "My beloved ace!" and what player hasn't felt that? We know that *as naz* metamorphosed into a three-card bluffing game called *poque* (related to the Gaelic for "kiss") as well as a close German cousin called *Pochspiel* ("the bragging game"). French soldiers brought *poque* to New Orleans around 1820, when it was played with a twenty-card deck. After a shuffle, five-card hands were dealt facedown to four players, who proceeded to bet on the relative strength of their cards. Without straights or flushes—let alone straight flushes—four aces, or four kings with an ace, were the only unbeatable hands. But even if you held no pair at all, the look in your eye combined with the size of your wager could force players holding much stronger hands to relinquish the pot, a tactic that seemed very much in the spirit of our fledgling market democracy.

As *poque* spread north on Mississippi riverboats, more and more folks wanted in on the newfangled chancing. The southern pronunciation was "pokuh," which as the game migrated north and east became "poker." The rules changed as well. The fifty-two-card deck was incorporated around 1837 to accommodate up to ten players and make for more lucrative pots. Flushes and straights were introduced, as was the option to draw three new cards. Fortunes in land, fur, gold, cotton, and tobacco changed hands on the turn of one card, or a bluff—who knew which?

One early problem was that skilled, ruthless cardsharps came to dominate much of the action. When they couldn't beat you with marked cards, a "cold deck" pre-sequenced to deal you the second-best hand, or an ace up their sleeve, they pulled a pistol or switchblade and took your money that way. For a long time it seemed that only a scoundrel or fool would play what was then called "the cheater's game." And yet it continued to flourish.

Cleaner versions of poker became widely popular during the Civil War, when soldiers on both sides took up the game between battles and survivors brought it home with them to every state and territory. Spreading west with the gold rush, it was played with the same reckless enterprise that the 49ers and Comstock Boys had brought to their claim jumping. Not surprisingly, poker on the western frontier retained its unsavory elements and picked up some new ones. In the town of Deadwood in the Black Hills of the Dakota Territory in 1876, Sheriff J. B. "Wild Bill" Hickok was playing in Carl Mann's Saloon No. 10 when Jack "Crooked Nose" McCall snuck up and shot him in the back of the head with a .45 caliber revolver. Hickok's national reputation as a gunfighter had been established eleven years earlier in a *Harper's* article by George Ward Nichols, so a yellow-bellied knave like McCall would never have drawn on Hickok face-to-face. Being the last man to be seated in the game, however, Sheriff Hickok was forced to play that evening with his back to the door, and it cost him his life. As the gambling lawman lay bleeding into the sawdust, still twitching, someone noticed that he continued to clutch his five cards, including two aces and two eights, which has been known ever since as the Dead Man's Hand. Today's hold'em players routinely fold an A-8 before the flop, even when there hasn't been a raise. They're avoiding serious kicker trouble if an ace or two happens to hit the board, but they're also steering clear of Hickok's bad karma. "I ain't superstitious," as Muddy Waters sang, "but a black cat just crossed my trail."

With its frontier cachet still intact, poker has become the most popular card game on the planet. Players continue to sport cowboy noms de guerre—Amarillo Slim, Texas Dolly, Kid Poker, Oklahoma Johnny—while tournaments are called things like Gold Rush, Pot of Gold, Wild Wednesday Omaha, and Texas Hold'em Shootout. (As a meteorological variant, the biggest tournament in Scandinavia, held in midwinter, is called the Helsinki Freezeout.) Even Sklansky and Malmuth's cerebral advice books feature a Colt .45, the gunslinger's weapon of choice, on their covers. Perhaps it's because after the final card, fifth street, gets dealt and the betting is completed, players still in the hand must engage in a *showdown*.

Pot-limit and no-limit Texas hold'em (called big-bet poker) have taken Europe, Australia, and some parts of Asia by storm. Under-the-table cameras and glass panels in front of each player on the celebrated *Late Night Poker* broadcasts over Britain's Channel 4 allow the audience to follow the betting sequence knowing who has the nuts and who's bluffing. (Without such information, watching real-time poker played in a television studio—as opposed to Hollywood dramatizations like *Rounders* or *The Sting*—can be like observing bears hibernate and smoke. The entire point of a player's demeanor, after all, is to *not* convey trustworthy information.) Tournaments modeled on Binion's World Series are now held in Costa Rica, Birmingham, Dublin, Melbourne, Sydney, Wellington, Bregenz, Prague, Amsterdam, Malta, Moscow, and St. Petersburg, as well as on cruise ships. Club Aviation on the Champs Élysées holds four big seasonal tournaments a year—four extra reasons that several touring pros make their home in the

City of Light. In November 2000 London's Ladbroke Casinos will stage the first PokerMi££ion, with a guaranteed first prize of £1 million and final-table action broadcast live to 300 million households in 140 countries. According to Victoria Coren of the *Guardian*, "Poker is the new black around here."

One result of all this is that after being dominated by Texans for almost two decades, the World Series has now crowned champions from the Bronx, Brooklyn, Boston, Grand Rapids, Iran, Vietnam, China, and Ireland. In 1997 twelve of the twenty-one WSOP titles were captured by foreign-born players, and the '98 championship went to Thuan "Scotty" Nguyen, who had emigrated at seventeen from South Vietnam in a small boat, almost starving to death with his younger brother before a U.S. Navy ship picked them up. Last year three of the final seven in the championship event hailed from a much smaller country, including the winner, Noel Furlong. George McKeever finished seventh and Padraig Parkinson, a fierce but good-humored native Dubliner, finished, as he puts it, "t'ird."

1. Noel Furlong	Clifton Lodge, Ireland	$1,000,000
2. Alan Goehring	New York, New York	$ 768,625
3. Padraig Parkinson	Dublin, Ireland	$ 489,125
4. Erik Seidel	Las Vegas, Nevada	$ 279,500
5. Chris Bigler	Felisbach, Switzerland	$ 212,420
6. Huck Seed	Las Vegas, Nevada	$ 167,700
7. George McKeever	Dublin, Ireland	$ 125,775

Parkinson used his prize money to finance a move to Paris, where he lives in the 6th arrondissement with his ravishing brunette girlfriend, Veronique. This year, of course, he wants to win the damn thing, and at age forty-two has committed to a regimen that would never have occurred to him in his younger days. Eating less meat and getting more regular exercise was the easy part. A devoted imbiber of spirits, he woke up on New Year's morning 2000 with a hangover but hasn't touched a drop since, and he won't until the Big One is over. "If you want to be a champion, I t'ink you have to behave like one," he tells me, with no small regret in his voice. Given his Dublin heritage and the city he's chosen to live in, it cannot be easy submitting to Spartan restraint. "Veronique helps on t'at front," he tells me. We wish one another good luck and make plans to toast the last hand of the tournament, the later the better for both of us.

Besides drawing record numbers of entries, the 2000 WSOP has also provided evidence that *Homo pokeriens* keeps evolving in salutary fashion. In the very first event, Limit Hold'em with a $2,000 buy-in, Hieu "Tony" Ma, another Vietnam-born maestro, defeated a record field of 496, including nine former champions. And check out these names at the final table, melting-pot lovers. Shrink back, Pat Buchanan!

1.	Hieu "Tony" Ma	$367,040
2.	Roman Abinsay	$188,480
3.	Hung "David" Tran	$ 92,240
4.	Ray Dehkharghani	$ 59,520
5.	David Stearns	$ 44,640
6.	Jimmy Athanas	$ 34,720
7.	Kevin Lewis	$ 24,800
8.	Reinhold Schmitt	$ 19,840
9.	Scott Brayer	$ 15,875

Word is, the stylish Mr. Ma has already won another $60,000 playing one-table no-limit satellites. Thank God he did not play in mine.

Chick power ruled in the second event, when Jerri Thomas, a forty-one-year-old commodities trader from Hamilton, Ohio, took the $1,500 seven-stud bracelet. (Because of the five extra cards potentially dealt to each player, stud is contested eight-handed, and the final-table lineup reflects that.)

1.	Jerri Thomas	$135,975
2.	Bill Gibes	$ 69,825
3.	Tab Thiptinnakon	$ 34,910
4.	Stan Goldstein	$ 22,050
5.	Richard Tatalovich	$ 18,375
6.	David Chiu	$ 14,700

7.	Dale Phillips	$ 11,025
8.	Rafael Perry	$ 7,720

Thomas's victory was all the more impressive because she had given birth to her second child only three months earlier. Clearly back in shape both mentally and physically, she wore a close-fitting red hooded sweatshirt, a diamond necklace, and her big diamond engagement ring to the final table, where she began play far behind the chip leader. As her husband, Harry Thomas Jr., and three-month-old Harry III looked on from the bleachers, she coolly dispatched her seven male opponents. Her sister Mel and twelve-year-old son, Mark, helped Harry with the baby-sitting, but during the fifteen-minute breaks granted every two hours, Jerri took Trey to the women's room herself for a diaper change. The Thomases' teamwork has paid off in other ways. Harry taught Jerri to play less than seven years ago, and they are now only the second married couple with a World Series bracelet apiece. (Dr. Max and Maria Stern were the first.) Harry, a Cincinnati land developer who won the $5,000 stud event in '85, underwent a quintuple bypass last September, when Jerri was five months pregnant, but seems to have fully recovered. Deeply religious, both Thomases are quick to credit Danny Robison, their Bible course instructor, for fundamental guidance with their stud games as well. Harry also points out that he and Jerri try to compete only against people who play for sport or entertainment, not from financial necessity.

"This has been a dream for a long time," Jerri told reporters while being photographed with the bracelet. "I don't think the layoff really hurt me. Harry getting well was such a blessing, and the baby has brought so much joy into our lives, that maybe it helped. It has really been a wonderful year."

And then, on May 5, Jennifer Harman took home the No-Limit Deuce-to-Seven bracelet. Because of its steep degree of difficulty, this event drew only thirty entrants and paid just five places, but the Deuce (in which the lowest hand wins, and aces and five-card straights are both high) is a title that poker pros covet almost as much as the Big One. No satellites are spread for it, so only by putting up $5,000 in cash can the cockiest, best-bankrolled rounders show their stuff. Harman won going away.

1. Jennifer Harman $146,250
2. Lyle Berman $ 81,250
3. Steve Zolotow $ 48,750
4. Bruce Corman $ 33,500
5. Lamar Wilkinson $ 16,250

Only the sixth woman to win a World Series title (not counting women-only events), Harman becomes the first to take a no-limit contest. The lean, blond thirty-six-year-old can still generate the aura of a cute but naive li'l sis, but opponents who read her as such are in for exorbitant lessons. Her short-sleeved Lycra tops reveal a mean Y-shaped scar on her left triceps, earned while protecting a friend's child from one of her ornery Australian blue cattle dogs. Even when Harman is not in a hand, the superfine hairs along her forearms bristle with static, though she also will sigh like a frustrated schoolgirl. Her nerves have been steeled by a decade of high-stakes lowball against the likes of Brunson, Chip Reese, Howard Lederer, Annie Duke, and Huck Seed, but until last week Harman had never played No-Limit Deuce. Neither had Duke, for that matter, but that didn't faze either one of them. They took a ten-minute lesson from Lederer, Duke's immense older brother, and put up their five grand apiece. Lederer, who once dated Harman, resembles a millennial Dead Head at the poker table, with the torso and beard of a Kodiak grizzly, towering stacks of lucre between his big paws. By way of further eclecticism, the strict vegetarian recently won a $10,000 proposition bet simply by eating a cheeseburger.

In his wrap-up report on the Deuce, Andy Glazer risked PC citations from outside Las Vegas by referring to Harman as "a stunningly beautiful woman," then hastened to remind his readers that he'd called a male player "ruggedly handsome" three reports earlier. It's from Glazer's fast and fastidious e-ports, as well as those of Mike Paulle and others, that the poker world knows Huck Seed took home his third WSOP bracelet (for razz) and Johnny Chan his sixth (for pot-limit

Omaha). Glazer somehow produces insightful and punny accounts within a couple of hours of the event's final hand. They often run to 3,000 or 4,000 words arranged in taut, stylish sentences. Before he sits down at the keyboard, the former Atlanta defense attorney hovers above the final table with a gray legal pad, furiously jotting down hands, flops, and positions, in the meantime coming up with his headlines and leads—for example, "Mom Defeats the Seven Studs" above the story of Thomas's victory. (As far as the runners-up were concerned, Mike Paulle's headline was a pip more emasculating: "Snow White Fends off Seven Dwarves.")

This is the first year results of the preliminary events are being posted on the Internet, and four million people have been rabidly following the action on casino.com, conjelco.com, binions.com, and a few other sites. The championship event will be covered live hand by hand, in addition to the usual TV and newspaper coverage, and the Discovery Channel is filming its annual documentary. Dan Abrams, the youthful producer, confided to me that he definitely wouldn't mind if a woman won the Big One this year.

"Right own," I told him. "That's a sixties expression that means, 'I agree with you.' "

"Thank you, sir."

For further context: no woman has taken a major open title in bridge or chess, either, let alone in a primarily physical sport. Math skill is crucial in poker, of course, but not nearly so much as in bridge and chess. Because men have fifteen or twenty times as much testosterone onboard, aggression with chips may also come more naturally to them. Women can compensate, however, with superior ability to read emotions and psychology. Poker should therefore be seen not as the last bastion of cowboy or riverboat chauvinism but as the contest in which women have the most democratic opportunity to prevail.

It took Thomas and Harman only nine days to almost double the women's bracelet count of the previous three decades, but the ball started rolling much earlier. In addition to Sonja Camenzind's breakthrough, Marie Smith won the pot-limit hold'em event at the Irish Poker Championships in March, and England's Lucy Rokach is now the third-ranked hold'em player in Europe. Outside the tournament circuit, cowgirls like Harman and Duke have been more than holding their own against the big—and good, and old—boys in the nightly $1,000-$2,000 "white-chip action" at the Bellagio, considered the toughest ring game in the world.

But no woman has yet won the Big One. In twenty-nine years only Barbara Enright, who finished fifth in '95, has even made the final table. For the sake of my *Harper's* piece (and Dan's documentary), I'm hoping this year will be different. I've already got four hours of tape on Liebert and Johnson and Thomas, and interviews lined up with Harman and Duke and some others. Having three daughters and three sisters makes me root even harder, I think, for one of the "chicks with decks" (as female reporters have taken to calling them) to break through next Thursday. Another line going around is that well-endowed women such as Enright and Johnson have unfair advantages in no-limit hold'em, since they start every hand with a big pair. Rim shot, groan, wince, clash of cymbals.

Even if the breakthrough doesn't happen this year, things are still a far cry from how they were in the days of *Roe v. Wade* and *Court v. Riggs*. In 1977, London gaming journalist David Spanier could write in the *Independent*: "No girl I have ever seen at a poker table has ever managed to win consistently. There are plenty who try, in the gorgeous palaces of Las Vegas and in Gardena [a poker mecca west of downtown Los Angeles], and in the workaday casinos of London, too. Women players, typically, are tense, beady-eyed, chain-smoking ladies . . . a far cry from the languorous cuties you see displayed in casino ads." Eyebrow-raising stuff, even coming from a spiny old-school stegosaurus, though for the most part it was probably accurate. But Spanier didn't stop there. "There are often girls around," he continued, "but a girl's fate is to sit on the fringe of the action waiting for her man to finish the game, which inevitably means waiting up half the night. By that time the girl is just about dropping with fatigue and looking like last week's laundry." Dude!?

Just before he died back in February, Spanier surveyed the new landscape: "Women are no longer considered as accessories to be brought to the poker table, but as equals at the game." Even so, he remained unafraid to stir controversy. "This is not to say that sex cannot enter poker. A woman at the table can alter the chemistry of the game," he suggested. "If a woman can exploit her sexuality by a certain smile, a look, a little flirting, to put a male opponent off his game, she is entitled to do so. Any man who responds, in the spirit of the occasion, should be even more on his guard. The object on both sides (one must assume) is to win the pot." Unless (one must assume) the reverse implied pot odds determine that a midtournament liaison would be a smarter bet—or more fun.

Who's the favorite among the women this year? Besides the ones I've already mentioned, the names of Melissa Hayden, Nani Dollison, Tracy Phan, Mimi Tran, and Spring Cheong keep coming up. With the exception of Hayden, all of these ladies are ethnically Asian, another major trend that bears watching.

The male player generating the most buzz—aside from the former champions here—is probably Chris "Jesus" Ferguson. Long and exceptionally lean, with three-foot chestnut locks, a full beard, and Jesus-like features, Ferguson is almost freakishly photogenic in his poker regalia. He shows up at the crack of noon every day in a Black Stallion cowboy hat adorned with silver medallions, and wraparound mirrored shades in whose reflection the action on the table is regularly exploited by photographers. Is he Richard Petty's hippie nephew? The rhythm guitarist of the Youngbloods? Robert Downey Jr.'s crack dealer? Actually, the thirty-seven-year-old stock trader from Pacific Palisades has been toiling studiously at UCLA, Jim "the Lizard King" Morrison's alma mater. No leather-pantsed, death-enamored bacchanalian, however, Ferguson's favorite hobby is swing-dancing, and he's thinking of launching a hedge fund. In the meantime he effortlessly crossbreeds poker's traditional badass Marlboro Man persona with its nonsmoking, more halcyon LA component. (He was named Best All-Around Player at the California State Poker Championship back in February.) Modest and soft-spoken in spite of his worldly success, when filling out questionnaires he lists his occupation as "student." Here at Binion's he has already reached three final tables and won the $2,500 stud event.

1. Chris "Jesus" Ferguson $151,000
2. Al DeCarlo $ 75,500
3. Perry Friedman $ 37,750
4. Kevin Song $ 22,650
5. Kim Nguyen $ 18,875
6. Fred Brown $ 15,100
7. Pierre Peretti $ 11,330
8. Larry Kantor $ 7,555

Continuing the brainy-guy trend, the bracelet for $1,500 Omaha (a variant of hold'em in which players begin with four hole cards instead of two) was captured by Ivo Donev, a forty-year-old chess player from Rousse, Bulgaria. His father, I. M. Donev, was the national champion of Austria and trained the East German chess team in the early 1980s. Ivo won the Moscow International Youth Tournament in 1989, then quickly rose to the rank of International Master. His final step up, to Grand Master, was impeded by the collapse of the Soviet Union, during which chaos and inertia ruled for three years in the chess world. In 1992 Donev and other young players tried to revive the game in Bulgaria, but, as he says, "somehow the magic was gone." Two years later he emigrated to Virginia with his wife and daughter. To support the family while he studied electronics, he taught for an online chess school, offering students (via e-mail and telephone) close tactical analyses of the Fianchettoed King's Bishop, the Maroczy Bind Formation, and the Hanging Center, all for $30 an hour. Unchallenged by the level of chess competition he found in his adopted country, he decided to take up an American game. Already steeped in a training discipline that used books and computers, Donev found it natural to learn poker by studying Sklansky and Malmuth and McEvoy, and by practicing on Wilson Turbo software. Playing here at Binion's in crisp white button-down shirts, he's a picture of masterful concentration, in contrast to some of his more insouciant opponents, with their loud shirts and motormouth prattle, chest hair atwinkle with jewelry. His peppery hair smartly groomed, Donev keeps what must be his lucky blue-and-gold tie in a neat Windsor knot at all times.

1. Ivo Donev $85,800
2. Thor Hansen $42,900
3. Martin Oliveras $21,450
4. Hassan Igram $12,870
5. Ben Tang $ 9,652
6. Charli Brahmi $ 7,510
7. Mark Scott $ 7,510
8. Barry Shulman $ 7,510
9. Dan Heimiller $ 3,430

(Brahmi, Scott, and Shulman—the swashbuckling publisher of *Card Player*—were all eliminated on the same hand, so the prize money for sixth, seventh, and eighth places was divided evenly among them.)

Three nights before I arrived, poker's evolution made quantum racial headway when Phillip Ivey took home the $2,500 Pot-Limit Omaha title, becoming the second African American with a World Series bracelet. (The first was Walter Smiley, who took the $5,000 stud title way back in 1976.) Playing out of Atlantic City, the twenty-three-year-old Ivey has been on the tournament circuit for less than a year, but his triumph was hardly a fluke. Four weeks ago he became the youngest titleholder at Jack Binion's World Poker Open, winning a hold'em event and "cashing" in three others. (Only the top 5 or 6 percent of entrants take home any prize money.) Here at the Binion's mother ship, Ivey had to come back from an $85,000-to-$400,000 chip deficit to defeat Amarillo Slim with a series of fifth-street miracles, all the while pointedly ignoring Slim's notorious coffeehousing— "friendly" verbal jousting designed to distract his opponent. In thirty years of World Series play, during which he's won four gold bracelets, Slim had never not finished first after making a final table.

1. Phillip Ivey $195,000
2. "Amarillo Slim" Preston $ 97,500
3. Markus Golser $ 48,750
4. Phil "The Brat" Hellmuth Jr. $ 29,250
5. Dave "Devilfish" Ulliott $ 21,940

6. Dave Colclough	$ 17,065
7. Hassan Kamoei	$ 12,190
8. Ali "Baba" Sarkeshik	$ 9,750
9. Chris Bjorin	$ 7,800

The straight-shooting Glazer toasted Ivey's achievement that night on casino.com: "Poker doesn't belong to white American males anymore. Poker books, computer programs, and worldwide legal cardrooms with codes of conduct have cut the head off the 'good old boy' network, even if the body does keep flopping around for a while. Poker now belongs to anyone with the brains, guts, and nerves to play it, and there's something about that level playing field that feels great, even to a white American male writer."

At noon on Sunday—T minus twenty-four hours—the Women's Tournament gets under way, but more than a few stars are sitting it out. Duke, Harman, Kolberg, Kathy Liebert, Melissa Hayden, and Linda Johnson have all found other business more pressing. Duke is at the other end of the room playing one-table satellites, and Hayden is a finalist in the $5,000 Limit Hold'em, a far more prestigious event.

"Actually," Mike Paulle informs me, "the one with the highest degree of difficulty is the Press Tournament." He's talking about the free, semiserious event I'm about to start playing. The idea is to give journalists and photographers a feel for what they'll be covering tomorrow, and to put a good taste in our mouths with respect to the Horseshoe as we write up our stories or edit our video reports. When I ask Paulle, who's in charge of this tournament, whether he's kidding, he says: "Believe me, this action'll get plenty loony."

But poker action of any variety is just what I'm looking for, since I'm desperate to fondle some cards. We're being given a chance to play no-limit hold'em with $10,000 in chips, just like the big kids. The top three finishers also get to assign checks for $5,000, $1,000, and $500 to their favorite charity. My more selfish reason is that the last nine survivors receive the same navy blue Binion's WSOP jacket as final-tablists of the money events. And I figure it will make for good practice, however amateurish or unpredictable the competition turns out to be.

"Don't bet on it," says Paulle. "Rounds only last fifteen minutes, so the luck factor'll be magnified by a factor of eight." A round is the interval between the doubling of the blinds. In order to neutralize luck as much as possible, rounds in the Big One last two full hours. Fifteen-minute rounds make it clear that the Horseshoe wants to wrap up the press tournament ASAP. Dealers and tables cost money.

What also keeps this from being great practice—and may even tip it over into a counterproductive exercise—is that half my opponents have never played poker before. We spend most of the first twenty minutes simply going over the rules *as we play*, often to people who do not speak Texan. With no money at stake, some folks are playing as though the rules *require* all-in bets instead of simply permit them. Two sixes? I reraise all-in! At the same table, sometimes on the same hand, you also have to contend with poker professionals like Oklahoma Johnny Hale moonlighting this week as journalists.

Informed at some length, with the help of a printed chart, that a straight flush and four-of-a-kind both beat a full house, a reporter from Seoul declares, "No, dealer, no!" Protecting her chips with her left hand and forearm, she turns over K-K, which combines with the board to make kings full of sixes, a true Genghis Khan of a hand. "Must fold!" the reporter insists, ruefully shaking her head and releasing demure little giggles. *Such a forlorn medley of cards have I welcomed!* Sixes and treys take the pot.

One blond—and, yes, ruggedly handsome—member of a Swedish TV crew speaks crystalline English but remains unclear as to who can bet, when, why, or how. Which makes it kinda hard to decide whether to play my A-Q against him after he pushes in most of his stack. Anxious to keep playing for a while, I decide that I should fold. As soon as I do, Ruggedly Handsome Guy turns over . . . the deuce and nine of spades.

"Twiggy!" says Oklahoma Johnny. His thick black Elvis Costello spectacles glint in the smoky fluorescence.

"Good bet," I tell Ruggedly Handsome Guy, trying to smile.

"A *great* bet, young man," adds a woman in a look-at-me hat, openly flirting with him. The blue-and-black eye of a peacock feather wafts to one side of her rouge as she beams. R.H.G. opens his palms. Handsome is as handsome does, so he rakes in the chips and restacks them.

Halfway through the second round, I'm dealt pocket queens in early position. As I would in a for-money tournament, I raise the $400 big blind to $1,600. Naively hoping to take it right there, I get *five* serene callers, creating exactly the sort of "family pot" that seldom occurs in serious no-limit action. We all watch the flop come 10-9-Q. After the guy in the small blind bets $1,000, Johnny Hale from the big blind tosses an orange $5,000 chip toward the pot. With top set, I decide to reraise all-in. With ten other pocket cards in action, I have to assume that somebody's holding a jack: J-K, J-Q, J-J, maybe even a J-8 with this loony mob. But my bet got the small blind to fold, so at least I have narrowed the field. I've put Johnny Hale on—guessed he has—a straight draw, but even if he makes a straight, I'll have fourteen "outs." That is, any one of the remaining three tens or three nines would give me a full house, and the remaining queen would give me four-of-a-kind; and so, with the same seven outs (10, 10, 10, 9, 9, 9, Q) on both fourth street and fifth street, I have fourteen chances to beat any straight, any flush.

Hale calls my raise and turns over K-J, the top straight. He nods when I show him my queens. At least for the moment, he's got me.

The turn is a four, the river an eight, and that's that. Gone after twenty-five minutes, I gather together my Post-its, pen, water bottle, and whatever is left of my pride. Hale stands up and warmly shakes my hand, then reaches into a knapsack and takes out a book, *Gentleman Gambler: The Life and Times of 'Oklahoma Johnny' Hale on Poker and Las Vegas*, which he opens and quickly inscribes. "At least I'm a gambler," he says, placing it into my hand. "You'll do better tomorrow, my friend."

I wish him well, mumble a thank you, shove off. Even though almost nothing was at stake, losing so swiftly has made me feel woozy, humiliated. Tomorrow's competition will be orders of magnitude tougher, and I might not flop a set of queens all day long. Plus why did I risk all my chips with a made straight so flagrantly in the offing? And couldn't the damn board have paired?

The cover of Hale's book has a photograph of him in the same gold chains, rings, medallions, and bracelets, the same black frames and white Stetson, even the same smile he has on as he sits back down to play with my chips. "In this account of his life and times as a Gentleman Gambler, Johnny takes you with him on his odyssey from poor country boy to the battlefields of Korea to unprecedented success in the construction business to near bankruptcy to" blah blah blah blah. I flip through the pictures—Johnny with Jack McClelland, Johnny with his wife and daughter, with Jerry Buss and T.J. Cloutier and Johnny Moss and Mike Sexton—then open it to the dedication page, on which the near-bankrupt has scribbled: "To McNus @ 31 WSOP, Stay Lucky, OK Johnny Hale."

Stay?

Still woozy, I head over to watch the conclusion of last night's $5,000 limit hold'em, the twenty-first—and second most lucrative—event of the Series. Every final table is played in the cordoned-off southeast corner of the room, with aluminum bleachers on two sides and a monitor suspended from the ceiling above the dealer. My press pass scores me a tableside seat and envious glares from the railbirds, but it turns out I'm sitting too low to follow the action; all I can see are the profiles of two poker faces, and the monitor is too staticky to make out the board cards. You can tell a face card from a seven and red cards from black, but that's it.

As each player loses the last of his chips, he's been given a round of applause. The new information gets handwritten onto a placard to the right of the table, with space for the winner's picture reserved near the top. Now that Men Nguyen is gone, Melissa Hayden and Jay Heimowitz are playing heads-up for the bracelet.

1. _____	$284,000
2. _____	$142,000
3. Men "The Master" Nguyen	$ 71,000
4. Steve Zolotow	$ 42,600

5. Gus Echeverri	$ 31,950
6. Fred Brown	$ 24,850
7. Michael Danino	$ 17,750
8. Hung La	$ 14,200
9. Harry Thomas	$ 11,360

Jerri Thomas finished eighteenth, I am told, so obviously the family continues to acquit itself impressively—sawed-through ribs, 4 a.m. feedings, aromatic Huggies, and all. Another story here is that Annie Duke finished thirteenth, and the $7,810 payout moved her into first place among women in lifetime WSOP prize money. Even so, it's the prospect of Hayden's becoming the year's third female bracelet winner that has galvanized the most press attention. A French TV crew has been joined now by one from Japan, one from Britain.

Hayden won a no-limit hold'em event at the World Poker Open and placed fourth in another. Like Phil Ivey, then, she is hot. Heimowitz, a Budweiser distributor from Bethel, New York, is gunning for his fifth World Series bracelet; he also finished third behind Brunson and Ungar in 1980, when he took pocket aces all-in against Brunson's pocket jacks, but got beat. There must be a quip in here somewhere about Michelob, poker, and Woodstock, but I'll leave Paulle or Glazer to come up with it.

Hayden's home base is Manhattan, where she works as a photographer and book-jacket designer. Her optical precision and deadpan, Duchampian humor grace the covers of some of the smartest books I've read in the last few years. The big rusty screw with a cobweb clinging to its grooves for dear life on Mary Gaitskill's *Because They Wanted To* is Hayden's work, as is the cliff-hanging tunnel of cards on Paul Auster's poker novel, *The Music of Chance*, as is the jagged bullet hole through the ace of hearts on Michael Connelly's *Angel's Flight*. She also did the green chalkboard on *Me Talk Pretty One Day* by my old student David Sedaris. David arrived at the School of the Art Institute in 1984 wanting to be a painter. He and Jennifer took the same painting and drawing classes, and they happened to be in the media center together when the *Challenger* exploded. An assignment that year in a bookmaking class required students to come up with a sixteen-page text, so David put together some fragments from his diary. The first book he worked on with me was *Do You Know What Time It Is?*, a wicked send-up of Raymond Carver complete with a library card and a clock with movable pewter hands. "Two miles outside of Selma, North Carolina," it began, "a ballpoint pen broke in Ted's mouth." Later, Ted dials 411 from his motel room to find out the time; his lover has been gone for a while.

> "Sir," the woman said, "this is information. If you want the time I'll be happy to give you the number."
> "I'm blind," Ted said.
> "Pardon?"
> "I said I'm blind and tired so could you please just tell me the time, I'd like to get this taken care of all in one call." He heard the woman ask someone the time. Ted had no idea what brought him to tell such a boldfaced lie. It was sort of exciting. The woman came back on the line and told him in a sympathetic way that it was 12:30.
> "Is that at night or in the day?" Ted asked.
> "AM. It's half past midnight, dear. It's dark outside."

Once he graduated, I hired David to teach a writing workshop, and he did a terrific job for us for a couple of semesters before heading off to Manhattan to clean apartments and write. But he did remember to thank me for hiring him with a piece called "The Learning Curve," which began: "A year after my graduation from the School of the Art Institute of Chicago, a terrible mistake was made and I was offered a position teaching a writing workshop." A few years later he gave our commencement address, in which he recalled a sculpture class he had taken at the School. "The assignment is to bring in a self-portrait and the fellow beside you shows up with two olives and a coat hanger. After a while, you can't help but notice the resemblance." David's address ended this way: "There is no escaping the people who love you, especially not today. Their gift is wrapped in a complex, difficult paper and tied with a ribbon five miles longer than your patience. When you open the package, remember to look surprised and behave with grace, as theirs is the gift that brought you here and will accompany you, kicking and screaming, to whatever future awaits you."

In the meantime, his latest book's cover designer has come back from dead last in chips, biding her time till she found a good hand to attack with. The blinds are now $5,000 and $10,000, with bets of $20,000 before and after the flop, and $40,000 on fourth and fifth street, so they're effectively playing no-limit. With $210,000 in chips to Heimowitz's half million, Hayden may seem hopelessly under-funded, but she's only one all-in hand from the lead. (When it works, this move is called "doubling through.") My problem is that I can see neither their hole cards nor the board cards as the dealer flips them over, and without that information, it's hard to appreciate the psychol-ogy of their hand-to-hand combat. For that we'd need under-the-table technology. If I knew Heimowitz was checking with, say, pocket kings, setting a lethal trap instead of just showing weakness, the tension would be infinitely greater as Hayden sat pondering her next move. Becky Behnen vetoed the cameras last month, citing copyright rea-sons; the patent owner, Henry Orenstein, was demanding too high a fee. Most of the players I've talked to are opposed to the technology, mainly because it would expose their tricks and tendencies to their fu-ture competition. Others have said they're afraid that information could be rerouted somehow back to another player at the table—via shortwave radio, hand signals from railbirds, what have you.

While we wait for her to act, I note once again that Hayden's dark sweater-vest is designed to show off her pale cleavage. Do I write down that fact or ignore it? I also have to wonder what Heimowitz makes of it. What about her mane of bronze-orange hair that hangs straight to the small of her back? Or her black ribbed tights, or what she told me during the last break are her lucky black Henry Zouir flats? Combined with the little black Prada bag under her chair, Hay-den is very downtown—very Agnès B, Jimmy Choo. The much more upstate Mr. Heimowitz has on moccasins, blue jeans, a black-and-white T-shirt. Is he ruggedly handsome? I don't want to say. But he's winning.

The reporter sitting to my left is another attractive downtown type:

black clothes, straight hair, not much makeup. She turns out to be Katy Lederer, Howard and Annie's kid sister. Katy is here to root for her siblings and write a few "Postcards from the World Series" for an Internet site. She also just made the finals of the National Poetry Series with a manuscript called *Winter Sex*, and has begun a family memoir called *Poker Face*. Of the three Lederer children, she's the only one who doesn't play poker.

"At least not for serious money," she tells me.

"What does a Lederer mean by 'serious,' though?"

"Oh, you know, for millions and millions."

I was right about her cultural provenance, which she now says is Brooklyn. Like me, she has always been taken with the tropes of the game: *betting on the come, backdooring a straight, steal-raising under the gun*. When the fifth-street card is especially cruel or unexpected, you say that it *spikes*: "Melissa spiked a gutshot straight to catch Jay's two pairs on the river."

This is what's happened, in fact. Hayden went all-in for $85,000 with an inside straight draw, hitting an eight on the final card to bring her back up to $170,000. Her inside straight draw was *gutshot* (or a *belly-buster*) in that it called for twice as much intestinal fortitude as an open-ended draw, which could have used any one of eight cards to make her hand a winner, instead of only four. Heimowitz still has a 3–1 chip lead, but if Hayden doubles through one more time, they'll be even.

Two hands later she goes all-in again with K-J. Heimowitz calls, turns over the 8 and 7 of spades, and makes a flush on fifth street. Fini. The finalists get up and shake hands while receiving a standing ovation, but Melissa doesn't look very happy. No bracelet. Unless they made a deal before starting head-to-head play, she'll have to settle for $142,000 plus knowing how far she came back from.

Listed as No. 116, right under Amarillo Slim Preston, my name now appears in black marker on the long white melamine board among the 238 players officially entered in the championship event. The "S" beside my name—just like the one next to Slim's!—indicates my seat was earned in a one-table satellite. "SS" means supersatellite, and no S at all means that person ponied up one hundred C-notes. Only a few dozen entries are S-less right now, but that number is expected to go up in the morning.

We'll see.

Slim, as it happens, is trying to lasso one last satellite before the big dance gets under way, but it doesn't look good for him at the moment. He's one of four contenders left at his table, but two of them are sitting behind imposing towers of brown and white chips, while he's down to three brown $100's.

"These boys is too good for me," he drawls. "Only place round here Ah can hold mah own is when I go to the men's room." Yeah, right. Besides one of his gold bracelets and what looks to be a twenty-four-carat—and twenty-four-*pound*—belt buckle, he's wearing his trademark pale Stetson festooned with the beige and silver skin of a rattlesnake that Slim now claims "bit me." As other reporters edge closer, he adds: "But Ah got 'im back, yessir. Killed the sumbitch with mah bare hands, skinned 'im and stuck 'im up here." The sumbitch projects, fangs ajar, from the front of the brim, aimed straight at whomever old Slim sets his sights on. You can almost hear it rattle and hiss.

Once Slim gets knocked out, most reporters and railbirds move two tables over to a satellite contested by Annie Duke in seat 6, a beefy guy called Crazy Paul in 7, and Tony Ma in 8. Dan Alspach, a talkative aerospace contractor from La Jolla, sits in seat 10. Over in 2 is Noel Furlong. Even with his bifocals, white hair, and paunch, he's been dubbed "the Irish Stu Ungar" not only because he's the champ but because of the menacing attack of his no-limit game. But at least it's with a lilting brogue that he gruffly says "Raise," then pushes forward $1,000.

He gets no callers until the action makes its way around to Alspach, sitting up plumply in his bright blue Hawaiian shirt. "I reraise the reigning world champion," he chirps, pushing in $4,000. This must be the La Jolla version of friendly respect, though Furlong seems little amused as he studies his cards and opponent. Finally, sighing, he folds. Flipping over the jack of clubs and four of hearts, Alspach drinks in the impressed reaction of the railbirds, and mine. Furlong smiles.

On the TV above them, a rail-thin young African man in a No. 91 Chicago Bulls jersey brandishes an assault rifle in one hand, a machete in the other. I can't read his lips, but from the way he's running the machete across his throat you can tell that he's making a threat. The TVs in here are usually tuned to either a baseball game or Sport Center, but local news coverage of the trial will come on occasionally. I also remember reading last week in the *Times* that guerrillas in Sierra Leone have boasted of cutting the liver and heart from a government prisoner and eating them raw. The only Bull who ever wore No. 91 is, of course, Dennis Rodman. Now that the picture begins to make sense, it's replaced by a stunningly handsome blond anchorwoman.

Sitting in the chair behind Furlong, I pull out my notebook. Due to deliver her third child in three weeks or so, Duke has her loamy bare feet propped on the empty 5 seat. Above them: black leggings, gray pullover, no makeup, brown hair in a casual pageboy.

When I ask her why she skipped the women's event, I'm treated to a wince of disdain. She rakes in the last of Crazy Paul's chips, stacks them up. "Not very interesting money," she says. "And I can't stand the smell of perfume," she adds, pregnantly macho.

Though she seldom stops coffeehousing, it's clear that she doesn't much cotton to answering questions. Which isn't to say that she won't let me know what she's thinking. "Nothing worse than a table full of women," she offers a few minutes later, folding her hand after Ma makes a preflop raise of $2,000.

Ma's hair is a tidy black helmet above precipitous cheekbones and almost-black aviator shades. He betrays less emotion than a viper would staring you down.

Alspach folds. Furlong studies. We wait. Hasan Habib sits just behind Ma, and they whisper back and forth from time to time. The players call this over-the-shoulder support system *sweating*, and it seems to go on at most of the satellite tables. Idle chitchat for the most part, it sometimes involves rehashing hands once they're over. Whether this is kosher has never been universally established. Here at Binion's it seems to depend on how friendly the rest of the table is. It's not as though Tony Ma needs anyone's help, but the rule is one player to a hand.

Furlong finally pushes his cards a few inches forward, and Duke folds without hesitation. Ma says, "Aces," while pushing his cards face-down toward the muck, then starts raking in the pot. Before the dealer has a chance to pull Ma's cards in, Duke reaches out and takes a quick peek underneath. "Just checking," she says.

Wow. I mean, *wow*. I watch as Ma, Furlong, Alspach, the dealer, and other folks surrounding the table consider this breach of poker etiquette—of much more than etiquette, really. It's an impudent breach of the *rules* to look at an opponent's mucked cards; to obtain information like that, you need to call him and risk the $2,000. In olden days, players were "given the gun" for much less pivotal infractions. If what Ma wanted his opponents to think—what he *told* them to think—turned out to be false, everyone's tactics would shift. And there's $10,000 at stake.

Now that the damage is done, the young male dealer turns to Duke and says mildly, "Players, please do not touch the muck," a perfunctory reprimand if ever we've heard one—like a referee warning Tyson not to hit below the belt right after he'd landed an uppercut to the scrotum.

"You're right," says Duke, glancing over at Ma. "I apologize, Tony."

Ma shakes his head but seems ready to drop it. What man, after all, can hammer an apologetic (and barefoot) pregnant woman, let alone give her the gun?

"Did he have 'em?" says Alspach. He's only half kidding, it seems—sticking the needle in, breaking the ice, jest fer fun.

The dealer, for his part, starts shuffling.

"I mean, we're all dying to know," Alspach says.

Clearly hoping her gaffe will blow over if she keeps her mouth shut, Duke simply nods. The fact is, she has information that no one but Ma could have access to. She could also be lying. (Later, when I ask Jack McClelland for an opinion, he says that the dealer should have called a floor supervisor to the table. A warning would have been given; either that or a ten-minute penalty away from the table. "She *did* that?" he asks. And he laughs.)

The next hand Ma plays, he makes a point of shoving his money out just *before* the flop gets turned over, putting a few extra degrees—

centigrade—of heat on anyone thinking of calling him. It's impossible
to tell whether he makes this move out of anger or not, but it works.

A few hands later Duke uses pocket kings to blow away Alspach, but
Ma still has her by about 3–2 in chips. Unless I've missed something,
neither proposes a deal now. Because of the peek that she stole? Because they both already have a seat? An unspoken agreement going in?

When I summon the courage to ask Ma why they haven't made a
deal, he shrugs (barely), and Duke gives me the impression she'd be
even less forthcoming. Which is not to say silent. "I'm the only one
playing $1,000-$2,000 every day who's pregnant, you guys. I know I've
got *that* locked up." She also insists that her babies were "all born at
home, where they're supposed to be."

Three or four hands later, Duke goes all-in, the beads and braided
leather rattling up and down her waterlogged wrists as she pushes forward the last of her chips. Ma calls the bet and turns over pocket tens,
and the best Duke can show him is an offsuit A-8. No ace appears on
the board, so it's over. Both Ma and Duke remain in their seats, ready
to play the next satellite.

The women's event winds up this way:

1.	Nani Dollison	$53,200
2.	Martine Oules	$26,600
3.	Elaine Douglas	$13,300
4.	Sheila Ryan	$ 7,980
5.	Jerri Thomas	$ 6,650
6.	Janice Newton	$ 5,320
7.	Connie Hughes	$ 3,990
8.	Robin Brown	$ 2,660
9.	Roxanne Rodman	$ 1,995

I can see what Duke means about the *relatively* uninteresting
money. It took Jerri Thomas almost fifteen hours to make her $6,650,
after all. A nice payday under any circumstances, though it did cost her
sleep, a precious commodity for the mother of a small child, especially
the night before the event every big-time player has focused on for the

previous fifty-one weeks and three days. For the same $1,000 buy-in, Duke needs only ninety minutes to contest one-table satellites potentially worth $10,000; on the other hand, she did forgo a chance to win $53,200. But my sense is that Duke is the brand of gunslinger who only wants to draw on the baddest hombres walking her streets. Her stunt with Ma's cards also makes it clear she will mess with them.

Room 1016, 2:07 a.m. My itch to get started requires more glucose, ethanol, and serotonin reuptake inhibitors than are currently onboard my system. What's also required is eight hours' sleep, but I'm scared that it may not be forthcoming. I swallow my Zocor with a double dose of Trazodone, then put in wake-up calls for 9:45 and 10:00. Is it possible to beg the operator to "Please don't forget" without sounding stupid or insulting?

Probably not.

I'd call St. Louis just to check in, or maybe leave a message asking Jennifer to call me in the morning, but the phone would ring at least three or four times before the machine came on, waking her up. I can hardly wait to tell her about Duke's "where they're supposed to be" line. Beatrice was born during an emergency C-section, so she and her mother would each have died a hideous death if we hadn't been in the maternity ward of Evanston Women's Hospital. Home-birth fanaticism has become one of our favorite subjects to gossip about, but it will just have to keep till the morning.

Bonaventure gave the jurors Sunday off, the first day they've had since receiving the case back on Wednesday. With no chance of catching any new developments, I click off the television and turn out the light. I'll be playing in the Big One in less than ten hours, so I should've taken the Trazodone closer to midnight, since 100 mg may leave me a little groggy tomorrow. And then I realize: *It was Mother's Day!*

Slim and Geraldo

DEATH IN THE AFTERNOON

> Over Descartian vortices you hover. And
> perhaps, at mid-day, in the fairest weather,
> with one half-throttled shriek you drop through
> that transparent air into the summer sea, no
> more to rise forever.
> —HERMAN MELVILLE, *Moby-Dick*

> OK, OK, so I was wrong.
> —BILL BUFORD, *Among the Thugs*

"**I**'m sorry I'm sorry I'm sorry . . ."

"Yeah, yeah, I'll bet." But the chill on the other end of the line is colored with humor, thank God. "We're coping, I guess."

"I still can't believe I forgot! With all the commotion . . ." On top of clichés of this magnitude, I actually start to concoct a sad tale of playing a three-hour satellite I couldn't walk away from until . . . I finally shut myself up. "Happy Mother's Day, Higgins." This last is my principal term of endearment for her.

"Oh gee, thanks."

"And please please tell Guigno I'm sorry." Her mother.

"That you can tell her yourself. And don't forget to call Mary-Mom," says Jennifer, reminding me again that I also failed to call my own mother. "But good luck today, Braino, even though you sure don't deserve it."

♠

After leaving a message on my mother's machine and a half hour of penitent backstroke, I open *Championship No-Limit and Pot-Limit Hold'em* and continue to cram for my first big exam since I was an undergrad twenty-eight years ago. Even during that addled epoch, my knack for making educated guesses was reliably measured, I think, by the epistemology papers and symbolic logic midterms I endured as a philosophy major, as well as by the ACT, SAT, and GRE marathons. Nothing's changed, really. Instead of using a No. 2 pencil to darken slot A, B, C, or D, today I'll be moving clay chips after divining whether to bet, call, raise, or fold.

Reviewing all twelve of T.J.'s practice hands, I pore over underlined passages to check whether I've absorbed the logic of his analyses. In Practice Hand 10, he gives the reader J-J in early position during the early stage of a tournament, then asks: "Do you bring it in with a raise, or do you just limp in?" (To limp into a pot before the flop means to match the big blind but not raise.) My plan is to raise two and a half times the big blind. Why so small? Because opponents may read a larger raise as a signal of weakness. Also, if an opponent comes back over the top with a reraise, you have to assume he has aces or kings, so you can't call his reraise with jacks. You forfeit your original bet, but at least it wasn't large to begin with.

T.J. covers the advantages of both limping and raising. Limping, he says, protects you against getting reraised before the flop; if a player acting after you makes a big raise, you just fold. What you want is to see the flop as cheaply as possible and have another jack hit the board. "Of course," he admits, "if you had raised before the flop, they may not have played those little-ace or K-Q hands," but that's the chance you take when you limp. From fifth position or later, T.J. advises a raise of three or four times the big blind, since the number of potential reraisers has now been cut in half. He also recommends playing pocket jacks much more aggressively as the tournament progresses, but I don't need to study that part yet.

Another passage I've tagged is, "Cardinal rule number one in no-limit hold'em is: *If you limp with aces, you will never get broke with aces.*" One of the classic WSOP debates is about whether to go all-in with A-A on the first hand (or during the first hour, or day), so soon after putting up $10,000, since you're never more than a 6–1 favorite. My plan is to limp with A-A if I find them in early position, hoping someone raises ahead of me so I can reraise all-in. This is called "getting cute" with your aces, a greedily high-risk attempt to start off with twenty thousand dollars, not ten.

It's getting on toward eleven o'clock, but I stay in my deck chair, memorizing passages I've marked with a star. "Where I was schooled in Dallas, the second raise probably would have been aces, and the third raise was like Ivory Snow: 99.9 percent pure aces." And this, from a few chapters later: "No-limit is a game in which you never actually have to build a pot. When you move in on them, there are a lot of players who will call a raise for all their chips with a hand like A-Q. They're not good players, but they are out there."

Aside from these tactical issues, my main concern is nerves—becoming a fawn in the headlights of a humvee like T.J. or some other badass. The best thing to help keep me calm would be huge cards to play and building up chips with them early on. The confidence I got from winning the satellite has already been neutralized by knowing I wasn't unlucky to be eliminated so fast from the press tournament: I simply failed to read the board and my opponent correctly. Bad Jim keeps arguing that it was "just bad luck" to flop a set of queens but not make a full house on the same hand that a big stack flopped a straight, but he would say that, wouldn't he?

T.J.'s remarks about luck might be called Texas Fatalism: "You can set up all the plays in the world, you can play perfectly on a hand, and you can still lose. And there's nothing that you can do about it." In one of the best poker novels I've read, Jesse May's *Shut Up and Deal*, the narrator points out that the game requires a combination of luck and skill, but then he says something less obvious. "People think mastering the skill is the hard part, but they're wrong. The trick to poker is mastering the luck. That's philosophy. Understanding luck is philosophy, and there are some people who aren't ever gonna fade it. That's what sets poker apart. And that's what keeps everyone coming back for more." If it weren't for the luck factor, the same five or six people would win every tournament. They'd be the only ones who'd keep playing them, however, so the prize pools would get pretty small.

Talismans, anyone? Just as Tiger Woods always wears a shirt with red in it on Sunday, Men Nguyen never clips the hairs growing from his moles before playing a final table. Kathy Liebert told me it's unlucky if she's asked to turn over her hole cards after she or her opponent has gone all-in, though the World Series dealers don't give her a choice: "On their backs, ladies and gentlemen." For Hans "Tuna" Lund, a toothpick is lucky *until proven otherwise*, which is pretty much my own attitude about hats. I have six to choose from this trip: the White Sox hat I got married to Jennifer in, two dark Bellagio caps and one pale Bellagio visor, the official red wool Binion's WSOP 2000 cap (with the $14.95 price tag still attached, for extra good luck), and my Yankee blue *Harper's* "H" cap, the one I plan to lead off with. The logic of my voodoo runs as follows: *Harper's*, Higgins, Hold'em, Horseshoe, hired by Lewis H. Lapham. And let's not forget that Oliver Wendell *H*olmes wrote that all beliefs, however superstitious, are essentially bets, educated guesses based on experience. Then there's the fact that Holmes's pal William James (whose brother *H*enry wrote a novel called, I believe, *The Hambassadors*) echoed this notion: "Truth *happens* to an idea. It *becomes* true, is made true by events." Or it isn't. Hello? Can there be any serious doubt as to which lucky hat I should wear?

The rest of T.J.'s advice I've reduced to four memorizable aphorisms:

1. Don't call big bets; fold or raise.
2. Avoid trouble hands like K-Q, K-J, or any ace with a kicker smaller than a king in all but the last two positions.
3. Don't steal-raise or bluff in the obvious positions like the small blind and button; slow-play A-A and K-K from them, too.
4. Draws are death.

This last one means: Don't risk your tournament life chasing big pairs with suited connectors, as is often the correct strategy in a limit game. You could win a big pot if you happened to make a straight or a flush, but aggressive no-limit players make it far too expensive to draw to straights and flushes against their big pocket pairs. Missed draws

(and other mistakes) are costlier by an order of magnitude when playing no-limit, and the chips you squander in a tournament can't be replaced by digging into your pocket—even *if* you had money down
there.

Amen.

Who wants to be a millionaire? Every last woman and man in this
throng of a line, though my guess is that most of them already are. No
credit cards are accepted, no checks, so a lot of these folks must be
packing $10,000 in cash.

It turns out that *all* of them are. I had to stand in line for five minutes before figuring out that the receipt I've been fingering sweatily allows me to elbow and excuse my way up through the crush and into
the tournament room without passing Go, without waiting.

Furious satellite action is still under way, even at six before noon.
From the looks in their eyes, a few of these hombres have been down
here all night, desperately trying to qualify. The record amount spent
by one person on satellites and supers without winning a seat is
$18,000, set last year. The press has been told the guy's name, but I
don't want to embarrass the sturdy, red-haired orthodontist. He must
have decided to make a straight $10,000 buy-in this year, since no S
graces his name on the melamine board. All of which helps explain the
high cost of braces in Davenport, Iowa.

For those less well compensated in their day jobs, satellite dealers
are doubling the blinds every three minutes instead of every twenty.
This eliminates players *tout de suite* but reduces the caliber of poker to
a series of all-in crapshoots. (I've even heard of one-*hand* satellites just
before major events but still haven't personally witnessed one.) In the
meantime, the overflow crowd in the room gets denser by the minute,
and louder. Railbirds are six or eight deep, clapping or whistling when
someone survives to gain entry, as camera crews roam through the
aisles. One guy they're focusing on is the tournament director, Bob
"Silver Eagle" Thompson. With his white hair, narrow-eyed gaze, and
big jaw, he reminds me of Tom Landry—in a Stetson, though, not a
fedora. He effortlessly personifies the American West, Texas hold'em
most in particular. And that's what all of these ranchers and farmers

and city slickers, these tough-looking dames, these cosmopolitan rakes and suburban leaf-rakers came here to play: cowboy poker.

Thompson runs the floor with his son, Robert Jr., who's wearing a business suit, white shirt, and tie, and a somewhat more slovenly giant by the name of Tom Elias. Robert's older sister, Kathi Wood, coordinates the administration. Kathi's Xeroxed fact sheet says that if five hundred entrants buy in, five tables will be paid instead of four—nine players more than the usual thirty-six. First place would pay $1.5 million, second almost $900,000, and all other payouts would escalate. With places 45–37 paying $15,000 apiece, my chance of making the money would improve by 25 percent. I'll have to survive an extra fifty or sixty players, but this is a trade-off I'm happy to make, especially since I only have to contend with eight of them at a time. If I can survive for two days, I'll make back over three times my investment. On the other hand, 91 percent of us not only will fail to share in the purse but will have donated our entire ten grand. What the rounders are thinking, of course, is *More dead money!* They're only too happy to wait while the cash-packing hopefuls keep filing like lambs through the doorway.

All of the side action has been moved downstairs (or down to the Bellagio), but one pot-limit game on Table 56 was allowed to carry on a bit longer, if only for pure entertainment value. The blinds are $1,000-$2,000, with the average pot building well into the upper five figures, every last cent of it sheltered by a pair of security guards packing blue-black revolvers. The floormen have cordoned off a wobbly parallelogram around the table, against which a few dozen tournament players are doing a lot of respectful mouth-to-ear whispering. But it's not hard to tell who is winning. A hyper young gaucho named Hector Jesus Leal (from Mule Shoe, Texas, he says) is sitting behind a magenta cell phone, two rolls of honey-lemon Halls, a hardpack of Marlboro reds, and a foot-square Plexiglas box overflowing with compressed wads of C-notes—$1.3 million being the most recent guestimate. The other big stack sits in front of a spiky Vietnamese dude called Tony D., who according to the whisperers "owns half of Saigon." Beefy, gray-haired Jim Bechtel, the 1993 world champion, sits to the left of Leal and seems to have hit a long dry spell. In

A.D. 2000, being named Jesus seems to help more than being named Jim, but maybe if I just bought some *Halls* . . .

Four tables over, Becky Behnen is posing for snapshots and wishing folks luck. This is her second World Series in charge, but it's hard to imagine that her heart is much in it. The black western suit and sober white blouse says it all. The people who murdered her brother may be set free any minute, while she gets to hear them woof about where they plan to hold their victory bash. Tabish wants to go to the Aristocrat, according to TV reports. Murphy wants to go to Piero's.

The rap against Becky, as I understand it, is that she cuts too many corners, from serving mediocre food in the buffet to reducing the gold in the winners' bracelets from 18 to 14 karats. The bracelets are no longer fashioned by Neiman Marcus, and their new design is flimsier, less elegant. On her husband's advice, she also sold her father's signature million-dollar glass horseshoe displaying the one hundred $10,000 bills, a must-see Las Vegas attraction since 1964. Before last year's tournament she and Nick replaced nearly every employee associated with her brothers, including poker-room managers Jim and Susan Albrecht and WSOP director and MC Jack McClelland, who now run Jack Binion's World Poker Open. It's out of loyalty to these people that Brunson and Chip Reese are boycotting the Horseshoe this year, but plenty of players not willing to take things that far still ain't happy. At least this is what I have heard.

Nor can the pressure of the trial be helping the general vibe. That a jury should be deliberating charges of first-degree S&M murder against Ted's friend and consort one block away during the final week of the tournament his father invented—well, this is either too much of a muchness, tipping toward the implausible, or it's the shapeliest tragic construction since Aristotle laid down the rules for these things 2,370 years ago. And yet, in the end, not so tragic. Ted had no shortage of flaws, but whether they amounted to tragic hubris visited upon his brow by Olympian gods is probably a dog that won't hunt. His wealth and status as heir of a town Founding Father may have elevated him in Aristotle's day, but to the postmodern sensibility he's merely a privileged, i.e. overprivileged, white male. With his penchants for gangsterly violence, hard drugs, stagy sex, and immoderate gambling,

Ted perfectly—if not tragically—incarnated *Homo stripiens*, otherwise known as Las Vegas Man. It's also kind of hard to ignore the inside-out parallel between Sandy and Ted and Bobby Kennedy and Marilyn Monroe. Monroe's longtime abuse of barbiturates naturally led to the question: Was she careless, suicidal, or had she been murdered? She had a "violent argument" with Bobby a few hours before she died; that much we know. Not that the attorney general snuck back into her hotel room and personally burked her, but still.

Ted's nephew Benny Behnen has had to step up as the male representative of his lineage. Lookswise, young Benny is a cross between the Elvis of *Heartbreak Hotel* and Bill Clinton at Oxford: tallish, dark, princely, a *GQ* cowboy hipster. Watching him work the room now in a gray pin-striped suit, you can tell hosting poker tournaments is right up his alley. For one thing, he plays the game himself for high stakes, and regularly enters events put on by other casinos. His natural affinity for the World Series actually began in utero, since he was born as the 1976 final table was being contested. I've heard that today is his birthday.

Right now he and Slim are ogling Johnny Chan's rattlesnake ring, fashioned by Cartier from thirteen large diamonds, each of them single-handedly putting to shame the three I bought Jennifer.

"Hooo, boy," Benny drawls, holding it up to the light. "Lucky thirteen."

Chan only nods. As his former bodyguard and tournament masseur has reported, "Johnny doesn't really open up for anybody. Not even his wife and kids," though he seems to get on well with Benny. We've all seen Chan's red Mercedes SL in the valet parking area, with the California plates reading 333JJ—treys full of jacks. As the all-time leading WSOP money winner with $2,570,494, and perhaps thirty times that in other spoils, Chan can afford the juice on his vanities. He now owns six houses to go with his six children, six bracelets, what is presumably a small fleet of cars, and one diamond rattlesnake ring. Up close, the Orient Express is smaller than he looks in *Rounders*, which accurately depicts him as a chilling intimidator. (That Matt Damon's character successfully bluffs him *on one hand* is absurdly meant to demonstrate that he plays at Chan's level.) Chan won the Big One in both '87 and '88 and came within a hand of three-peating until Phil Hellmuth, then a twenty-four-year-old wunderkind from Wisconsin, finally derailed him with a pair of pocket nines.

Standing next to Chan amid so many corn-fed middle-aged guys with goatees and beer bellies, Slim still looks clear-eyed and rangy at seventy-seven in his pressed khaki trousers, platinum belt buckle, mother-of-pearl buttons on his crisp western shirt. To underscore the slender cowpokiness, his beige and tan boots have SLIM worked vertically into the leather. He also *sounds* confident: "People who sit down with me are expectin' to lose and, goddammit, I don't wanna disappoint 'em."

Once Chan departs, Slim launches into a story about getting kidnapped in 1992 by Pablo Escobar. He was down in Bogotá, it seems, for the opening of a casino when Escobar's men confused him for an undercover DEA agent. "I was wired up, not tied up," he insists, then taken by helicopter from Cartagena and told he would be dropped into the jungle. When they realized their mistake, Slim was unwired and shown around the country in style, personally escorted by Escobar, who sent him a set of emerald shirt buttons by way of apology. Slim also claims that mail addressed to "Slim, Amarillo TX" will reach him without any problem.

Apropos the gaggle of female reporters, he tells one that the population of Amarillo has been the same for thirty years, that in fact it never changes. How come? "Because ever' time some woman gets pregnant, some man leaves town."

"You're bad, Slim," the reporter informs him, but with light in her voice and her eye.

"Ah don't mean nothin' when Ah talk bad, okay?"

"I understand," she says. "I read your book, you know."

Joining the informal parliament of champions is Linda Johnson, resplendent in silver and black geisha garb to set off her single gold bracelet. Beside her is Walter Clyde "Puggy" Pearson, the '73 world champion, decked out in a gold and lemon silk Genghis Khan outfit, including a crown with raised and tasseled earflaps, to go with his eponymous pug nose and Abe Lincoln whiskers. "Some crowd here this mornin'," he observes with a Tennessee twang. "Lotta pretty ladies, all rot."

This is true. A few of the younger women have on what can only be called boudoirwear: lacy nothings hung with spaghetti straps over plush torsos, unignorable goads for opponents if the late David Spanier was right. Yet despite the tradition of look-at-me threads at the Big One, the leading sartorial choice of this day remains Poker Practical: baseball cap, sunglasses, sateen casino jacket, relaxed-fit Gap denim. *C'est moi.*

Bob Thompson's dulcet basso voice comes over the PA to announce that last year's record of 393 has been shattered. We're already at 457, in fact. With the sign-up line still snaking three players thick out the door, and a couple of satellite tables going strong, we'll no doubt reach five hundred entries. But since no cards will be in the air for a spell, I sit back and make a few notes, most of them under the heading POMO. Because the evidence before my eyes says the World Series of Poker has evolved from its good-old-boy roots into a stronghold of, yes, *functional multiculturalism*, proving if nothing else that there is such a thing. Most of the academic versions, of course, have long since degenerated into monocultural zealotry, diverse as to race or gender but in almost no other respects. The term has even taken a pejorative cast of late, correctly associated with tenured politicians swimming in schools of resentment, apparently aiming to prove that ideology is indeed a form of brain damage.

Certainly no real-life arena attracts poker's multiplicity of age groups, body types, political opinions, or income and education levels, inviting the dewy and working-class to compete on an equal footing with affluent and/or pointy-headed nonagenarians. Even planetwide sports like soccer and basketball are still the exclusive province of speedy young mesomorphs. Baseball's World Series is contested mostly among North Americans (including, of course, those born in the Caribbean, though no one knows *when* they were born), just as the World Cup is contested primarily among Europeans and South Americans, chess among Caucasian Jews, cricket among Brits and the formerly colonized, football among male Americans, X sports among middle-class teenagers, jai alai among the Iberians. Americans don't fight bulls, Tanzanians don't curl, Swedes don't go in much for cricket, too few Hibernians luge, and Charlie don't surf. But everyone these days plays poker, Charlie especially. Scanning the tournament results in *Card Player*, it seems as though half the winners of hold'em events are named Nguyen.

This year's world championship field is an ecumenical crazy quilt of players from twenty-three countries on all six inhabited continents, among them Hasan Habib from Karachi, Jason Viriyayuthakorn from Bangkok via Hamilton, New Jersey, and, from Pamplona, a Carlos Fuentes. Any all-name team would also have to include Tab Thiptinnakon, Chip Jett, Exxon Feyznia, Sirous Baghchehsaraie, Toto Leonidas, David Plastik, Sam Grizzle, Somporn Li, Lin Poon Wang, and Spring Cheong, as well as the '96 champion, Huckleberry Seed. (Seed siblings Caraway, Apple, and Cotton don't play poker.) Among toned jocks like Seed, Jerri Thomas, T.J. Cloutier, and Layne Flack we have about equal numbers of the obese and the skeletal, plus people in bare feet and wheelchairs and dance shoes. Evangelical Christians are competing with Larry Flynt and Devilfish Ulliott, CEOs and dotcom zillionaires versus call girls, masseuses, and poker dealers. We also have gay men and lesbians, cowgirls and golfers and artists, black poker professionals and Jewish physicians, Jewish pros and black docs, at least one Aramaic scholar and rabbi, and several Vietnamese boat people. All told our number is 512, breaking last year's record by 119 and bringing the purse to a staggering $5.12 million.

Bob Thompson must now read all 512 names, along with our new seat assignments, while the Horseshoe staff scrambles to somehow come up with a dozen extra tables, at least that many more dealers, plus another half million in chips. Once he has read all the names, Thompson announces that in order to cut the huge field in half by tomorrow, we'll have to play two extra hours tonight.

I would love to.

My assignment is Table 20, Seat 6, and I take it as a terrible omen that I've been shunted down the escalator to what used to be the supersatellite area. Should I feel petrified or vindicated that Keller and

Duke and Liebert and Chan are all down here as well? And now looming up behind me comes Hellmuth. Last seen on the Discovery Channel whining his usual exit tirade—"the guy over here with *two* outs *calls*
me?!" as though *he* never gambled and won—Hellmuth is even taller
than he appears on TV: six six at least, topped off by a black leather
jacket and ultimatebet.com hat. Andy Glazer's in-progress biography
of him is called *Poker Brat*, a sobriquet Hellmuth apparently relishes.
Last year he boorishly challenged the guy who knocked him out of the
tournament to play heads-up for a million dollars. Once he calmed
down, though, he checked himself into Esalen to work on his temper,
having promised Linda Johnson to control it as a condition of writing
for *Card Player*. But he still makes no small plans for himself: having
already won six gold bracelets, he wants *nineteen* more. "If I could stay
healthy and get lucky and win twenty-five WSOP bracelets over my
lifetime," he posted modestly on philhellmuth.com, "then I may well
be considered the best poker player of all time."

This year he's pulled out every stop, budgeting almost $200,000 for
the World Series month. To have access to the Bellagio's health club
and pools, he's spending $1,100 a week to bunk there, not counting
what he admits is "the world's most expensive room service," plus
$1,800 to rent a Lincoln for the seven-mile commute to the Horse-
shoe. The side action has cost him as well. One day last week he donated $80,000 to a game of Chinese poker (in which players compose
three separate hands with their cards) against Chan, David Chiu, Annie Duke, and two other experts, all this on top of the $90,000 Hell-
muth budgeted for World Series buy-ins and rebuys. He even decided
to skip Saturday's $5,000 limit hold'em event because its final table
was scheduled for the night before the Big One. Instead he flew home
to Palo Alto to relax with his wife and two young sons, then flew back
to Vegas this morning. But at least this year he has shown up *on time*.
I'm told that he often sleeps through the first hour or two of play, letting his chips be slowly blinded off, a display of raw hubris his opponents both savor and resent.

Every reporter I talk to down here considers 512 to be more than a
little flabbergasting, not only because of the five-figure buy-in but because the World Poker Open ended only a week before the World Se-

ries began. "All that money hasn't had time yet to filter back down into the poker community," says the guy from *Casino Player*. "Most of it's still deep in the pockets of the winners." Hundreds of other tournaments now compete with the WSOP on the calendar. There's also the relative decrepitude of the Horseshoe facilities; most affluent players would much rather stay—and play poker—at the Bellagio, out in LA, or in Europe. Yet as Slim Preston has pointed out, "The Series is so big and successful you could hold it in Pahrump, out there where Teddy had his silver buried, and people would show up."

Andy Glazer cites the Nasdaq being north of 4,000, the prestige of the WSOP's being the oldest and largest tournament, and the extra week of satellites Becky had scheduled. "Eight hundred sixty-two, altogether," he tells me.

"Then why didn't eight sixty-two show up this morning?"

"Because lots of folks won more than one," he (somewhat) patiently explains. "Tony Ma won seven or eight by himself . . ." I can tell he is nervous, however. After weighing the decision for weeks, he's just put up ten grand of his own to participate in, not just report on, the championship. Since neither of us can take copious notes while we're playing, we'll have to rely on Mike Paulle's report on Day 1, and on "hearsay."

It may be worth noting how common it is for poker reporters to play the events they are covering. When someone like McClelland or Glazer or Hale buys into a tournament, it isn't a literary stunt like George Plimpton trying to quarterback an NFL team, or Mike Ditka trying to coach one. A lot of folks dealing the cards, adjudicating the disputes, or writing the Internet accounts are formidable players themselves; it's just that their bankrolls are a bit on the thin side this morning.

"Take your seats, tournament players. Cards will be in the air in one minute . . ."

For the tenth or twelfth time, Glazer and I wish each other good luck. Then I find Table 20, plunk myself down in Seat 6. This puts me slightly to the left of center while facing the dealer. Two seats to my left is a Filipino woman in a little black dress, while the pasty ghoul beside her in 9 has on a satin tuxedo. Two to my right is a wild-eyed

black guy in a cloth airman's helmet—red with white polka dots—
hung with a dozen pink and yellow rabbits' feet. Seat 5 was allotted to
a member of the Lynyrd Skynyrd International Fan Club, or so claims
his T-shirt. Am I confident of my ability to see through the moves of
such adversaries? No, I am not. The absence of stars at the table is
cause, though, for slightly less pessimism.

Once we show him our receipts, the dealer pushes each of us
$10,000 in chips: one orange five-thousand, three white and royal blue
"dimes," two black and yellow five-hundreds, seven slate-colored hundreds topped by a dozen green "quarters"—the same stack that lasted
me twenty-five minutes last night. In 1969, I paid twenty bucks to a
scalper for a seat on the floor of the Amphitheater to see the Rolling
Stones. For the tenth anniversary of our first date, Jennifer and I forked
over almost a thousand for two seats at Charlie Trotter's kitchen table,
and twice we've paid a similar amount for a pair of Bulls play-off tickets.
So ten grand is twenty times more than I have ever paid for one seat.

"All right now, dealers. Shuffle up and deal!"

The cards finally go in the air at 1:36. The blinds start at $25 and
$50, no antes. Our dealer, whose nameplate says ZIRCON, has a shaved
cueball head and big teeth. (If his name or his skull is an omen, I
haven't unpacked it as yet.) He flicks out a card apiece, clockwise, to
determine who gets the button—the privilege of betting last on hand
No. 1. And with the Hebrew king of spades, that would be *moi*.

Zircon regathers the cards, shuffles the deck four more times, deals
the first hand. I inhale. What I find between my thumbs is an ace and
a six, both of clubs. I exhale. No fewer than five of my opponents limp
in. By tossing $50 in the pot, each one is trying to get a cheap look at
the flop. But hey, not on *moi*'s watch! I make it $250 to go, get no
callers, and with $10,250, take the lead in the tournament.

I've been admonishing myself for five months to play like a solid
farmer, not a gambling fox: conservative, rocklike, waiting for big
pocket pairs. So why did I just force the action over such a piddling
pot with nothing stronger than a suited baby ace? Why not just call
and hope for a flurry of clubs? Granted, I'll need to steal enough
blinds to let me play big hands for free, but I'm afraid that I raised out
of fear. Fear of *not raising*, that is. But if any one of those five limpers

had reraised, I wouldn't have been able to call. The only way I'd get any action, in other words, was if I was beaten. I also made my move from by *far* the most obvious steal-raise position. Yet here I am leading the Big One.

Not for long, of course. I keep betting too impulsively, overriding my blueprint by entering pots with small pairs, K-J and suited 5-4, getting smoked. Is someone else pushing my chips forward, or making my mouth say, "Let's raise it"? I have a solid plan of attack somewhere near the front of my cerebral cortex, but my right hand refuses to follow it.

The main person making me pay is an unfearsome cowpoke three seats to my right. Wearing the same puzzled grin as he rakes in pot after pot, he reminds me of Henry Gibson playing Henrik Ibsen on *Laugh-In*. Ha ha. My worst ha-ha-hammering comes when I turn an overset of queens—make three queens on fourth street, that is, with no higher card on the board—and bet $2,000, a foolish amount at this stage. Looking more puzzled than ever, Henrik smooth-calls me. The board is now 5-3-7-Q, with two spades. When a red jack on fifth street fails to either improve my hand or put a three-flush or an overcard on the board, Henrik bets $2,000. Instead of raising all-in, I just call, since he *could* have a straight. My guess is that he's been calling along with two pairs, though he could also have a smaller set than mine. Winning this pot will put me back up to even: lesson learned, tabula rasa, ready to start playing solid. But the little shit shows me a seven-high straight! Déjà vu all over again, and this time it counts! A bubble of silence engulfs my numb head, interrupted by buzzing, by ringing, though I'm happy, I guess, to report that I'm not the only person at the table who gasps, that baffled shrugs and wavelets of sympathy are directed my way from all quarters. *Yikes!* cry these wavelets. We're in here with a maniac! Thank God *I* didn't get dealt those three queens!

Controlling my voice, I must ask: "You call me preflop with six-four?"

Henrik is busy restacking my chips. It looks like he's going to say something, but he holds himself back. Zircon shuffles. I compliment myself for not having blurted *with fucking six-four*, but part of me wishes I'd said it, especially as I begin to understand that restacking my chips is his answer.

"Appears that way," says the tuxedoed ghoul with deep Transylvanian contempt, for Henrik or me I can't tell.

Zircon deals.

"*Suited* six-four," Henrik says.

By the first fifteen-minute break I'm down to $2,200 and change. Shell-shocked and nauseous, I skulk up to my room and call Jennifer to give her the ball-crushing news.

"Oh, *sweetie*," she sighs. "Oh, that sucks."

"How did I manage," I ask, sincerely expecting a useful, time-reversing answer from her, "to lose four fifths of my stack in two hours?"

"What you need is a kiss and a head rub, I think."

"You think? That's not a real good explanation, but please please please *please* come out here and give me one anyway."

"Plus you still have well over two thousand . . ."

"Don't you realize how little that is?! Don't you GET IT!?"

Further pissing and moaning only depresses my testosterone level to four parts per googolplex. It plummets another big fraction when Grace starts to wail in the foreground. Why can't she be more of a man!

"Here, Gracie," coos Jennifer. "There. You're fine now. Okay? Mama kiss it."

Yeah, sure, comfort *her* . . .

It turns out that all Jennifer can provide from St. Louis is a suggestion to page through my brag book, the 4x6 album with pictures of our girls and my two other children. "Just keep it in your pocket and think about all of us. . . . Well?"

It's truly a sorry idea, but since I don't have a better one I retrieve the damn thing from my suitcase and carry it with me downstairs.

My goal all along has been to get in bed tonight still alive, and it's clear that I ain't gonna make it. Yet I have zero reason to be surprised by this turn of events. Competing against inspired professionals, I'm not even heeding my pedigreed battle plan. Forget about Ted or Phil Hellmuth—my entering this event was the real act of hubris. I should have figured out a way to cash in my satellite win and gone home with

$10,000. Even if they quadrupled the stakes in my home game, even if I started losing on a regular basis, that bankroll would have lasted ten years.

The only surprise is that I have *any* chips to my name. And "the good thing," as my relentlessly practical wife pointed out before we hung up, is that the sooner I bleed off the rest of them, the better job I can do covering the trial and the female contenders. When the words were coming out of her mouth they filled me with loathing and despair, but I have to face facts. I'm a writer, after all, not a poker player, and my teenagerly addiction had made me forget that.

Bad girl, Dat! Bad Jim!

The floorpeople consolidating the tables have high-carded me upstairs to Table 37, Seat 8. As we're sitting back down, word spreads that Keller, Harman, Pearson, Ivey, Seed, Flack, and both Men and Scotty Nguyen have already bitten the dust, along with thirty-two others. So that's something. Have I "beaten" these people? Not really. All I've done is outlast them. But I still should be thrilled to be stroking my orange-free stack.

Maybe the reason I'm not is that, right behind me, Geraldo Rivera is yucking it up for the cameras. He's here, he is pleased to report, doing a story for MSNBC about high-stakes gambling, but when Katy Lederer asks him whether he plays poker, he says, "I played strip poker as a kid, that's about as far as I went."

Did he ever lose?

"I *always* lost!" he brays toothily. "I *threw* them!"

Also on hand is the mayor and, worse, he is armed with a microphone. After praising "the fabulous Binion family," he puns on his own first name by telling us that Bellagio's owner, Steve Wynn, "has comped you all front-row seats for 'O.' " This is the Cirque du Soleil extravaganza with acrobat swimmers, not the aquabatic musical version of Pauline Réage, a production I'd line *up* to see, comped or not. But I have to wonder if Oscar was also pulling our legs when, speaking of Tony Spilotro, he told *The New Yorker*'s Connie Bruck last May, "Better to murder than to be a rat." Very classy.

Right now another reporter is asking him whether he's ever played in the World Series of Poker himself.

"Oh, no, no. Too rich for my blood," he says, arch but imperious. "You know, I have trouble paying my valet tips."

The players I'm seated with couldn't care less about either Geraldo or Oscar. All they want, it appears, is to eliminate me and each other.

But not me, oh my brothers and sisters! I may not have much discipline, see, but now I have *pictures*. I've positioned the brag book on the cushion behind my short stack, opening it to the page on which Jennifer reads *The Big Hungry Bear* to our Bea; to intensify the luck here at Binion's, I've put on my pale gray Bellagio visor. B, b, b, b. I can't lose. Almost as important, the front of my cerebellum seems to have finally whipped my right hand into shape. It feels good. Because in short order I fold pocket nines from an early position and K-Q on the button when someone has raised it in front of me. The only pot I enter of the first twenty-three I do so with kings, raising to five times the blind. No one calls.

In the next four hours I manage to steal a few blinds and to take down a decent-sized pot when my pairs of queens and jacks hold up over one pair of aces. (I was in the big blind, and the player with aces had limped.) And so, with my new leather ass and my talismans, I manage to hang around till the nine o'clock dinner break, when I've scratched my way up to $16,450.

First, up to my room to call Jennifer. I may brag a little about my newfound steal-raising prowess, but I still give her most of the credit. She lets me. When she dubs me "Excitable Boy," I savor it as a compliment as I head back downstairs to the cafeteria. There, instead of prime rib and an alp of mashed potatoes, I judiciously select a few slices of turkey, a soupspoonful of potatoes, a nest of green salad. If snake, sprouts, and bean curd were part of the modest cornucopia, I'd probably choose them as well.

With no empty tables or booths, I have to impose on a trio of southern California players, among whom I find a pair of bad-beat horror stories already in progress. The entire second floor of the Horseshoe, in fact, seems to have become the locus of a vast bad-beat conspiracy. "Kings cracked by sevens . . . but she spikes the fucking trey on the river . . . aces sucked out on by *jacks*!?" Good Jim noshes greens, orders a glass of iced tea.

Loosely defined, a bad beat is any second-best hand that draws out on the best starting hand, held by you. Sklansky calls it: "Having a hand that was a big favorite defeated as the result of a lucky draw, especially when the person drawing was playing incorrectly by being in the pot in the first place." Brunson defines it as follows: "When you get a big hand cracked [beaten] by someone who was a big *dog* against you and made his longshot draw." There are subtle gradations of badness, of course, from coin flips that don't go your way, slight favorites like Q-Q getting caught by A-K, up to severe long shots like 3-7 sucking out on A-A. The worst beats of all involve your opponent sucking out after making a ludicrous, odds-defying call when the amount you had raised on the flop would have chased any reasonable player.

The only other issue on my fellow players' minds is the smoke. All week it has been relentlessly pointed out that California card rooms are entirely smoke-free and the smokers still play there; T.J. Cloutier and Scotty Nguyen are often mentioned in this context. Even in "chimneys like Europe," the majority of tournaments are nonsmoking affairs. Becky's compromise policy is that only the players can smoke here, though her ventilation system is hardly a match for the number who do. Nor has the rule been strictly enforced along the rails.

Then there's this from a guy blowing smoke rings one table over: ". . . so he puts me all-in with his flush, and I nail him when the board pairs on fifth street."

Back at the poker table, I grab myself by the collar and *demand* that I wait for big pairs in all but the last three positions; and for the next couple of hours I listen, sitting and folding as *other* folks gamble with draws and small pairs. The bad news is that escalating blinds and a stretch of cold cards grind my stack down to $14,000 at midnight. We still have two hours to go, but I'm not even slightly fatigued; if anything, I'm afraid my adrenaline might rupture an eye or an artery. I've heard this event called "four days of intense boredom interrupted by brief moments of sheer terror," but I've yet to feel bored for one second.

As of 12:17 we're still at Level 4, anteing $25 a hand with $100 and $200 blinds. The longer the levels, of course, the more poker skill comes into play, and much of the Big One's prestige has to do with its two-hour levels. Three more days of this pressure would require some genuine stamina.

Down to $13,850, I can't wait forever to play. Of the 169 possible two-card starting hands, only thirty-five or forty are considered playable, fewer than a dozen from early position, even fewer than that in a no-limit tournament. Though you wouldn't know it from watching Bad Jim this afternoon, it's easier to be patient early on, when the blinds and antes are minuscule compared with your $10,000 stack. But now we are at Level 5, and it's hard to stay patient with the blinds at $200-$400 and $50 antes. It's costing me $1,050 a round just to sit here and fold all my rags, so unless something gives I'll be down to the felt before bedtime. Since premium hands like paired face cards, aces, or suited ace-king show up so seldom, A-8, 10-9, etc. are starting to look downright raiseworthy. My right hand is itching to play them.

Finally, *finally*, two off the button, I peek between my knuckles and discover a pair of red jacks. Not a monster, exactly, but the best hand I've seen in three hours. It's also one of the most dangerous hands you can play in no-limit. Raising to $1,200, I get three nasty callers, but the flop comes a ravishing K-J-8 rainbow. (The three different suits of a rainbow greatly reduce the chances of someone else's making a flush.) With the overcard king and all these damn callers, I bet $1,500, both fearing and hoping for action. Seat 7 folds, but the Japanese yuppie on the button weirdly makes it $3,000 and Shaved Head in the small blind says, "Call." It's going to cost me every last chip to keep playing this hand, and without the mortal nuts (at this point, three kings) I'm petrified of set over set; even worse are the obvious straight draws. Yet if I don't get my chips in with this hand, when am I going to? Never, I decide, as I call and watch fourth street come a darling, a beautissimous, a sideways-infinity 8, providing my first full house of the day—in two days, in fact, since it's Tuesday. Check, check. Realizing too late that maybe I should have checked too, set a trap, I find myself nudging the rest of my chips about eight inches forward, redundantly announcing, "All-in." My heart bashes out through my shirt, but evidence of fear is okay now, since I want both these suckers to call me.

Japan meditates his options for a minute or so and then folds, flashing two queens in disgust. A pretty good laydown, but still: a queen could be next off the deck. Either way, *Sayonara!*

Shaved Head mutters, "Call," in a tone that suggests he is holding K-K. Oh my God. Since one of us (me, unfortunately) is all-in, no further betting is possible, and we both must turn over our hole cards. His are the . . . 10-9 of clubs, *not* the cowboys (or the other two eights), so it's over. The river card even rubs salt in his wound by giving him a useless club flush.

The pot contains $36,900. Stacking it next to the brag book, I'd love nothing better than to jump up and dance to the elevator, but we still have seventy minutes left at Level 5. I order hot chocolate, sit tight. A half hour later I fold pocket sevens from a middle position, even though no one had raised.

Good girl, Dat!

Thompson finally calls a halt to our march at nine after two. Sheets are passed around with places to record name and chip count, and mine comes to $35,325. Tom Elias recounts them, signs my sheet, stuffs chips and sheet into a Ziploc bag, staples it shut. I congratulate other survivors and weather the torrent of bad-beat chronicles as a herd of us waits for the elevators.

Back in smoke-free 1016, the message light blinks. The Horseshoe doesn't have voice mail, so I have to call the operator. "Mr. McManus? Your wife called." But she didn't say "call any time." It's 4:35 in St. Louis, too early for either Beatrice or Grace to be up yet.

I ask for a wake-up call at 10:00, brush my teeth, get in bed. My rush while it lasted—one hand!—has gladdened my heart as much as any quatrain or fuck or narcotic or shot glass of silver Patrón, as much as any three of those things. It takes an extra 50 mg of Trazodone washed down by a glass of room-service cabernet, then a long, hyper stretch of replaying hands in the darkness—oh, right, *now* I see, you played a *suited* 6-4! Ha ha ha!—to finally fall off, I'm so wired . . .

The six authors of *Super/System*

♣ ♥

BOOK-LEARNED

♦ ♠

The old maxim that sex and reading have a lot in common is probably true. Both rely on our ability to make up fantasies and believe in them—or at least to suspend disbelief long enough to get something we need.

—DEBORAH GARRISON, reviewing Nicholson Baker

Luck is the residue of design. The more prepared you are, the more you study your game of choice, the luckier you'll become.

—ANDY GLAZER, paraphrasing Branch Rickey

A klieg-light sliver blasts through a crack along the edge of the curtain. As my bladder chimes in with a Wagnerian reveille, I jerk up my head. Terrified that it's already noon, I exhale—almost whistle—with relief when the clock radio indicates 8:57. But wait. Did I miss any birthdays or goddess's festivals last night? Poker Widows Day? The Ides of Spank Bad Jim Month? I hope not.

I've lived in this room for a week now, by far the longest stretch Jennifer and I have been separated. Even stranger is that she and the girls are in Missouri and I'm in Nevada, on the road but in separate places. Except for the miniature shampoos and fresh towels every day and my suitcase splayed open on the bed, 1016 is starting to feel like home, at least for a moment or two. Then it passes.

I dial June's number in Creve Coeur, though I'm guessing the four of them are already out and about. (The butterfly house and the train ride at the zoo, I believe, were the first two stops on what I'm sure is a crowded and meticulously organized itinerary.) When the machine beeps, I recap yesterday's highlights, emphasizing how right about the brag book Jennifer turned out to be. I tell them which pictures I featured, how I positioned them on the cushion in back of my chips, giving "you and the girls" all the credit. "I'll try you again at the break. Give 'em large hugs for me, Higgins." Once I hang up, the rush of desire to hug them in person almost douses my lust to play cards. Then it passes.

As I put on my swim trunks and sandals, I consider the logistics of getting them out here: two or three round-trip tickets with no advance purchase, reserve adjoining rooms when the Horseshoe is full, gate-check the stroller and car seats, all this multiplied by the odds of my being eliminated before they even left for the airport. Jennifer coming out by herself makes more sense, but that would require June to skip work and take care of the girls. If I manage to survive today's action, having my babycakes with me tomorrow might make all the difference—though each time I bet, she would cringe. She also might slip a naltrexone mickey into my mineral water, or persuade Bob Thompson to cash in my chips; this would defeat the entire logic of a freeze-out tournament, but men have done crazier things to make Jennifer happy. And even if June *volunteered* to baby-sit two kids in diapers, she couldn't take off days from work on a moment's notice unless there was a genuine crisis. But isn't that what we're talking about here, the good kind of family emergency? Jennifer is still nursing Grace, though, so the baby-sitting option is out. I'd have to make the money tonight before I could rethink three airfares, etc. Right now what I need are a couple of hours to study.

Suddenly in more of a rush, I grab sunglasses, key card, pen, and the three books we're likeliest to be tested on this afternoon, then head out the door—without sunscreen. The lock clicks behind me. Do I need it at nine in the morning?

I don't.

Only two of the four elevators go up to the pool deck, and this morning the wrong two—the two farthest in from the hall—keep arriving on my floor. I dash back to my room for the sunscreen before hitting

Up again. *Ding!* The same one as last time has been waiting right here all along, politely refusing to believe that no one on ten needs a lift. I chop through the air with the edge of my palm, breaking the plane of the doors. Nothing happens. I put one foot inside and press Mezzanine, slipping back out as the doors close. Fifteen or twenty seconds later I dare to press Up again. *Ding!* The same doors slide clear again, openly mocking me.

Fuck.

This time I wait a good minute, shifting the books from my left to right hand. I even turn around to hit the Up button on the opposite wall, trying to alter my luck.

The next elevator that opens is the *other* wrong one. A trio of maintenance guys lugging heavy-duty plumbing equipment stare blankly ahead, waiting for me to get on. The royal suite's toilet has overflowed, probably, His Highness is toe-deep in Charmin and turds, and I'm holding his rescuers up. I point to my swim trunks and hold out the books in the crook of my arm, as though these might explain why I'm not getting on. Yeah, right. The bathing suit maybe, but what do three books have to do with it? By now the plumbers have decided I'm too self-important a dufus to ride with them. I'm some prig who reads books with a *pen* . . .

As the doors finally close, one of them guffaws, shakes his head. I don't blame him. And then, even more absurdly, a curly-haired guy about my age comes jogging down the hall. I peer around the corner, watching as he reaches the other end and heads back this way. Mickey Appleman? Long nose, sad eyes, wild ash-blond hair restrained with a sweatband, this to go with a sweatshirt, shorts, track shoes. It's him. As he jogs by again, I tell him, "Good luck today."

"You too," he says, running in place. Then he's gone, disappearing through a stairwell door at the end of the hallway. This must be his routine when it's too hot to run outside before a long tournament day: oxygenate blood, pump it from legs up to brain, facilitate ion exchanges. By the time a viable elevator arrives, I'm ready to follow his lead—to hustle and wheeze my way up thirteen flights, zigzagging my way to the pool deck then down, and skip swimming laps till tomorrow.

Once I'm finally in the pool, though, I'm glad I persevered. The water is brisker this early, making me wish I had access to a rooftop desert pool every morning. Maybe I should simply quit teaching, move out here and live at the Horseshoe, play poker full-time. If I paid by the month, I could probably negotiate a reasonable rate, though with all the money I'd win the rent wouldn't matter much anyway. I could write in the mornings, play no-limit tournaments from noon till 2 a.m., then play side games and party with my fellow rounders at Cheetahs till dawn. Between the big tournaments I could make up lost quality time with my girls and their mother, who'd be living just a mile or so away in Ted's old neighborhood, where I hear they have pretty good schools. If Jennifer started to get anxious about this arrangement, one of our neighbors would write her a prescription, or I'd buy her a ragtop Mercedes. If she *really* started to miss me, she could always smoke dope with the gardener or take up with one of my friends . . .

To blot such fantasias, I swim laps from 9:22 until 10:00 by the Alvarez clock. Muscle throb, sweet sigh of lung burn, sun on my shoulders, cool water. I've had almost nothing to drink three nights running, so I don't feel as groggy as I normally do in the morning. I may also have lost a few picograms. As I execute one last turn in the far corner, I resolve not to drink *at all* until I'm eliminated from the tournament, when I'll be forced to knock back a goodly number of anti-celebratory shots of Patrón.

Like a somewhat less pudgy Odysseus, then, I rise majestically from the chlorinated sea wearing little more than SPF 50. Calypsonian sunbathers look up from *People* in awe as I towel off, pick up my T-shirt. *No, no,* they silently cry. *Leave it off, we beseech you!* With the haughty discipline of Apollo, I ignore them and open my book, find my place. Horseshoe pen poised to underscore the timeless wisdom of poker's Olympians, I humbly petition the oracle.

> By the time you get to the middle stage, you should know which players are moving in which situations, which players are liable to call you and which ones are not.
>
> You will also know that the worst play you can ever make is to bluff at a bad player. Bad players will not lay down a hand, even

in a tournament. They don't know any better. If you're going to run a bluff, you should run it at a good player because he's not afraid to lay down a hand. In the first round when the blinds are relatively small, there may be some occasions when you can bluff, but mostly you're just waiting for a good hand and the right opening to try to trap your opponents. Usually, it is the weaker players you're waiting to trap, not the strong ones. The strong ones are waiting to do exactly the same thing to you!

Which is all well and good, but how am I supposed to know who the strong players are the minute I sit at the table? Our seating positions have been redrawn at random, so each of my eight opponents will be a blank slate when we start again at noon. Suppose I get reraised all-in holding nothing but, oh, say, two queens on the third hand we play? . . . I guess this is one of the advantages that tournament veterans have over rookies: they know each other's tendencies cold. Yet that can cut both ways, of course. Knowing what their fellow pros expect of them, how hard can it be to throw change-ups? Since they've had little chance to watch *me*, however, they may read my mistakes as bold moves and thus treat my raises with even less respect. Assuming my first mistake wasn't *fatal*, in which case respect becomes moot. That's the thing about being a no-limit amateur: one bad read and you're trudging back home to your day job.

What I need to do this afternoon is hang in. Reraised all-in before the flop by a bigger stack, I will fold any hand except aces. Even kings? Even kings. Because right now the idea of reporting on the action instead of participating couldn't have much less appeal. I'll still be taking notes on my Post-its while observing the women at my table, but most of my focus will be on just staying alive. Once it's over, I'll have a few weeks to interview the dozen highest finishers and write up the action for Lewis.

T.J. goes on to advise that the middle stage of a tournament is the time to step it up a little, to become what he calls semi-aggressive. "Taking a few more risks means picking spots when you can be the aggressor, when you can be the first one in the pot—when you can do the pushing, not the calling. For example, if you're in a middle position, you might raise it up with a suited A-10 or K-J, whereas you may have passed with those hands earlier." Good. That makes sense. I should *slightly* lower my standards for hands to get involved with. Pocket jacks or tens from early position, in addition to queens, kings, and aces. What about raising with pocket sevens or eights from middle position, or calling a raise with them from the button? "Just be sure that in these situations you are the aggressor," says T.J. three paragraphs down. "You are not reacting to your opponents, *they* are reacting to you." Got it, big guy. Raise or fold. First one in the pot or forget it, unless I latch onto a monster.

With so much real money at stake, drilling myself under T.J.'s precision tutelage feels a little like plotting a bank robbery. *Be sure to bludgeon guard seven-eighths inch above temple . . . extract combination with muzzle to senior vice-president's tonsils . . . transfer currency packets to black Nike gym bag with prelubricated titanium zipper . . .* Actually, I *hope* this is how things turn out, but it's gotten too viciously hot to keep reading up here. A lot of my swimming high has melted sideways over my love handles, plus even through polarized lenses the glare off the paper is nuclear. And it's still only 10:17.

I lug the books down to my room, order oatmeal and OJ and coffee, then jump in the shower. Rinsing away all the sunscreen and sweat and chlorine juices me up again, too. Getting dressed, I'm able to get the prong into the third notch of my belt instead of the second, so I tip the busboy an extra two dollars. Because that's the kind of mick I am, fella.

What is it that Jane Fonda and Wayne W. Dyer and Deepak Chopra always say—*Today is the first day of the rest of your life?* Well, they're right! (Or is it *I've got to get organized?*) And doesn't Deepak or Wayne recommend that we *Fold an unsuited A-Q in all but the last three positions?* I thought so. Because that's how I'm feeling on this, the first radiant, well-organized morning of the rest of my life: I'm *proud* to be reading self-help books! Stirring milk and banana slices into my oatmeal, I have Doyle and David and T.J. already open in front of me.

As Jared Diamond (good name) demonstrates in *Guns, Germs, and Steel,* when Francisco Pizarro and 168 Spanish soldiers defeated Atahuallpa's army of 80,000 Incas at Cajamarca in 1532, the decisive factor was the Spaniards' ability to read and write. That's why we call this *Las Vegas*, not the Inca or Aztec term for The Meadows. Because it may seem as though civilizations master each other with avionics and viruses, blunderbusses and Tomahawk missiles, but really we do it with books. (Relative levels of book-learning are a function of the shape of the continent you hail from, believe it or not, but that's a whole other discussion.) "Literacy," Diamond makes clear, "made the Spaniards heirs to a huge body of knowledge about human behavior and history. By contrast, not only did Atahuallpa have no conception of the Spaniards themselves, and no personal experience of any invaders from overseas, but he also had never even heard (or read) of similar threats to anyone else, anywhere else, anytime previously in history."

Poker is another form of combat that repays literate groundwork—in spades, as it were. The first time an opponent checkraises you (tempting you to attack by checking, then ambushing you with a raise), you tend not to know what to do. Many novices are even offended by such tactics, sometimes adopting house rules that prohibit them. Not very sporting, old chap. Most ungentlemanly. These people fail to appreciate what is not only a legitimate tactic but the nature of poker, the art form of what Lakota Sioux warriors called the trickster coyote.

Decades of experience can provide some hilariously expensive lessons by trial and error in how to respond to a checkraise. (You can reraise all-in, for example. You can fold. You can learn to read clues that a checkraise is coming and decline to bet, thereby obtaining a free card that may give you a stronger hand than the guy who wanted to checkraise is holding. You can tempt someone *to* checkraise by feigning weakness on an earlier street when you're actually holding the nuts.) Weapons like these don't come fast or cheap, or at least they didn't used to. But these days you can add them to your arsenal in a couple of weeks by reading the right books while enacting their advice on a computer program—in theory, at least. (*Don't tell us how it works in practice*, my postmodern colleagues insist. *How does it work in theory?*) Certainly the cost of the programs and books is an infinitesimal fraction of the bankroll required to play uninformed no-limit hold'em for even a session or two, let alone year after year.

As Peter Ruchman explained to me, today's younger players need books because they don't have the training ground available to them that the road gamblers had. Legends like Brunson, Preston, Moss, and Pearson had to "fade the white line" of the highway for decades to hone their raw skills, while today we have primers, computers, and smoke-free, air-conditioned card rooms to learn on the cheap. We don't even have to worry much about cheating, since cameras and nonplaying dealers have all but eliminated that peril.

Some of the surviving road gamblers regret this trend more than a little, and it's hard to blame them. For the first eight years, the World Series was pretty much their private jousting field under Benny Binion's auspices, a fiefdom in which his fellow Texans took turns modeling the laurels. Now that they have to cope with hundreds of annual challengers, no Lone Star denizen has taken the Big One since '78.

The person likeliest to get these boys back in the win column is probably Cloutier. Although born in northern California, he has lived in Richardson for over two decades and is now considered to be among the last of the Texas road warriors. After retiring from football, he'd worked as a food wholesaler with his father and brother-in-law; when that business failed, he drove a bread truck for Toscana and later became night manager at the Wonder Bread bakery in San Francisco. In 1976 he moved to Dallas to work as a wildcatter, playing poker first on his days off then pretty much every day, as the oil boom sputtered and he gradually learned the game's subtleties.

Championship Hold'em is actually Cloutier in taped conversation with Tom McEvoy, the 1982 world champion and a Grand Rapids native. Their ideas (maybe 80 percent Cloutier's, 20 percent McEvoy's) have been transcribed and edited by Dana Smith into a kind of oral history of their no-limit hold'em experience, intercut with manly asides and violence-flecked "Tales from T.J." to remind us where most of this wisdom got learned. Poker's gunslinging past is the visceral subtext of all the advice that the former tight end has to offer, and he frequently reminds us how much time he has spent with hombres who settle their differences with ruthless finality, who would put you all-in in the primo no-limit encounter. "The Big Texan was a whale of a man and he ran the best game in Dallas," goes one tale, explaining why the author is hesitant to offend the guy in charge of his main source of income. T.J. restrains himself even when the Big Texan accuses him of making an illegal raise and literally slaps him on the hand. "Well, I rared up and was really going to let him have it because I never cared for him one iota anyway. But I thought better of it because I needed that game; it paid all my expenses for the year." The Big Texan then has the gall to tell T.J. that if he had hit him, he would have gone for his gun. "Buddy," says T.J., "if I had hit you, you'd never have had a chance to get that gun out."

McEvoy's own book, *Tournament Poker*, covers general strategy for the most popular games. His advice on satellite and super-satellite strategy is indispensable for anyone hoping to win her way into a high-buy-in tournament. He also explains how to make the most of your stack, tall or short, at various stages of the tournament proper, and how to negotiate deals at the end. His tone is humane, folksy, sensible: "Don't worry about second-guessing yourself because you have only a limited amount of chips to play with and you have to double up at some point anyway. So don't be too concerned about being the first player eliminated. Tenth place pays the same as second place in a ten-handed satellite: nothing." With a degree in accounting from the University of Michigan, McEvoy spent a dozen years as a CPA before moving his family to Las Vegas and trying to support them as a poker player. Though his financial straits have been dire at times—he told me he's "the poorest famous person I know"—he now owns four WSOP bracelets and has won almost 10 percent of the tournaments he's entered.

Dana Smith used to teach high school English and journalism, so she knows her way around a gerund and a comma splice. She's also savvy enough to let some bowlegged grammar barge its way into the prose ("on the flop, on fourth street, at fifth street"), letting the lead author sound like a pugnacious tight end and wildcatter: "a man is a stone fool any time a pair hits the board and he's drawing to a middle-buster or an open-end straight." Who wants no-limit hold'em advice from some pointy-headed grammarian anyway?

When T.J. calls more blandly analytical experts "poker mathematician types," he is referring, above all, to Sklansky and Malmuth. He says that they fail to adapt to the ebb and flow of tournament competition, implying that this is because they've lost touch with poker's outlaw heritage. McEvoy interjects that their play is "too mechanical," then ups the ante by charging that "they lack flair." Whether things like adaptability and flair can be taught in a book is an interesting question, and I don't know the answer. It reminds me of Edward O. Wilson's remark in *On Human Nature*—that neurobiology cannot be learned at the feet of a guru, just as philosophy "must not be left in the hands of the merely wise."

Guru cattiness aside, what *Championship No-Limit and Pot-Limit Hold'em* mainly offers is solid advice proven lucrative over decades of roadhouse games and high-stakes tournaments. There are sections on the three main stages of tournaments, reading your opponents, avoiding trouble hands, defending—or not defending—your big and small blinds, how to practice, whether to play satellites or super-satellites when your bankroll gets thin. (T.J. recommends the former because you begin with more chips to maneuver; supers, he argues, are relatively mindless all-in affairs in which luck becomes too large a factor.) What about whether to concentrate on side games or tournaments? Not a close call. "There is so much dead money in tournaments that good players have a huge overlay, especially in pot-limit and no-limit games, because the skill factor is so much higher in these games than it is in limit." In keeping with his roughhewn image and tone, T.J.'s chapters never take long to get down to the nitty-gritty: which hands to play when. Should you enter a raised pot from late position with the 6-5 of clubs? (Writing in 1997, T.J. frowns on this move much more than Brunson did nineteen years earlier.) What about when you "flop middle set"? That is, when playing pocket jacks, the board shows A-J-6, and your opponent leads off with a bet. "You don't try to shut him out" with a big raise, says T.J.; instead, you should "flat-call" the bet—call when a raise is anticipated. Why not move all-in, trying to win the pot then and there, especially against the chance that a second ace will appear on the board, providing mediocre hands like A-J or A-6 with a bigger full house? (Aces full of sixes beating your jacks full of aces.) T.J.'s answer: "Columbus took a chance, so I'm going to take one, too." If his opponent turns over a better hand on fifth street, or reaches for a sidearm, the big man from Richardson presumably will knock him unconscious then rake in the blood-spattered pot.

Still, the mother of poker advice books remains Brunson's *Super/ System*. First published in 1978 with a $100 price tag, it sold out almost immediately and changed the face of poker forever. Much like *The Simpsons, The West Wing,* and *The Sopranos,* it was written by a half dozen maestros. Mike Caro covers draw poker, Chip Reese seven-card stud, Joey Hawthorne the three most popular lowball games, David Sklansky high-low split games, and Bobby Baldwin limit hold'em. Brunson himself covers no-limit hold'em, the section I'm reviewing right now over my third cup of coffee.

Brunson apportions ninety-seven loud-and-clear pages to what he calls "the Cadillac of poker games." (The other chapters average under seventy.) His message? Attack! After that, attack some more. Bludgeon your opponents with big pocket pairs, with suited connectors, with nothing. Just don't forget to reraise, to put your opponents all-in. "I'm a very aggressive player," he redundantly states at one point. "I'm reaching out and picking up small pots all the time. I'm always betting at those pots . . . hammering at them. And I *don't* want anybody to stop me from doing that. I *don't* want anyone to *defeat* my style of play." What part of this message, dear reader, do you *not* understand?

Like an unchallenged warlord dressing down lily-livered recruits, he tells us exactly what to do in slippery situations, while making painfully clear the importance of attitude and table image. Some players, he says, make dainty little bets when trying to win a large pot, a tactic he refers to with unvarnished scorn as a "Post-Oak bluff." "Well, that's a *gutless* bet," Brunson continues, then uses a footnote, of all things, to reiterate in boldface, "*I NEVER make a Post-Oak bluff," before the main text swaggers onward: "The tight player who made that weak bet on the flop is asking me to take his money. And, in most cases, that's exactly what I'm going to do when the next card falls—regardless of what it is. I'm going to move in on that tight player because I feel confident he's going to throw his hand away and *not* put his whole stack in jeopardy."

Well over two thousand years ago, in *The Art of War,* Sun Tzu illuminated what may seem at first blush like mere testosterone-drenched saber rattling: "What discourages opponents from coming is the prospect of harm." Brunson's updated version goes like this: "My opponents are afraid to play back at me because they know I'm subject to set them all-in." The benefits he reaps from striking fear in their hearts can become exponential. By accumulating a series of small pots, seldom much more than the antes and blinds, he can afford to "take the worst of it" (have the odds be slightly against him) when a big pot comes along. "I've already got that pot paid for with all the small pots I've picked up." Once he wins one of these big pots, subsequent small pots fall into even greater jeopardy, and the snowball keeps building. Avalanches like Ungar and Moss are famous for playing this way.

Super/System was launched with maximal authority because Brunson had just won the no-limit championship at Binion's in '76 and '77 and narrowly missed the hat trick in '78, a few weeks after the book was published. He finished second that year to—who else? His coauthor Baldwin. And then second to Ungar in '80.

There's no rhyme or reason, by the way, for that slash in his title, and throughout the book's 605 pages punctuation follows the rule of "It seemed like a good idea at the time." Still, no one doubts that it changed the game for good, adversely affecting Brunson's bottom line. Putting down in black and white his trade secrets has proven roughly akin to Coca-Cola's publishing its recipe, the Dallas Cowboys their playbook, or the CIA names and photographs of its field agents. Most poker experts have learned to keep their favorite tactics a secret, or at least try to camouflage them for as long as possible.

If Brunson is the reluctant dean of strategy authors, David Sklansky remains the best teacher and wonkiest theoretician. Nicknamed "Einstein," Sklansky got an Ivy League education at Penn, then worked in the corporate world before quitting to play poker professionally in Gardena and Las Vegas. He was only twenty-seven when Brunson invited him to write the "High-Low" chapter of *Super/System*, and it made Sklansky's name. While Brunson regrets publishing his modus operandi, Sklansky has savored his guru status and produced nine widely respected books of his own, which cover and extend the state of the art of nearly every variety of limit poker. Sklansky's logic, strategic insight, and creatively applied mathematics have proven so sound that his books are assigned to trainees at Susquehanna Partners and several other options-trading firms. No poker writer's books sell as briskly.

His *Theory of Poker* is the definitive philosophical statement of the game's fundamentals. Beginners read it to ground themselves in the basics, veteran pros to plug holes in their games and get a better handle on the logic behind their more artful moves. It's a book to reread every three or four years and dip into periodically, especially before a big game. As its title predicts, *Theory* offers little in the way of nuts-and-bolts advice. Instead, it clarifies the questions to ask when making all poker decisions.

Sklansky writes like a somewhat pedantic calculus or logic professor, a tweedy juggernaut of probability and syllogism. He has the math down, of course, often to the fourth or fifth decimal, and this, combined with hundreds of icily rational directives for playing "correctly," has left some readers feeling browbeaten or intimidated. A taskmaster for his students, Sklansky is frankly contemptuous of the pedagogy of his rivals. Rating the relative value of J-10 suited, he snorts: "Those writers who have called this the best hand, even in full games, are out of their minds!"

The heart of his philosophy is what he calls the Fundamental Theorem of Poker: *Every time you play a hand differently from the way you would have played it if you could see all your opponents' cards, they gain; and every time you play your hand the same way you would have played it if you could see all their cards, they lose. Conversely, every time opponents play their hands differently from the way they would have if they could see all your cards, you gain; and every time they play their hands the same way they would have played if they could see all your cards, you lose.* Sound simple? It is and it isn't. Of *course* you'd win more if you were privy to your opponents' pocket cards, but reading those cards as they lie facedown on the felt is an inexact science at best. Sklansky teaches you to make highly educated guesses based on previous plays, current position, and a host of related criteria. He also makes clear how much correct play depends on the pot odds—that is, on the ratio of the size of the pot to the bet you must call to continue with the hand.

Arranged in twenty-five chapters, the subjects in *Theory* range from

simple things like why it's better to raise than to call, through relatively advanced stuff like reverse implied pot odds and randomizing
bluffs via game theory. A typical chapter begins with a clear definition
of, say, the semibluff: betting with a hand you don't think is currently
the strongest but which has a reasonable chance of improving to
the best hand. A flush draw with no pairs on board, for example. After showing how this tactic conforms to the Fundamental Theorem,
Sklansky gives practical reasons to semibluff. (It withholds a free card
from your opponent; often gets *you* a free card on subsequent betting
rounds; adds deception to your game, since when you do hit your
hand, it will be harder for opponents to read its strength, helping you
win larger pots; gives you a chance to win the pot immediately, possibly against a superior hand.) Even getting caught in a failed semibluff
can be valuable "advertisementwise," as Benny Binion would say. Once
you reveal yourself as a bluffer, you tend to be paid off more handsomely when you do make your hand.

Sklansky isn't afraid to repeat points for emphasis, and his self-
published books often read as though they were also self-edited. He's
writing sophisticated primers, he wants us to know, not well-crafted
short stories. (He went to Penn, goddammit, not Iowa!) In the preface
to *Hold'em Poker for Advanced Players*, cowritten with Malmuth, the authors stipulate preemptively that "the purpose of this book is not to
get an 'A' from our English teacher. Rather it is to show you how to
make a lot of money in all but the toughest of hold'em games." They
even mock the notion that writerly elegance amounts to much, anyway. "So if we end a sentence with a preposition or use a few too many
words or even introduce a new subject in a slightly inappropriate
place, you can take solace from the fact that you can buy lots more
books by Hemingway with the money we make you." If only they
knew how strenuously Papa's so-called final drafts had to be burnished
by Maxwell Perkins, they wouldn't be quite so defensive. And maybe
they'd hire an editor.

In *Poker, Gaming & Life*, Sklansky takes on issues outside the poker
world. To keep stealthy crimes from becoming "good plays" for criminals, he proposes that sentences be made "more severe even if the

crime itself is no more heinous than others where it's easier to be caught. If this results in especially severe punishments that are deemed unconstitutional, amend the constitution." In other words, burkers beware! Sklansky's forte is revealing a counterintuitive idea to be the sane or correct one. He has persuasive opinions about advertising, cheating on your taxes, airline seats for children, racial diversity, and risking your life during wartime. Looking back at Vietnam, he says we can judge "whether the soldiers who were taking maybe a 1 percent chance of dying were getting a fair risk vs. reward ratio. If we had won, Vietnam certainly would have been a little different than it is today, but would that difference have been worth more than 50,000 American lives?" To get the reverse implied odds, we'll have to ask some of the Nguyens.

Unfortunately for me, Sklansky's poker counsel is geared mainly for limit hold'em played for medium stakes; he has yet to address at serious length either no-limit or tournament strategy. (This changed in 2002. See Bibliography.) Since these are the areas I need the most help in, I've spent most of my time on this trip rereading Brunson and Cloutier. We may never face down a bat-wielding enforcer, but those of us T.J. refers to as book-learned types have other advantages, I hope. We're used to processing the world off the page, translating printed language and numbers into ideas and action. Some of us are better at this than others. I'm thinking of liberal-arts majors like Duke, Liebert, Kolberg, and Hellmuth (whose father is a dean at the University of Wisconsin), not that these folks haven't also learned plenty by the seat of their pants, as well as via their genes. And what about lawyers? Despite the Gregory Peck–Atticus Finch stereotype, most attorneys work alone in a room, eyes to print with their mouths shut, and aren't particularly handsome, but their clients go free or to prison—or forfeit their money, or get strapped to a table—because of what did or did not get perused in some fusty old casebook. Perused *and picked up on*, that is. Likewise, veteran readers of literature know how to unpack information and meaning from what can be some rather belligerently cryptic sources. Complex as no-limit hold'em may be, fathoming Dante's matrix of Beatrice, three, and God's grace, for example, or making post-structuralist sense of the last and first sentence of *Finnegans Wake* can't be too much less tricky than calculating the reverse implied pot odds while drawing to the nut flush with one pair already on board and $1.5 million at stake, all this without the tactical implications of your thought process showing up on your features, now can it?

MAE WEST: Is poker a game of chance?
W. C. FIELDS: Not the way I play it.

— *My Little Chickadee*

When I saw the camera motorcycles pulling up to me, I put on a mask of pain. It was the ideal script, a chance to play a little game of poker.

— LANCE ARMSTRONG

I arrive back downstairs to the black-on-white printed reality of my name on page one of the five-page, single-spaced leader board. Two hundred and fourteen players have chips, and my $35,325 puts me in forty-first place. No literary construct or Baudrillardian simulacra, these are the plain, sunlit facts.

With par at $23,933, I may even have enough ammunition to survive a small blunder or two, although Mehul Chaudhari, the leader, has me almost tripled with $92,500. I remind myself to stay out of pots with him, or just about any pot contested by players with much bigger stacks than my own: my satellite rivals Habib and Jacobs, for example, in fifth and fifteenth place, respectively. Kathy Liebert is in seventh, T.J. nineteenth, Noel Furlong right above me in thirty-ninth. Bunched near the middle of the pack are Melissa Hayden, Annie Duke, Erik Seidel, Barbara Enright. Mansour Matloubi, the 1990 champion, has $18,975, Chan $14,550. Down under twelve thou-

Slim and Kathy Liebert

sand are Heimowitz and Sklansky, Hellmuth and McEvoy and Viriyayuthakorn. All of these folks are my heroes.

Fewer costumes got pulled out of mothballs this morning, and everyone's mood is more businesslike. The buy-ins of the 298 players eliminated yesterday come to almost $3 million in dead money, this on top of the $2.14 million of our own money still to be won. The action today will eliminate 169 more of us. Each of the forty-five survivors will be guaranteed at least $15,000 and be on a freeroll for the gold bracelet and $1.5 million. Four women are in serious contention, another five still in the running.

Am I ready for this? Maybe not. My first huge mistake comes only forty minutes in, when one behind the button I'm dealt pocket kings. Still juiced about being here at all, I decide to limp in, calling the $400 big blind instead of making it $2,000 or so, like I know I'm supposed to. What I'm hoping, of course, is to flop another king, build a pot, then ambush my foes at the showdown. The danger is failing to raise out hands like A-10, A-J, and the drawing hands, any of which could jump up and bite me on the flop.

The button and small blind have both limped as well, so four of us take the 7-9-7 flop. Check. Check. Scared of a seven but ecstatic that no ace has reared its ugly spire, I bet $2,000. When the button and small blind both call, I doubt that I have the best hand anymore. I'll have to outplay them or fold.

The next card to fall is a genuinely hideous eight. The scraggly, three-color mustache in the small blind tosses four white $1,000 chips toward the pot. I call, God knows why. The button studies the board, then his hand, then the board. Tick tick tick. He peeks at his cards one more time, dilates his nostrils, and folds.

Fifth street comes a harmless trey of clubs, for 7-9-7-8-3. Without a three-flush on board but an eminently possible straight, Mustache tosses out five more white. Now, a good poker player would swallow his medicine here by laying down kings, but . . . But nothing. Just fold! But I already have $4,200 invested in the pot, with no overcard ace on the board, so I call. And Mustache turns over J-10.

As Jerry Lundegard, the wife-murdering Oldsmobile salesman in *Fargo*, would say: What the Christ else would he have? Although how did he call me, with only four outs, on the flop? Even harder to swallow is knowing that Mustache would almost certainly have folded J-10 if I'd made it $2,000 preflop. Watching him rake in my pot, I have to wonder when I became a person on whom everything is lost. This game was *designed* to blast drawing hands from the battlefield, imbecile!

Down to $28,000, I resolve for the umpteenth time to play solid poker, but why should I think I might listen? It also seems fair to assume that the Royal Hibernian poker gods have deemed me unfit for any more aces or kings, given that I play them so poorly. I have little choice but to go into rock mode, that relatively safe but monotonous zone where you fold all hands lower than suited K-Q, this while the antes and blinds hack away at your stacks with machetes. My only consolation is knowing I richly deserve it.

It's almost 4:30 when, from the small blind, I manage to slip into an unraised pot with the J-9 of clubs of all things, the hand people call "T.J. Cloutier." It's me vs. the regally corpulent Arab in the big blind; he got moved to this table fifteen minutes ago carrying a stack roughly twice the size of mine. And he checks.

The dealer turns over a dream flop: the trey, ace, and queen, all of clubs. So I check. Prince Faud makes the bet I expected, a teaser of $3,000. Not having raised before the flop, he could easily be playing something as weak as the K-2 of clubs, which would give him the nuts. But I doubt it. He's probably betting a pair, treys much more likely than queens; or perhaps one of each. Since I really don't know him from Adam, he could also be slow-playing aces. The big blind is the perfect position from which to get cute with them, too. So I raise him all-in, before he gets a chance to improve.

The dealer cuts $3,000 from my stack and counts down the rest. "Raise twenty-six seven."

Having turned almost sideways in his chair, Faud looks me over while riffling one of his stacks. The good news is that he's already taken too long to be holding the K-x of clubs. I gulp as discreetly as possible, look away *so* very casually. With roughly $55,000 left, he could call, lose the hand, and survive fairly comfortably. He also could use a more subtle cologne, a leafier diet, and slightly more regular exercise. His lungs have a job on their hands.

From the corner of my eye, I watch him separate $26,700 from his stacks and recount the rest; the two stacks are almost identical. Then his eyes are upon me again. To encourage him to call, I imagine myself plunging naked into an ice-clogged river—the Neva, for example, in February—trying to generate a chilled-scrotum look on my face.

But as Faud pushes forward one stack, I'm convinced I've misread him. I have no alternative but to show him J-9. He places . . . 3-3 right beside it. My flush makes me about a 4–1 favorite, but Faud still has seven outs twice to make a full house or quad treys. With the board reading 3-A-Q, the ten and king of clubs would be nice, but miracles are best never prayed for. Any ace, queen, or trey and I'm through.

I've never played pots even a tenth of this size, and my ocular nerves are processing dread with unsteady camerawork. Instead of the table, the dealer, the pot, and three cards, what I see is Analytical Cubism. I slap my cheek, trying to focus. The dealer thumps his fist, burns the top card, pauses, turns over the seven of spades. Prince Faud keeps breathing; I can't. The dealer thumps his fist, burns the top card, pauses for about half an hour, turns over the . . . red . . . queen? No, king! It's the *king*! (King of hearts, Ted's card, not that it matters.) In my marrow, my lungs, my intestines, I feel as though I've just delivered myself of a perfect, magnificent dump.

"Good hand," says the prince.

"Yep. Sorry. Thanks."

"You had me since the flop. I should have raised you out."

"That flop made it tough not to come." But what am I saying? He made a mistake by not raising before the flop, and after three clubs hit, I trapped him, induced a bad call, and he didn't suck out on the river. There's surely no need for me to apologize, though I'm still shaken by how easily he could have spiked a full house. In which case I would have been "busted with honor": good play, disastrous outcome. Instead, I have new ammunition.

A dozen hands later, I call a good-sized raise from late position while holding 10-10. When the bony Vietnamese raiser checks the

2-2-2 flop, he seems to confirm what I put him on before the flop, A-Q or A-K, though he also would've checked with a deuce. But would he have raised before the flop with just one? Of course not. Maybe with two, but not one. But couldn't he have raised with paired face cards or aces? Of course.

When I wager the size of the pot, he thinks long enough to fry a platypus egg on his pocky, overheated forehead, while breathing with great consternation. Tick tock, tick tock, as Hannibal Lecter would say. Pocky Charlie glares down at his cards one more time—have they changed?—before spitefully mucking them, hard.

By the 6:20 dinner break I have $98,000. If I hadn't wasted a call with A-3 a couple of hands earlier, I'd be sitting with the magic One Large.

When my colleague Matthew Goulish, the Goat Island performer and writer, heard I was going to cover the World Series, he asked whether I'd read Yasunari Kawabata's *The Master of Go*. Matthew was surprised when I told him I hadn't, since he knows I've used Kawabata's *Palm-of-the-Hand Stories* in my short-fiction workshop. Two days later I found a brand-new copy of *The Master of Go* in my mailbox. "Be inspired. Matthew." He's recommended enough keepers to me over the years that I took it home and read it that night. Forty-one very short chapters, 182 uncrowded pages. Not only was it not about poker, it chronicled a game I had no idea how to play. The lapidary prose could not have been further removed from the cowboy advice books towering precariously on my night table.

Go, I learned, involves placing white or black stones into one of the 361 "points" on the board. Alternating stones with your opponent, the object is to surround, and thereby capture, enemy stones while averting the capture of your own. Kawabata's account of a 1938 match between an invincible master and his much younger challenger was originally serialized in a Tokyo newspaper. The epochal match lasts almost six months, and it's fair to say that it spells the literal death of the loser. Yet more is at stake than the life of one man. The entire tradition of Japanese aristocracy is being indirectly illuminated. Kawabata reworked these articles extensively after the war, trying to produce an elegiac metaphor of Japan's defeat in 1945. His new narrator follows the glacial action from below and outside. "I was not so much observing the play as observing the players. They were the monarchs, and the managers and reporters were their subjects." An amateur player himself, Kawabata hopes to "report on Go as if it were a pursuit of supreme dignity and importance—and I could not pretend to understand it perfectly—I had to respect and admire the players. I was presently able to feel not only interest in the match but a sense of Go as an art, and that was because I reduced myself to nothing as I gazed at the master." His translator, Edward Seidensticker, explains in the introduction that the book was conceived as a *shosetsu*, "a faithful chronicle-novel" that Westerners might read as a kind of reportorial memoir: "embroidered or colored but essentially nonfiction all the same."

In the end, as the victor sits "motionless, head bowed," hands resting "side by side on his knees," I couldn't help thinking of the chest-thumping, crotch-thrusting war dances American athletes treat their opponents and fans to after touchdowns or dunks. Even poker players—Men Nguyen and Devilfish Ulliott come to mind—have been known to agitate booty while singing renditions of Elvis after winning big pots. Both are improvements, at least, over smacking the table and hissing a venomous *Y-e-e-e-sss!*

Instead of hissing, or belting out "Jailhouse Rock" if I rake a huge pot, or reducing myself to nothing, my plan is to write a *shosetsu*.

Forty minutes after the dinner break, I get high-carded out of my seat next to Faud. (As players are eliminated throughout the event, others are randomly chosen with a deal of one card apiece to move to the nearest shorthanded table.) Now, for Level 5, we've cashed in all our black chips for yellow $500s, and the blacks left over are removed by means of a "race." The dealer distributes one card for each remaindered black, and the highest cards receive an extra yellow.

With $93,500, I'm now in Seat 2 of a table with Hasan Habib in 1, J.J. Bortner in 3, Kathy Liebert in 4, Mickey Appleman in 6, and Daniel Negreanu in 8. It's ridiculously stiff competition, but a great chance to study a pair of my subjects up close. Bortner, on my left, is a thirtyish woman with short wavy hair above blue cat's-eye spectacles. Without exception, people I talked to this week characterized her game as inordinately, even "outlandishly," aggressive. I'm surprised to see that she's Asian—Chinese, I would guess—since her name had me picturing a Texas moll draped with a gunbelt and fringe. More disjunction: she works (she tells me) as a CPA in San Francisco but keeps a ceramic rattlesnake coiled on top of her stacks, which she's just un-CPA-ishly shoved all-in, snake and all. Liebert and Appleman fold. So much for demure Asian ladies.

Appleman had already won a WSOP stud high-low title when Alvarez profiled him in '81. Since then he's won two more bracelets: for the Deuce in '93 and a limit hold'em event three years later. He's been on the poker circuit for twenty-five years now, though he makes his main living these days as a sports handicapper, a job he described in a *Card Player* interview as "applying nonquantifiable angles." This evening he's wearing a white Massada baseball cap angled slightly leftward over his profusion of curls. And he's losing.

Negreanu is whippet thin under his teal San Jose Sharks jersey and ultimatebet.com hat. Barely twenty-five, he's already been living for six years off his poker skills, a good deal of which he picked up in his hometown, Toronto. Besides much success in high-limit side games, he's won twelve good-sized tournaments in the last three years, including a pair of WSOP bracelets. Fresh off a win at the United States Poker Championship and an impressive showing in Tunica, he's brimming with humor and confidence behind his devilish ginger goatee.

"Let's be honest here," he tells Habib in a faintly Canadian accent, this after a flop comes off A-7-7. "You've got the seven. Why are you trying to walk it?" As Habib tries to maintain his poker face, Negreanu grabs a dozen orange chips, corkscrews around like he's going to throw a left hook, and *wings* the chips into the pot—which he goes on to win with A-10.

A half hour later, as I'm folding my two-dozenth hand in a row, word comes that Hellmuth, the last former champion still in the hunt, has just been eliminated in sixty-fourth place. With sixty-three players left at seven tables, I've drifted back down to $82,500. We'll play on tonight till we lose eighteen more, but I have no idea how long this may take. With the blinds at $1,500-$3,000 and $500 antes, it's costing me—costing everyone—a minimum of $9,000 per round. The leaders at this point are Duke, Habib, Liebert, and a guy called Captain Tom Franklin, a silver-bearded Vietnam vet sitting two tables behind me. All four of them have in the neighborhood of a quarter of a million in chips. I resolve to keep playing conservatively, waiting for a monster I can sic on the big shots, or anyone.

In the meantime, how about an injury update? On top of a half numb, half tingling ass and a slight nervous headache, handling the cards and chips for two days has given me a nasty pair of hangnails. Normally, in the absence of clippers, I'd nip them right off, but with so many cameras I can't. Deposits of felt are also embedded under the nails of my right index finger and thumb. Yet somehow I suck it up and keep playing.

Sitting one behind the button, Negreanu just raised to $6,000. Fold. Fold. His friendly insouciance makes him extremely hard to read, but I've heard and now seen how aggressive he is. Sitting in the big blind with an A-J unsuited, I reraise to $12,000. He seems plenty happy to call.

The flop comes a 7-5-J rainbow. With top pair, top kicker, I check. Smiling and shrugging, Negreanu checks, too.

The turn: four of clubs. To head off a low straight draw (and praying he hasn't hit a small set), I bet $12,000. He calls, just like that.

The river is an overcard queen, which I hate. So I check.

Negreanu looks me over for a second or two, taps his finger. Since he called my bet on the turn, it's up to me to show my hand first. Two jacks, ace kicker. Not that I'm overly proud of it. Negreanu nods twice, mucks his cards, and it's over.

Whew! Blasé can be way more intimidating than fierce, can it not?

As I'm raking the chips, a commotion breaks out right behind me, and I'm convinced someone *else* won the pot—that I'd inadvertently cheated, or that Negreanu has duped me somehow: *he* won the pot, as a matter of fact, and now the railbirds and press wanna mock my reaction. The dozen extra cameras nosing in around the table confirm it. One huge white lens has just banged my elbow, surfacing out of nowhere like the white shark Roy Scheider was chumming for.

The quarry, however, is a Stetsoned goblin in a pink and blue shirt suddenly looming behind Kathy Liebert: Slim Preston. Kathy swings around in her chair and looks up. And now, with a terrified look on *his* face, Slim runs a serious butcher knife across his own throat. Is it real? Yes it is. Is he pretending to be Kathy's anti-O.J. or something, the pale Amarillo Othello driven mad by her poker unfaithfulness?

Nope. I was not even close.

The story is that way back in '73, Slim offered to have his throat slit if a woman ever won this event. Now that Liebert is in position to do so, photographers want to capture Slim's yolky trepidation. We get it. But as he and Kathy pose, I gather from other reporters that Slim said he'd submit his throat to the blade only if a *particular* woman, a braggart named Vera Richmond, took home the bracelet. Then Slim himself takes up the story: "A little past the halfway point, Vera was the chip leader. During the next break she walks up to the reignin' champion—me—and says, 'Mr. Slim, what do you think about a lady gettin' hold of that many chips?' and Ah says, 'Ah think it's great.' 'Well,' she has the nerve to blurt out, 'it's a dead certainty that I'm gonna win this World Series,' and that didn't set rot with me. 'Vera,' Ah told her, 'if you win the World Series of Poker you can take a dull knoff and cut mah throat.' But she didn't even come *close*." And we laugh. Slim clearly savors all the heat he caught back then from "the gals, the lesser lady players, although when Ah told the good ones how it was, they knew Vera and understood what Ah meant by my remark. To this day, Ah'm still quoted incorrectly." He also seems to relish how much better copy the misquote is making for now.

Nor can there be any doubt that Liebert wants to concentrate on the business at hand. Aside from the money at stake, this is her chance to make history. Still, she's being a pretty good sport, though I'd be smiling, too, if I had big straight white teeth and $270,000 in front of me.

Slim and his convoy of press finally move to the table behind us, where he strikes the same pose above Annie Duke. As the microphones jab down and flashes go off in her face, Duke appears less amused than Liebert was. Yeah, whatever, she seems to be thinking behind her sweet, pregnant smile. Just shut up and deal.

Like Sandy Murphy, I realize, Liebert and Duke are both around thirty, and all three came to Vegas in their mid-twenties to make their fortune. Duke had grown up in Concord, New Hampshire, in a brainy and word-happy family. She got a B.A. at Columbia University (English and psychology double major) and completed her coursework and research for a Ph.D. in psycholinguistics at Penn. Her dissertation topic was "syntactic bootstrapping," evidence by itself that a high-powered career in academia beckoned. True love, however, and perhaps fear of tweed, intervened. She proposed to and married Ben Duke, a handsome Montanan she'd met at Penn, moved back west with him, and started a family. In the meantime, with Ben's and her big brother Howard's support and a steady diet of Sklansky on her new reading list, Duke began earning good money playing poker in bars around Montana, as well as during longer and longer sojourns to Vegas, especially during the spring. She and Ben continue to fine-tune their child-rearing and work schedules in a way that impressively redefines flextime. However they work it, it works.

Duke's persona at the card table makes her especially relish taking pots from male players. "My mere presence enrages them," she believes. "Guys can be, on the whole, winning players, and when they come up against a woman, they can't help themselves. They can't stand to be beaten by a woman. It happens again and again. They just call, call, call, when they should be folding." Little syntactic bootstrapping is required to understand that Duke thinks the vast majority of men are neurotic nonmensches, a surprisingly quaint strain of feminism for a woman born in 1969. Other takes on Duke I have heard more than once are that "she thinks she's Annie Oakley" and that she tends to cope with self-esteem issues by being "a complete bitch." Rene Anker, a friend of Duke's since they were in eighth grade together, says this: "Annie's very opinionated and sure of herself in a way that doesn't always make you well-liked, but she was so smart that people respected her even if she drove them nuts." Fair enough.

Liebert is much less combative in trying to prove herself. She grew up in Louisville and on Long Island, then graduated from Marist College in Poughkeepsie, where her B.S. may have involved the definitive prepoker curriculum: major in business with a concentration in finance, minor in psychology. (That both Liebert's parents have a Ph.D. in psychology, and that Duke's father is a language columnist with a Ph.D. in linguistics and her mother scored 1600 on the SAT, no doubt were also big factors in the poker success of the daughters.) Liebert was hired as a stock analyst by Dun and Bradstreet but immediately got bored with the Wall Street routine, as Duke had been in the budding groves of academe. Planning to enter law school in California, Liebert moved to San Diego in 1991 to begin establishing residency. But then, on a gambler's whim much like Murphy's, she took a vacation to Vegas. While Murphy played blackjack at Caesars for $500 a hand and Duke was being tutored by Howard, Liebert tried her luck in a $4-$8 hold'em game at the Dunes. She not only won a few dollars, but was struck by the camaraderie at the table, as well as by the game's cerebral challenges. She went home and boned up on books by Shane Smith and on McEvoy's *Tournament Poker*, returning the following year to play in a small Vegas tournament. Her first event, Omaha with a $120 buy-in, drew 470 entrants. Liebert outlasted 468 of them and agreed to a deal splitting first- and second-place money with her more experienced opponent; in effect, she had won her first tournament. Three days later she finished second in a hold'em event, bringing her prize money to over $30,000 for the trip. Next stop, the World Series, where she "cashed" in her second event and has never looked back. By 1997 she'd come within a hand of winning the $3,000 no-limit hold'em event, taking home $124,000 for second. She is currently fifth on the women's all-time prize money list.

When I had lunch with her last week, Liebert told me how determined she is to make poker her business. "In some ways I'm a big risk taker. In other ways, definitely not." She has homes in LA and Las Vegas, spending about five months apiece in each town. The other two months she travels the circuit to Foxwoods in Connecticut, the Taj in Atlantic City, and now the Horseshoe in Tunica. In her *Poker Pages* column, "Techniques for Women," she concedes that they "tend to play a more passive style than men" but insists that women can use this to their advantage. "First of all, if a woman holds a very strong hand, she may want to sometimes play it passively to allow the overly aggressive male to put money in the pot. By sometimes checking and calling you can induce people with weak hands to bet your hand for you." She suggests that many men play women "as if they were open books. Often if a woman checks the man will assume she is weak and will bet. If a woman bets or raises they will often give her credit for a good hand," even when the woman is bluffing. Liebert's column also recommends Sklansky's *Theory of Poker*, Sklansky and Malmuth's *Hold'em for Advanced Players*, and Cloutier and McEvoy's *Championship Hold'em*. The McEvoy recommendation is especially unsurprising, given that the columnist currently lives with him.

Liebert and Murphy, then, both came to Vegas from southern California to make their fortune as gamblers, and both fell in love and moved in with a middle-aged man. (Tom McEvoy and Ted Binion were both born in 1944.) Kathy and Tom have broken up a few times, and marriage doesn't seem to be in the cards for them, but they have remained intimate friends and sometimes travel together, this as Tom continues to coach Kathy on how to write up and publish her poker experiences. Ted and Sandy handled their breakups a tad less maturely, it seems. Whereas Annie and Ben are very much together, and then some.

During the next break, Negreanu sidles up alongside me, smiling and shaking his head. "I had you back there, mister writer." No malice at all in his voice, just letting me know how close he had come to ironing out my A-J.

Only slightly offended, I whip out my Post-its and ask him to explain.

"You trapped yourself, man. That strange little reraise you made before the flop—like you *wanted* me in there against you. But all you had was ace-jack! No way can I fold when you're raising that puny amount, but you're playing the hand out of position and pretty much forcing yourself to hit a big flop." He hunkers down over an imaginary table, imitating a dufus desperately hoping to hit a big flop. This would, uh, I guess, have been me.

"What did *you* have?" I ask him. "Ace-king?"

"Three-five of spades, man." He laughs. "On a steal. But the thing is, you trapped your*self*. The way you played it, you were either gonna win a small pot or lose a really big one, since if I hit my hand you probably wouldn't have been able to lay down top pair-ace kicker." In other words, I'm talking to the express train I obliviously dodged, which has been around the track a few times and just came within a whisker of hitting a straight against my measly jacks. Again, nothing hostile or threatening about it, just helpfully stating the facts.

So I thank him.

With a dozen eliminations to go till we reach forty-five, I basically hang around for two hours, actively avoiding confrontations with stacks the same size as or larger than mine. The two times I raise (with A-Q and 8-8), people like Hasan and Kathy come blasting back over the top of me, so I lay the hands down—chickenhearted and costly, of course, but not fatal. By the time we're down to fifty survivors, however, my stack has been whittled to $38,000, almost exactly where I started the day. The difference is that I'm now on the bubble, far below the $102,400 average. If I don't play my cards right the next time I enter a pot, the bubble is going to pop.

My table was already a terrifying convocation, but when Daniel's A-A gets him busted by a set of nines, he's replaced by—oh, *shit!*—T.J. Cloutier. It gets worse. In his new seat for less than a minute, T.J. has already raised it to $5,000, and the white-hatted cowboy in 9 and Hasan have both folded. My action. One off the button, perfectly happy to sit here and wait for a monster, I look down and find yet another A-J.

Don't call big bets, I remind Bad Jim harshly. *Fold or raise.* Since A-J is hardly a reraising hand, that means I should fold, does it not? Good Jim's content, not contentious. Yet he's also aware that strong players target the weak ones, especially when the pressure is on, and he can't shake the feeling that T.J. has pegged him as a tight-weak reporter. It's time to cowboy up.

"Call," I say, flipping one orange chip toward the pot. It's an asinine play, and I know it. A cowboy would reraise all-in.

Jerry, the mustachioed Latin dealer, turns the flop: A-9-6 rainbow.

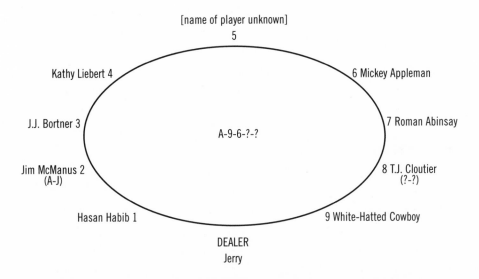

T.J. glares down at me, making me glad we are separated by the length of the felt. The Texas afro that another tight end, Mike Ditka, achieved with a perm for a while sprouts naturally in gunmetal gray from T.J.'s huge head. While there's nothing overt about it, the man comfortably embodies a lethal threat, even from the seated position. If it happens to suit him, he can reach across the table and rupture key vertebrae with his bare hand, and everyone sitting here understands this down in our helical enzymes—in *my* helical enzymes at least, not to mention my looping and straight ones. Doing my best to meet his jagged scrutiny, I decide not to taunt him about his 'fro, his book's punctuation and grammar, or the stench from his Salem wafting into our sinuses. The best way to take care of that is to break him and make him go home. In the meantime, I'd love a few tokes off that Salem myself. Should I ask him to share it with me?

Tapping one massive finger, he checks.

I've put him on a medium ace, which is also the way I'd describe my own hand, unfortunately. He may have a bigger one, of course, or A-9 or A-6, but with top pair and a half-decent kicker I feel there's no choice but to push forward four orange chips.

"Bet twenty thousand," says Jerry.

I meet T.J.'s glare for a second or two, then study the smoke-marbled distance. I must appear terribly frightened, however, because

T.J. moves in with alacrity. *Wham!* Plus a checkraise on top of it all.

"Reraise," says Jerry. "All-in."

T.J.'s total stack is smaller than mine, but only by three or four thousand. If I call and get beat, that's all I'd have left. As the new ministack at this table, I'd become the prime candidate for going out next. But I still think I've got T.J. beat.

"Call," I say, nudging all four of my stacks toward the pot. One topples over pathetically.

Now it's T.J. who don't look so happy. "I think you've got me outkicked," he growls hoarsely, exhaling long plumes of Salem.

We'll see. I skim my two cards off the felt and turn them over respectfully. The railbirds don't sound too impressed. "He calls an all-in raise with ace-*jack*?!" Yes, I have. Because that's the kind of mick I am, fellas.

T.J. makes me wait while he snuffs out the butt, then turns over . . . *A-10!* My heart hurdles four of my ribs, lands in stride, keeps on sprinting. Linda Johnson has been watching all this from just behind Jerry, and she shoots me a big, crazy grin.

What a call!

The turn card is a nine, so the board reads A-9-6-9, giving both T.J. and me aces up, with my jack still outkicking his ten; no flush or straight draws for either of us. He's a goner. I try to relax, to look a degree or two cooler, but I don't think it's working. At all. I figure that since only one of the three remaining tens can beat me, I'm a 44–3 favorite not only to win a huge pot but to punch out the number-one badass.

Jerry raps the felt, burns a card, turns over the . . . nine of clubs. Whoa! There's a choruslike gasp off the rail, and Kathy Liebert says, "Oh my God!" With so much blood roaring back and forth between my hemispheres, I'm unable to parse either the buzz of commentary or the funhouse display of slack jaws and raised eyebrows. All I know is that T.J. is grinning and shaking his head and *not standing up*. Even after Jerry announces, "Split pot," and is echoed by dozens of railbirds, it takes me another long moment to fathom that we both just made nines full of aces. *That is so fucking scabby*, I think but don't say, not only because it's T.J. who sucked out on me but because I've resurrected a phrase I haven't used since fifth grade. *Sucked out on me*, of course, is a better way to put it, but I can't say that either, out loud. I stare at the three nines in shock as Bad Jerry shoves me my measly half share of the chips. I try to restack them by color, but my fingers don't work very well.

Linda squeezes my shoulder, and I take the opportunity to whine, "It really has to come the third nine?"

"Actually, any king or queen would've got you a split pot as well."

It would've? "Oh . . . right." Since either would have outkicked my jack.

"You still played it perfectly, though. And you made a great call."

Eavesdropping on Linda and me is a nerdy bald guy with a press badge who's at least as agitated as I am. *His* excuse is that he's talking on two phones at once, eyes darting left, darting right as he tries to follow three conversations. The moment has arrived, I decide, to nibble off one of these hangnails.

As I publicly gnaw my torn digit, Mike Paulle comes over the public address: "Jim, we can move the press back if you want."

"Hey, I want *more* press, not less." This is not true, not at all, but it's all I can think of to say, I'm so *pissed* . . .

Careful not to let myself steam on the bubble, I sit tight for the next twenty minutes. Kathy meanwhile keeps the table pretty much under control. Her friendly if not quite angelic features don't keep her from maneuvering her $300,000 stack like some cute Vegas Rommel, blitzkrieging antes and blinds, setting us all-in if we even *think* about drawing against her. Watching T.J. watch Kathy, and Kathy's awareness of that, I recall that George Patton had studied Rommel's book about fighting a desert war, too.

Down to forty-six of us, all six tables are shorthanded, with either seven or eight players, and we're forced to proceed hand-for-hand. The next player eliminated receives zero prize money; everyone else gets at least $15,000. Jerry and his colleagues hold up their shuffle until all six tables complete the current hand, waiting for Bob Thompson to say, "Go ahead, deal." This is to keep the short stacks at one table from stalling till someone goes out at another. At the same time, it's only natural that we all want to think long and hard before calling big bets, or entering a pot to begin with.

Some of the holdups last eight or ten minutes, so now seems a good time to pee. When I try to get out of my chair, the tendons in my legs yank me forward. Even once I've stretched them a little, the crowd around the table is too thick to penetrate quickly. I have to get down and crawl through a forest of denim and Nike—and one sleek pair of calves—before standing back up and hobbling into the men's room.

Jesus Ferguson mans a urinal in his trademark black hat slung low over convex, mirrored shades. (I've kept my shades on as well, so as not to let my rods and cones get used to unpolarized light.) The only thing off about Ferguson's getup is the elegant little black dancer's shoes—till I remember his hobby is swing-dancing.

"Still have chips?" he asks cordially, heading back toward the sink.

"Sort of," I tell him, not turning around. "What about you?"

"I'm still doing all right. Hey, good luck."

"You, too. By the way, do you prefer Chris or Jesus?"

"Oh, both, I guess."

Both? I shake and zip up.

"Either one," he amplifies. "I like them both the same."

Helpful.

And now here's Andy Glazer. Having been eliminated late last night, he's back in reporter mode, poorer. We acknowledge this unhappy fact, as does Chris. Hand on my shoulder, Andy suggests I "might wanna slow down at this stage."

"Brother, the last thing I want is to keep mixing things up, but the cards haven't given me any choice."

"No choice with ace-jack, huh?"

"My right hand keeps grabbing the chips and tossing them into the—"

"Almost as though . . ." Chris puts in, suddenly spooky-voiced, strobing his bony fingers toward my face in psychedelic fashion, "you've been hyp-no-tized . . ."

"Y-e-e-e-s . . ."

"Yeah, that sounds about right," Andy says.

Says Jesus, "We understand perfectly."

Before sitting back down, I survey the other five tables. Jacobs and Duke have big stacks, as do Captain Tom and Mike Sexton. But according to the floormen's official count, Liebert still dominates the tournament, with Duke and Habib close behind.

The tiniest stacks are at our table, too, where Appleman is down to $4,500. Roman Abinsay, a handsome Filipino about my age who's been moved to Seat 7, has roughly twice that. One mistake by either of them wins me $15,000 in cash.

And vice versa.

Three hands later I find myself in the big blind with the 8-9 of hearts. Jennifer and I had our first date in 1989, and Beatrice was born in '98. Since then I've always played suited 8-9, especially when it's in hearts. Even now? Even now. Maybe even *especially* now . . .

Everyone folds to Hasan in the small blind, and he raises to $20,000. I recount my stack: $36,100. Good Jim advises, Just let him have the blinds and wait for a better hand, fool. But I'm starting to get a feel for Hasan, and I think he's on a steal. So I call. Not that I ever would fold the 8-9 of hearts . . . yet only a suicidal nut job would call for most of his stack at this stage with nothing but suited connectors. Plus, if I thought Hasan was stealing I should have reraised him, not called.

The flop comes 9-J-8, with two diamonds, no hearts. I'm feeling pretty proud of myself, pretty lucky, until Hasan puts both hands behind his gi-normous stacks and starts pushing. "All-in."

Jesus Christ. Two pairs may be better than what Hasan has right now, but if he hits a set or a flush while I fail to improve, it's me who'll be going out instead of Appleman or Abinsay, and in the worst of all possible places. Hasan may *already* have a set or a straight, plus I shouldn't even be *in* this fucking hand to begin with! My sentimental voodoo is about to cost me $15,000, plus whatever else I might've . . .

Calm down now, says Good Jim. Hasan is probably semibluffing before his own hand gets made, forcing me into a decision he knows I do not want to make. Only a fool wouldn't do so with the scare cards out there, and Hasan is no fool. But I'm the one who has the best hand. So I call, putting me down to the felt for the fifth or sixth time in two days.

It turns out Hasan was attacking with the K-Q of diamonds, so it isn't the end of the world yet. The deck Jerry's holding contains nine other diamonds, but the eight or the nine fills me up. Add the four tens (for a straight) and Hasan has eleven outs twice. Drumroll, *si'l vous plaît.* Here we go.

Fourth street is red, but a heart. Just the deuce. He now has eleven outs *once.*

Fifth street is black (five of clubs), so my two pairs have doubled me through to $78,500. I'm scared I'm about to start weeping. Linda Johnson fans herself, shaking her head like I'm crazy.

"Good call," says Hasan.

"Thank you, my friend."

"But I don't know how you made it, you know?"

"I never fold the eight and nine of hearts." As I further explain, his dark olive features suggest that my voodoo made sense, in a way.

The next hand I muck a Q-7, but it takes fifteen minutes for us all to complete it, mainly because a short stack at the table to my right thinks forever before calling all-in with two pairs; but he wins with them as well. Much applause.

On the next hand, with Liebert in the big blind, Appleman folds, leaving him with barely enough to post the next blind. Maybe he won't have to, however, since Abinsay just pushed in his entire $10,500.

Let's get this over with, shall we? Appleman, of course, desperately wants someone to call and knock Abinsay out forty-sixth, but no one ahead of me calls him. With 8-4 off-suit I can't call either, lunatic though I may be. Neither can J.J., who shrugs. Which leaves it up to Kathy to play sheriff. She already has $3,500 invested in the pot with her big blind and ante; she can easily afford seven more. And she calls, matching the $10,500 and turning over K-Q unsuited.

Appleman's face hasn't changed expression all evening and it doesn't change now, even when Abinsay turns over . . . aces. Liebert smiles, shakes her head. The flop comes Q-7-3, so she needs either of the two remaining queens or a king. I'm praying for her with my toes.

Fourth street comes a seven, for Q-7-3-7, apparently helping neither of them.

When Kathy's king also gets paired on the river, a few railbirds whoop; another starts chirping that we're "done for the night." And no one wants to believe him more than I do, but a second quick look at the board makes clear what Kathy's big sigh has just indicated: aces and sevens beat kings and queens, all night long. That's about how long we've been playing, in fact, though it feels like the *real* action is just getting started.

The next blind forces Appleman to post his last $1,500 with a pitiful 7-3 off-suit, but the 7-Q-7 flop quadruples him through to $6,000. He shrugs.

I'm now more determined than ever to stay on the sidelines, let other folks deal with this pressure. Even when under the gun I find aces, I seriously think about mucking them, especially since watching Negreanu get busted while playing them. Aces get cracked all the time, as a matter of fact. *Boo-hoo-hoo.* In the end it's too easy to imagine me kicking myself fifteen minutes from now, let alone what I'd do in fifteen years. And so, forced to act first and still a bit gun-shy from my recent Apocalypse Nows, I bet only $12,000. Fold. Fold. Fold. Fold. Fold. Fold. But the white-hatted cowboy in Seat 9 says, "Call," and I don't have a very good feeling, even when Hasan also folds.

The flop comes J-4-2 rainbow and I bet out $12,000, hoping to win the pot then and there, but with part of me sensing that Cowboy will raise. I can't see his face very well because Jerry's in the way, just the crumpled straw bill of the hat and a droopy blond mustache. I already hate him, of course, but when he smooth-calls again I realize I'm trapped by three jacks.

The pot contains about $65,000, almost half of it mine, but I have to get away from this hand. If I make no more bets and then fold, I'll be down to $40,000, enough to survive one more ouster, I hope.

Fourth street is the five of hearts, for J-4-2-5, giving me an inside straight draw to go with my now meager aces. I can't put the cowboy on anything higher than three jacks, since he wouldn't have called my first raise with A-3. (Or *would* he?) But I almost *prefer* that he have jacks as my right hand picks up fifteen blue chips, breaking them down into three crooked piles on the felt. I don't want to bet, but I have to, praying he has queens or kings.

And Cowboy smooth-calls me *again*! Now if I lose I'll be down to almost nothing, plus I'm so pot-committed I'd almost have to call even if another damn jack hits the board, or such is my manic illogic. I can no longer cling to the hope that he has anything less than a set.

Thank God in Heaven the next card is the—*aaaaaahhhhhh*—trey of spades, backdooring me into a wheel. (Giving me, in other words, an unexpected five-high straight on the final two cards.) No way has Cowboy been horsing around with 6-6 (for a higher straight), and since the board hasn't paired he couldn't have filled his three jacks. So I check, hoping against hope he'll at least *represent* the six and I can checkraise all-in. He had me trapped good and proper back there on the flop and the turn, but he let me keep drawing and now I believe I have him.

When he checks and turns over two jacks, I turn over an ace for the wheel. And then, for good measure, the other, which Cowboy don't seem to appreciate. I don't blame him, but neither do I care. I suddenly have almost $200,000, second at this table only to Liebert's three-fifty or so. If Abinsay, Appleman, or someone at another table had gone out twenty minutes ago, I'd be sitting with maybe a tenth this amount; or I could have been bounced out myself. Yet I feel not a dust mote of guilt.

I spend the next two hands (10-7, 6-7; fold, fold) reminding myself to avoid pots with Habib and Liebert before, back on the button again, I find an A-Q and think, *uh-oh*. When the action gets folded around to me, I raise it to $12,000. As soon as Bortner folds, who else but Liebert reraises to $24,000. She probably thinks I was trying to steal her big blind, and I wish I could have told her I was raising with a genuine hand, though nothing *half* genuine enough to be able to call a reraise with. She probably knows both these things. Then again, on the theory that big-time pros want to push me around, and failing for the dozenth time to heed T.J.'s advice about raising or folding, I call.

The flop of 2-7-Q bails me out, in a way. Top pair, top kicker again. But when Liebert taps a slender pink finger to check, I catch a faint but distinct whiff of checkraise. As the odor becomes more pronounced, my overmatched brain seizes up—*ckcheckcheckch*—but my thumb and middle finger manage to toss forward two pink tenthousands without even pausing to consult with their boss. In Chicago we say George S. Halas used to toss nickels around like they were manhole covers while negotiating contracts with his players. And so, in his honor, I'm treating these pink chips like nickels.

Kathy appears unconcerned as she fingers her chips, breaking off $20,000 in white to show me how niggling a dent this would make in her fortress. Then she stares me down hard for a while, right through my polarized lenses, like some chick laser surgeon zinging my capillaries. Do they smoke? Do they sizzle? I look off into ∞, trying to impersonate a guy who'd be *thrilled* to get called but without making too much of a production out of it. In any event, I don't flinch (I don't think). But I'm excruciatingly aware that Kathy's retracing our sequence of bets, narrowing down what I have. My scariest hand, from her point of view, is Q-Q. I believe she is holding 7-7, 10-10, or J-J; K-Q again *maybe*, though that would be simply too beautiful. Whatever queen she's playing I've got her tied or outkicked, but what if she's slow-playing two of them? And what about aces or kings? She reraised before the flop, after all, and those are the reraising hands. That decides it, in fact: if she puts me all-in, I will muck.

After weighing and squeezing her miniature soccer ball for over a minute, she cuts out a stack of fifteen orange chips—$75,000— fondling them as though ready to move her hand forward, all the while watching me closely. I stare away from the table for another ten seconds, then pointedly look back at her. I like her a lot, and she knows that. She also knows that my article will be stronger if a woman wins the championship, especially a woman with whom I have a few hours of Q&A on tape. Yet as Miles Davis perfectly phrased it, so what. All that matters now is this pot.

When she finally mucks, I exhale, then flash her my queen in what I hope will be seen as a comradely gesture. "Show one show all," demands Abinsay. When Jerry seconds the motion, I pick up both cards from the edge of the muck, flip them over. Kathy nods, but she doesn't look happy. With over a quarter of a million in chips now, I'm already learning to live with it.

You think *that* was brazen? Two hands later, after T.J. has raised to $10,000, I find an eminently foldable A-5 unsuited, an *automatic* fold for those with double-digit IQs. But I can't shake the feeling that my new favorite author wants to pilfer our antes and blinds, though I may also be stoned on some high-test adrenaline. But the longer I measure the odds of him stealing—*when everybody is trying to survive to get into the money*, as he says in Chapter 3, *you can pick up a mountain of chips*—the more convinced I become that he is, so I call. That's right, I call a big raise with A-5. That's right, I don't reraise. Understanding my stupidity better than my brain does, my heart thumps out signals visible, I'm sure, all over my body—fingers, neck, pupils, complexion—of how petrified I am. (More specifically, this is my candyass limbic system, the neurons and hormone-secreting cells just below the putatively thinking portion of my cerebral cortex, all of them whimpering, "*Boo-hoo-hoo-hoo-hoo!* Me ascared!") But couldn't my twitches and trembling fingers also be read as elation? As in, "Yeah! I'm finally gonna get T.J.'s chips!"

Not in this lifetime, you wanker.

But I camouflage (I think) my relief when the flop comes A-3-2, giving me another belly draw to go with top pair and pitiful kicker. When T.J. raps his fist on the table I'm convinced I'll be checkraised, but even if I bet and he comes back over the top, I'd still have enough to survive. I pluck two pink chips from the top of one stack, toss them forward. *En garde!*

"Bet twenty thousand," says Jerry.

Now it's T.J. who's staring me down again, an altogether more visceral experience than my face-off with Kathy, or even the first time T.J. had me in his sights. It's impossible not to think of Jack Palance staring down Billy Crystal: *I crap bigger'n you, city slicker.* I'm afraid to let on that I'm scared, and God only knows how that translates into body language.

But he mucks it, God love him! Showing me queens, he seems both proud of his lay-down and irked at the gall of me, slick little east-coast book-learned weasel that I am, even if it's *his* goddamn book I been learnin' from. I show him my ace, rake the pot.

Amid the ensuing buzz, I can hear Andy speaking for the record into Katy Lederer's tape recorder about "how spooky things are getting. A few minutes ago he was a writer trying to hang on, and suddenly he's messing with Kathy and T.J.?" Hey, with T.J. perhaps, but I certainly didn't think I was messing with Kathy. I read them both to be messing with *me*, each time with less than a premium hand. (Dead wrong on T.J.'s Q-Q, but no matter.) All I did was refuse to lay down my hands even though they were who they were and I didn't have the absolute nuts. I've also been bailed out by flops.

So even after I get pocket kings cracked by the all-in Appleman's K-10 when the board makes him a straight, everything's still copacetic. Because on the very next hand an unfortunate guy at the table to our left gets busted in forty-sixth place. Everyone applauds for the guy and for us as Thompson finally calls it a morning.

"I love this," says Linda, planting a medium-sized kiss on my lips to go with a warm, creamy hug. The *Card Player* people, especially Andy and Linda and Tom, have become my new family out here. Sugar from Linda is the perfect nightcap, though perhaps just a snifter of cognac wouldn't hurt anyone either . . .

Suddenly back in columnist mode, Linda wants to know, "How does it feel?"

"Uh, this is the most fun I've ever had in my life?"

As she scribbles this heresy into her notebook, I'm too exhausted to tack on the standard "except for making love with my wife and the birth of our children." I also don't know whether that caveat is even true. Not that those things didn't feel good.

Three answers later I borrow Linda's phone to call Jennifer, waking her up. "We're in the money, Higgins. Sorry for calling so late."

"We are?" she says, groggy.

"Uh, yup. I'm sorry . . ."

"That's good, right? I mean, are you out?"

"No, I'm in, but let me give you the details tomorrow, okay?"

"Good, good, I knew you would do this good, Jimmy . . ."

You *did?*

Once I hang up, Linda wants to hear about my *Harper's* assignment, the Bellagio connection, how it felt going up against Kathy and T.J., how I could even have *thought* about calling Hasan's raise with 8-9 on the bubble. Unaccustomed to being pressed to go on by reporters, my mouth doesn't work very well. Even when it turns out that my $276,000 is good for third place, just behind Liebert's $283,500 and the English bloke Barney Boatman's $282,000, I need another hug, not more grilling. I've gathered that poker people are used to staying up—and standing up—later than I am, though am I not one of them yet? Either way, it's heading toward 3 a.m. when Linda says, "When did you start playing poker?"

"Girl, I must crash now," I beg, holding her waist and pretending to almost keel over, except I'm not pretending.

She props me up, gives me a smooch. "In the morning."

SONG FOR TWO JIMS

There are few things that are so unpardonably neglected
in our country as poker. . . . Why, I have known
clergymen, good men, kindhearted, liberal, sincere,
and all that, who did not know the meaning of a
"flush." It is enough to make one ashamed of one's
species.

—MARK TWAIN

Two Jims. Who knows why?
—LAURIE ANDERSON, "Song for Two Jims"

What Linda eventually found out—not that night—was that my education as a poker player began when I was nine. My family had recently moved from the Bronx out to Lisle, Illinois, twenty miles southwest of Chicago, from a four-room tenement apartment in an Irish ghetto to a five-bedroom white clapboard house with black shutters in a subdivision called Oakview. My father was a sales rep for a steel company, and my mother stayed home with Kevin and Sheila; Ellen and I, the two oldest kids, went to St. Joan of Arc School. In June, Ellen and I flew back to New York to spend the summer with our grandparents. Grandma Grace, my father's mother, had an apartment along Fordham Road. My mother's parents, Tom and Betsy Madden, lived in Parkchester but were building (not having built) a summerhouse in Mahopac, forty miles upstate near the Hudson. Ellen and I would platoon between these ambiguously parallel universes. While

Tom Madden's monogrammed chips

Mr James L. McManus
U. S. S. Baltimore
c/o G. P. O.
London

1918 envelope addressed to James L. McManus

she lived it up for a week with the Maddens, I was overfed, pampered, and smothered by Grace, then vice versa.

Tom and Betsy took us fishing, to Tony's Italian "gin mill" on Webster Avenue under the 3rd Avenue El (where I became enthralled with the word, and the use of, *spittoons*), and for picnic lunches at Belmont Park racetrack. I still remember betting on Blue Boy and Savage Sailor at Grandpa's behest, but not whether either horse finished in the money. I also recall that in spite of the frolicsome Madden lifestyle, Grandma Betsy's cooking and discipline were on the Spartan side. "I will hit" was her trademark admonition, upon which she never delivered, but still. Grandma *Grace* wouldn't say such a thing. The packs of baseball cards I craved, Grandma Betsy prohibited; I could read the box scores if I wanted to follow baseball, she said, or listen to the radio. To her mind, the stiff pink slabs of bubble gum that came with the cards were "a pox." Once, when I tried to impress upon her my sacred obligation to stay abreast of the latest Topps offerings, she jammed her salty index finger between my lips and convincingly mimicked a dentist's drill boring sideways into a molar. "You want that? Is *that* what you want?" Swearing not to chew the stupid gum, to let her watch me throw it away, made no dent at all in her veto. "I know you, Jim, don't I?" She did.

Grandma Grace took me to Mass, bought me cards, tried hard to fatten me up. She weighed Ellen and me the day we arrived and sent home weekly "progress reports" to our parents. Her devout Catholic husband, the man I was named for, had died of a heart attack in 1928, age thirty-five years and one month. My father was seven months old. In one version of the story, he was nursing at Grace's breast when his father, who was reading the *New York Times* and sipping iced tea, suddenly hugged himself, choking, and toppled off the green wicker sofa. He did not have life insurance, either privately or through Steinway and Sons, where he'd worked as an accountant. Grace's mother had to look after the boys while Grace went to work as a bookkeeper at a bank in Mineola. Five months later, after the stock market crashed, the bank laid off a third of its employees, including every woman. Only male heads of families kept their jobs.

Having raised two fatherless boys during the Depression, Grandma

Grace took extra flesh as a sign of prosperity and good health. During the summer of 1960 she lovingly poured whole cream over my Farina and Corn Flakes. I got Hershey bars after lunch, two or three egg custards for dessert of an evening. Within weeks she had me hooked for life on sugar, LDL cholesterol, and polyunsaturated fats. If I die, as I almost certainly will, before my threescore and ten, it will be thanks to Grandma Grace's dietary regimen combined with Grandpa Jim's genes. No wonder I want to be Bad Jim in the too-little time I have left!

Bad Jim was born that same summer, in fact, up in Mahopac. Tom and Betsy's house had a roof and a floor but no solid walls yet. We slept on army surplus cots or in hammocks hooked up between joists, grilled burgers over a charcoal fire, made long trips for ice, deployed lanterns. "Our shanty-Irish campgrounds," Grandma Betsy called the house. "Not like your lace-curtain grandma's." We also lacked plumbing that summer, and somehow it fell to the eldest nonadult male to empty the "slops" in the woods every morning: one galvanized bucket and a couple of milk bottles, each with an inch of tea- or champagne-colored fluid sloshing around in the bottom—tea-colored, mind you, from the filterless Chesterfield butts floating in solution. As far as turds were concerned, Grandma Betsy declared we were "all on our own," i.e. we went in the woods, and I'll always respect her for that particular edict. *Sinn Fein!*

When Betsy was off somewhere else, Grandpa Tom and his divorced, alcoholic son, my Uncle Thomas, introduced me to tools, tackle, blueprints, pinup girls, cigarettes, and Irish whiskey—for me, cut with ginger ale. There was also a ten-year-old Italian girl named Margie staying up the sandy dirt road from us, and I was tauntingly encouraged to visit her there. And I did. She had brown hair, brown eyes, tiny scabs on her knees, and a tan—what more could I want in a woman? *Should we bring Margie with us to the lake? . . . Now, Jimmy, what have you and Miss Margie been up to?* It was humiliating, repulsive, and thrilling. For a few weeks I thought that I loved her, whatever that meant, and dreaded my returns to Fordham Road. But I never told Margie, of course. And besides, what I *really* cared about that summer was baseball, especially now that it had confronted me with a shattering moral dilemma. Caught between my Bronx-born loyalty to the Yankees and the fever I had as the Go Go Sox competed for their second straight pennant, I couldn't decide whom to root for. I was president, after all, of the Lisle chapter of the Nellie Fox fan club and had "doubles" of most of his teammates, plus I already hated the Cubs— yet my navy blue NY cap looked so sharp, and the Yankees had Whitey and Yogi and Mickey. When Uncle Thomas took me to see the Sox play in Yankee Stadium—decent seats down low along the right-field line, outside the 296 mark—I sipped beer and waffled from inning to inning. Because of Margie and the Maddens and baseball, I needed to go to confession, and Grandma Grace made sure I did. *Bless me, Father, for I have sinned. My last confession was seven days ago. I've had a hundred and twelve impure thoughts, Father. I sipped beer and whiskey, disobeyed my grandparents, rooted for two teams at once. For these and all of my sins I am heartily sorry.* I liked words like *whiskey* and *rooted*.

Evenings in Mahopac we listened to Yankee games on a transistor radio, munched watermelon and spit the seeds outside through the walls, and played poker. The first few times, the grown-ups let me use a "cheat sheet" listing the ranks of the hands, but soon I was insisting I'd never needed it. We played mostly five-card draw, the rules of which were set forth by that ultimate authority, Edmond Hoyle—or, in Grandpa Tom's argument-settling citations, "Dat's accawdin' to Hurl." Each player was dealt five cards facedown, and you needed a pair of jacks or higher to open the betting; once someone *else* opened, however, you could raise and reraise them with anything. Before the next round of betting you could turn in as many as three of your cards and get three replacements, and the new five-card hand was what you bet on and took to the showdown. With all the draws and bluffs I ran I must have lost steadily, but even when I busted out of chips Grandpa let me play what he called Relief Poker, though Hurl doesn't mention this variant. I couldn't bet any more but could still win half the pot if I had the best hand at the showdown. Then I went back to nonrelief status.

Among other stunts, I loved standing pat and raising with nothing, but I'm told that my worst tactic was calling with hands like the ace and four of diamonds. So long as I had a suited kicker, I was perfectly happy to draw three to a flush; I could also make cool things like *wheels*. I must have filled these ridiculous long shots, or made aces up, more than my fair share of times because I distinctly recall being scolded for recklessness—"Fold dem hands, Jimmy! My Gawd!"— while scooping huge pots from the grown-ups. "Doncha know the odds against that?" I didn't; I didn't care, either. Getting shipped a big pot on a bluff was the first wicked thrill of my life, unless it was grappling with hard, golden, slippery Margie in the deepest, coldest part of Lake Mahopac. Her two-piece blue swimsuit had ruffles fanning out from the bottom that fluttered against my hands or face as we pretended to "save" one another. (It couldn't have been more than a year or two earlier that I'd gaped at the slack, pale cleavage down Grandma Grace's blouse and decided: so *that* was where ladies' crotches were.) But as much as I loved saving Margie, I absolutely cherished the sound, the very idea, of a *flush*, maybe because the lack of a functional toilet made my mornings so cringe-worthy. Even forty years later, drawing to flushes can still remind me of the Mahopac house, which then makes me think of Richard Pryor's urine-sample routine: *Outta the way! I'm comin' through with the piss now!* I also hear, "Fold dem hands, Jimmy!"

Grandpa Tom's copy of Hurl didn't survive all their moves, but a few years ago I became the reverent beneficiary of seventy-seven of his monogrammed poker chips. Thirteen red, thirty-nine white, twenty-five blue molded plastic disks, each with TMN stamped in gold on one side. Thomas Nicholas Madden, 1900–1973, beloved grandfather of Bad Jim McManus. From the size of the taped-together box the chips came in, the original set must have had twenty-five each of red and blue, to go with fifty whites. In a faded blue scrawl on the top is his table determining payouts:

300–340	2¢
350–390	3¢
400–440	5¢
450–490	10¢
500–540	15¢
550–	25¢

My guess is that the buy-ins were ten cents apiece for six players, since the small folding table we played at couldn't seat any more than that. My opponents that summer must have been Tom, Betsy, and Uncle Thomas, along with a neighbor or two. (I don't think Margie's parents played with us, since she would have come, too, and I couldn't have focused on poker.) To make the stakes feel higher, Grandpa Tom must have multiplied the chip values by ten—hence all the zeros in the left column. I've noted as well that by winning just 25 percent more chips than the fourth-place finisher's 440, your prize would be five times as lucrative. And *still* I would draw to those flushes!

Late that August, Grandma Grace flew back to Chicago with Ellen and me and moved into our house in Lisle, escalating the war for my soul between her—and, implicitly, my dead grandpa, Jim—and the Maddens.

James Loughlin McManus had been born May 20, 1893, into a devout Irish Catholic family living in Providence, Rhode Island. (Two of his brothers were later ordained Jesuit priests.) Jim was working as an accountant in Newport when the U.S. declared war on Germany. He immediately enlisted in the navy and wound up serving as a fireman first-class aboard the minelayer USS *Baltimore* as part of Squadron 1 in the Northern Mine Barrage. He also got his start as a writer.

None of Jim's shipboard letters survive, nor do any he received. All we have is one small empty buff envelope addressed to him in what looks to be a young woman's handwriting: *Mr. James L. McManus, U.S.S. Baltimore, c/o G.P.O., London.* Affixed upper right is a brown three-ha'penny stamp featuring King George V's bearded profile. Canceled in Edinburgh at 2:30 p.m., 12 September 1918, the letter most likely reached Jim before he sailed back to New York in October. No one in our family has any idea what happened to it after that. If the envelope was scented with perfume, that, too, has faded into premodernist oblivion.

We also have the shipboard journal he kept in a notebook of five-by-eight-inch blue-lined paper. The first entry is for March 4, 1918, as the coal-powered *Baltimore* steams out of New York Harbor. Jim's shipboard duties include putting out fires, coaling and cleaning the boilers, taking on mines, laying them into the ocean. The primitive hundred-and-twenty-pound booby traps often detonate prematurely, maiming or killing dozens of his fellow sailors. *Commenced mining at 5:15 a.m. At 5:35 a violent explosion was heard. This was followed by many others. It was learned that the mines were exploding through some defects. We laid 180 and had two explosions. Was on watch in the engine room at the time. Felt an almost indescribable thrill when the first explosion occurred as I thought we were under fire. Expecting to meet a part of the German Navy at any time.*

Safely across the Atlantic, finally, and into the Irish Sea, he makes not one reference to his ancestral island. But steaming up the Clyde past Glaswegian shipyards, he writes: *The workmen pause in their efforts to defeat the Huns to wave a greeting. Shipbuilding was not the only work in progress. Aeroplanes could be seen in the yard of the Albion Motor Car Co. Another place was making the much talked about "Tanks." They were being tried out on ground especially prepared for them. Whilst different workers came out to greet us, we were surprised to note that young women were amongst them. They were clad in khaki overalls.*

During eight months at sea in a war zone, including fifteen days of shore leave in various Scottish cities, this is the single mention he makes of any woman other than his sisters—and it's sociological, not amatory. What he thought about the woman with the Edinburgh postmark or what she wrote in her letter, he doesn't set down in his journal.

His entry for March 23, a Saturday night he spent on liberty in Glasgow, reads in its entirety: *Had an amusing evening watching the odd dances.* Yet the next day, Palm Sunday, he waxes on proudly about finding St. Patrick's Catholic Church in time to make nine o'clock Mass, adding: *Received evergreen instead of palm. Visited Fr. MacMahon S.J. of St. Aloysius Parish.* On Good Friday: *Attended Tenebrae at St. Aloysius. Received a host from Fr. MacMahon S.J. Wrote to Joe.* (Joe is his brother, a Jesuit.) Two days later, on Easter: *Went to church in the morning and evening.* As his great-granddaughter Bridget Madden McManus would say, "*What* the?"

Jim's main secular interest is baseball. The best players from each American ship compete in games on shore, and Jim tracks the *Balti-*

more team's progress. On May 20 he turns twenty-five. *Celebrated my birthday doing a good day's work.* He often jots quietly lyrical passages about the Highland scenery—*Sunrise unveiled a very quaint town, situated at the front of a chain of hills*—but never a word about drinking, fights, card games. The only acknowledgment he makes that any American sailor is tempted by even a wee dram of Scotch comes on May 30. *Went to the movies after purchasing a few souvenirs. Most of the "party" were in great spirits returning—mostly distilled.* Both puns combine with that "most" to suggest that he himself didn't imbibe. He doesn't mention it in the journal, but at some point he picks up a five-inch conch shell, which he eventually carries home and presents to the American girl he will marry in 1923: Grandma Grace. In the meantime, though, there he was: twenty-five, money and seashells in his pockets, neither married nor betrothed, at large in a friendly foreign port among war-weary lassies most of whose menfolk are off in the trenches or already dead. Jim gives no hint that he's tempted.

But for me, one of his four journalist grandchildren, the biggest surprise and frustration isn't what he leaves out but a pair of matter-of-fact revelations. On July 5 he notes in passing that he "wrote a piece for *Fleet Review*," and on August 1 that he wrote another "for the *Mine Force Semi-Monthly*." No word, however, as to their subject or the reception they received from editors, shipmates, or family members. No word that he plans to write more.

Upon discharge early in 1919, his character is rated "good," the two alternatives being "inaptitude" and "undesirable." He is five feet seven inches, a hundred and forty-three pounds. Eyes gray, hair brown, complexion "ruddy." On a scale of 0–4 ("0, Bad; 1, Indifferent; 2, Fair; 2.5, Passing; 3, Good; 3.5, Very Good; 4.0, Excellent"), he receives the following grades: "Seamanship, 3.0; Ordnance, 3.0; Signaling, 3.0; Marksmanship, small arms, xxx [NA, presumably]; Mechanical ability, 3.3; Knowledge of marine machinery, xxx; Ability as leader of men, 3.1; Sobriety, 4.0; Obedience, 4.0; Average standing for term of enlistment, 3.33."

Like the others who served Over There under fire, my grandfather was certainly a hero. No slugger, no ladies' man, no sailor-poet, no gambler, but a man to respect and look up to. A literate, sober, and

God-fearing man you could count on to squarely face moral and physical challenges. And a fledgling journalist on top of it. Better than Passing Jim, not quite Very Good Jim, he is solidly, officially, Good Jim.

After the war he lands a job as an accountant at Steinway and Sons in Astoria, Queens. In June 1922 (as *Ulysses* is being published in Paris) he meets Grace Lynch, a red-haired bookkeeper living with her mother and two sisters at 61 West Eleventh Street in Greenwich Village. Jim and Grace fall in love, become engaged. After saving as much as they can, they marry on August 25, 1923, at St. Joseph's Church on Waverly Place. No bohemians, they buy a house out in Carl Place, a tiny Long Island town nine miles east of the Steinway plant, tucked up against Mineola. Grace is twenty-five, Jim is thirty—on the old side, in those days, to be starting a family. (Betsy and Tom were married at the more typical ages of sixteen and nineteen.) But not *too* old. Their first son, Donald, is born eleven months later; their second, Kevin Joseph McManus (my father), on October 20, 1927. Calvin Coolidge is president, Prohibition in force. The Yankees have just won their second World Series. During the regular season, Babe Ruth hit sixty home runs, more than any other *team* in the major leagues, and Charles Lindbergh flew solo from New York to Paris. The Jazz Age is roaring along, the stock market booming, the country at peace. And people are buying pianos, especially Steinways.

If Jim did any writing since his days on the *Baltimore*, no evidence has ever turned up. Grace never mentioned it, either to their son Kevin or to any of Kevin's seven children, five of whom eventually became writers. Perhaps Jim was waiting until his growing family was financially settled before he took up his pen again. What is certain is that on June 20, 1928, he had a heart attack on the porch of the house in Carl Place. He died the next morning, age thirty-five years and one month. Don was almost four, my father not quite eight months. In effect, he would never meet his own father.

Even more than most families during the thirties, the McManuses were downwardly mobile. My father used to claim that even though movies cost only two cents when he was a kid, he and Don could seldom come up with four cents to go see one, let alone the dime it would take to really make a day on the town. (His context was usually the "scads" of loose change to be found atop the dryer or between the cushions of our couch.) Yet somehow Grace kept them afloat. She also made sure that Jim's Jesuit values were taken to heart by his sons. When my father graduated from high school, he was voted "Most Respected" by his classmates, and most people who met him later in life considered him a mensch and a half. After serving six months in the navy at the end of World War II, he graduated from Fordham University in 1950 with honors in English and immediately took a job as a salesman to be able to marry my mother, as well as help Don support theirs.

Mary Madden had known Kevin McManus since grammar school. Her own Irish Catholic family was better off financially, less bookish, and far less devout. Her father, Tom, and grandfather, Peter, had been asbestos workers at the Brooklyn Naval Yard during the First World War, exempting them from uniformed service, and both went on to prosper in the building trades. Her grandfather's name appears on a plaque in the lobby of the Empire State Building honoring individual union craftsmen who constructed it, with Peter Madden representing the asbestos workers. It was the first time working men earned $1.00 an hour, an almost Ruthian wage when admission to movies cost two cents and bread was three loaves for a nickel.

Tom Madden married Betsy Madden in 1919, and ten months later the first of their four children was born. Years afterward, their only daughter (my mother, born in 1928) worked out a little routine in which she struck an inbred-Hunchback-of-Notre-Dame pose and snarled, "Who says my parents were cousins!" They weren't, as it happened, but that didn't hinder the jokesters.

By 1925, Tom had become a building inspector for the City of New York. His job was to spot-check tenements for vermin, overcrowding, fire-code violations, or evidence that apartments were being used as breweries, stills, or bordellos; he then made reports to both the city and the landlord. Or he didn't. The details are murky, of course, since his daughter and wife are the principal repositories of lore about the family, but the fact is that slumlords, bootleggers, madames, and pimps wanted to make Tom Madden happy. With Betsy working part-time for the buildings department as well, the couple had double the power to move paperwork along much more slowly or swiftly. Without a signed and properly executed certificate of occupancy, for example, no landlord could rent out his property. A prostitute would lose her apartment if Inspector Madden chose to report her. Bribes could have taken the form of contraband, money, or favors. Did my grandfather take them? Seven decades later, my mother recalls that if her father had a white envelope peeping up from his breast pocket, her parents "would seem more relaxed." Perhaps it was only his paycheck.

What no one denies is that Tom developed a reputation as a dandy, a rake, and a gambler, a man who spent most evenings at "the gin mill" both after and before Prohibition was repealed in '33. Even Betsy, in her day a dyed-blond flapper eminently capable of fending for herself, always told us: "Your grandpa liked the ladies, and the ladies liked him." She was bragging, of course, not admitting. "She kept very close tabs on him," my mother reports on what is probably her least favorite subject. "She had to, and she did."

I believe her.

Throughout the Depression, most New York City employees were kept on the payroll by Mayor Fiorello La Guardia. (He is still considered a hero—or saint—in our family, even when we're forced to fly through his dysfunctional eponymous airport.) Though their pay was cut in half for a while, the Maddens were comparatively well off through the Second World War and beyond. Decades later, their Marxist-feminist granddaughter, Ellen McManus, now a Ph.D.'d rhetorician, re(de?)constructed things this way: "The Lynches and McManuses were very middle class in values, aspirations, and manners—'genteel' might be a better word than 'devout' in this regard—while the Maddens were pretty solidly working class. Because of Grandpa Jim's death, the McManuses were on their way down socioeconomically, and partly because of unions and the political power of the Irish in New York, the Maddens were on their way up, and Mom and Dad met at that intersection." Exactly! When Mary Madden married Kevin McManus on June 17, 1950, the honeymooning couple could afford $68.52 for two nights in a suite at the Plaza, a pair of $8.80 orchestra seats for *Gentlemen Prefer Blondes*, and round-trip airfare to Virginia Beach, almost unheard of extravagances. Otherwise, their means were quite modest.

I was born on March 22, 1951, a drizzling Maundy Thursday three trimesters to the evening after the nuptials. My timing was fortuitous on military grounds as well, since five weeks earlier my father had received a draft notice. He'd already served in the navy, but as a twenty-three-year-old childless male he was rated 3A once again. Conceived in the nick of time in Room 1214 of the Plaza under the auspices of the Holy Roman Catholic and Apostolic Church, Father Vincent J. Hopkins, S.J., presiding, the new James Loughlin McManus would spare his dad a tour of Korea.

Born on the Upper West Side of Manhattan, in St. Elizabeth's Hospital, I was brought home to St. Brendan's Parish in the Bronx. (Very little was accomplished by Irish Americans in those days without a saint or two getting involved.) My parents' apartment was at 300 Reservoir Place, near the intersection of Perry Avenue and 205th Street. Over the next nineteen years they brought home six other children: Mary Ellen, Kevin, Sheila, Brian, Terence, and Colleen. Although Terry plays blackjack sometimes and Brian trades futures at the Chicago Board of Trade, not one of my siblings plays poker. (Asterisk: During the seventies Ellen McPersonus, as we'd christened her, belonged to a discussion group at Barnard called Women's Issues Poker, in which, she recalls, "I believe I was the only straight member, and by far the worst player." She hasn't played since.) Neither of our parents played, either. So how did a nice Catholic boy like Good Jim remain hooked on such godless recreation? Didn't Jesus Himself banish gamblers and money changers from the temple? Turn Lot's wife to salt? And don't even mention what went on down the road in Gomorrah . . .

In October 1960, just a couple of months after my initiation into the pleasures of saving Margie and drawing to flushes, I began serving 6:30 a.m. Mass for Father Frederick Beller, O.S.B., on the altar of St. Joan of Arc Church. Grandma Grace always knelt in the first row of pews, right behind me. Did I enunciate my *Introibo ad altare Dei* crisply enough? Refold Father's chasuble with sufficient precision and reverence? Grandma Grace was convinced—and worked night and day to convince her "little lamb," Jim—that if any member of one's immediate family became a priest, every member would go directly to heaven the instant they died. ("As soon as one person dies, do they *all* die right then?" "No, dea', of cawse not.") Whereas people from priestless households risked centuries or millennia in Purgatory, and some went to Hell *for eternity*. I hadn't read Augustine or Dante or Sartre yet, so for me Hell was the puke-inspiring stench of spent matches *times a million*, caverns of fire crawling with (somehow unscorched) talking serpents, plus the absence of God's love (the one torture I thought I could deal with). Didn't I want to guarantee that no one in my family would ever be sent there? I did. Yes, I did. And by pulling strings with Father Beller to allow me to become, at age nine, the youngest altar boy in our parish, Grandma Grace had paved the way for my scholarship to a seminary and, by the time I turned twenty-one, my holy ordination.

In the meantime, I took my acolyte's duties quite seriously. I scrubbed behind my ears (once, until one of them bled down my neck) before setting foot on God's altar, and made sure my Latin responses were flawless. *Dominus vobiscum. Et cum spiritu tuo.* ("The Lord be with you." "And with your spirit." *Not* "You're damning us, Nabisco." "Matt cums parting her tutu," as the daringest altar boys muttered.) While the rest of the fourth graders were at 11:20 Mass every day, I got to stay behind in the classroom and help Sister Doris distribute the little red and white milk cartons, a perfect opportunity to sneak peeks into girls' desks and lockers. What kind of sandwich was Ruth Ann Patten having for lunch today? Did this new silver locket mean Laurie Neff liked A1 LeClerque? Outside, on the public diamonds, I learned to my horror that Gordie Halliday, the third baseman on my Little League team, wasn't Catholic—and therefore could not go to Heaven—so I secretly redeemed him. *I baptize you, Gordie, in the name of the Father, and of the Son, and of the Holy Spirit*, this while applying a thumb-smear crucifix of tap water to his forehead as he lay prostrate on our couch with his hands pressed together and "pointing towards Him." I'd made Gordie wear a white long-sleeved shirt to receive the holy sacrament, and I called him up the next few Sunday mornings to make sure he'd gone to Mass—until his parents called mine and

Gordie went back to being a Lutheran. God, damn him! I consoled myself with the thought that, while Gordie would now go to Hell, at least our hot-corner guardian had been spared an eternity in Limbo. *Amen.*

By junior high school, thank God, some things began dawning on wretchedly sanctimonious Good Jim. Recruiters from Jesuit seminaries as far away as Boston and Florissant, Missouri, continued to visit our house, but I was forced to admit that I no longer positively, absolutely "felt the calling." It occurred to me that sports, poker, drinking, and girls might somehow be preferable to lifelong chastity and celibacy, much to Grandma Grace's chagrin. In her own gentle manner, she guilted me for all she was worth. "Oh, Jim," she would moan if I cursed, or even if I combed my hair like Brian Jones. "What, Grandma? Jeez!" Eyes downcast, shaking her head, she went off to Mass by herself. The little lamb was taller than her now, he knew where her crotch was, and all this new stature and wisdom had steeled his resolve to be Bad.

During the summers I still caddied, went to church-sponsored mixers, played baseball and tennis and golf, but my job on the golf course rekindled my appetite for poker. My friend John Collins and I got thoroughly schooled in the caddy shack of the Hinsdale Country Club by the full-time professional caddies, guys with names like Doc and Tennessee. These worldly dudes must have drooled on their stubble when the cocky little Catholic-school striplings showed up after a couple of five-hour loops and put our entire eighteen or nineteen dollars on the table. The game here was seven-card stud, with one-dollar betting limits, made even scarier by playing with actual bills. (We also played hearts for twenty cents a point, so shooting the moon even once could be worth a day's pay.) Nothing school, church, or family had to offer could compete with the rush of taking down a twenty-dollar pot, or with the gutshot devastation of losing two days' wages on the turn of a card. My father picked me up late on a Sunday afternoon, took one look at my poker face, and somehow got me to confess that I'd blown every penny I'd earned. The Hinsdale caddy shack was off limits to me for a while, so I had to go loop out in Naperville, where they played five-card draw, jacks or better—my game. And sooner or later, I prospered. So another thing Grandma Grace was up against was the vow of poverty priests had to take. Even Good Jim liked money. He had a savings account at the First Bank of Lisle and spent languid hours gloating over the balance, which soon rose well into the low three figures. Bad Jim's wads of poker cash were sealed in a baggie, then stashed under the gravel of our crawl space.

During high school my friends and I hung out, smoked, drank, and played cards at whichever house our parents had abandoned for the evening, or where they would leave us relatively unsupervised so long as we stayed in the basement. My best friend, Reid Schaefer, lived in a treeless Lisle subdivision called The Meadows, which on parentfree gambling nights we referred to, sensibly enough, as Las Vegas. One guy we knew from St. Procopius College brought along his girlfriend, Frances Bender, though maybe it was the other way around. Like Reid and me and most of our friends, Bender Over went to Benet Academy, the Benedictine prep school across Maple Avenue from St. Procopius, so it must have been she who brought the guy to our games. Either way, she also persuaded other Benet girls to show up, and this led to untold and wondrous liaisons. Booze and grass soon got added to the mix, along with spin-the-bottle and strip poker, though there always seemed to be at least one money game also in progress. Playing for serious dollars against stoned or drunk teenagers, the tricks I'd picked up from the Maddens and professional caddies—*don't call, fold or raise; don't draw to backdoor flushes or inside straights*—were especially profitable, even though I was usually ripped myself.

As we all got better part-time jobs (mine was unloading trucks at Consolidated Freightways on the south side of Chicago), we played for more extravagant stakes. We spent our winnings on albums, beer, cigarettes, gas, guitars, vodka, lids of fifth-rate pot laced with God knows what ratsbane; on Stones, Doors, Hendrix, and Dylan concerts in the city, or seeing the Cryan' Shames or the Apochryphals, Joe Mantegna's badass cover band, at the Blue Village in Westmont; or on sojourns to New York abortion clinics, an eighteen-hour drive if you pushed it. Unable to swing one in time, Paul Nurbiss and Susie Gonda gave their baby up for adoption, while Jack Kavanaugh and Linda Tilley "had to" get married. On Halloween 1968, even Good Jim had something resembling conjugal relations with a blush-prone senior whose nickname, owing to her somewhat off-center green eyes, was Picasso but whom Bad Jim considered a number. Our "scene" went down upstairs in Jack Kavanaugh's twin sisters' bedroom, more specifically on the orange shag carpet under their Barbies and homework and *Rubber Soul* poster, which as a Stones person I could hardly approve of. Picasso's favorite singer was Joni Mitchell, which baffled me almost as thoroughly as the shifting tectonics of what we were up to. That same fall, one of my close friends was killed and another made quadriplegic as they drove home drunk in a rusty white Corvair from one of our games out in Naperville.

Girls, booze, drugs, cars, and cards—for my generation at least, poker was integral, for better or worse, to becoming a man of the world. Mostly worse. And for the next decade or so, I took these manly dicta a smidgen too much to heart. My only excuse is that they were reinforced by every song, book, movie, and slogan I was exposed to in those years. "Under My Thumb," "Rainy Day Women," *The Hustler, The Story of O, Lady Chatterly's Lover,* "Purple Haze," "Light My Fire," "Satisfaction," *The Cincinnati Kid, Portnoy's Complaint, Justine, Naked Lunch, Tropic of Cancer,* or anything else Grove Press published. The movies and songs had more visceral power, the books more complex human substance, but they all provided more or less identical counsel: get some, get off, get over, get down; get your kicks, get it up, get it on. These dicta were reinforced by neither of my parents, but what did they know? They opposed this behavior tooth and nail, for which I mocked them behind their backs, redoubling my efforts to thwart them. Grandpa Tom and Uncle Thomas were always interested in any girl I brought home, mainly to determine whether she was a number, a cutie, a looker, or a knockout. (My younger brothers liked to wrestle with the numbers, especially Patty Gerhardstein, whose name yielded several bad puns.) All Grandma Grace wanted to know was whether the girl was "nice." If she wasn't, if she was "that" kind of girl, the next time I went to confession I'd be told by the priest to say fifteen Our Fathers, fifteen Hail Marys, and make twenty-five ejaculations. *Nothing Portnoy and I can't handle*, Bad Jim guffawed, knowing he was about to take over.

What my family calls Jim's Lost Years went on, so they tell me, ad nauseam. I don't know whether I was a revolutionary during the Nixon administration, for example, but I certainly was revolting. While I laid back self-righteously stoned in some "crib" in New York or California, both Grandma Grace and Grandpa Tom died, she of a heart attack, he of asbestosis, a lung disease caused by inhaling the fibrous chrysotile dust back in Brooklyn. I made neither funeral. This was in '73, that *annus horribilis*, the year I met my first wife, the year my father had his first heart attack. Bad Jim remained at large in the world. His first marriage ended in 1988, just before his father died after being ravaged by a series of strokes. He met Jennifer Ann Arra in 1989, married her in '92, and became Good Jim again for a while.

Grandma Betsy's heart failed on January 19, 1994, her ninetieth birthday. Genetically, then, I was still drawing to a heart flush as I metamorphosed again into *Homo suburbanus*, this time as a father of four, sometime husbander of college funds, swallower of Prozac and Zocor and aspirin with my OJ and oatmeal each morning, uxorious consort of Jennifer. I wrote poems and fiction, including three novels published by Grove, and got a job teaching. Baptized James but called Jim, eldest and prodigal son of a motley Irish Catholic brood, naturally my hero was Joyce, which could hardly help resolve the Good-Bad imbroglio. Much like my hero, I drank, spent, complained way too much. Both of us lived, though too briefly, in Italy, put our writing ahead of our family, were superstitious, right-handed, no chef, and graduated from a public university, the best we could afford. Like James Aloysius himself, I had contempt for Catholicism but from time to time thought of myself as a priest of literature. My second novel was a pastiche of the *Odyssey*, too; Joyce's hero was an ad salesman, mine a left-handed pitcher, so of course *his* book wound up slightly higher than mine on the list of the century's greatest novels. But we both had weak eyes, bad teeth, skinny fingers, loved Homer and Dante and Shakespeare and Svevo, and were mostly monogamous sexual perverts obsessed with James Joyce.

Emulating the Joyce of *Pomes Penyeach*, I wrote a mediocre poem when my father died.

MY FATHER'S SUNGLASSES

"The best things in life are pink."
My father let me in on this fact
twenty-six years ago, as we waited
outside the First Bank of Lisle

for my mother. It's a Saturday
morning, late June or early July,
muggy and blindingly sunny,
even with my hat pulled down low.

"And it's hotter than Hell," he adds
from behind his brown, sweatstained
tortoiseshell sunglasses. I'm in
my itchy red Bronco League uni,

clutching a new green passbook
in my oily, broken-in Mantle.
My account has one line, $160.00,
money I'd got for graduation

plus some I'd made as a caddie.
I was rich, I thought then, but
I've started to feel kinda nervous.
Are pink, for Christ's sake? Than in Hell?

I need to look into his eyes.
We're gonna be late for my game,
I'm pitching, and I've got no idea
what my father is talking about.

A few years after he died, Jennifer and I took my mother and Bridget to Ireland. We swung by the Lough Derg of Heaney's *Station Island*, climbed Croagh Patrick with a performance-art troupe and 38,000 other penitents (not a few of whom ascended the jagged shale barefoot, spackled with blood to their shins), got searched at checkpoints in Belfast and Fermanagh, followed a stretch of Bloom's route through Dublin. We tarried, for Jennifer's sake, at the Irish National Stud and wagered extravagantly, for mine, on more than a few of its progeny. After losing steadily one long afternoon at the Galway Races, I happened upon a bookie named Kevin McManus. (Scores of private books were arranged in a big rectangle next to the track, each with a little kiosk posting in chalk slightly different lines on the horses, using binoculars to spy on each other's shifting prices.) I introduced Kevin to my mother, and she and I regaled him with parts of our family history. "You don't say," he said several times, "tat's amazin'," all the while gallantly flirting with "Morry." She loved it. Just before the second-last race of the day I bet forty punts, comeback money, on a stallion named Oh So Grumpy, strictly because he matched my wagering mood at that hour. He went off in the nine-furlong steeplechase at 27–1, and he won by five lengths. With an equivocal show of mock regret, Kevin McManus forked over a thick stack of blue twenty-punt notes touting Yeats' haughty visage, along with a couple of green and brown tenners that featured the ex-banker, Joyce. *Banc Ceannais na Heireann*, asserted their fronts, while their backs murmured, *riverrun, past Eve and Adam's, from swerve of shore to bend of bay, brings us by a commodious vicus of recirculation back to Howth Castle and Environs.*

I thanked him.

♣ ♥

TENSION-DISCHARGE

♦ ♠

Nothing is so powerful in drawing the spirit of a man
downwards as the caresses of a woman.
—AUGUSTINE

The commonest mistake in history is underestimating
your opponent: happens at the poker table all the time.
—GENERAL DAVID SHOUP,
President Kennedy's adviser
during the Cuban Missile Crisis

Seven and a half hours later I have unwelcome company in the Alvarez pool. The strong swimmer splashing away my tranquillity—and
preventing diagonal laps—is a dark, beefy guy with a mustache. When
he finally climbs the hell out, I recognize him as Humberto Brenes, a
Costa Rican player I met a few days ago. He showed me his World Series bracelet (for Omaha in 1993) and invited me down to San Jose to
play in his poker club at the Hotel Corobici. The laminated four-color
business card he gave me features a toucan with a foot-long nutcracking beak. Even if I don't make the trip or see Humberto ever again, it's
the kind of thing that will always look great in my Rolodex. I go back
to swimming diagonally.

The Vegas bookies have fixed the over-under for the winner's age at
forty-three, so after I get out of the pool and reintroduce myself, I ask
Humberto the obvious question. It turns out we're both forty-nine. I
have four kids, Humberto has three; he has a bracelet, I don't. So he's

Ferguson and the author, with Cloutier in foreground.

got me. We wish one another good luck, though Humberto insists I won't need it, given the size of my stack and how well he has heard I am playing.

What's the Spanish for *Oh, you are too, too kind, Mr. Nutcracking Bullshitter*? Anyway. "Yeah, you either," I tell him.

Forty-nine, overs, well exercised—but still full of shit—we chuckle riding down in the elevator.

What Andy Glazer has dubbed "the Fabulous 45" have been randomly assigned new seats. As far as the over-under is concerned, a quick glance around the five tables says that fewer than a dozen are obvious unders, another good reason for me to bet the over, assuming I had any money. Whatever our age, our task is to play freezeout until six of us are left. How long that might take, no one I've talked to has any idea. "Till dawn, if necessary," is the least, or most, optimistic guess I've heard. Normally they play down to nine on Day 3, but this year's final table has been trimmed to six for the sake of the Discovery film. Too many contestants might spoil its hour-long format.

Humberto, with $101,000, is at Table 48, the most hazardous of the five. Plenty of chips to win there if you catch cards and play well, but with Boatman and Liebert wielding huge stacks, you risk being set all-in each time you enter a pot. Tom Jacobs' $229,000 makes him the boss of Table 47, which is way out of balance, with four stacks under $38,000. Annie, Hasan, and Mike Sexton are all at Table 54, the second most chip-laden group and perhaps the most talented. Annie and Hasan are both playing well, and Sexton is coming off a victory at the European No-Limit Hold'em Championship in Paris. A French TV crew has him miked for the action today. I've already heard him claim that unlike several of the other chip leaders, he's "no mathematician." Instead, he's "a pokeratician."

At Seat 6 of Table 55 sits its putative bully, yours truly. I've fantasized for decades about having a World Series stack imposing enough to make brutal sport of my opponents, but I have zero actual experience in the role. Do I feel any pressure? Of course not. I open the brag book to the *Big Hungry Bear* reading session then pour out my baggie of chips, stack them by color, recount them. Not that I think anyone would have stealthily siphoned a pink or an orange this morning, but still: $276,000, all present and accounted for. Does it make sense to say that one *loves* little towers of tinted clay disks? Did Grandma Betsy shit in the woods?

I spent the first two days gasping and thrashing and spluttering to keep my nose above water, with no one like Margie to save me. My new, much more glamorous job is to Jet-Ski along the surface—against the current, unfortunately, since my four most chip-laden opponents sit immediately upstream, to my left. Larry Beilfuss in 7, with $121,000, is a black-haired, bespectacled, all-business Milwaukean around my age; last month he made the final table of the championship event in Tunica, so he's gunning for two in a row. To his left in 8 is Dae Kim (high forehead, clear glasses, impenetrable black eyes) with $127,500, Hung La (gray hair, named Hung, enough said) in 9 with $197,000, and mean-looking Anastassi Lazarou in 1 with $125,000. Since chips tend to flow clockwise around a table, I'm in lousy position, despite my big stack, to kick major butt. *Boo-hoo-hoo-hoo, sniffle sniffle. Boo-hoo-hoo-hoo-hoo-hoo-hoo!*

Only two women have survived to this stage, though both of them arrived with colors flying. The other good news is that two out of forty-five (4.4 percent) marks a respectable uptick over the ratio of 18:512 (3.5 percent) who entered the starting gate Monday. Four point four percent must also improve on the rate at which women get indicted for first-degree murder, but I need to find out about that.

In the meantime, here on my right, I have a curly-haired Parisian by the name of Angelo Besnainou. He greets me with a smile and what sounds like Cuban salsa leaking from his earphones. Guitar, congas, drums, all from a half mile away. The jewel box reveals it to be Nocy's *Flames of Spain*. The young woman dancing in flames on the cover reminds me a little of Sandy. Barbarella in Hell, cha-cha-cha.

"You would like," says Angelo, pointing to the jewel box, "to hear?"

Is he kidding? "Not right now," I say. "Thanks."

He slides off the earphones. "I will get you a copy?"

Yes, please, I tell him, deploying immaculate French—not only to be amicable but perhaps to subtly intimidate him. Polyglots of my caliber must also be masterful pokerists, *non*? And now for the clincher: "*Merci.*"

Angelo has heard about my assignment and wants me to send him a copy of the finished article, so between hands we exchange addresses and phone numbers. Besides Linda Johnson and maybe Chris Ferguson, he's about the sunniest person I've met here so far. Even sunnier is the fact that he sits to my right with only $64,000, which I plan to relieve him of stat.

Par is now $115,000. At Level 11 the antes alone are $1,000 (three times the buy-in for my home game) with blinds of $2,000 and $4,000. At $15,000 per round, the average stack would be blinded off in about seven rounds. I have more leeway, of course, with my four yellow five-hundreds, fourteen blue-and-white thousands, twenty-four orange five-thousands, and fourteen hot pink ten-thousands. (And yes, I'm convinced of it: love is *exactly* the word.) The floormen have requested that we keep all our pinks to the fore, this to give opponents a fair chance to measure with whom they want to tangle. Or not.

As expected, the first player eliminated, over at Table 62, is Eric Shulz, who finished last night with a single $500 chip. An old poker adage says that all you need to win is a chip and a chair, especially since Jack "Treetop" Straus pulled off this miraculous feat in the '82 championship. But starting from so far behind at a table with Mel Judah, Cloutier, and Ferguson, that's what it remained for Mr. Shulz—an old adage. Even so, that single yellow chip flecked with black just earned him $15,000, the same prize the next eight eliminatees will receive. One of which, of course, could be me.

By the time the applause for Shulz dies away, Mickey Appleman has played three good-sized pots at our table, winning all three. Sitting next to Angelo in the 4 seat, he has just raised all-in once again. Angelo folds, and I'm in no position to play trouper holding Broderick Crawford (10-4), especially since I couldn't beat Appleman last night with K-K. After mucking my cards, I brush away what looks like cocaine or powdered rock salt from the baize in front of my chips. Was someone snorting lines or noshing Saltines here last night? I notice that the snowy debris is even more copious over by Angelo's stacks . . .

After studying for a minute, Beilfuss decides to call Appleman; Kim, La, and Lazarou fold. Pair of fives for Appleman, A-9 for Beilfuss. The flop comes A-A-5, a fire-breathing monster for Beilfuss but an even bigger one for Appleman, unless the case ace or a nine spikes. But fives full of aces holds up, ruining Beilfuss's morning while giving Appleman $180,000. What a rush the guy's on! It seems like he was down to felt only a few minutes ago. Plus it's good now to have all of those damn chips on my right.

In the meantime, the white mess turns out to be sugar and the culprit turns out to be Angelo. Catching him sprinkle out *more* of it, I stare at him, shaking my head. *"Monsieur, si'l vous plaît . . ."*

"For sweet life. You know?"

"No, I guess I don't," grumbles Bad Jim.

"Raise," says the guy in the 3 seat.

Mickey and Angelo fold. After folding 6-K, I brush away more of the sugar.

In the course of the next few rounds, always politely waiting until both of us have folded, Angelo explains that Tunisian Jews, of which he is one, have a tradition of sprinkling sugar on portentous objects: a new house, a tractor, a child . . .

"Like launching a ship with champagne," I suggest, pronouncing the word with two and a half froggy syllables.

"Eef you weesh."

I have to admit it's a beautiful concept. In *substance*, however, it combines with the moisture on our fingers to sugarcoat the cards as we play them, to say nothing of the chance of marking them inadvertently.

"Like your beautiful daughters," he says.

"Not really, Angelo. But thank you."

"Oh yes."

What can I say? I wish grains of sugar were my biggest problem right now. What I really need to be concentrating on is the ill-tempered Beilfuss and the inscrutable Kim snapping me off with reraises each time I've tried to steal their blinds. Have they no damn respect for the bully?

Down to $220,000, I decide to back off for a while. But when sitting on the button a couple hands later I find the same red jacks that came to my rescue on Monday, I raise Hung La's big blind with two hot pink chips. The best things in life are pink, motherfucker. So fold.

La shows how frightened he is by blasting back over the top of me without a half-second's pause. "All-in for one eighty-five," says the dealer.

Fuck you, Hung Chi Minh, you agrarian socialist prick! I should sic the Mad Bomber again on your rice-munching, chopsticks-brandishing ass! Why, I oughta . . .

I can tell he can tell I am scared.

The question, of course, is whether Hung Chi is counterattacking with a legitimate monster, unleashing his own Tet Offensive, or the reraise is just a knee-jerk retaliation for what he thinks is yet another positional raise on my part. He's probably showing the bully how sacred his Communist blind is. *Don't tread on me, Mr. Pictures! Mr. Lyndon Baines Johnson from Texas!!! Mr. NIXON!!!* Is that what he's thinking? Who knows! Not me, I can tell you. Instead of studying his face for the last hour, I've been chatting on Frenchly about saccharine hexes and Nocy, so I have no read on La whatsoever. It's also starting to sink in as to why you don't want to raise from the obvious steal-raise positions, though I was hardly on a steal with J-J. I study La's face for a twitch, blush, or arrogant confidence. Nothing. I don't think he has kings or aces, but I wouldn't put queens or a suited A-K past him. Nope. A-K is probably the *least* he is holding . . .

Tick tick tick . . .

Kissing my $25,000 good-bye, I put my tail between my legs and fold the damn jacks, and La mucks his hand without showing. It *oits.*

After licking my fingers and wounds for an hour, I'm only too happy to call, with K-K, a newcomer to our table who's just raised his last $28,000. Brown beard, blond bangs, long hair in back—a mullet, I believe it is called. Very stylish. Suitably embarrassed, he shows me K-10. *Oh* yeah, I gloat, mentally pumping my fist. I'm almost a 9–1 overdog, so it's time to get back in the game! But the Q-9-3 flop gives Mullet a belly-buster draw (9-10-x-Q-K) and me a sharp crimp in my lower intestine. Diverticulitis? No, terror. And when, sure enough, the beardless jack of clubs arrives on the turn, my chip count and confidence plummet to $97,000, a piddling sum at this stage. Just in time, too, for Level 12, when the blinds jump to three and six grand. So I'm doubly screwed in one swoop.

It gets worse. Subject to more realignment, I get high-carded to Seat 7 of Table 48. Waiting for me there, blood-flecked saliva dripping from their canines, are Hasan Habib in 4, Mike Sexton in 5, Jeff Shulman (the chip leader now, with almost $500,000) in 6, Tom Jacobs in 8, and in 9, T.J. Cloutier. Wonderful. My only chance here to catch up is to wait, not too long, for a monster to materialize between my knuckles, raise big, and hope I get called by a worse hand and don't get sucked out on. And then I have to do it again. And then I have to do it *again*. That's my plan.

Hands like 4-7, 7-4, Q-2, 7-4, and 5-J make it easy to sit out the first round or so. At least the person dealing me these rags is a ravishing woman whose name badge says Red, presumably because of her fox-colored, shoulder-length locks, these to go with wide hazel eyes and sly grin. Be that as it may, rags are rags.

T.J. has just raised Jeff Shulman's big blind, and the kid sits and thinks for a while. When he folds, T.J. "graciously" shows him K-K. Shulman laughs, mocking what he admits was a serious misread. "I'd put you on a medium ace."

T.J. laughs, too. "I was working my jaw, trying to make my heart pound through my shirt." Trying, in other words, to look scared and weak. He then chose to advertise the strength of the hand he had raised with. An A-9, A-10, or a medium pair he probably would have kept to himself: no need to come off as overly aggressive. Showing kings tends to prove he is cautious, which will buy more respect the next time he chooses to bluff. Not that he needs any more.

I try to bear all this in mind a few hands later, when it gets folded around to me and with a suited K-J, I raise T.J.'s blind to $20,000. This may not be the smartest move I've made this week, but I need to steal *somebody's* blind to avoid being blinded out myself. When T.J. mucks his hand, it feels like lead sinkers have been tenderly unhooked from my scrotum. Good girl, Mr. Cloutier! But just because a debatable raise worked *this once* doesn't make it a wise move in retrospect. I counsel Bad Jim to slow down.

Under the gun six hands later, Good Jim summons the discipline to muck pocket tens, a hand Bad Jim raises with from just about any position. So I feel pretty proud of myself, especially when Tom Jacobs follows my fold by raising the blind to $20,000 and T.J. smooth-calls him. Pretty proud? I am *thrilled* to be out of their way. I feel even better when the flop comes ace of hearts, eight of hearts, four of clubs, missing my tens by a mile. Now I can sit back without pressure and observe these two good old boys from up close, as Tom bets $30,000 and T.J. smooth-calls him again. As big as Tom is, T.J.'s bigger. Much bigger. And that seems to add to the drama. Not that heads-up action between physically smaller players (Chan and Jen Harman, say) can't be "Hector-Patroclus: The Rematch," but Jacobs and Cloutier are straight out of central casting: chain-smoking, cocky as hell, more than a little belligerent.

The turn card is the trey of hearts, for A-8-4-3 (with three hearts). Tom goes all-in. I immediately put him on a heart flush, of course, but when T.J. without hesitation calls for all of *his* chips, I have to put him on one, too. The question is, who has the heart king? Since it usually takes a better hand to call than to raise, I've got my make-believe money on T.J. Tom has him outchipped by $125,000, so if T.J. loses the showdown he'll finally be outta here. Good! Intimidating as Tom is, he scares me a little bit less, so I have a strong rooting interest as Tom flips over A-8, top two pair (with no hearts), and T.J. reveals . . . pocket fours. But of course. T.J.'s bottom set was good all along, and he knew that. My embarrassing little secret is that neither of them had even a flush *draw*, let alone an actual flush. My only solace is that when I made these dead-wrong reads I didn't have chips in the pot.

T.J.'s new $400,000 stack threatens to make him boss hoss, the role he was surely born to play, and it takes him one hand to start bullying. Raise. Raise. Raise. Reraise. When it isn't him attacking, it's Jeff Shulman again. And with Shulman's vast stacks on my right, I'm developing a severe case of big-stack envy, somehow made worse by Red sitting there in the box. (All the dealers wear white shirts and long black bow ties with HORSESHOE printed vertically down each dangling end, and on Red it looks quite fashion-forward.) With the blinds at $3,000-$6,000 and $1,000 antes, the raises have been to at least $20,000, so it's risky to try to fight back. The rest of us know that they're probably stealing with half of these raises, but we're also aware that sometimes they're attacking with genuine hands, and it would be just our luck to play back when the raiser holds aces or kings. Ruthlessly taking advantage of our uncertainty isn't Shulman and Cloutier's right, it's their *job*, which makes me despise them no less. Even when I find pocket queens I'm shy about betting them, for fear of a volcanic response from yon glowering chimney or an isolating reraise from Shulman. I nonetheless raise it a third of my stack, which comes now to $31,000.

T.J. stubs out a butt, fingers chips. As I cower at the prospects, Tom Jacobs, cur that he is, must smell my fear, because *he* decides to reraise all-in. The only good news is that T.J. elects not to compound my peril; nor does anyone else at the table. With the third best starting hand possible, I have no real choice but to call with my last sixty thousand. Gasping for oxygen as inconspicuously as possible, I show Tom Q-Q and watch him turn over . . . *whew* . . . nothing scarier than the J-10 of clubs. Big-time bluff. And since I have the queen club he has even less of a chance with his draws.

Red burns and turns: ace of diamonds, seven of clubs, jack of hearts. Harmless enough pair for Tom, I tell myself, panting, but no straight or flush draws, thank God.

Red once again burns and turns: six of hearts. *Eggselent!* With a club flush no longer in the cards, only a jack or a ten can save Tom, and who in God's name expects that? Besides me. The cameras loom down and poke through. I exhale. Red's job is to milk the suspense just a little, and under any other circumstances it would be my great pleasure to watch her. Right now all I can concentrate on is the spot on the baize where her right hand is placing the dreaded, the gloriously redemptive, the red . . . diamond deuce.

"Good hand," says Tom.

"Thanks."

"And good call."

As Red shoves me the lifesaving pot, I'm tempted to slide her a blue-and-white chip, as a tip. Since she wouldn't be able to cash it, however, I beam via heart waves and dilated pupils my gratitude. Given a spit test right now, my testosterone would spike through the roof.

As though Red gave me unfair advantage, however, someone decides three hands later that it's time for new dealers. Bad Jim considers protesting.

"Thanks, Red," I say, with what feels now like genuine love.

"Good luck, players," she says, getting up sveltely, to be replaced by a young guy named Paul. Maybe it's just me, but the valences of the table seem to shift microscopically. It could be the hour, the cameras, the prestige and money at stake, or just me missing Red, but it's different.

Right away Hasan puts the short-stacked Anastassi Lazarou all-in. Both of them show us an ace, but Hasan's kicker is a nine, Lazarou's only a six. The flop comes 5-5-K, the turn is an eight, the river a jack. As Lazarou gets up from the table, Paul shoves the pot to Hasan. *Way to go, Hasan,* I am thinking, *one less player between us and tomorrow's big money,* when a commotion erupts along the rail and Lazarou explodes through the crush and arrives, breathing hard, at the table. "The pot was split!" he yells. "Give me my money back!"

By this point the cards have been mucked, but T.J. and Paul still try to reconstruct the hand. Bob Thompson arrives behind Paul, switching off his mike before asking for a recap. With my scant short-term memory—the last ninety seconds being my diciest period—all I can do is observe. Everyone else agrees that Hasan had A-9, Anastassi A-6. The board cards are also conceded, especially now that Paul has retrieved them from the muck and laid them face up: 5-5-K-8-J. To me it still looks as though Hasan won with . . . *whoa.* The winning hand was 5-5-A-K-*J,* not 5-5-A-K-9. Once the jack fell, Hasan's nine no longer played over Lazarou's six. We'd all been expecting it to, and that was how we'd seen it. A similar sequence developed last night, when my A-J split the pot with T.J.'s A-10, but that time the dealer had noticed; if he hadn't, of course, T.J. would have quickly let him know. It does make me feel less oblivious now that no one else noticed *this* tie: not Paul, whose job is to call the best hand before pushing (or splitting) the pot; not T.J., a pokeratician who seems more in charge than the dealers and whose laser eye I've seen guestimate a messy pile of multicolored chips to within fifty dollars; not even Lazarou, whose tournament life was at stake. Only Phil Hellmuth, sitting and chatting with Andy Glazer two rows behind the action, had caught it. (As Hellmuth later explained, he "saw the split coming" and felt he had no choice but to mention it to Lazarou. "The cameras would have caught it anyway," he said, "and that wouldn't have been good for the tournament.") This is the plainest evidence I've witnessed of the measureless card sense the top players have. Geniuses like Hellmuth and Preston and Chan (and usually T.J.) not only see things that other players don't, they see them before they even happen.

After the exact size of the pot has been deduced from the antes, blinds, and bets, Hasan passes Lazarou half of the chips back: one white, seven orange. Hasan seems to take it in stride. "No prrroblem, buddy," he tells Paul, who is busy apologizing for the third or fourth time. (Red, of course, would have kept everything straight to begin with, and looked smashing doing it; in fact, if she had been dealing, Bad Jim would have won the whole pot.) I'm forced to concur with all the pronouncements that this was "the right thing to do," but I also imagine how it would feel to give back chips I'd already been fondling. Ouch.

Meanwhile, on the chicks-with-decks front, two big developments. Annie Duke has been high-carded over to our table, sitting down with an unborn child and $325,000 in front of her, but no shoes or socks; and Kathy Liebert has been bounced from the tournament. Her announced prize money for seventeenth place comes to $39,120, but missing the final table and a shot at the bracelet must be shattering for her, especially because of how long she was running in front. While our table was settling the Lazarou mess, Liebert got tagged with a freak one-two combination. Entering a big pot with queens, she was caught by K-10, then lost the rest of her chips five hands later when Mike Sexton called *her* K-10 raise with Q-Q, and that time the queens held up. Brutal. I also can't help thinking of the $30,000 chunk I took out of her last night with A-Q. Having those three extra pinks when she raised tonight with her queens might have kept her opponent from calling with a toilet-paper hand like K-10. Physicists have known for a while that the process of observation changes the thing you're observing, but in this case it feels weirdly unsporting and personal—as if I helped to determine whether Liebert was a wave or a particle.

But as much as my journalist self now wants Duke to advance, I can barely keep from whooping when, sitting in the small blind, I find pocket kings, this after Annie has already raised it four pink. I reraise eight more, flashing her what I hope is a friendly but confident smile. Her response is to say, "I'm all-in."

Terrified of aces, I still have no choice but to call. She's got me outchipped by about seventy thousand, so it's me, not her, who's all-in. I timidly turn over my kings as she snaps down . . . queens. This is good, is it not? Getting all my money in the pot as the 4–1 favorite? I hope.

The flop comes 2-7-A, leaving Annie about a 43–2 underdog: the other two queens vs. every other card in the deck. So why don't I feel more exuberant? It must have to do with the way our table has suddenly become the matrix of Annie Duke fandom. At least fifty people are ferociously pulling against me, the women in particular training miasmas of estrogen onto my innocent cowboys, willing them to be bushwhacked by queens. (Who was it that called poker "the art of civilized bushwhacking"? Freud? Kenneth Clark? Barbara Bush? Kate? Larry Flynt?) Bob Thompson's amplified reminder that Duke is the last woman left in contention only whips them up further.

"*Annieeeeeeeeeeeeeeeeeeeee!*"

"*You go, girl!*"

"*C'mon, QUEEEEEEEEEEEEEEEEEEEEEENNNN!!!!!!!!*"

A third queen, they seem to believe, would confer some amorphously millennial Gender Justice, paying Bad Jim back *personally* for two hundred years of poker domination by men, plus thousands of years of the other kind. But their vibes and miasmas (I won't say hysteria) have a rational aspect, of course, since their girl is a better player than I am, period. On top of her skill and high-stakes experience, she is backed by the cumulative poker acumen of Howard Lederer, Jen Harman, Melissa Hayden, and the other circuit regulars watching this, all of them beaming *malocchio* onto my neophyte, outsider gall, conveniently ignoring that no one wants this woman to win the event more than I do, *just not this pot.* They're also willfully downplaying the fact that Poker Justice says kings should beat queens every race, or at least four times out of five. But even my new friend and fellow writer Katy Lederer is Fury-ously rooting against me.

Hysteria.

Fourth street comes the seven of clubs, making their calls for a queen even louder, more desperate. Duke herself sits there with stoical coolth, probably not buying into that Gender Justice crap for a second, God bless her! To counter her earth-mom fecundity, my brag book is open to the same bathtub splash fest that presided over my hand against Tom Jacobs, even though I'd also been helped by Red's loveliness, although—maybe not. Maybe the splash fest was and still is enough by itself to make this next card a nonqueen. Hows about a king, for good measure?

But no. Jack of diamonds, missing the queens by a pip. Thank you, fair-minded poker gods, poker goddesses. Thank you, splash fest. Duke gives us all a brave smile, but it's clear that she's pissed. Barefoot and pregnant and pissed.

Her fan club will have to get over it.

With almost $380,000, I can afford to wait for big pocket pairs, letting other folks play the riskier hands. When I enter a pot from now on, I'll be able to raise with aplomb. Unscared money is always less vulnerable to intimidating wagers in no-limit (as compared to the limit games I'm used to). The brag book has also been helping me trick myself into almost not caring about the money involved. The *tao* of the beautiful wife, of the happy and beautiful children. Even if I happen to lose all my chips the next hand I play, it will not be the end of the world. Fifteenth place pays $46,640 on my $4,000 investment, and look what I have to go home to.

Midwestern Guy thus can gaze with Far Eastern serenity as Rabbi Steve Kaufman raises from one off the button and Mark Rose reraises all-in. Kaufman calls right away, as why should he not with A-Q? When Rose flips over 3-3, we have the classic hold'em showdown of a pair vs. overcards. With five cards to come, the pair is about an 11–9 favorite, but when the flop comes all rags (but no trey), Rose becomes a much heavier favorite. Kaufman spikes a queen on the turn, though, instantly whipping 3-3 into underdoghood. The river produces no trey, so as the dinner break arrives we are down to fourteen contenders.

My fellow journalists keep asking how it feels to be in this position, but I don't know how to answer them, especially while trying to pee or, now, eat. Most often I say, "It feels great" or "I'm in shock, but I feel very lucky," both of which are perfectly true. Back in the men's room, to spice up my answer a little for an *R-J* reporter who knows I'm also covering the trial, I said, "It feels like what Kramer's ex-lawyer stipulated about the breasts of Seinfeld's ex-girlfriend. Spec*tac*-ular." But I don't think he'd seen, or remembered, that episode.

"The very last one," I said, killing the joke even deader. "The one where they all go to prison?"

"Sex is good but poker lasts longer, you mean?"

"Something like that. Though I guess it depends on—forget it."

"Consider it forgotten," he said, though I sensed he would use it to make Bad Jim look like a pig—not the most challenging journalistic assignment he'll ever have, come to think of it.

What I haven't brought up to anyone is my discovery that winning big pots on Day 3 can quicken the blood, shall we say. I've read about this phenomenon but never experienced it personally, though I don't think I should be too surprised. David Spanier, among many others, claims that poker "has an intimate connection with sexual drives," then quotes psychoanalyst Ralph Greening on its procreative cadence: "There is a rhythm of tension-discharge, which is constantly repeated." Greening further proposes that poker showdowns may be equivalent in the unconscious to comparing penises with other men. What they might do for Jerri Thomas or Annie Duke is much harder to say.

Waxing ever more kinky, Spanier quotes the Freudian analyst Edmund Bergler, who asserts that compulsive gamblers are motivated by "psychic masochism," a desire to punish themselves for Oedipal transgressions. Such players, argues Spanier, "feel they are above the laws of probability. They trust to luck, usually personified in the feminine as Lady Luck . . . a will-o'-the-wisp deity forever beyond their call, for although sometimes she smiles upon them, in the long run she always spurns them." Long-run or short-run, poker in Spanier's view is about erotic titillation. "Playing with poker chips, counting them out, stacking them up, the smooth shapes and glistening colors, the sensual pleasure of handling the cards . . . it's all of a piece." With what? Masturbation, he says, most often related to submissive or dominant urges. After making his case in more scholarly terms, he cites an unnamed bisexual friend who confided to him: "I got a huge erection when I was losing one night really heavily. . . . In a dreadful way it was pleasurable. But then when I managed to win some of the money back, the excitement faded."

Can there be any doubt psychic masochism was part of the reason that Ted, having lost his mother, been left by his wife, and banned by the Gaming Commission, immediately fell for the tough-talking Murphy, a lean, blond Cruella DeVille in a G-string? *Lemme take you shopping at the handcuff store, honey.* We should also recall that Murphy's losing blackjack binge at Caesars Palace was what had forced her to take a get-even job dancing laps (not that anyone had to twist her arm), so masochism was probably part of her psyche as well. Lady Luck had just spurned both Ted and Sandy, and they needed to punish themselves. This makes the rhinestone-studded manacles they picked up (also at Caesars, that block-square toga party, shopping mall, and chancing emporium) perfectly natural accoutrements to their more public mating displays. If Spanier and Bergler have it right, a taste for rough sex and restraining devices may spring from the same psychic aquifers as do penchants for blackjack or horses or tumbling dice, especially when bruised ids and egos get stirred up with vodka and smack, and with smacks. It doesn't make rough sex a crime or even vaguely suicidal (or any less fun), but it can predispose the participants to scarier outcomes than tender caresses in the missionary position might. *La morte douce* thus becomes the logical extension of "rough stuff" prosaic as nipple clamps, pinches, handcuffs, and hip checks. We aren't bonobos, thank God.

In *Crime and Punishment*, the vodka-swilling Marmeladov's masochistic guilt provides him with intense pleasure as his beautiful young second wife drags him across the kitchen floor by his hair, in part because both of them are being financially supported by Sonya, his prostitute daughter. In suffering this penance, Marmeladov not only experiences sexual gratification but justifies, or pays in advance for, his *next* drinking binge, and the mouthwatering cycle continues. Literary psychoanalyst Louis Breger points out that Dostoyevsky's Underground Man longs for "the highest and best" in his relationships with women, even while admitting to debauchery with prostitutes. "Worse yet," Breger writes, "he recognizes that there is a kind of sexual pleasure in his own vileness, in his very attack on the romantic ideal." Nor can we doubt that what many folks think of as vile or unromantic was arousing to Ted Binion, too. (Good Jim is shocked, *shocked*, to be forced to consider such things, while Bad Jim is nodding and blushing.)

Lusting for a slap in the face, the Underground Man explains his own psychic masochism: "Despair can hold the most intense sorts of pleasure when one is strongly conscious of the hopelessness of one's position. And here, with the slap in the face, it is forced in upon you what filth you are smeared with." For all his tough-guy posing, Ted must have felt such despair. The worse his legal and domestic problems got, the more he craved strippers and wild sex and heroin, but the worse he was able to perform, leading to greater despair. And the longer the cycle continued, the less he was willing to support his resident hooker in the style to which she'd become accustomed. Finally cuckolded, handcuffed, poisoned turkey baster shoved down his throat, bare-breasted whore on his chest, her vagina still slick from congress with another man—Ted on that horrible Thursday morning wound up as filthy and "forced in upon" as a masochist is likely to find himself.

Dostoyevsky's own guilt about his simultaneous addiction to Paulina Suslova, a seductive twenty-year-old literary opportunist, and roulette closely parallels his narrator's bondage to a woman and the wheel in *The Gambler,* most of which takes place in a masochist's paradise called Roulettenberg, a stand-in for the Black Forest resort town of Baden-Baden. As the tormented author wrote in a letter to his sister: "Blessed are they who do not play and regard the roulette wheel with loathing as the greatest of stupidities." Writing much later to his second wife, Anna Grigoryevna Snitkina, he further develops the correlation between bondage and gambling: "Can you believe it, Anna, that my hands are untied now? I was shackled to gambling, body and soul." In his fiction, in his personal life, Dostoyevsky was determined to go, as he writes to his sister, "everywhere and in everything . . . to the last limit." Precisely as Tolstoy had been—the Tolstoy of *War and Peace* and *Anna Karenina*—before he turned himself into a boring, pedantic old saint. Precisely as Ted Binion had been. Only Ted went much further than either great Russian, of course. Ted preferred what was *literally* no-limit action, and he never sought canonization.

Was it Sandy or her "Teddy Ruxton Bear," as she called him affectionately, who wore those designer shackles at first? Once the metal clicked shut around one pair of wrists, how did their respective fantasies play themselves out in these high-octane rituals? We cannot guess all the particulars, but we know that each of them was the most reckless, obsessed sort of gambler. It also seems reasonable to accept R. J. Rosenthal's thesis that gambling is "an acting out of a meaningful fantasy, in which someone is doing something to someone else. There are rewards and punishments, with specific meanings, both conscious and unconscious, assigned to winning and losing." This echoes Breger's argument that high-stakes gamblers get "an illusion of power and control as a way of defending against depression and loss, uncertainty, helplessness and fragmentation, being overwhelmed by the uncontrollable" in other parts of their lives. Loss of control is vital to the handcuffed submissive's ecstasy, the fulcrum on which pain can tilt into pleasure, bondage into its opposite. It also sheds light on Ted's decision to hire someone as laughably undependable as Tabish to build a "secret" underground vault in which to squirrel chocolate chips and bars of silver, not to mention introducing him to his horny young girlfriend. (Snorting heroin and fraternizing with hit men like Fat Herbie Blitzstein fit the pattern just as neatly.) Even when we're not consciously aware that this is what we're up to, it's always a thrill to tempt fate. At bottom, the thrill is erotic.

Having chosen Sandy as his consort in the spring of '95, Ted never had a chance to get better. The acute psychic masochism shared and nurtured by Sandy got him permanently banned from the Horseshoe and strung out worse than ever, cuckolded and burked on the floor of his den, burglarized twice in the bargain. Dostoyevsky, on the other hand, was eventually able to kick his self-destructive roulette habit, but only after his true-blue second wife let him get it all out of his system. Anna also made him a father for the first time at age forty-seven, and surely that enhanced her salutary influence. But before that she went so far as to grant him permission to pawn their winter coats and wedding rings—on their honeymoon, no less!—to enable him to play more roulette. *My nature requires this*, he'd pleaded to her. *This is how I'm made!* Anna knew what she'd let herself in for. They'd become engaged only after she took down in shorthand his frenzied dictation of *The Gambler* in twenty-seven days to meet a deadline, and by succeeding earned three thousand rubles. Had he failed—had *they* failed—by even one minute, Fyodor Mikhailovich would have forfeited the royalties not only on *The Gambler* but on *all* of his books to his viciously opportunistic publisher. Talk about a gamble! Talk about going all-in! (And talk about "enabling" behavior on Anna's part.) Yet Dostoyevsky *lived* for contests like these. For him, gambling and genius and Russianness and love were gorgeously braided together, like Anna Grigoryevna's brown hair. To take risks, challenge fate, was an act of high poetry. *Once I hear the clatter of the chips*, he desperately explained to her once, *I almost go into convulsions*. Hear, hear! But even in Bad Jim's most out-of-control fantasia, pawning winter coats would never occur to him. Wedding rings, maybe. Not coats.

Jennifer Ann Arra has turned out to be my own brown-haired savior of a second wife, and when she dolls herself up to go somewhere with me, she often plaits her two-foot-long tresses—without even looking!—into a thick, glossy, intricate braid. Three years ago we were guests for five weeks at the Rockefeller Foundation's Villa Serbelloni in Bellagio—the one on Lake Como, where Fyodor and Anna spent part of their extended honeymoon, not Steve Wynn's pixillated facsimile. Villa Serbelloni sits several hundred feet above the town, at the tip of a thumb-shaped peninsula called La Punta Spartivento, the point where the wind is divided, and where the three arms of Como converge. The deepest freshwater in Europe, the lake here is hemmed in by Swiss and Italian Alps, fringed with gardens and hundred-foot cypresses. The site has been what can fairly be called an alpine destination resort for twenty-six hundred years, ever since a band of Celts built a fort there. Virgil and Catullus lovingly refer to the place, as do both Plinys, who had a summer home there, the Villa Pliniana, in the years just after Christ was born. The present villa was commandeered in 1943 by the SS, who deployed it as R-and-R quarters for Luftwaffe pilots. Ella Walker, the whiskey heiress, had purchased it in 1928, and she refurbished it after the war. She died in 1959, having bequested it to the Rockefeller Foundation, whose president that year was Dean Rusk. It was Rusk who decided the villa should be used as a haven for artists and writers and scientists.

The room Jennifer and I were assigned, No. 9, faces west and south, with views of the Lecco and Como arms. The director, Gianna Celli, informed us that President Kennedy had slept in Room 9 back in June of '63. He'd just made state visits to several European capitals, and an audience at the Vatican was scheduled with Pope John XXIII. But when the pope died before they could meet, Kennedy suddenly had a problem on his hands. *Air Force One* had already landed in Rome, but our first Catholic president's attendance at a papal funeral would make him appear unduly in thrall to the Vatican, as had been widely predicted he would be during the 1960 campaign against Nixon. Rusk, who was now secretary of state, persuaded his boss to lay low at the Villa Serbelloni instead.

When Jennifer asked what Jackie had thought of the place, Ms. Celli fixed her with a meaningful look. "Mrs. Kennedy did not accompany 'im at all to Europe. She must stay 'ome with their two children. But your president, he did not sleep alone." She said this as though we'd be shocked. The reason my eyebrows were raised was that it may have been Jack's final dalliance.

During our own romantic interlude at the villa, Jennifer and I must have had twenty-five days of brisk autumn sun, which gave first the Lecco arm of the lake a blindingly platinum glitter, and then, as we got dressed for sumptuous dinners, the Como. Beatrice Mairead was conceived near the balcony window of Room 9, just before one of those dinners.

We all burp and straggle back from the steak house or cafeteria to antes of $2,000, blinds of $5,000 and $10,000, with the last fourteen players redivided as follows:

Table 1	Table 2
1. Mark Rose, $223,000	1. Mickey Appleman, $540,000
2. Annie Duke, $130,000	2. Roman Abinsay, $330,000
3. Hasan Habib, $620,000	3. Angelo Besnainou, $70,000
4. Chris Ferguson, $305,000	4. Tom Franklin, $450,000
5. Jim McManus, $450,000	5. Jeff Shulman, $440,000
6. Steve Kaufman, $400,000	6. Anastassi Lazarou, $105,000
7. T.J. Cloutier, $540,000	7. Mike Sexton, $385,000

Annie has barely enough for a few rounds of antes and blinds, but if she can double through even once she'll be back in the ball game. Look at Hasan, though. And what a player Appleman must be, having started the day with $6,000! I'm glad that the draw kept us separated, though obviously Table 1 will be no picnic, either. Perhaps, for more sweet life, Angelo could switch with Hasan.

We proceed once again hand-for-hand, aiming to get down to six while making sure stalling won't pay. Between shuffles I get up and watch Angelo's A-6 lose to Jeff Shulman's A-10. Standing here with me, Katy Lederer is friendly as ever, even to the guy who just pissed in her big sister's Cheerios. Being from one of the most successful poker families on the planet, Katy knows better than I do how these things tend to go. "It ain't personal, Jim."

"I hope not."

She elbows me in the ribs, adds, "You monster," then gives me a drag off her Winston.

I remind myself how much seven-handed action changes the value of pocket cards, since you only have to beat six other players. Trouble hands like K-Q or medium pairs are now cautiously playable, even from early position. I need to not only lower my standards a notch, but account for the fact that my opponents will, too.

The most amazing thing to me is how calm I feel now, as though vying for the lead late on Day 3 of the Big One is all in a long evening's work. Yet the stack in front of me amounts to seven times my salary, three times the size of our mortgage. In real life back home, I make sure the kitchen faucet handle points toward Cold before rinsing a sippy cup; otherwise our water heater might burn an extra hundred and twelfth of a cent's worth of gas. Tossing five- and ten-thousand-dollar chips around like they're Monopoly bills makes the cosmos feel perfectly phat. (That's Hip-hop Jim talking, not to be confused with Hip-Replacement Jimbo.) I can't see every stack on Table 2, but I figure I'm in fourth, third, or second right now, and I understand that I can win. I can *win*. When the blinds double to ten and twenty thousand, in fact, I'm happy, not scared, since it feels like it's to my advantage to have the short stacks in twice as much jeopardy.

The next hand I play turns out to be one of the most widely discussed of the 2000 World Series, far more controversial than the dealer's mistake that almost eliminated Lazarou, or even the incident Monday night when a drunkenly abusive player was carried out in rhinestonefree handcuffs by Horseshoe security. This one starts innocently enough, with Chris Ferguson in the small blind making what has become our standard preflop raise to $60,000. With jacks in the big blind I'm happy to call him, especially since I've read his raise as positional. Hasan, who weirdly limped in from the button, also calls, so the pot's giving me better than 3–1 odds on my money. I've risked only sixty so far, but we're likely to take it much higher, which triggers the blend of *oh, shit* and *oh, well* that's been percolating down through my cranium each time I play a big pot, although jacks have been good to me all week.

When the flop comes A-Q-2, it's more like *oh, shit* and *oh, shit*, one apiece for the queen and the ace. The fecal sensation becomes more pronounced as Chris moves both palms behind his stacks, clasps them together with pale, bony fingers, and pushes them slowly toward the pot, making sure not to topple any of his precious pink towers. I ask

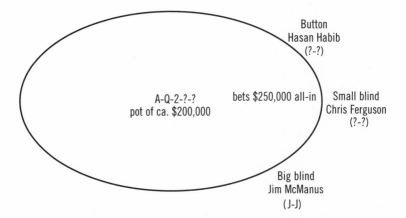

him to count it. "Two fifty," he says, without counting. I believe him, and the dealer confirms it.

Does it make sense to call an all-in bet with two overcards on the board and possibly more on the way? Of course not. At the same time, I don't want no Fred Astaire wanna-be going by the name of *Hey, Zeus* to be shoving me off my two jacks. I mean, no fucking way. And another thing: With the beard and the hair and the cheekbones and all, *Chris* ain't ironic enough for him as a nickname? What's next, stigmata? Another thing pissing me off is that Bob Thompson keeps vacillating between "Jesus" and "Chris" as he commentates, for which I blame Mr. "I like them both the same," and not Bob. If only it was the queen *or* the ace sitting out there on the board, and not both . . .

Nolan Dalla is sitting behind the dealer, taking notes for his *Card Player* column, which will have this to say: "McManus put his head down on the edge of the table and solemnly pondered his decision." Solemnly? Who am I now, Grandpa Jim? The image I have of myself runs more along the lines of Steve McQueen, blue eyes glinting flintily (glaring ferally? glowing frostily?) across the table at Edward G. Robinson, but I suppose we have to take Dalla's word for it.

T.J. and Annie and Sexton have been getting their share of the photographers' attention, but *Hey, Zeus* has become the new darling. His convex mirrored lenses must make for some swank photographic effects, so I'm sure they're all pulling for him to win the whole thing, as opposed to some puffily unphotogenic dad-type like me. But darn it all, I'm bad as well! Not only is my Volvo station wagon turbo-charged, it's *black*, thank you very much, with a black, yea black *leather*, interior. Can't they also appreciate my space-age titanium shades, or the four-color tatts of Sade and Réage on my scrotum, the latter inked in during my last stretch in Folsom . . .

Have I lifted my head from the table by now, Mr. Dalla? I hope so. Because I seem to have noticed that Hasan stands a few feet away from you, and he's speaking to Tony Ma. At first I assume that Hasan must have folded out of turn, but then I'm convinced I passed out for a spell and they played on without me. For a keener perspective, here's Dalla's column again: "McManus's deliberation captured much of the crowd's attention and lasted a considerable amount of time. Mean-while, Habib was still in the hand—but had not acted yet. He had stood up from the table and approached the rail. It's important to point out that Habib previously had taken a number of breaks while away from the table when he was not involved in a hand. So his action didn't seem to be out of character. Nevertheless, approaching the rail and talking to a bystander in the middle of a hand was a clear violation of tournament rules." Dalla goes on to point out that the bystander is in fact Tony Ma, the 1999 Player of the Year. "Without doubt, advice from a player of Ma's caliber would be priceless at the final stages of a tournament . . . It's certainly possible, even probable, that the two players were discussing strategy—specifically whether Habib should call Ferguson's all-in bet of $250,000. Witnesses reported that Ma seemed to shake his head. Habib subsequently went back to the table and mucked his hand when it became his turn to act."

This must have been immediately after I pushed my jacks into the muck. In the end my decision was simple: too many overcards, no read whatsoever on Chris. Even if I thought that Hasan might improve my pot odds by calling, I still couldn't risk all my chips.

As Chris rakes the pot, Bob Thompson announces, "All you play-ers, remember: one player to a hand." Amid the lights, cameras, chat-tering railbirds, I'm not even sure what he means. (It isn't until a month later that I read Dalla's *Card Player* account, including his com-ment that Thompson's directive was "sort of like making the announcement that robbery is illegal after the money has been stolen from the bank.")

In any event, that was *nothing*. Because three hands later I look down and find what certainly looks like Big Slick. I squeeze the cards harder, then peer in again to make sure. Yessiree: king of hearts, ace of diamonds. Swallowing as discreetly as possible, I wait my turn before pushing ten orange chips toward the unraised pot. "Fifty thousand," the dealer announces. The instant Rabbi Steve mucks his hand, T.J. shoves forward a tall stack of pink, snarling, "Raise." He may not have actually snarled, but that's how it registers down in my helices. And whatever the verb, it's another $100,000 to me.

In the final chapter of *Super/System*, Brunson says that A-K are his favorite pocket cards because you'll win more with them when you make a hand, and lose less when you don't; whereas A-Q, just one pip below it, is a hand that he famously refuses to play under any circumstances. T.J.'s book stresses that you have to win pots both with and against the A-K. "It's the biggest decision hand in the tournament." He considers the ability to play it effectively so crucial that in four of his twelve practice hands, the reader is given these pocket cards. And be still my computerized, book-learnin' heart and suck in my unChristlike cheeks, but I just have a feeling that T.J. is making a play while I'm holding it. Yet with two hundred large in the pot, what the hell is a feeling? The short answer runs something as follows: T.J. says that when *he* gets raised holding A-K, his response depends on *who made the raise*. I've studied the passage so obsessively, I believe I can quote it verbatim. "There are times when I will just flat call the raise. There are times when I will try to win the money right then by reraising. And there are times when I will simply throw the hand away. It all depends on what I know about my opponent." Not to get overly granular here, but I know T.J. thinks he can push me around, so I *feel* I should give him a call. Reading his book and playing against him since Tuesday afternoon has left it abundantly clear he's a dude upon whom nothing is lost—just his chips in this case, if I'm right. If I'm wrong, I'll be out of the tournament.

"Call," I say, pushing in $100,000. Having put him on a medium ace, I plan to torture him if either an ace or a king hits the board, otherwise to call him all the way down if he bets.

The flop comes a baby rainbow: deuce of clubs, five of hearts, four of diamonds. I still have boss overcards, plus a belly-buster draw to a wheel, but I also have nada. Same draw for T.J., I'm guessing, since he's not the kind of guy to reraise with A-3—unless he has kryptonite balls and assumes he can bluff me with toilet paper, both of which are probably operative. I also recall that in Practice Hand 4, the reader has A-K and the flop comes three babies. If Player A bets, T.J. quizzes the

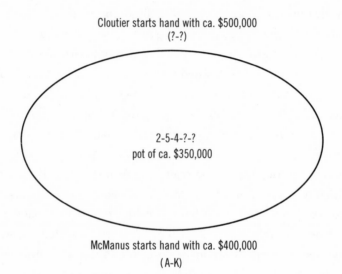

Cloutier starts hand with ca. $500,000
(?-?)

2-5-4-?-?
pot of ca. $350,000

McManus starts hand with ca. $400,000
(A-K)

reader, what do you do? "You throw your hand away. Why? Because you have nothing. In no-limit hold'em, you never chase"—this being the dozenth time he's repeated the never-chase maxim. Assuming he knows that I've read this, I'll chase. And maybe we both have A-K. At this point, I *crave* a split pot. (I'd even take 40 percent!) So I check.

The instant I tap the felt, T.J. mutters, "Two hunnerd thousand," and his entire stack of pink disappears into his hand, to be deftly redeposited on the felt in four stacks of five—orderly, easy to count, in my face. His fingers don't seem to be trembling.

Once again I am forced to recall what T.J. and Andy and everyone else have advised me. In crunch time, don't call. Fold or raise. And

$200,000 is a darn healthy wager in the face of the strength I represented by calling his previous bets. Bottom line? No way should I call with an inside straight draw and two measly overcards, but that's what I think I will do. Chalk it up to a braincramp borne of testosterone, impatience, and youth. I'm only forty-nine, after all. On the other hand, am I ready to exit the tournament?

"Call," I croak finally, making a virtue of necessity by trying to sound and appear as though I've just lured poor old T.J. into my devilish trap, an impression I hope isn't risibly belied by my fingers fumbling to count out $200,000. It's excruciatingly clear that I should have reraised him all-in on the flop, or before. But I didn't have the nerve at the time, and now it's too late: he's got too many chips in the pot to seriously consider a laydown.

I can't bear even to glance in his direction, so I cannot say how he reacts to the turn card, the seven of diamonds, which as far as I'm concerned changes exactly nothing. The board now reads 2-5-4-7, and T.J. is *not* sitting there with 6-3, lemme tell you. I check.

"I'm all-in," he says. No surprise here, since he's been trying to buy the damn pot all along. A third enormous bet doesn't scare me any less, or any more, than the first two did. Except now he has put me all-in.

Auto-advance cameras click, video cameras and writers with notepads edge closer. I stare hard in T.J.'s direction, not into his eyes, for what is later reported by Glazer to be "perhaps twenty seconds." Right now it feels like just one. But don't go all squishy now, Jim. Go all-in. Because as Slim often says, *It feels better in,* and this has long been my experience. Slim, as it happens, is standing behind my left shoulder, kibitzing with Bob Thompson and Benny. Bob turns his mike on to note for the gallery that "T.J. has Jim covered by a hundred thousand or so." What he doesn't say is that if T.J. has made even a pair of deuces, I'm finished.

"I call."

Am I dead?

We will see.

T.J. turns over an ace and a nine in two suits, muttering something I can't quite make out because of the buzz off the rail. When I turn over macho Big Slick, there are oohs, aahs, applause, and T.J. appears mildly shocked. No straight, huh? Not even a *pair*? So then how in the fuck could you call? Amid the gathering uproar, Thompson announces our hands. A trey will give us both wheels and a split, a nine and I'm kevorked. Anything else, the pot's mine. Yet my sense, as the dealer's right fist thumps the table, is that T.J. will catch the same nine that jumped up to save him last night . . .

"Jack of clubs on the river!" says Thompson into his microphone. "Jim McManus wins $866,000 and becomes the new chip leader!"

I hear Benny drawl, "Je-sus Chrahst."

"Ah'd bet on that boy," Slim drawls back. "He's got the heart of a cliff divah."

"T.J. taught me everything I know about this game," I hear myself saying. "Read his book and you'll see." If I had my copy on me, I'd brandish it aloft for the cameras, since I can't really say what I'm thinking.

T.J. stubs out a Salem, not pleased. "It didn't teach you *that*, boy," he growls, with what I hear as a trace of contempt. So maybe he *can* hear Bad Jim singing *Move over, Rover, and let Jimi take over. Yeah, you know what I'm talkin' about. Yeaa-uh!* But the last man on earth I would openly taunt is T.J. Cloutier. I also remember how showing my queen to Kathy Liebert didn't seem to assuage her, not that it's my job to assuage either one of them . . .

This *former* cliff diver, though, is gonna sit good and tight with his chip lead, at least for a couple of rounds. After thirteen hours at the table and staring down T.J.'s three barrels, I've got cobwebby spermatozoa floating through my vitreous humor. So I'm not even tempted to play a 10-8, a 10-J, or even a suited A-8. Me too shaky . . .

A half hour later I find jacks again and decide that it's time to wield my big stick. I also decide not to raise, but to limp—to use my big stick as a crutch. Pretty cute, huh?

Annie Duke, on the button, cooperates beautifully by raising to $60,000. Time to reraise, I decide. *Big Mac's Mammoth Stack Attacks Annie Duke with Jack-Jack* . . . Hasan and Chris fold. Hasan stands up, yawning and stretching, to watch. And then I'm yawning, too—out of nervousness, mind you, since I've never been more wide awake. My yawn is tailing off and I'm pulling my fist away from my mouth as I start to move $150,000 toward the pot; having glanced at Duke's stacks, I've gauged this would set her all-in. The next thing I know, both Rabbi Steve Kaufman and the dealer are citing me for a string raise.

"He never said 'raise'!" says the rabbi, again.

"You never said 'raise,' sir."

I realize they're right. I apologize. My hand must have started forward then gone back to my stacks for a second big helping of pink. This is illegal, of course, since otherwise you could watch your opponent's face while stringing together the size of your raise. The dealer now has to determine how many chips of what color were in my hand when it originally started forward. "Sixty thousand," he says, which happens to be the minimum allowable raise of Annie's original bet. And *boy*, she's not happy. She turns to her entourage for a moment, then glares at the ceiling. "This is the worst thing," she shrieks, "that's ever happened to me in a tournament!" And *shrieks*, I'm afraid, is the word. "Let me call that *myself*," she chides Kaufman, and for a moment I'm cheering her on, till she adds, "I would've been *glad* to let him go to his stack for more!" She runs a hand up through henna'd brown bangs, jangling her wristload of beads, braided leather, plastic bangles. "Oh, *man* . . ."

That she "would've been *glad*" if I'd put her all-in suggests she has a premium hand; that she was so overwrought when she said it makes it hard to believe she was acting. I have to put her on something better than a lousy pair of jacks, do I not? But so why, after my raise was scaled back to sixty, didn't she simply reraise me all-in? Have professional feminine wiles been deployed to mislead poor Jim? We will see.

The flop comes A-Q-8, about as bad as can be for my johnnies. I check to the shrieker. "All-in," she says, breezily sliding what's left of her stacks toward the pot. She has a live human being inside her— whose name will be Lucy, I've heard—but that's not the main reason I fold. No way can I call even $90,000 more, though the pot odds are certainly tempting. Nine more pink chips is too much to risk with those overcards squatting pregnantly there on the baize. It isn't the

toughest laydown I've made, but it still smarts to have to muck johnnies again. This is, after all, two-card chicken we're playing, and
things can change fast on fourth street and fifth street . . .

"I changed my mind," Duke announces to the crowd, then graciously flashes me an ace before mucking. I nod once to show her I
saw it, a second time to express my appreciation of the gesture. Otherwise the hand could have kept me awake nights for years. But I wonder: Should I reach out and peek at her other card now, set off some
World Series drama? Before I can decide what to do, the dealer has
mixed both her cards in the muck. "I mean," Duke continues, "that's
the *best* thing that ever happened to me in a tournament!"

Whoops, laughs, applause from the rail. *"Hang in there, Annie! . . .
Chicks ruuuuuule!"* Harman, Hayden, Katy, and Howard Lederer, plus
a guy I assume must be Ben, all sport immense, stupid grins. I silently
vow to write unflattering things about them in my article. *While sporting immense, stupid grins, the partisan idiots whooped for their pregnant . . .*

Yet whom can I blame but myself and Steve Kaufman? If I'd been
competent to set Duke all-in before the flop, when all she probably
had was a medium ace, she almost certainly would have folded; but for
only an extra $60,000, she was sufficiently tied to her hand to make a
crying call correct. Then she caught a huge piece of the flop. So my
little snafu just cost me $120,000 and handed Jeff Shulman the lead. If
I'd simply said "Raise," I'd be sitting on over a million.

To stem this new ebb tide, I resolve to fold my next fourteen hands
unless I find aces or kings, although queens might be cause for a rethink. What about tens or jacks on the button?

No such luck. I'm not the only one battening down, though, because two rounds go by without a single flop, a modest raise being sufficient to capture the blinds. Meanwhile, on the other table, Sexton
and Lazarou get bounced on consecutive hands.

We are ten.

Playing five-handed, Hasan just bet $100,000 on a flop of Q-2-3
and T.J. has reraised all-in. Good Jim studies both of them, trying
to pick up a tell. But each of them bets with an absolute minimum
of anima. Zero. He could care less, he couldn't care less: take your
pick.

Once Hasan calls, T.J. discloses two treys; Hasan shows Q-5. When trip treys hold up, T.J. is back to almost half a million, where he was before I called down his bluffs. We've had the big guy on the canvas a couple of times, but he keeps finding ways to get up. Not a good sign, I'm afraid.

During the next break, I smoke my own borrowed Winston with Katy and let her explain all the things I did wrong against Annie. "You had kings in the big blind, and so—"

"I had jacks, but no matter."

"No *matter*?"

I shrug, take a drag. It tastes good.

"We thought you had kings."

"That was last time. This time, just jacks."

"Everyone thought you had kings. But anyway, Annie had raised near the button with A-7. You reraised her, but not by enough. Someone like T.J. or Kathy—"

"Someone smart . . ."

"Someone smart. Ha! But what *they're* gonna do is try to get that original bet of Annie's right there *on the spot* and just pick up the pot. Even her rag ace would have been a threat to your hand, so it would've been good to have gotten her out of there."

Blushing, humiliated, dizzy from carbon monoxide, I nod. All of this intake is killing me, but at least I don't have an erection. Katy is cute, she's a writer, she's friendly, she's certainly generous with poker advice, but my testosterone level is foundering.

"You'd at least want to raise her a *little* bit extra, to get a better price on your jacks."

"Not to mention to find out if she had aces, ace-king . . ."

"Of course. But you basically priced her in. She knew you probably had the best hand, but she was forced to call by the new odds you set for her." She takes out a cigarette. "Her complaints, you know, Jim, they really had nothing to do with you. It was just that you were pricing her in and she didn't want to play."

"He's learning, he's learning," says Andy Glazer from behind me. When I ask him if he has any tips, he seems to believe I'm expressing false modesty. I assure him that I'm not. "You all saw me blow my big chance to reraise . . ."

"I just feel a little strange giving tips to someone who's on the kind of roll *you're* on . . ."

"Hey, man, just gimme 'em. Any little thing that might help. When Annie Duke rattles her bangles, or her water bag breaks, does that mean she's still on a draw?"

Katy smiles.

"Just remember how much the hand values change," Andy tells me. "Five-handed's real different from seven. And not too much calling, although the way you smooth-called T.J. back there . . ."

"That was one lucky guess."

"That, my friend, was the hand of the tournament, so far at least. But you still should be raising or folding for the most part, not calling."

As other reporters crowd in, much is made of my being in contention to win the event I came here to cover, that it's the first one I've played, and that "a rank amateur has made the final ten of the Big One." That's what I would be saying as well. But I have to remind a reporter for *Las Vegas Magazine* of how when I was two or three off the money, my short stack came under assault from Liebert and Cloutier and Habib; and how I'd won my way in to begin with. I simply want to counter the notion that beginner's luck could carry *anyone* through three days of no-limit hold'em. "I've been playing the game forty years, plus teaching a course called the Literature and Science of Poker . . ."

"Someone said *Harper's* put up the ten grand for your buy-in."

"Not true. Lewis Lapham sent me out here to cover the trial and the tournament. He told me to 'have fun,' which I'm doing. But all he put up was an advance for expenses, and I used that money—my money—to play a one-table satellite . . ." Shit! *All* he put up, did I say? Did I *say* that? . . . Even I understand how defensive this must sound, how ungrateful, not to mention uncool and vainglorious.

"How much money?"

"Four thousand. But look, methinks I'm protesting too much."

"You think I am—"

"Anyway . . ."

"Meaning?"

"I've got to get back to the table."

Level 15 brings $3,000 antes, $15,000 and $30,000 blinds. Even at this hairy altitude, my chips are still copious enough to let me stay patient, to breathe without oxygen canisters till I'm dealt a big ace or a pair. Anyone in his right mind would follow this plan, but as soon as I find an A-9, I flash back to what Annie just did to me with an even shittier ace. And so, as Hasan has, I call Chris's baby raise to $60,000. Exhale.

When the flop comes A-Q-5 rainbow, Chris's calm, reedy voice says, "All-in."

Hasan and I sneak a peek at each other, then stare hard at Chris. I can see both my faces in his twin silver bubbles. Other than that, I see nothing.

"Jim has about $700,000 in chips," declares Thompson, "Chris and Hasan, oh, I'd say about half that."

Hasan folds, leaving it all up to me to keep Jesus honest.

If I call him and lose, I'll be crippled, yet winning this pot would not only guarantee my playing tomorrow, it would give me the far inside lane in the sprint for the $1.5 million. Yet every last piece of advice I've received says no *way* do you call in these situations unless you're holding the nuts or close to it. I do have top pair, but I lose to any set or—more likely—any ace with a kicker of ten or above. If only I had some kind of read on our sweet, sneaky Savior. He's not only capable of bluffing, he's been yanking a few loaves and fishes from his swing-dancing butt since the break. My mouth for this reason says, "Call."

And I'm liking how pale Jesus looks as he turns over . . . how about that! His *own* mediocre A-9. I pause long enough to give him a decent psychic scourging before I let him off the hook and show mine. Shaking our heads as the crowd goes bananas, we triple-check the board for a flush draw; finding none, we both burst out laughing. Wrist to her forehead, his lean, foxy wife stands behind him, recounting the split on her phone. The fact is, we're both overjoyed with our half.

And then, on the very next hand, Annie Duke raises all-in, only to have Jesus call her and show pocket aces. Revealing the fateful A-9, Annie slowly gets out of her chair. Her supporters are cheering with gusto, but not even one nine appears on the board, let alone the pair of them she requires. That's it.

Thompson announces that her tenth-place finish is the highest by a woman since Barbara Enright came in sixth in '96. "*And*, this $52,160 makes Annie the leading female money winner in World Series history." Another big ovation for that, including from the guys at the tables. But I doubt this will cheer Annie up much. She's a cowgirl who was playing for the glory this week, not the money. But at least she is free to get out of this smoke and go have her baby *at home*.

Down to nine men, we are ranged at one table: Ferguson in Seat 1 with $800,000, then Habib with $400,000, me with $950,000, Cloutier with $550,000, Abinsay with $420,000, Appleman with $240,000, Shulman with $1,100,000, Franklin with $600,000, and Kaufman with $220,000. Let's see. This makes us Jesus, the Middle Eastern guy, the writer (or "the guy with the pictures"), the cowboy tight end, the Roman Filipino, the melancholy Harpo Massada, the whippersnapper, the captain, the rabbi.

No doubt most of the smart money is on Jesus and T.J. Sitting one to my left, T.J.'s in perfect position to hammer his student, as he's been itching to do for two days. Plus he now has revenge as a motive, even though I've heard that the pros don't play "personal poker." We'll see. A chair has been moved behind us to serve as our ashtray-and-extra-hat table. I open the brag book on the cushion beside T.J.'s elbow, then assemble my chips into three stacks of twenty pink, four of orange, squaring them against the side of my drink holder, which holds a new cranberry juice.

For the next fifty minutes, the standard preflop raise of ninety or a hundred thousand is usually enough to take down the blinds. From time to time one of us comes over the top, but in each case the original raiser gives the reraiser credit by folding. But then, in short order, this happens:

Abinsay, from under the gun, brings it in for only sixty, and Appleman calls with his last $58,000. With the J-10 of spades I'm tempted to make it a cheap three-way date, but I follow the Don't Chase commandment. Thank God and Cloutier, too, because none of my straight or flush cards appear on the board as Roman's A-K easily holds up over Mickey's A-10. Mickey has just "won" $74,980 and a lengthy ovation, but he looks even more melancholy than usual. As he tells a *Card Player* reporter: "When you get that far, it's a once-in-a-lifetime opportunity to seize the moment. I didn't do it, so I have to live with that fact. The championship event is not just the bracelet, it transcends that. It's the ultimate test. It's putting your mark on the world of poker."

Two hands after that, Captain Tom Franklin wagers his last $118,000 before the flop, and Ferguson calls him, shows tens. Where does he *get* all these hands? When the captain shows fours and the board gives no help, we are seven.

We've been playing for more than thirteen hours already. One more unfortunate bet and it's bedtime. But since nobody's ready to finish in seventh, a kind of aggressive inertia takes over again: not one all-in bet gets a call for the next twenty minutes. As in every WSOP event, the last nine players receive commemorative final-table jackets; this year's are navy blue, with red collars. There's also a hefty difference in prize money: $146,700 for seventh vs. $195,600 for sixth. But the main reason for our lull in aggression is that tomorrow's final table will seat only six. When Thompson announces that starting next year the last *nine* will play on Day 4, it's gotta be something of a pisser for Franklin and Appleman.

The guy forcing most of the action is Jeff Shulman, taking advantage of the caution flag to build up his chip lead. At twenty-three, with a mop of dark hair, crooked silver frames and clear lenses, he's the younger half of what is already one of the best father-son combos in poker. The iron-haired older half, Barry, owns *Card Player*, but he's also a pretty mean tournament player himself. Right now he's standing a yard behind Jeff, obviously worried but proud.

We non-family members would love to know whether Junior is pounding us with legitimate hands, but apparently no one is catching good enough cards to find out with. One mistake against Jeff and you're finished, whereas he can guess wrong and play on.

Finally, *finally*, one off the button, I find aces, the first time I've seen them all day. *I don't seek, I find*, said Picasso; and as Bozo said, *Hey, folks, that's me!* But my ecstasy ratchets down notch by notch as Rabbi, then Jesus, then Middle Eastern Guy muck their hands. Bozo the Cubist wants raisers! I'm tempted to limp in to entice one, though I know it would be read as a trap. The $66,000 in antes and blinds I'd win here by raising is hardly chump change, but when you're packing pocket rockets you want to *eviscerate* people. Masking my chagrin, I make the minimum raise to $60,000, hoping someone will come blasting back over the top of my show of timidity. Not the tight end, however, who even deigns to shoot me a rare little smile as he folds—*nice try, punk*. Roman and Jeff are also untempted to call. *Boo-hoo-hoo.* Raking the miniature pot, I feel like I've *lost* half a million.

Three hands later, Shulman raises to $200,000 from the button. Stealing again, I assume, but what can I do with Q-3? Kaufman ponders defending his $15,000 small blind for a moment, then mucks, leaving Chris, in the big blind, to reflect on his options for another half minute or so.

"What would Jesus do?" a shrill railbird wonders aloud, eliciting about an equal number of shushes and guffaws. It's a fair question, though, and the answer is: move all seven of His tidy stacks into the pot, reraising $650,000. Hasan and the rest of us scram. Jeff stares at Chris for a couple of seconds, then shrugs almost meekly and calls. When he turns over pocket sevens—not really much of a hand to be calling a big stack all-in with—there are whispers and cries of astonishment. In response, Chris flips up . . . *sixes!?* In absolute crunch time, this cool, preppie kid made a veteran read of his hirsute opponent, leaving Jesus with only two outs. Jewish, Luciferian Jeff looks pretty proud of himself, as does Barry. And why should they not? To paraphrase God the Father in *Paradise Lost*: getting all your chips in the pot as a dominating favorite is about as strong a play as you can make at this stage of celestial history, just before he goes on:

> *Effulgence of my Glory, Son beloved,*
> *Son in whose face invisible is beheld*
> *Visibly, what by Deity I am,*

And in whose hand that overpair of sevens
Makes you one Hell of a Card Player . . .

As auto-advance cameras fire and the railbirds go silent, the flop comes ten of hearts, three of hearts . . . *six* of hearts! As my mother used to say to avoid any blasphemy: Oh, my garden of roses! Having flopped a miraculous set, Jesus vaults from his chair. But as plenty of people are pointing out loudly, Jeff, for all his hellacious bad luck, has a flush draw, since he's holding the seven of hearts. This gives him nine outs right there, to go with the two other sevens. Chris's wife has both palms pressed hard against her ears, a Munch screamer, as dozens of voices cry out for sevens or sixes or hearts.

When the five of clubs hits on the turn, Jeff has a straight draw as well, though Chris is "still almost a two-to-one favorite." If I had twenty more minutes I could've done the math in my head, but T.J. has saved me the trouble by muttering the odds back toward Benny. Thirteen of the 44 unexposed cards will give Jeff the pot; 31 cards work for Chris, who probably figured this out a month and a half before anyone.

The dealer turns fifth street: the red king of . . . diamonds. No heart flush. No seven. No straight. As Lucifer slumps in his chair, Jesus is dancing from his, the sooner to be locked in a tango embrace with his wife. No celebratory peck for these two, but a lingering soul smooch while they twirl one another around.

"Jesus Makes 6-6-6," I suggest as a headline, "Takes Over Chip Lead, Molests Wife in Public."

"Molests Girlfriend in Public," a railbird amends me.

"Even better," I say. But the truth is, I'm dying inside. Not only is Jennifer not here to tango with me, it's starting to sink in that to win this damn thing, I'll not only have to catch a few monsters, I'll need to catch them when someone else holds one a single pip lower. I'll have to play well for three or four days just to be in a position to get lucky when the big money goes in the pot. *If only, if only,* I snivel. If only I'd caught aces on *this* hand . . . till it dawns on me that if I had, I would've lost every one of my chips.

Never mind.

But of one thing I'm certain: Smooching Jesus is due for an epic correction. Overdue, actually. *Way* overdue. Having cashiered Annie Duke with aces and Franklin with tens, he now spikes a two-outer and doubles through Jeff to the lead? What he needs is a quick crucifixion, if only to give his strawberry-blond Mary Magdalene something to hug him about. Everyone at the table would love to just nail him right now, yet we're terrified of taking him on. He not only has the big stack, he's got a vibrating horseshoe lodged nineteen feet up his ass.

T.J., of course, isn't terrified, even when Bullying Jesus raises the very next pot to $90,000. T.J. had witnessed hundreds of rushes like this before Chris was even born. How do I know this? From the way T.J. says "Raise" as soon as the action gets to him, and from the way he shoves $290,000 toward the pot. Roman folds in a hurry, but Jeff has the nerve to reraise T.J. all-in. He must be on tilt from the epochal beat he just swallowed. And speaking of which, here comes Chris, *re-reraising* all-in himself! I fold my 8-7 and glance up at T.J. The big guy can't seem to believe what has happened, but he lays down his hand like a man. "I'm gonna get outta their way," he mutters, then snorts without mirth. "All *I* had were jacks." We believe him, of course. What are jacks, after all, once Beelzebub and Jesus H. Christ get involved? And it turns out to be a shrewd laydown because Jeff now reveals, with K-K, that he wasn't on tilt after all. But then Chris shows us aces again!

"Get. The fuck. *Outta* here!" comments a gentleman sitting behind me. Says another: "You cannot be serious!"

The board renders no poetic justice, either, because this time the best starting hand holds up easily. Just like that, Jeff is out. Seventh out of 512, with $146,600 in cash and a commemorative nylon jacket for his trouble, but he is out nonetheless. A couple of minutes ago he was running the table, with a lock on another huge pot, only to be eliminated one off the movie. He congratulates Chris and the rest of us, then Chris one more time, and then, with his dad's arm around him, walks away like a man with a future.

At least for this evening—this morning—we're done. Once the floormen have counted and bagged all the chips, I'm surprised to be told

I'm in second. It feels like I haven't won a pot in a day and a half. Except for the aces, on which I got zero action, I haven't hit a big hand since—when was it? Tuesday? It's 1:55 Thursday morning. We'll be back in ten hours to settle things once and for all, with Mr. Ferguson packing slightly more ammunition than the rest of us.

Chris Ferguson	$2,853,000
Jim McManus	$ 554,000
Roman Abinsay	$ 521,000
Steve Kaufman	$ 511,000
Hasan Habib	$ 464,000
T.J. Cloutier	$ 216,000

I may have the second most chips, but four of us are basically tied for second behind Chris. And with a stack less than half the size of mine, T.J. is at least twice as dangerous.

After giving a couple of dazed, incoherent interviews, I call Jennifer on Dan Abrams's phone. "Jimmy?" she whispers after only one ring.

"We made the final table."

"You're kidding!"

"Did I wake Gracie up?"

"For a second. She's already sleeping again."

"All I had to do was look at that one of you reading *The Big Red Strawberry* to Bea and the pros had no chance . . ."

"You sound totally wasted."

"I am."

"And totally wired."

"I am."

I make some additional noises to summarize the last hour's action.

"You gonna be able to sleep?"

"That's the question."

The next one involves whether she should fly out tomorrow, but it doesn't take us more than a minute to nix the idea; putting the girls through a couple of four-hour flights just wouldn't make sense. I give Jennifer the addresses of web sites that will broadcast the tournament live. June doesn't have Internet access at home, so they'll have to find a neighbor who does.

Somehow we wind up musing about places we'd been before we had kids—Unalaska, Going-to-the-Sun Road, Harris and Lewis and Venice and Paris, the Black Stallion Motel in Shorewood, Wisconsin—and about how bizarre it feels for me to be here and her to be there with our girls. "Although maybe it's better this way," whispers Jennifer. "You're in such a groove now, you might lose your concentration." This is her secret, I realize. This is the source of my luck. She gives me permission to be in the world, and to gamble, so I don't need to gamble so much.

Knowing I won't be able to sleep right away, I catch up with Dan at the Horseshoe's main bar. It's at the very farthest corner of the joint from the tournament room, over by the high-stakes craps tables, right around the corner from where the million-dollar display used to be. The courthouse is just out the door, down the street.

"No sign of T.J.," Dan jokes, referring to Cloutier's well-known addiction to dice.

"He's gone off to powder his nose, freshen up."

"He'll be here."

"A lot of guys betting on him for tomorrow."

"I know *I* would."

"Me too."

"But you won't."

"Don't have no money to bet with."

"Good point. You will, though," says Dan. "C'mon, *boxcars* . . ." He shakes a pair of imaginary dice in his fist, rolls them out onto the blood red carpet, offers to buy me a beer.

I accept. When I start to complain that my Trazodone hasn't always been up to the challenge this week, Dan offers me something better: two Ativan. To accept delivery I keep my hand under the bar. The pills are so small that they stick to my palm, and one of them falls to the carpet. Here I am, then, on my hands and knees on the dark, grimy floor of the Horseshoe, scratching around for illicit pharmaceuticals. Even more gonzo, I find it, unless it's a mouse turd. When I stand up again, I feel dizzy. I totter, perhaps. Slur my words. Watching me guzzle the pills with a Harp and another of Katy's Winstons, Dan suddenly needs reassurance that he hasn't endangered my health.

"No worries, my friend." Guzzle, guzzle. "I mix Prozac and Trazodone and Zocor with booze every night." I'm slightly amazed to hear myself say this, even more so to know that it's true.

"So it isn't just Ted who plays fast and loose with his downers."

"That's why I love the guy, dude."

"Better watch your liver then, dude."

"I'm watching, I'm watching . . ."

I sip.

Dan wants first crack at me for an interview in the morning. He also plans to do follow-up profiles of the finalists in their homes, and he wants to set up a "classroom situation" with a few of my students. Since he's bribed me with lager and long-distance minutes and dope I have to say yes, though I would have agreed to it anyway. *Harper's* should also be pleased.

John Gerhart, the dealer of last Wednesday's satellite, has taken the stool on my left and ordered a beer. I'm happy to see him until I remember: his tip!

"I'll catch you tomorrow," I promise. "I mean it."

"Don't worry, bud. You played really well back up there."

Yet John and Dan agree that I'm calling too much. "And remember," says John, "it only takes one good hand to double through, so you're really not that far behind Chris. Let the other guys take him on for a while." We discuss which hands will be playable, even raiseworthy, when it gets down to five- or four-handed. "Just make sure you don't choke," Dan advises, grabbing his throat before making his hands into an old-fashioned camera with film crank.

"If I do you'll be watching?"

" 'Fraid so."

And now, after citing impressive credentials as a masseur, John suggests I could use a massage before going to bed.

"From you, do you mean?"

"Help you uncoil a little . . ."

This is an offer I will have to decline. Ungrammatical, sexist, redundant, tautological, or not, *No male masseurs* is my rule, however therapeutic their intentions. If John here were Red, I'd say yes, even if she had *no* credentials, and I'm way too exhausted to worry about all the moral and political ramifications of such a policy. I look at my watch, sip some Harp. "That's an extraordinarily generous offer, my friend, but it's three before three and I have to go hibernate." I go on to thank him four times.

"Hey, you're welcome. You're welcome."

Bidding them goodnight, I carry the dregs of my Harp back through the dinging and flashing west side of the casino, then up the crowded elevator to Room 1016. Home. I put in a wake-up call order, take my Zocor and Prozac with Harp, watch local news with a big stupid grin on my face. Make that *immense* stupid grin, and one that I can't wipe away. The jury has asked for more read-backs, mainly Montoya-Gascoigne's testimony about being sent home early, which means they're considering the charges specifically and seriously; either that or they're looking for a technicality on which to hang reasonable doubt. As the Ativans eventually start to kick in, the question becomes, Do I care?

THE LAST SUPPER

> Isn't God intervening all the time, even in the
> order of nature?
>
> —AUGUSTINE, *The Testimony*

> There are those men who say, "There is no
> happiness for a man if he has not the pleasures
> of the flesh." These are they whom the Apostle
> censures, saying, "Let us eat and drink, for
> tomorrow we shall die."
>
> —AUGUSTINE, Sermon 62

Shaking off Ativan nightmares in the pool Thursday morning, I can't avoid fantasizing about what second-place money, $896,500, could buy us. Ferguson's ludicrous chip lead keeps me from thinking too much about the $1.5 million, but finishing second would still put us in the 38 percent bracket, so right away we'd be down to $500,000 and change. *Boo-hoo-hoo.* After paying off the mortgage and investing a big chunk in a college fund, we could probably afford a Dublin-London-Paris poker vacation, with business-class plane tickets and fancy hotels. The new Cross Country, with the wraparound bumper and 144 speakers, might also make sense; or else the Mercedes ML. But first we need a fence around the side yard, to keep the girls out of the alley, and inside the fence a new patio, with the bricks laid out in that scallop design the sidewalks in Italy have. The rest of our house is perfectly adequate, although finishing the basement or adding a second story would give us more room to spread out. Bridget and James

The author arriving at the final table

could each use a car and a trip, and there's a Telecaster James has had his eye on. Plus I want to keep playing these tournaments.

Boning up one last time, I find T.J.'s advice on final-table strategy a bit vague and obvious: "Remember that any time you're all-in, you have to win the pot or you're gone. . . . Know your players and avoid making any bonehead plays." He must figure that if you've made it this far, you're starting to know what you're doing. Or maybe he's got a few secrets he feels would be best not to share.

Oatmeal, banana, grapefruit juice, coffee. Jennifer has left a message on her mother's machine: tornadoes are spinning through eastern Missouri, they haven't found a computer yet, the girls are both fine, I shouldn't be nervous, she loves me.

The gymnasium-sized tournament room has been converted to an intimate poker studio, if there is such a thing. In place of last night's four tables are twenty rows of seats facing a thirteen-foot projection screen. Aluminum bleachers have been erected along one side of the final table, flanked by more rows of seats at both ends. Otherwise, standing room only. The table is lit with four banks of lights and surrounded by monitors, cameras on tripods, a podium on heavy black risers. Thank God, amid all this lunacy, my Las Vegas family is here: Linda and Tom, Andy and Katy and Dan. Good morning, good morning, good morning. "And thanks for the pills, bro. They worked."

"Shhhhhhhh."

Dan is all business, of course, surrounded by mixing boards, anacondas of cable, a broad bank of monitors. Everyone else wants to interview the finalists, but he has first dibs. One of his tech guys wires me for sound, winding the line up through the fly of my jeans and clipping the mike to my collar. *Test, test . . .*

Hasan, who has already been wired, shows me the sheet with our new seating order. Chris drew Seat 1, where he'll start off with almost $3 million in chips; then comes Hasan in 2, me in 3, T.J. in 4, Roman in 5, Steve in 6. All told we have $5.12 million in chips, with which we'll be vying for $3,762,360 in prize money. (The other $1,357,640 has already been awarded to places forty-five through seven, with the long money reserved for the top two or three on the pyramid.) Our equity in the purse makes each dollar chip worth roughly seventy-three cents in cash, but the ratio will go down each time one of us gets eliminated, until the entire $5.12 million in chips is worth $1.5 million in cash to the winner. When we started on Monday, the ratio was exactly one to one. The highest it got was early Wednesday morning, when Shulz's last $500 chip was worth $15,000 in cash, or thirty to one. I recall Mason Malmuth's advice from the Masque program: "The more chips you have, the less each individual chip is worth, and the less chips you have, the more each individual chip is worth." Translation? Hanging on by your fingernails pays.

The guy who was stomping on mine Wednesday morning, Hasan, chooses this moment to tell me he takes medication for obsessive-compulsive disorder. Three weeks ago, down in Tunica, his old stuff stopped working: his neck twitched, he couldn't stop blinking, and his hands shook so badly he couldn't move chips or turn over his hole cards. "I was all messed up, buddy." When he got back to LA, his doctor wrote him a new prescription for Anafranil, but it didn't kick in until the second week of the World Series, just in time to help him finish second in the Omaha event. He still needs two hands to look at his hole cards, he says.

"I've noticed that."

"Of *courrse* you have, buddy," he says. "That's how you called with eight-nine." He looks me now square in the eye. "I'm so nerrvous I think I might die, Jim. Rright herre on camerra." He smiles to show how melodramatic he knows this must sound, but I can tell that he's perfectly serious. He means keel over dead, just like that.

When I put my hand on his shoulder, he lightens the mood by telling me that on Monday morning one of his friends offered to buy him in for $10,000 in exchange for a 50 percent stake in his winnings, a stake now worth at least $97,800. "I was tempted, but that would've cost me plenty, you know? But good luck to you, buddy."

"And good luck to you."

As we hug one another, I'm startled to realize that I meant what I said. For eight days and nights we've been throwing haymakers at each other over critical pots, but that makes me love him a little. Plus we'll both need some luck from now on.

Then again, maybe not. Because as we're letting go of each other, Hasan suddenly asks me if I've "heard about the deal." I have not. And he looks a bit peeved. "Jim, we were looking all over for you . . ."

"Who—when was this?"

It turns out that while I was swimming a tentative agreement was reached among at least three of the finalists: we would play on as hard as we could for the bracelet, but prize-money-wise we would settle up early. Chris was to receive a million dollars even, the rest of us $552,000 apiece.

"Is it still on the table?"

Hasan regrets to inform me that T.J. has already nixed it. T.J. is after the bracelet, and he won't have it tainted by even the hint of a deal. Bob Thompson apparently cornered each of us—either last night or this morning—to strictly proscribe any "chop," especially in front of the cameras. As he told me last night by way of apology for the warning: "It's a tough way to make an easy living."

"That's that, then," I say.

Hasan shrugs fatalistically. Nods. "We'll just play it."

But first we must fill out more forms: poker experience, hometown, date of birth, occupation, waivers in triplicate for the Discovery people. I even sign five or six autographs. Finally, a little after noon, Bob takes the mike and introduces us, beginning with seat number 1. Chris, at thirty-seven, has already won the $2,500 stud event, to go with the 1999 California State Championship, a few lesser titles, his new Ph.D., blah blah blah. I hear Andy note that his nickname stems not from delusions of grandeur but from his hair and "the kindness of his features." Next we are told that Hasan used to own a video store in LA but has now, at thirty-eight, been a pro for ten years. At the World Poker Open he finished second to Hellmuth in the $1,000 no-limit hold'em event.

Now me. On their Internet radio broadcast, Glazer and Hellmuth are calling me "the family man's family man," presumably because of the brag book and calls to St. Louis on other people's phones. Thompson mentions that I'm covering the World Series for *Harper's*, playing in my first poker tournament, and that most of my no-limit strategy "comes from T.J.'s blue book." Down I sit.

T.J. needs no introduction but gets a rather lengthy one anyway, followed by a standing ovation. This is his fourth final-table appearance at the Big One. At sixty, he's won four smaller WSOP titles, fifty international events altogether, and garnered the second most prize money in World Series history. "By placing first or second today, he'll move past Johnny Chan into first." But hey, watch them tenses there, Bob. Mr. Chan stands ten feet away with his back to me, shaking with laughter.

Abinsay, a fifty-two-year-old Filipino living in Los Angeles, has already placed second in the $2,000 limit hold'em event; in this one, he's come from the farthest behind as of Tuesday. Kaufman, fifty-four, is a rabbi as well as a professor of languages ("Hebrew, Aramaic, some others") at Hebrew Union College in Cincinnati, sufficiently high-powered as a scholar to consult on the Dead Sea Scrolls. After playing tournaments since '96, he made the final table of the Big One in Tunica, so this makes it two in a row. He's also a bit of a noodge.

Our mean age, we are told, is forty-eight years and four months, which must be the new over-under. Four of us above, two below. We pose for a short round of photos. With the TV lights hot on my neck, I order an OJ with ginger ale, open my album to the page on which Jennifer is reading to Beatrice. T.J. has developed a cold since last night, but he still sits bolt upright and smokes, his gray Binion's polo shirt tucked into beige sans-a-belt slacks. The chair with his ashtray is against my left elbow; when I ask him to move it over he seems a bit miffed, but he does it. I try to let him know one more time how terrific his book is, but he doesn't wanna hear about it. Instead of a compliment from an appreciative reader and fan, he seems to think it's some kind of gamesmanship. Maybe he's right. Yet it's obvious to him and everyone else who the novice is here, the chaste book-learned tournament virgin. No question, all five of these guys see my $554,000 as their most plunderable target.

Oh yeah? I think, looking around at them, each in his turn. *Zat so?* This is how Doc Holliday and Wild Bill Hickok and Johnny Moss intimidated their adversaries, you see—with hard, silent glances while thinking confrontational thoughts. You talkin' to *me*?

Hand 1. The blinds are still $15,000 and $30,000, with $3,000 antes. T.J. can't wait very long to make a move, but it's Hasan who puts in the first raise, to $70,000. I'm tempted to call with 2-2 but come to my senses—um, *duh*!—in time to consider reraising or folding. I fold. When T.J. and Roman fold, too, it looks like Hasan may have executed the last day's first steal; but then here comes Professor Kaufman blasting over the top of him in a language we all understand: twenty pink. Once Chris folds, Hasan has our first gulp-worthy rethink. After gazing at Kaufman for maybe ten seconds, he mucks his two cards with a sigh. Both he and Chris look a bit shaky.

Hand 2. After everyone passes, Roman makes it $100,000 to go from the button, a likely positional raise. Politely but firmly, Chris says, "All-in." Roman calls, pushing the rest of his half million forward, then turns over A-Q. For Chris? Pocket eights. Here we go. Sitting two around the bend from me, Chris appears nervous and pale, and I hope I'll be able to read him this well when playing a hand against him while his cards are face*down*. I'd like to observe Roman, too, since I have so little experience against him, but T.J. is blocking my view.

Bob Thompson narrates the 7-2-7 flop, followed by a trey and a five. Adios. Roman stands up from the table to abundant applause. His ouster has just guaranteed me fifth-place money, almost a quarter of a million dollars, but that's the last thing I care about. I wanna cast Jesus and the rabbi and this other pair of money changers from the temple and rake in the *serious* shekels.

My testosterone buzz gets muffled somewhat when I happen to glance at a monitor. Ha! Who's that little homunculus hunched in the seat next to T.J.? I realize it's me just as T.J. is moving all-in. Could this finally be it for him? I hope so, I really do hope so, but . . . Nope. No one calls, certainly not the L.H. with his homuncular little J-5. T.J. elects to show us the A-10 of diamonds, just in case we were wondering. Is there anything worse than a *slippery* badass? There isn't.

On the next hand, Hasan moves all-in. I sure can't call with a 7-6 offsuit, and neither can anyone else. On the following hand, Chris raises to $100,000, Hasan folds, and with suited 8-6 so do I. So do T.J. and Steve. We've thus let Chris extend his lead by another $63,000. He builds his new chips into the two solid triangles in front of him, one set on top of the other: ten pink twenty-chip columns in a 1-2-3-4 configuration ($2 million right there), topped by six of less regular color scheme arranged 1-2-3. Kinda scary.

Thinking that must mean I'm scared, right? That I'm playing today with the liver and heart of a Perdue Oven Stuffer? I've already bled away 10 percent of my stack, after all, while the others are letting it rip. To regain the momentum I had when I called T.J.'s bluffs, I need to bristle up fairly soon.

My next three hands are unplayable, but on Hand 9, in the big blind, I discover the A-Q of clubs and get ready to raise. Fold, fold, fold. But Hasan, in the small blind, raises all-in right in front of me. *Bawk, buck-buck-buck.* I shoot him a curious glance, do a double take: he's radically changed. I don't know when he put them on, but he's now wearing Darth Vader shades beneath a black ultimatebet.com hat with the brim pulled down low. What to do.

Suited A-Q is a better hand to raise than to call with, but still. Five-handed, it can fairly be called, *pace* Brunson, a monster. Granted that Roman's A-Q got him beheaded six hands ago, my read of Hasan is that he's caught up in a spasm of all-in steal-raises. I mostly discount the tremble I see in one hand, but I read his macho glower as weakness. It's that passage from the "blue book" that sticks in my craw: "When you move in on them, there are a lot of players who will call a raise for all of their chips with a hand like A-Q. They're not good players, but they are out there." Yet I don't think Hasan has a better one.

"Call," I say, pressing my seven stacks together and pushing them forward. Cameras roll, cameras click, bleacher bums catcall and whistle. I believe that this puts me all-in. I definitely should've counted, of course, comparing my stack with Hasan's, but—too late.

Hasan turns over an ace and a four, both of hearts. What a call. I mean, What A *Call!* When I flip up my suited A-Q, everyone sees why I'm tickled.

But now comes the flop of Hasan's and my life: a nine, then a six, then a king—all of spades. So far, so fantastic. Justice will be served in Las Vegas, at least in the poker arena. Dead to the three remaining fours, Hasan grimaces, groans, shakes his head. Every other card in the deck gives me the $970,000 pot and a real shot at challenging Chris. Unless, I suddenly realize, we get runner-runner spades for a flush and split pot. Dearest God up in Heaven, in whom I have always believed, always will, puh-huh-huh-*leeeez* just do not let that happen!

The crowd, for its part, must be bellowing dozens of things, but all I can hear is the Habib Society pleading for fours. Terrorists all of them, I can only assume, with scimitars and scary-looking Arabic glyphs decorating their flag. Burn the Stars and Stripes! Incinerate the arrogant American! Kill the Great Satan! Kill! Kill! "Ha-san Ha-*beeeeeeeb*," someone croons. Habibians also have a specific card to ask for, so their chants have a more succinct density, at least on *some* delicate eardrums. Four! *Four!!* FOUR!!! *FOUR!!!!* Even so, in my bubble of silence and calm, I've come to understand that I'm going to win not just this pot, but the tournament. One and a half million dollars. The bracelet. I'll be poker's new Heavyweight Champion.

My faith is confirmed when fourth street arrives as the sacred, the numinous, the preternaturally chic five o' diamonds. *Close* to a four, I gloat to myself, but no sucking-out-on-me cigar. Its brilliant red diamondness reduces the chance of a pot-splitting flush to, hmmmm, let's make sure we calculate these odds as precisely as possible . . .

Zero!

Hasan knows all this, so he's already out of his chair. You can tell from his posture and how he holds his right arm that he's getting ready to shake my hand. I actually feel sorry for the guy. He's a pro, I'm an amateur, and this is the second time in a week that I've beaten him out of serious money. On the other hand, what can I say? My heart pounds like Keith Moon on Methedrine, but I'm still feeling thoroughly confident as the dealer thumps his fist, burns a card. Not only that, my A-Q *deserves* the whole pot, much as my cowboys deserved to subdue Annie's queens. It is morally, theologically, statistically fitting and just, not to mention pokeraticiously. So that when the fifth street card—*what?*—is the—*what!*—four of hearts, I "reel," according to Glazer's live feed, "in stunned silence," even though a chorus of f-words and blasphemes and fours is screeching through my skull like a squadron of Pakistani banshees on tilt. Both Hasan's fists fly into the air, the left one narrowly missing my chin. As I try to get up from my chair, I seem to black out. "What the—"

As Glazer is thinking right now and will write in his Internet coverage: "Jim hadn't suffered too many indignities at the hands of fate in the last couple of days. Most of his leading hands had held up. But now, at the worst possible moment, he'd taken a punishing blow." Punished and reeling, then, away from the table—God knows where I think I was going—I have to be told by Hasan, "You had me coverred. Don't worry. You'rre still in therre, buddy. Keep playing."

Though it feels like I died, I have life, if only $105,000 worth. Hasan and I are still clasping hands, it turns out, shaking our heads in amazement. We realize that this is what happens in poker sometimes, that fifth street could have just as—*more!*—easily gone the other way, the towers of pink and orange chips being raked a foot to the left instead of a foot to the right.

I get up, let go of Hasan, and borrow a nonmenthol cigarette from a guy in the bleachers, who lights it as well. (This must have been where I was heading twenty seconds ago.) When I get back to the table, T.J. shoots me a look. "What, are you kidding me, Jimmy?"

I'm not. And I'm suddenly struck, almost literally, by the fact that Grandpa Jim was a smoker, an eater of sweets, all but certainly an LDL cholesterol chart-topper, but a 4.0 in Sobriety, a 4.0 in Obedience, and that he died at thirty-five of a coronary. A *four* point oh, huh? I drag on my Marlboro Light although not very deeply, but deeply enough to trigger a twinge in my chest. And again. I also would love some tequila.

Three hands later I find an A-2, one of the most deeply pathetic hands you can enter a pot with. But I have barely enough chips to post the next pair of blinds, so I probably won't see another ace, let alone the big pair I've been babbling post-structuralist novenas for. I move in for $96,000.

T.J. folds, perhaps out of pity, but Steve Kaufman not only calls me but moves in himself, all $600,000 or so. He wants to knock me out on the cheap by making sure it stays heads-up between us. No doubt he can beat an A-2. Once Chris and Hasan muck their hands, Kaufman turns over the ace of hearts and the . . . queen of clubs. Perfect. That I'm now in the same suck-out posture Hasan was just in somehow inspires an ever more bottomless gloom. Sure, sure, when Dante was spiraling down into the antarctic bowels of Hell he may also have been ascending, without realizing it, toward Paradise, but here in Las Vegas, another barren desert peopled by faithless demons, three-outers don't spike twice in a row. Forget about how long the mathematical odds are against it, I *know* it's not going to happen. But it still doesn't keep me from hoping. If a queen doesn't fall, one of the other three deuces would save me. Any low cards that miss me could also turn into a wheel.

But the 9-6-K flop gives me neither straight draw nor flush draw, let alone a sweet deuce. No queen for Satan, at least, but I no longer hope to be saved. I hear a few ravishing sirens melodically pleading for deuces, but maybe they're all in my head. In the end, with an ace on the turn, a ten on the river, it's not even close. The Satanic Prince of Noodges has forked me down into the pitch.

Many zooms. Many clicks. Many claps. For Polyglot Beelzebub? Because I managed to survive till Day 4? Because amateur hour is over? Who knows. I shake the rabbi's graciously proffered hand across the table, then turn to hug Hasan. "I'm sorrry therre, buddy," he says. I believe him.

"You played well," T.J. says, engulfing my hand in his turn.

"Your book changed my life."

"Hey, Jimmy, I hope it made a difference."

And now here is Jesus coming around the table for a warm, bony hug. "You played great." He shakes my hand, says something else.

"What?"

"What?"

"Anyway, thanks, bro."

The dealer is shuffling again. Time to go.

Thompson and Glazer and Hellmuth and all the other commentators are telling the assembled and far-flung poker universe that I just won $247,760 by finishing fifth out of 512. What it feels like, lemme tell ya, is fifth out of six. As I stagger away from the action, it hits me how alive I had felt since last Wednesday and how dead I feel now. A swift rigor mortis of soul overtook me when that four hit the table. My head feels constructed of Styrofoam.

Up on the podium, Becky shakes my hand, pets my arm. "You were wonderful, Jim. And last night. Oh my God! Congratulations!"

I tell her she's put on a phenomenal tournament, and it feels right to add, "I hope the right verdict comes through." Surprise flickers briefly across her small, heart-shaped face—that I've brought up what's being deliberated a hundred and fifty yards down the street. So maybe I shouldn't have. This is her moment to bask in much sunnier notions—the way she's extended her father's legacy, for example, with another record field. Yet for all his shenanigans, Ted loved the Horseshoe as much as anyone did, so mentioning him is my way of . . .

Pumping my hand, his nephew snaps me back to reality. "That four was brutal, Jim. *Bru*tal! You were playing so awesome last night." Yeah, last night. When I take the opportunity to ask whether I can interview him sometime tonight or tomorrow, he seems almost honored. "You bet, man. You kiddin'? Just find me, okay? Or else I'll find you."

Tom Elias ushers me a few steps to the left, where a payout booth has been fashioned. From his unbashful spiel, I gather that "big winners" have to tip the dealers and staff "between 2 and 8 percent." Do I have to decide that right now? "We have to take care of our people, Jim. So, I mean, yeah, you do." Did I mention that Tom is quite *large*? Quite forceful as well of *vibration*? In the meantime he's scrupulously counting out forty-two . . . forty-three . . . forty-four lavender $5,000 chips and sliding them into a rack. "Forty-five . . . forty-six . . ." Rims flecked with gold, slightly bigger than regular chips, these are the ones that supplanted the chocolates Ted pilfered four years ago. Surely I can spare three or four of them.

Tom asks my address as he fills out the W-2G form for "Certain Gambling Winnings." I sorta like the sound of that, too—to be certain of winning while gambling. But then comes the time to *pay up*! In the din and commotion, however, Tom hears me say Maryland Avenue instead of Wayland. (In Chicago everyone hears it as Waveland, that horrible bastion of Cubdom.) Watching him print "Maryland" on the form, I neglect to correct him, imagining this might somehow invalidate the form and I won't have to pay any taxes. My social security number he manages to get down precisely.

"Thanks, Tom."

"You're welcome."

I sign it. Let's see. Eight percent of $247,760 is about . . . twenty grand. As a *tip*? Get the fuck outta here! Two percent comes to almost $5,000, and surely that must be enough. Looming down over me, smiling, Tom says, "You really played great. I mean, wow." What he means is, *Under twelve grand and I'll smack you.*

I decide to tip $7,500, plus another $300 for John Gerhart. Altogether, this comes to 3.3 percent of my profit. It's also vastly more money than I'd ever played poker for, or made in a week, or a month, doing anything. And Tom is now thanking me so profusely I'm afraid I overdid it. Like Hasan's A-4 raise, all that 8 percent noise was a bluff.

Even friendlier now, Tom details a Horseshoe security guard to escort me downstairs to the cage. As we press through the crowd past a monitor, I see that Hasan has just been bounced by Chris, who is adding my columns of pink to the expanding top triangle.

God *damn* it, I wanna keep playing!

I start to understand it's all over when one of Dan's technicians starts removing the sound pack. "If you undo your belt, I'll just reach in through here and . . ." Whatever the opposite of an erection is, that's what I have. *Acorn* sounds accurate, or else an acute case of what Breger would call psychic sadism.

At the cashier downstairs, I play hurry up and wait with bucket-toting slot players, then start signing form after form. Jay Heimowitz is waiting to pick up a check, and he suggests I should get one cut for myself. Good idea, if only it wouldn't take them another half hour. C'mon! I have to go be a reporter again, even though it's not my first choice.

I finally slide check, tax forms, and tip receipt into a lockbox, keeping some blacks, greens, and reds—and one lavender—in my pocket. By the time I make it back up the escalator, the action is down to T.J. and Chris. It takes me a while to get close to the table because of all the film and press people—*other* press people, I realize. They're still playing with $3,000 antes and blinds of $15,000 and $30,000. According to Andy, T.J. has just made a series of brilliant playbacks, building up his stack to $1.5 million, with Chris hanging tough at $4 million. Another reporter points out that when the action began this morning, Chris's count was thirteen times greater than T.J.'s, $2,853,000 to $216,000. When they got down to heads-up, T.J. had only a sixth as many chips. "Cloutier's got him," he says, giving his otherwise reasonable prediction a smidgen less authority by pronouncing T.J.'s last name *clue-TEER*.

Right now play has been stopped to allow a phalanx of Horseshoe security to deliver the traditional cardboard box, setting it on the table between the two finalists. Benny pulls out wads of cash and hands them ceremoniously to his mother, who stacks them at T.J.'s end of the baize. Each wad consists of five hundred C-notes subdivided by five yellow-and-white paper bands marked "$10,000," these in turn held together with rubber bands doubled near the ends of the bills. When Becky has finished there are thirty such five-inch-thick wads stacked in a ramshackle cube three wads high, five across. This is officially one and a half times as many wads as have ever been awarded at Binion's World Series. Becky lays the gold championship bracelet across the second tier of cash, facing T.J., and T.J. can't help staring back. It's the thing he wants most in the world.

The bracelet aside, this will be the most money ever awarded to a single winner of a sporting event. (Boxing purses are fixed in advance, win or lose, plus they have to be split with armies of trainers and managers.) The poor guy who finishes second will get 179 lavender chips and some change, totaling $896,500. For context, the *winner* of the Masters, Vijay Singh, just earned $828,000, and Fusaichi Pegasus' owner got $888,400 for winning the Kentucky Derby. The winner of the Jack Binion World Poker Open took home $238,620, and the three-day Tournament of Champions paid its winner $248,346, almost exactly what I'm taking home. Altogether, the 2000 World Series of Poker's 4,922 entrants competed in twenty-two events for $15,392,500 in prize money.

I finally bump into Hasan and ask him what happened. "I had king-queen," he purrs wistfully, shrugging. "Chris had ace-king." Enough said.

Pen poised above his legal pad, Andy wants to know if I feel like a rock star.

"If the ace-queen stands up I might still be in there, but right now I feel like a back-up band."

"You got your money in the pot with by far the best hand, and that's all you can do."

Hasan agrees.

"Yeah, but who would we rather be, the guy who does that or the one who sucks out and plays on?"

They nod their assent. "Not even a close call," Andy says.

As we edge a step closer, Chris makes it $175,000 to go from the button. T.J. calls. When the flop comes K-K-6, T.J. checks. (In heads-up action, the player on the button bets first before the flop, second on subsequent rounds.) After thinking for over a minute, Chris wagers $200,000. When T.J. flat-calls, there's three-quarters of a million in the pot. Fourth street arrives a black trey. Check, check. Street five: jack of diamonds, for K-K-6-3-J. No straight draw, no flush draw, but does either of them have a king? T.J. at least represents having one by betting $600,000. A come-with-me tease or a steal? We will see. Then again, maybe we won't.

Chris takes a while to decide, then calls and turns over a Q-J, as T.J. turns over . . . K-10. His check on the turn, letting Chris pair his jack for "free," earned him six more big dimes and put him in the lead. He now has $2.65 million to Chris's $2.45.

"Only in no-limit," says Andy.

Two hands later Chris makes it $175,000, again prompting T.J. to come over the top for another half million. Chris shows how frightened he is by responding, "All-in." Without a blip of reluctance, T.J. says, "Call." Whoever takes this pot is the champion.

Bob Thompson requests that they show us (and the cameras) their hole cards. "Ace and seven of hearts for T.J., ace and deuce of spades for Chris." An uproar, then relative silence. It's basically the same confrontation Hasan and I, then Steve and I, had: dueling kickers, with the remote possibility of a flush draw for one or the other. A few feet away from his booth, I can hear Dan Abrams's directorial whisper: "Camera Two, give me Jesus." Because Jesus is dead to a deuce or a flurry of spades and we all want to see his reaction, there's a lens planted next to his cheekbone. From my vantage point he looks nervous, unhappy, and pale. After starting the morning in total command, it looks like he'll wind up the bridesmaid.

The flop comes off trey of *spades*, ten of *spades*, queen of . . . *hearts*. Though still a 3–2 underdog, Chris's four-flush gives him nine extra outs to go with the two other deuces; anything else, T.J. wins. Both of these guys have proven they have solid brass balls, but right now all four must feel just a tad on the clammy side.

When fourth street arrives king of *hearts*, T.J. picks up his own flush draw, and the yelling commences for hearts, spades, and deuces. On fifth street, however, the ten of diamonds shows up, yielding 10-10-A-K-Q for each of them and *another* chopped pot. Coitus anticlimaximus! T.J. stoically picks up a smoldering Salem; Chris looks tapped out but elated. How many deaths and resurrections can the Son of Man suffer per hour? Even the Texas centurion pretends to wipe sweat from his brow, as a joke, while exhaling long plumes of smoke.

The next two small pots go to T.J. when Chris is unable to call even modest $100,000 raises, but on the following hand Chris wins a decent pot with a raise on the turn. They're back to dead even. The hand after that brings no preflop raises, and when the flop comes king of hearts, trey of hearts, eight of clubs, Chris checks again. T.J. bets a mere hundred grand, Chris calls, and we all sense a trap being set. The question is, who's trapping whom? Because when the seven of spades hits the turn for K-3-8-7 (two hearts), this time it's Chris betting a puny $150,000 and T.J. who appears to be warily calling. The last card is the four of clubs, and both of them check. While they stare at each other, Chris flashes what must be a king. T.J. mucks.

They've been at it four and a half hours now, about half of that head-to-head. Hardly a marathon, but still a long time with this much at stake and dozens of lenses and mikes jabbing into your poker space. It's humid and hot, high-noon bright, airless as a visitors' locker room.

On Hand 93 of Day 4, T.J. raises to $175,000. Chris thinks for a second, takes another peek at his cards. He has pulled back into the lead, very slightly, about 2.6 to 2.5 million. Time to attack or consolidate? The latter, apparently, because when he reraises $600,000, T.J. moves in like a shot.

The pulse in T.J.'s cheek makes me think that he's finally got Chris where he wants him. Raise, reraise, re-reraise—doesn't this always mean somebody's flying American Airlines? "Where I was schooled in Dallas, the second raise probably would have been aces, and the third raise was like Ivory Snow: 99.9 percent pure aces."

Or not. This is heads-up, after all, when the hand values rise dramatically. So T.J. may not need twin steeples to push all his chips in the pot, even against a reraiser.

Chris thinks for almost two minutes. He scratches his cheek through his beard, shakes his head, exhales. Then he thinks for another two minutes. I can't speak for T.J., but no one else seems to begrudge all the time Chris is taking. We wait.

And we wait.

"Call him, Jesus!" shouts a rowdy fan twenty rows back. T.J.'s eyes narrow as he drags on his umpteenth Salem. He puts his left fist to his mouth, clears his throat. Won't somebody give him a Halls?

"T.J. likes his hand," Andy whispers to me, "and I think Chris has ace-nine." I remember the matching A-9's Chris and I turned out to be holding last night, how the untranquil mood had been suddenly scalpeled by laughter. Unlike last night, Chris suddenly removes his hat, then his sunglasses—*whoa*—in an instant defanging his aura. Slightly thinning hair above his temples accentuated by the length of the strands, brown eyes a tad bloodshot and sunken, he also looks much more like Jesus. Crowned with thorns, bound to the whipping post, trudging up the hill with the cross.

And he calls. As the low-dB buzz from the previous five or six minutes rises to a crescendo, he turns over the ace of spades and the . . . nine of clubs. T.J. immediately shows him the ace of diamonds and the . . . *queen* of clubs. The crowd gasps and whistles.

"Pretty astonishing call," I tell Andy.

"Chris has been calling with any—"

"No, *yours*. You didn't even wanna say 'medium ace'?"

He modestly shrugs, as though he hasn't been making reads of this caliber the whole tournament, then elbows my arm. "Ace-queen look familiar?"

"Oh, boy . . ."

The flop—four of hearts, deuce of hearts, king of clubs—keeps T.J. in the lead, amid much delirium ringside. Neither of them has a heart.

The king of hearts falls on the turn. Furiously jotting on his pad, Andy groans, "Not again!" Because now any deuce, any four, will give us *another* chopped pot: K-K-2-2 (or 4-4) with an ace. Exuberant Ferguson boosters entreat the poker gods for a nine, though my guess is they'd take a split pot. Surely Chris would. Cloutier fans may be somewhat more numerous, but it isn't clear what they should beg for. Hollering "Let's go, T.J.!" is pretty much all they can do. The rest of the crowd is bellowing both of their names, for a queen, for a nine, for a split . . .

I see Jesus leap from his seat with his fists in the air and T.J. thrust a huge paw across the table before I see the last card. What else could it be but ". . . a *NINE*," Bob Thompson ejaculates, his microphone feeding back piercingly. No one in the dense mob surrounding the table, especially not Bob, seems able to believe it. Chris reaches back across and clasps T.J.'s hand. "You outplayed me," he says, in the din. T.J. shakes his head, disagreeing. That he just got harpooned through the ventricles doesn't register on his vast, craggy features. He's *smiling*!

Cathy Burns and the Fergusons are all over Chris now. Hugs, kisses, pogo hops, shimmying. Chris makes his way around the table to where T.J. is standing with his pretty wife, Joy—green eyes, dark blond bouffant, quite a tan—inside a crush of reporters. While Chris is almost as tall, when the two men embrace their difference in mass is straight out of vaudeville: mesomorph-endomorph, steel-wool ringlets meshing with yard-long chestnut locks, the burly tight end being held by the sinewy swing dancer. How else could he keep him from rumbling downfield on a post pattern? "Are we still friends?" Chris asks him.

"Of course! Don't feel bad. You played great." But once they let go of each other, T.J. says, "You didn't think it would be that tough to beat me, did you?"

"Yes, I did. *Believe* me, I did."

By now Glazer and Hellmuth have latched onto T.J. "Chris is the one who should be getting the attention," he pointedly tells them.

A British TV reporter is noting that four of the five eliminations at the final table involved an A-Q: Roman's against Chris's 8-8, Steve's against my puny A-2, T.J.'s and mine both beaten when our opponent's smaller kicker got paired on fifth street.

"That's poker," says T.J. Smile. Shrug. Next question.

When I congratulate Chris, calling him Dr. Ferguson, he invites me upstairs to "the dinner. We'll talk."

"I'll be there."

Suddenly hungry, I try to tell T.J. how brilliantly he played. "All those times you came back from—"

"There's a lotta luck in poker," he rumbles, "and if you're gonna play this game you better get used to it." Next.

"What about fifth street?" a female reporter shouts up to him.

"I felt the nine coming off at the end. When I get in that zone, I can feel the cards coming. But you should be talking to Chris. He's the champion."

Directly behind him, Mike Sexton is explaining to the French TV audience that not only is T.J. the all-time World Series money leader, he's also the leader in overall tournament winnings. "Nobody's even close." Adds Glazer, nodding: "All true, but Chris earned this title. He walloped the little stacks when he was supposed to, he played cautious when he was supposed to, when he didn't want to give T.J. easy double-throughs. He was also more aggressive when the two stacks got closer, and when it was finally time to gamble, he picked the right moment."

"Oh, man, did he pick it," I say.

T.J. swings around now, still grinning, but I cannot suppress a slight cringe.

On my way to the steak house elevator, I pick up a copy of the *Sun*. The lead story has Trent Lott threatening to bring to a second vote a bill that would ship nuclear waste to Yucca Mountain, ninety miles northwest of Las Vegas. Senators Harry Reid of Nevada and Tom Daschle of South Dakota, however, have "called Lott's bluff, saying they would rally Democrats and sustain Clinton's veto again." I also learn that Fusaichi Pegasus is a 3–5 favorite in the Preakness on Saturday, and that UNLV blew a four-run lead in the final inning to lose 7–6 to San Diego State in their Mountain West Conference tournament opener. I know how they feel.

At the bottom of page one is a flattering photo of Becky: bright eyes, big smile, glowing cheeks. She looks both relaxed and in charge. The headline reads: "Behnen Confident Jury Will Reach Fair Decision." The reporter, Jeff German, quotes her: "The first time I saw them, I could tell they were extremely conscientious. It was 110 degrees in the courtroom, and they sat there and didn't move and hung on every word." German notes that the jurors have been deliberating for over nine days, a new record for Nevada, before quoting Becky again: "I'm very impressed with them. There must be a great deal of pressure to be in this position. I think they know they're going to be quizzed a lot after the verdict, and they want to show that they looked at everything. . . . They're not going to embarrass themselves." German also reports that the foreman had said in a letter to the judge that they were "moving in the right direction, taking the time required to give the defendants a fair and just trial by this jury."

"To the best champion ever!" says Tom Ferguson, hoisting a bubbly flute of Moët & Chandon toward his son. Chris bows his head, tugs a few dangling strands of hair back behind his left ear, then returns his dad's gaze, reraising his emotion.

"Hear, hear!" say we all, clinking flutes.

Chris sits across from me, in the middle of the long, narrow spread: snowy tablecloth, jumbo martinis and shrimp, much Moët. I didn't catch everyone's name, but among Chris's friends and family are Cathy; Randy Leavitt, his best friend from high school; his older brother, Marc, and Marc's wife, another (much prettier) Chris Ferguson; Dave and Tish and a few other friends from LA; and Perry Friedman, whom Chris dispatched in third place in the stud tournament, but who seems, two weeks later, to have recovered. And once again, "Cheers!" With thirteen of us at the table this unholy Thursday, twenty-three stories above Glitter Gulch in the Horseshoe's Ranch

Steak House, we're a perfect Las Vegas Last Supper. As the toasting continues, I swig what is left in my glass and pour myself seconds, stanching the overflow with two salty fingers while recalling my promise to toast with Padraig and Véronique. But I wish we were drinking to me, or at least that I'd finished in "t'ird." That honor, along with $570,500, went to Steve Kaufman, whom I silently toast with an Olde English expletive. I'm sure he'd be able to translate.

The Clark County courthouse is too close to see from this angle, but according to the local news (which I watched for a few minutes in my room while on my way up here) the jurors are still down there, deciding. A mile or so south, past the Stratosphere Tower, the diagonal Strip glimmers warmly in horizontal sunlight, leaving its parallel rows of neon and video plumage almost invisible, at least for another ten minutes.

Who's Judas, I wonder. Who wants to betray the world champ for a couple of pieces of silver? How about for a few bars of bullion? Not me. (Wait a sec. How many bars, did you say?) For one thing, Chris has made it clear that he realizes how lucky he was, which makes it much easier to appreciate how brilliantly he played throughout the World Series. Four final tables, two first-place finishes, $1,672,260. That was skill talking, folks. I also can't imagine that his modest, congenial spirit is a front he's maintained for three weeks. (As Ted might say, "No one is that good an actor," and in this case he wouldn't be wrong.) Maybe I'd feel differently if Chris had driven a splintery stake through my heart a few times, the way he did to Perry, Jeff, Annie, and T.J. Either way, he's going to finish his dinner, retire downstairs for some celebratory lovemaking and a solid night's sleep, then drive home in triumph to Pacific Palisades with his girlfriend, his family, his new Ph.D., a huge check, and a pair of gold bracelets. As much as any player can in a poker tournament, this guy earned them.

Not that he didn't have some advantages. His dad, we may recall, is professor emeritus of game theory and statistics at UCLA. Gray-haired and lean, Adam's apple visible through his peppery beard, Tom has the same deep-set eyes and bushy eyebrows that his younger son has. Behind his thick lenses, pens and glasses case protruding from the breast pocket of his shirt, this is the man who taught Chris how to think. Tom doesn't play poker himself, but he brought home games like Nim and Othello for his sons, nursing their tactical skills. Their mother, Beatriz Rossello, did not make the trip from Los Angeles. I'm told she is firmly opposed to all things Las Vegas—even more so than Tom is—but that even she caved this morning, bought a ticket, and drove down to LAX. She wound up missing her flight, though, and had to follow the play-by-play via cell phone. When it turns out that Mom has her own Ph.D. in mathematics (her topic was point set topology, the study of forms that bend and stretch), you have to wonder if any further evidence is necessary that genes, education, and pure Beatrician encouragement can help you play no-limit hold'em. It surely can't hurt that her son can take the fifth root of a sixteen-digit number, or multiply four-digit numbers—oh, let's say, 3,789 times 8,387—in his head quite a bit faster than I can with paper and pen.

"Three one seven seven eight three four three," he says maybe twelve seconds later, then waits.

"That's . . . shit. Excuse me," I mutter, carrying a six to the left. "This pen doesn't work very well. Could you say that again?"

"Thirty-one million seven hundred seventy-eight thousand three forty-three."

More bemused waiting as I add my eight columns of digits.

"That's right," I admit. "That's . . . real depressing."

"You wanna know his *favorite* parlor trick?" Cathy asks.

Yes, I do.

"He has you take one card from a deck, then he looks at the other cards one at a time and says which one you pulled. Works every time."

Palms up, Chris modestly shows me his hands. Look, Ma, no nail holes! "That's a trick we learn pretty early on. No big deal."

What I'm trying to calculate now is all the ways talents like these could help him against me in poker. "Yeah, right."

And yet as the entrées arrive what Tom wants to talk about are the hands "where he got lucky." The hands, in other words, in which game theory and computational firepower came *least* into play. And not just the final hand, either. The three big split pots that baled Chris out earlier seem to be the ones that impressed Tom the most. "I mean, *wow!*" he half yells, referring to the hand where Chris spiked the ten for a split. "Otherwise, bye-bye," he says, shaking his head in wonder.

"Lucky?" asks one of the LA contingent, this as a pair of young couples cruise by, pausing to gape at the champion. "This guy, lucky?"

"Who, him?" Perry Friedman asks pointedly.

Chris nods and shrugs at the general hilarity, then leans into another Cathy Burns smooch on his cheek. Missing Jennifer even more fiercely, I slice off a piece of three-inch-thick Montana porterhouse, chew for a minute or so, wash it down with a guzzle of '91 Mondavi reserve cabernet. (Becky has pulled out the stops in comping the champion's party, and we hear she's done the same for the Cloutiers.) This time I sip cabernet *before* the meat goes in my mouth, silently toasting the Binion Money Machine while I chew. Nine days of cafeteria turkey and mash, of lemonade, iced tea, and the local bottled water, makes all this taste extra yummy. *This is the end, dum-dum-dum-dum, my only friend, the end* . . . There's nothing like red wine and beef and the feel of clay chips pressing against your upper thigh or clacking between your moist fingers, especially when one of them's worth five thousand dollars, to put an old song in your heart.

I'm still obsessed, of course, with Hasan's diabolical four, and with the hand I had aces but couldn't get even one caller. I have to force myself to maturely recall that if I hadn't drawn out on the cowboy's three jacks back on Tuesday, or if T.J. had paired his nine kicker last night, or Annie Duke spiked a third queen, my run would have ended much sooner. But what keeps ambushing my imagination is the three hundred grand I effectively lost when this morning's near-deal got kaboshed. Jennifer and I could have closed out our mortgage with that kind of dough, even after paying the taxes. Maybe even covered a semester of college in 2016 . . .

When I ask Chris what he'd thought of the deal, he gives me a curious look. "First I've heard of it," he says, then suggests that T.J. must have nixed it before Hasan could propose it to the guy who'd get only a million. Both of us have heard that T.J.'s arrangement with his backer—Lyle Berman, the Lakes Gaming mogul who buys him into tournaments and covers his travel expenses—doesn't permit any deals. And why should it, when T.J. has already won fifty big tournaments outright? In any event, Chris says he would have declined. "Not with the chip lead I had. No way."

After flipping the cassette in my tape recorder, I ask him to talk about his table image and how, especially in tournaments, first impressions can make all the difference in how other players respond to your bets.

"Anything to throw you guys off," he says, noshing salad. Crisp salad.

It finally dawns on me that I need to let the guy eat in peace.

"But he also cleans up real nice," Cathy says, beaming. When Chris shoots her a mock-doubtful look, she leans up against him—a full-body nudge of affection. She's wearing the seven-stud bracelet on her slender, lightly freckled left wrist, this to go with the new one on Chris. He's the only double bracelet winner of the 2000 Series, one of the very few folks ever to accomplish that feat.

"I'll probably put the nine of hearts on this one," he says, referring to the gold he has on. Ever the numbers wonk, he notes that the stud event he won was, in fact, "the ninth event of the World Series." I make a mental note to send him some Dante annotations. The Pinsky and Mandelbaum are especially good on Dante's obsession with nine and three, as well as with Beatriz's namesake.

Cathy points out that her guy is "still" wearing the same blue, white, and beige checkered shirt that he wore to the stud final table—where he came from dead last, down 1–10 in chip count, to win. One of her friends wants to know who'll wear "the" bracelet when they go out.

He stifles a yawn with his fist, swallows food. "I'll probably just stick it in a safety deposit box." More chewing. "I didn't sleep at all last night," he tells us, explaining the yawn.

Cathy confirms it. "He was worried he wouldn't be able to concentrate . . ."

". . . but after the first few hands I was able to focus a hundred percent on the action."

One of the LA folks asks how he finally decided to call with ace-nine.

Chris taps his fork on the tablecloth. He's probably answered this question thirty-seven times in the last ninety minutes, yet he's game for another crack at it. "T.J. came out raising a hundred and seventy-five thousand, and I reraised him four and a quarter. When he came back over the top of me all-in, I wasn't too happy. But I've already got six hundred-what-odd in there . . ."

Did game theory help him make the call?

He shrugs. "Didn't hurt."

Someone else wants to know whether he subjected the call "to a Bayesian statistical analysis."

Though the question sounded serious, all Chris does is laugh. Then he stops. "I really feel terrible for T.J. I can imagine how brutal losing like that can be. He was definitely the best player today."

"What about that hand you and Jeff played last night?" I ask him, unable to stop myself. "The sevens and sixes."

"The blinds were at fifteen and thirty thousand," he says gallantly, then looks away for a moment and squints, recalling the hand with his usual scary precision. "I had about eight hundred thousand, Jeff a little less than twice that . . ."

"Jeff's on the button, you're in the big blind . . ."

He nods. "Jeff made it two hundred thousand to go, about twice the usual raise, which told me two things: he had a hand, and he didn't want any action. Being the disagreeable person I am, I decided to move in with my sixes and put him to a really tough decision. He deserves just a huge amount of credit for making that call with his sevens."

"No question," I say, but someone else chimes in with, "Sort of."

Chris disagrees. "That was a spectacular call."

A couple of miles behind him, the Strip glows and twinkles. Sunset officially over.

"You know," I say, resolving to ask no more questions, "I gotta admit I was nuts to be calling you with ace-nine last night."

He laughs, shakes his head. "I *hated* that call. I just hated it."

"One of us shoulda been a goner."

"No question. I mean, ace-nine sucks, if you ask me. Especially to be making your call with. Or mine," he says, referring to the last hand he played.

336 ♣   POSITIVELY FIFTH STREET

"But ace-queen sucks worse," I inform him.

He nods—doesn't smile, doesn't smirk—then picks up the closest Moët bottle and pours what's left into my flute.

There are two ways to sleep like a baby. The better way is to fall asleep as soon as your head hits the pillow and stay asleep until you wake up, cheerful and well rested, your problems and pleasures in more lucid perspective, in the morning. The other way is to sleep for an hour, cry for an hour, sleep for an hour, cry for an hour . . .

I opt for the latter, of course.

Five a.m. seems as good a time as any to abandon my siege of gut-soothing, brain-cooling slumber, so I put on my sandals, head out. Down the elevator, through the nearly empty casino and out onto Fremont, heading west toward the train station for a slight change of scenery. As I pass the Pioneer Hotel, a narrow-eyed blonde falls into step alongside me, yet my sense of Gulch etiquette is that I don't have to stop or say howdy. A dozen strides later she speaks to me, loud but not clear. From the thickly guttural syllables she's hurling my way, I take her for a refugee, from what I have little idea. Bosnia? Loveless-ness? Russia?

Hungary. Is that what she said to me? *Angary?*

I stop, turning halfway around. Teeth chattering in the predawn desert air, filthy Adidas warmup hanging open, one erect nipple projecting through Kurt Cobain T-shirt, the girl stops as well. Turns to face me. We stare at each other, at least one of us desperate to pick up a tell.

"Here you go." I peel a crisp twenty from my gangster roll, hold it out between us. "Are you hungry?"

Shifting her weight from one jangly foot to the other, she glowers—at me, at the bill, at the roll, back at me. Her dark eyes get less and less narrow. Finally she plucks the twenty by its uppermost corner and holds it like that. She lowers her head, then suddenly raises her chin toward my face. Doesn't smile. Is she going to slug me or kiss me?

Neither one, I'm relieved to find out, as she mutters her version of thank-you and angles back over toward First Street.

EITHER WAY

A bird in the hand is better than no bread.
To have your cake is to pay Paul.
Make hay while you can still hit the nail on the head.
For want of a nail the sky might fall.
—PAUL MULDOON, "Symposium"

The discourse flamed, the jurors sang, the lapdog strained its leash—
When I went forth to have you found the tenured took the beach
With dolloped hair and jangled nerves, without a jacking clue,
While all around the clacking sound of polished woodblocks blew.
—SUSAN WHEELER, "Shanked on the Red Bed"

The front page of Friday morning's *R-J* features a big color picture of Chris with his fists in the air. The white-haired dealer, who has just peeled the nine of hearts off the deck and laid it on the table, stares glumly ahead, as though he'd been rooting for T.J. According to the caption, the dealer's name is, of all things, Johnny Moss. Behind him, reacting, are Bob Thompson, Annie Duke, Phil Hellmuth, and a few other folks I don't recognize. T.J. is not in the frame. A smaller picture below it shows Becky laughing as Chris holds the ace of spades and nine of clubs against the mountain of money and chips, resting his head on the top like a four-year-old hugging his pillow. ATOP THE WORLD, says the headline. The story lists names, nicknames, prize money, and order of finish before concluding with a comment from Becky. "Asked about rumors the World Series would be sold to another property with more space and resources, Behnen said the World

Outside the Clark County Courthouse

Series would remain at her casino. 'It started here, and it will stay here,' she said. 'If we have to, we'll play outside.' "

On page three is a gossip column by Norm Clarke, whose picture has him sporting a toothy smile and rakish black eye patch. Below that, a photo of Ted's open safe on display in the Horseshoe. Clarke reports that the safe is misbilled as far as being formerly owned by Wyatt Earp or emptied by parties unknown. Evidence? "Bobby Fechser, grandson of Horseshoe founder Benny Binion, on Thursday disputed both claims. He accused Becky Behnen, Ted Binion's sister and president of the Horseshoe, of exploitation, saying, 'She wants to get as many people in there as possible.' "

Clarke's next item involves Oscar Goodman. The mayor, he writes, while "trying to remain neutral as to not offend any constituents, seems to be rooting for an acquittal. 'It's never a good story if it's a conviction,' he said at his weekly press conference Thursday. 'It's only a good story if it's an acquittal.' " Oscar also had some lawyerly advice for the defense team: he'd be "screaming bloody murder" each time it was referred to in the media as "the Binion murder trial," because no one had been convicted of murder. Good thinking, O. Best not to mention the m-word.

Item three is the Quote of the Day, "See you tonight at Piero's," which Clarke attributes to Sandy Murphy while she was speaking to John Momot on the way to her jail cell on Wednesday. Clarke goes on to explain that it was at a Piero's urinal that Tabish made Binion's acquaintance.

After dishing dirt on Julia Roberts, Brad Pitt, and Sammy Davis Jr., Clarke ends his column with a quote from Mike Tyson. The former champ was on campus in Wilberforce, Ohio, not far from where he was convicted of and served time for rape, to receive an honorary doctorate from Central State University. "I don't know what kind of doctor I am. But watching all these beautiful sisters here . . . I'm debating whether I should be a gynecologist."

Tearing them away from the rest of the paper, I add these new pages to the four-inch stack already packed in my suitcase. I had to buy a monogrammed Horseshoe suitbag to accommodate all the clippings, magazines, tournament reports, free poker books and

CD-ROMs, shot glasses, hats, decks of cards, pens, shirts, final-table jacket and commemorative, albeit unmonogrammed, towel, to go with nine days' worth of dirty laundry.

After scouring the room for loose chips and Post-its, I head over to the courthouse for one final chat with reporters and trial freaks. But nothing has changed; the story remains, Still No Story. Virtually no one doubts that the couple killed Binion, but after nine days of deliberation a lot of folks are predicting either a mistrial or "a flat-out not-guilty." But when? *Sun* reporter Kim Smith tells me "we're screwed if the jury comes back today." The *Sun* is an evening paper with a 10 a.m. deadline, but over the weekend they publish a joint edition with the *R-J*, making it impossible for either paper to scoop the other on events that occur after 3 p.m. Friday. Like most reporters, Smith believes the verdict will not be revealed until Monday.

I wish I could stay here to see it, though I don't think it makes any difference to my article whether I watch it on TV while sitting at home or in Vegas. My flight leaves at midnight, and the plan is to finish packing then play a little poker at the Bellagio before heading to the airport. The girls will be just waking up as the cab gets me back to our house.

After closing my lockbox and cashing my chips I literally bump into Becky, who's on her way up to her office. With her wan, frazzled smile to go with a pale blue western-cut suit and white moccasins, she looks like she just got through hosting a five-week party for three thousand people, one of whom still hasn't left. We congratulate each another again, and I perfunctorily ask if she'll answer a few questions. I'm more than a little surprised when she says, "Of course, Jim. C'mon upstairs." She rides with me up the escalator to a suite marked Executive Offices. A decent reporter, of course, would have already known where they were—just around the corner from the elevators on the second floor, across from Gee Joan, where I had orange chicken last week. I've walked by this door a few dozen times since last Wednesday.

Off to the right, past a warren of cubicles, Becky's waiting area and office are sizable but unprepossessing, not what you'd expect for the head of a Money Machine, even one that may soon be in bankruptcy. No windows, for one thing, and the ceiling can't be more than eight feet. Framed family pictures line a few bookshelves, and an impressive pair of longhorns is mounted on the wall behind her desk. To the right is a charcoal drawing of her dad in a buffalo-hide coat, grinning confidently from under his trademark beige 20-X Stetson.

His daughter invites me to sit. "What do you want to ask me, Jim?"

My subject may be anxious to get to the point, but I hardly know where to begin. I apologize for having to grill her, mentioning that because of the way we met, she probably doesn't think of me as a reporter. For that matter, neither do I. But I also have a feeling that this has enhanced our rapport. Even so, is it seemly, or even useful, to ask how she "feels" about her feud with one brother while a jury deliberates the guilt or innocence of her other brother's killers? "What about the balloon payment due to Jack on July 1?" is the question I settle on. I tell her I've heard that if she misses the payment, the Horseshoe reverts to her brother's control. "I've also heard that he might take the tournament—"

"Oh, no no no, Jim," she says. "The payment was due *last* July, and that's all taken care of. The World Series, everything, is staying right here."

Now, this contradicts what I've read in both papers and heard from a slew of reliable sources, but again I decide not to mention it. Why? Because I'm a crappy reporter. Because of all the success she and I have enjoyed during this World Series, and who wants to cancel that vibe? Because her and Jack's brother was viciously murdered by people who might get away with it. Because I asked her a question; she answered it.

Becky nods toward a porcelain angel at the front of her desk. "Ted gave me that when I was six." The blond figurine clutches a little green bucket; there's a crab on the sand near its feet. Becky and Ted are both boomers, like me. Same pop songs, same haircuts, same movies, same waistlines, same presidents. My mother and sisters have tchotchkes exactly like this one.

Becky hands me a picture of Ted at maybe sixteen or seventeen looking chipper and tousle-haired astride a quarter horse; beside him on a bigger horse is a full-grown man in a cowboy hat. Not Benny, too old to be Jack.

"Who's this other guy?"

"Oh, that's an in-law who's no longer an in-law."

I nod. Same divorce rate as well. Same vintage tint in the snapshots.

Becky changes the subject by telling me about the time thirteen-year-old Ted snipped the wicks off the candles of their church's Advent wreath, then mimicked the look on the bishop's face when he tried to light the candles. "Teddy had sort of a wild streak."

Absurdly, I've had to borrow a notepad and pen from her to scribble down what she tells me. Yet the more we talk about our families, the less I write down, and the longer we go on—for over an hour—the more it turns out we have in common. Stay-at-home mothers and ambitious fathers, bankruptcies, prison time, drugs, Catholic school in the fifties and sixties, and poker. But the main thing is that in the past three years Becky and I have each lost a brother. My brother Kevin wrote for the *Washington Post*. He was strong, forty-one, in bionic-man shape (aside from having leukemia) when he was admitted to Johns Hopkins, the place we'd been assured had the best treatment center on earth. But he still didn't make it. His wife, Anne, an editor at *U.S. News and World Report*, is raising their two children alone, as Doris Binion is now raising Bonnie in Dallas. Bonnie's Aunt Brenda lives in Amarillo these days, having long been a close friend of Slim's.

Becky and her husband have another son, Jack, who's autistic. After the usual twenty-year "rough patch," as she calls it, his mental health has improved to the point where he's able to deal blackjack downstairs. "Jack is our project," she tells me, "but he's also our pride and joy." His therapist showed the family how to use "pin downs," firm, loving, on-the-floor hugs to pacify him during his fits. "What used to be eight-hour ordeals now take ten minutes," Becky tells me, then waxes at length about what a terrific big brother Benny has been all these years. My daughter Bridget works with autistic kids, and Becky wants details. She also recalls going into premature labor during the 1976 World Series, and how she and Nick decided to name the child Benny, then adds, "That was the year Doyle won, I believe . . ."

"Yeah, it was."

I note but don't mention that Becky and Nick named their first son after her father, their second after the sibling to whom she was closest growing up, that being Jack. But I do ask Becky how she thinks the trial is going—"if you don't mind my asking."

"I feel those two prosecutors really did a good job," she says brightly, before her small voice trails off. "But, you know, I don't know." When she talks about how much weight Tabish lost this past year, she sounds much less vengeful than sad, especially about his long separation from Kyle and Amanda, his young son and daughter. Her voice has more energy when she talks about Murphy, referring to her as "that girl" or with pronouns. "But neither one of them will ever have another good day, either way."

Either way? This reminds me of something her father told historian Mary Ellen Glass back in '73, about his being "very capable of easily takin' care of" his family's enemies "in a most artistic way." Will Murphy and Tabish be artistically taken care of if the jury acquits them? Is this what we're talking here—wet work? It's a question any competent reporter would manage to ask, but I can't. The right phrasing simply won't form in my brain, let alone on my tongue. My only excuse is that, anxious as Becky may be to "put the trial behind us," there's a catch in her voice as she tells me she still might not be able to attend the reading of the verdict. "It would be bad enough if the jury went the wrong way, but I don't need her taunting us again." I assume she's referring to Murphy's habit of turning around to leer at Ted's friends and family whenever the defense scores a point. I can't help thinking of her and Rick's ultimate taunt—making Ted watch them fuck before killing him. I would "take care" of them, too. Can I say this?

"You know," Becky tells me, "when I talked to the jury, every person seemed so caring, so intelligent. And with all of this press, they don't want to embarrass themselves. So I really don't know who'll be celebrating. Certainly *we* won't be . . ." Tears in her eyes, she reaches across the desk for a Kleenex.

This is my first conversation with the relative of a murder victim. (I interviewed Michael Jordan during the '97 NBA Finals, but our subject was basketball only.) I'm also not used to writing down verbatim what a person is telling me, even on happier topics. Sitting here with her notepad and pen feels macabre.

"Either way," she repeats with some force, "they'll never have any good days."

Now I get it: she *wants* me to ask what she means. Should I say, Because they'll be so wracked with guilt? That's a laugh. More likely, she means it's because they'll always be looking over their shoulders, knowing that Jack, Nick, Becky, Benny Jr., and company will deliver their own brand of justice. Does she want to use *Harper's* to help put the frighteners on Murphy and Tabish, whether or not they're in prison? I continue to nod in a *meaningful* way, but nothing comes out of my mouth.

Becky is dabbing her eyes with a tissue when I surprise myself again by proposing to accompany her to the courtroom for the reading of the verdict—"assuming you'll be there yourself." Maybe then I can ask what she meant. The worst she can do, to me if not them, is say no.

She says yes. Her assistant takes my room number, expressing surprise that the *Harper's* reporter isn't packing a cell phone. Becky ushers me out through the warren and hugs me good-bye.

"I'll see you. And thank you. Tell Benny I'll see him there, too."

My plan all along had been to rely on Court TV and the *Sun* and *R-J* web sites for my account of the verdict, but being in the courtroom with Becky and the rest of Ted's family is a chance I don't want to pass up. It would cost only $75 to change my ticket, although since I don't know what day I'll be leaving, I'll probably have to fly standby. The real issue is that I haven't seen Jennifer, our girls, or Bridget or James for ten days, and Jennifer's dead-on imitations of Bea asking "Where Dat?" don't make my quandary easier. I could also wait around for a week only to have Becky decide she can't bear to be in the courtroom, though at least I'd have funds to play poker every day in the meantime. I'd probably have to go lease a cell phone.

To help me figure out how to play this, I take one last swim on the roof. Another thing goading me to stay is the latest manure from the mayor, the mouthpiece that couldn't stop woofing. *It's only a good story if it's an acquittal.* That so? The bottom line, however, is that I'm getting pretty desperate to see my wife and children again.

Now that Humberto has flown home to his in Costa Rica and *La Niña* has returned to the Meadows, driving temperatures over a hundred, I have the pool all to myself. It's the first time I've been shirtless under Vegas's afternoon sun, and it's probably scorching my shoulders. *I'll scream bloody murder, do you hear me, if anyone dares call this a murder trial.* Honestly. As I'm changing direction in the far corner, I hear and then see a helicopter hovering off to the south. The Alvarez clock says 3:47, too early for traffic reports . . .

I get out, grab my stuff, rush downstairs. My phone light is blinking—seven messages, though I have time to hear only two because the second is from Becky's assistant: jury back, verdict to be read at 4:30, meet Becky inside Courtroom 4.

The east facade of the courthouse resembles a four-story sheet of powder blue Peg-Board, a place to hang an Oldenburg gavel, if not one's hopes for a swift and fair verdict. On the lawn below are two portable TVs, each with a dozen folks lounging in a half circle of beach chairs, passing around french fries and water bottles. Kids in tuxes and gowns mingle with oldsters in Hawaiian shirts and flip-flops, presumably here to dissemble their way out of tickets. Others press in around monitors of the local news teams. It's a party.

It takes fifteen minutes to make it through metal detectors and the final cordon of security. Upstairs, in the crush of the hallway outside Courtroom 4, reporters who've been covering the case for twenty-one months jostle forward, and I feel a shade guilty elbowing and excusing my way past them. When I get to the door I knock on it softly, politely. No answer. I give it another few raps, wait several seconds, give it six or eight more. Eventually the door slowly opens a foot and I'm facing a stern, hefty bailiff.

I tell him my name, show my pass, making sure he sees the side that says "Press," not the side that says "Binion's World Series of Poker 2000." Trying to sound as unprivileged as possible, I tell him, "The victim's sister asked me to be with her in there." I repeat that I'm working for *Harper's* and that "Becky Binion is expecting me. Would you tell her I'm here, please?"

He nods, in a way, while closing the door in my face.

"You might wanna back up, I were you," this from a hyper reporter whose hipbone is nudging my ass. I take this proposal as hostile, an expression of resentment or a trick to get past me, but the young man and others manage to convince me that it's for my own good. It turns out that a pregnant reporter for Channel 8 was standing right here half an hour ago, when one of the bailiffs flung open the door and the knob punched her abdomen so hard she was taken away in an ambulance. There's no room to take a step back, but I do *lean* away from the door.

It's 4:35 when it finally opens—so very slowly again, and this time I understand why. The bailiff takes me by the shoulder and steers me inside, escorting me to the last seat in the back row, far right. The walls of the small, crowded room are paneled in cheery pale maple. Behind the bench is a slab of gray marble with the great seal of Nevada in the center. A plaque above Bonaventure's desk reads: "The truth takes few words." In the front row on this side sits Bobby Fechser, Brenda's lanky blond son, his pale slacks and cowboy boots poking out into the aisle. Behind him sit Benny and a middle-aged black woman I haven't seen before. I give Benny a thumbs-up when he finally turns around, and he nods. Behind him are his parents; behind them is Becky's assistant alongside Benny's girlfriend, Andrea, whom I met early on at the tournament—a twentyish brunette built like Murphy, but facially sweeter.

Becky looks composed in pearl earrings, which she must have put on to formalize the pantsuit and moccasins. Nick Behnen is a husky six two or six three, making Becky look tiny as she steps across the aisle to introduce us. When she adds, "Jim made the final table last night," Nick politely pretends that this matters. If I hadn't, however, I probably wouldn't be standing here.

Directly across the aisle from me is Mary Jane Stevenson. She has long, heavily freckled legs unobstructed by nylons beneath her gray suit. Beneath a garland of fox-brown hair stiff with spray, her complexion is blotchier than it appears on Court TV, though she still looks attractive and smart. As the jury comes in, she stands up, but gets told to sit down by a bailiff. Because of all the photographers flanking the jury box, we can't see the back row of jurors. One woman, a heavyset young blonde, has on sunglasses, which Stevenson tells me required special permission from Judge Bonaventure. Craning my neck, I see that at least three other jurors wear shades. (As Michael Baden said later, "No one could remember having ever seen such a sight in a jury.") At the far left of the front row is a big white-haired gent, untucked white golf shirt clinging to his belly. This must be the aerospace engineer, and he looks like someone I know but can't place. To his right is a black woman, then an older white woman, then what appears to be a very short man, also in sunglasses. Together they look like a group on its way to a VFW picnic or, even stranger, a poker tournament.

Over on the bride side, I recognize Bill Fuller's white pompadour. This is the guy who supposedly spent a few million dollars on Murphy's defense, leased her a swank apartment and a Mercedes convertible, then proposed that she marry him. No word yet on Sandy's answer, but given her MO she will probably accept, even if Rick is exonerated.

Guilty? Not guilty? I do.

At twelve before five the lawyers file in. Davids Roger and Wall—both nondescript from the back, in dark, lumpy suits—take their seats at the prosecution table. The more Italianate Momot and Palazzo, et al., remain standing near the table to my left as the defendants are led in by three bailiffs. Murphy is thin, almost pretty. She's wearing a black four-button pantsuit and white blouse, her mouse-brown hair in a short, simple braid. Schoolmarm chic. Do big teased blond hair and flashy designer outfits imply less aversion to suffocating a guy for his money? In the view of Murphy's pollsters and attorneys, who get paid lots of money to know, there seems little doubt that they do.

Even more than he does on television, Tabish resembles a younger John Momot. With their beady eyes and marmot profiles, their slick suits and haircuts, they look like a father-son duo of tall, natty rats. But at least Momot's cheeks have some color. In this sunburnt desert May, Tabish is so white he looks blue, hewn from skim milk. Together with spry Mr. Fuller, these are the three men in Sandy's new life. The flirtatious whispers and grins she's lavishing on Momot suggest that, for now, he's the favorite, but this is likely to change any moment.

The only other person in the room that I recognize is the detective Tom Dillard, in a gray suit and blue shirt and tie, sitting sideways in the front row behind David Wall. Maybe Bill Cassidy, Oscar's "eccentric" pollster, will whack Dillard right here while we watch, and Oscar will *still* get him off. Everyone in the room is a witness, so we all would be gunned down like elk.

Finally Judge Bonaventure makes his entrance. Clearly Sicilian, he's much less rotund than he looks on TV. His bright eyes and boyish gray moptop give him the tough but beneficent aspect of a Gangsta Beatle, in spite of the robe and the jowls. After whispering something to his clerk, he swings his chair around to face the jury. "Ladies and gentlemen, have you selected a foreperson?"

As a group, not altogether in sync, the jury says yes; at the very least, no one says no. My overwhelming sense is: they're deadlocked. The holdouts, having been crying all day, need to cover their eyes with dark glasses. See you tonight at Piero's.

"Who is that foreperson?" asks the judge, with more than a trace of a Rhode Island accent.

"I am, sir." This from the big, white-haired gent.

Bonaventure asks him to stand, and he does. "Have you arrived at a verdict?"

"Yes we have, Your Honor."

Well, well.

"Ms. Murphy, Mr. Tabish, would you please stand up?"

Along with their lawyers, they do so, all of them facing the jury. Bonaventure asks the foreperson to hand the verdicts to the bailiff. Dead silence. Sitting in the very last row, my vantage point needs to be higher, but I don't have permission to stand. I decide to split the difference by letting the spring-hinged cushion go up. Sitting on the metal front edge, I can see that the judge appears to sigh as he peruses one royal blue verdict sheet. His right hand strays up to his mouth and chin, his thumb absently massaging his lips for a good fifteen seconds.

He sniffs as he reads through the second one. If they both say not guilty, Murphy and Tabish will be walking out the same door that I do, headed for Piero's, Valentino's, wherever. Celebration fuck in the limo, with a chuckle or two about Ted, then a quiet little booth to drink some champagne, have some filets and bordeaux, sign a few movie and book deals. If the sheets both say guilty, they'll be in prison for more or less ever. Tabish will never spend time with his children again. Murphy won't have any, period.

What's been obvious all along is that they acted in much the same spirit as Aegisthus and Clytemnestra, Lord and Lady Macbeth, Clyde and Bonnie, Girolamo Cardano's wife-poisoning son. Murphy is also the wicked stepdaughter of Helen, of Claudine Longet, Robin Givens, Michelle Triola, Anna Nicole Smith, of the various Bouviers, Trumps, and Gabors. By refusing to mate with males not at the top of the food chain, trading beauty and youth for big money and calling the transaction "love," they short-circuit healthier affinities. *Basically a whore*, Bonnie Binion's terse read of Murphy, nails most of these ladies right on their cynical noggins.

Yet it's mainly the specter of Nicole Brown Simpson that haunts these proceedings. Her arrangement with O.J. spookily parallels Murphy's with Ted: dyed-blond California Girls mounted and stuffed as trophy consorts, beaten up when the mood descended upon their illustrious husbands. Like a sheer black stocking, however, the parallel gets yanked inside out when Sandy actually *does* what Nicole must have thought about—namely, whacking the dude who'd been slapping her around. The race card won't play here, but that O.J. beat Nicole to the punch *and got off* has caused most people following this case to think that while guilty, both Murphy and Tabish will walk.

The other specter here is the victim. Ted was born with entire bars of silver in his mouth, to say nothing of a spoon; he's the ultimate privileged white male. Like Agamemnon, he sacrificed a daughter to his appetite for conquest and concubines, only to be cuckolded and murdered at home. He cheated on his wife, beat up his girlfriend, abused both prescription and street drugs, liked kinky sex. The sort of folks who show up on juries may well think that Ted's having lived by these swords makes the swordsman and -woman who slew him somehow not guilty of murder, that all they really did was accelerate the tilt Ted himself *chose* to be on . . .

"Mr. Foreperson, please read the verdicts aloud, starting at the very top and working your way down."

"Yes, Your Honor. Any particular defendant?"

"The one on top will be fine."

"In the *State of Nevada v. Richard Bennett Tabish*, we the jury in the above entitled case find the defendant, Richard Bennett Tabish, as follows. Count one, conspiracy to commit murder and or robbery: guilty of conspiracy to commit murder and or robbery." Shuddering, Becky rests her head on Nick's arm; he gently moves it against his chest and swings his arm back around her shoulders. I don't know the law, but it sounds as though in one fell swoop both Murphy and Tabish have just been convicted, since who besides Murphy could Tabish have conspired with? Tabish is keeping his chin up, a beady-eyed Dracula sporting *way* too much gel for his big day in court. Murphy, from my angle, looks frightened but under control, even upon hearing ". . . two, conspiracy to commit extortion: guilty of conspiracy to commit extortion. Count three, conspiracy to commit kidnapping: guilty of conspiracy to commit kidnapping." I can't see his face, but Benny seems not to have reacted yet. I wonder where Brenda and Jack are—though both of them live out of state and we had less than two hours' notice.

Count four against Tabish is first-degree kidnapping with use of a deadly weapon, and the verdict is the same, with the foreperson adding a dash of conviction when he says the word "guilty." The same for count five, false imprisonment with use of a deadly weapon; six, extortion with use of a deadly weapon; and seven, first-degree murder with use of a deadly weapon: "*guilty* of first-degree murder with use of a deadly weapon." Use of a deadly weapon confers doubled jail time, so no steak tonight for Rick Tabish. No lap dances, either, from Sandy. No taunting. The last four counts are robbery with a deadly weapon, conspiracy to commit burglary and or grand larceny, burglary, and, finally, grand larceny. Guilty, guilty, guilty, guilty.

"Read the other, please, Mr. Foreman."

"In the *State of Nevada v. Sandra Renee Murphy*," he reads, enunciating every word crisply—Noel Furlong, I realize, is the guy he reminds me of—"we the jury in the above entitled case find the defendant, Sandra Renee Murphy, on count one, conspiracy to commit murder and or robbery: guilty of conspiracy to commit murder and or robbery."

Becky's shoulders fall slightly. She trembles, sags further against her husband. The extortion and kidnapping charges haven't been made against Sandra Renee, so the next count is "seven, murder with the use of a deadly weapon: guilty of murder in the first degree." It's a heavy-water phrase, *murder in the first degree*, but it also means Murphy has been spared the doubled sentence, apparently because she only used her *weight* on Ted's chest and her *hands* on his throat. Maybe Bill Fuller still has a chance now, since in twenty years she'll be only forty-eight, he just a hundred and three. (In the meantime, can murderers in Nevada receive conjugal visits? Would prison guards loan out their handcuffs?) Murphy is shaking her small, demure head back and forth. No whining or ululations, however, as many trial watchers expected. Counts eight through eleven against her are identical to the ones against Tabish: robbery, burglary and or grand larceny, burglary, grand larceny. All guilty. Still in strong voice, the foreperson concludes: "dated this nineteenth day of May 2000."

Bonaventure asks him to hand the blue sheets to the bailiff again, then turns to the defendants. "You can sit down if you want. It's up to you."

Murphy sits. After two beats of manly forbearance, Tabish does, too. Bonaventure asks the clerk to read back the verdicts and verify them. The clerk reads them through, giving feminine voicing to all that the foreperson declared, word for word. This takes a long time and strangely involves (for me) some suspense. Once again, though, they're found guilty. "Ladies and gentlemen of the jury," the clerk finally concludes, "are these your verdicts as read?"

Tearfully, hesitantly: yes.

Both sets of attorneys want them polled.

"Juror number one, are these your verdicts as read?" More suspense as, one by one, each juror says yes, even though numbers five and nine are weeping behind their dark glasses. Murphy shoots them daggerly glances while Tabish glares off toward the ceiling. The sixtyish juror No. 11, denim blouse hanging over the tops of her jeans, is openly sobbing. Tabish puts his hand on Murphy's hand, or her arm. Whichever part he's touched, she makes a point of pulling it away from him and leaning ten degrees more toward Momot.

Tears wet Becky's cheeks as Nick escorts her up the aisle. Boxed in by Court TV's camera crew, I get separated from the family in the rush to get out the two doors. The crush in the hall, down the stairs, is pythonic. By the time I catch up, the Behnens have pushed through the glass front doors to a heroine's welcome. "It's the sister!" Scores of Las Vegans press forward, applauding and giving thumbs-ups. Becky waves but shrinks back. The trial, after all, has attracted its fair share of nut jobs. Out of nowhere, what appear to be the same Horseshoe heavies who delivered the cardboard box yesterday have surrounded their boss. Taking their cue from Nick, the khaki-clad giants recontour themselves as a phalanx, sidestepping their way toward the corner of Third Street and Carson, where a white Binion's limo pulls to the curb with impeccable timing. As I jog alongside him, Benny tells me they'll be back at the Horseshoe in forty-five minutes. "We all can catch up with you there." He follows Andrea and his dad into the back of the car. Off they go.

Halfway back up the courthouse steps, Tom Palazzo is haranguing a clutch of reporters about the Binion Money Machine and how "stupid" it is that his client "must forfeit his freedom based on evidence developed outside normal police channels. This is America? Please." He's wearing whatever was left of the gel in Rick's tube; in the heat, though, his hairdo is melting. Behind him, a rail-thin man in Desert Storm camouflage pants and no shirt yells, "Junkie drug addict! Not Guilty! Not Guilty!" A young black man nearby brandishes a pair of hastily hand-lettered signs. One says: "Ted Binion *Heroin! User Drug Addict* Hard Facts." The other says: "?Burking? *Rick and Sandy* Are not that *Smart*! Try *Malpractice*." All three of these guys call to mind that wonderfully absurd Paul Muldoon poem: "You can lead a horse to water, but you can't make it hold / its nose to the grindstone and hunt with the hounds." But most folks out here seem convinced and quite pleased by the verdicts.

Twenty feet down the sidewalk, Bobby Fechser is being interviewed by a dignified anchorwoman type, though her microphone is covered in ratty fake fur. "I wanted to be here," says Fechser, "to show support for Ted, that he did not commit suicide." After answering two other questions, Fechser trots out the line he must have been nursing for weeks: "Bill Fuller should have taken that money and shot dice at the Horseshoe." The reporter nods deferentially, neither smiling nor frowning, then waits for Fechser to continue.

I can't. Already the scorching wind has driven grit through my lips, so I need some AC and a lager. Walking back along the east side of Second, I pass a tall man in a double-breasted tuxedo tugging one earlobe obsessively. The woman beside him has on a matching tuxedo. At least I believe it's a woman, but because of the glare I can't tell. At the far eastern tip of the Pacific time zone, Las Vegan sunsets come early. Even at 5:49 of a May afternoon, even through polarized lenses, there are horizontal shafts you must squint your way through, ricochet dazzlements forcing you to shade your eyes, sudden glares making you *duck*. Then there are thermal traps where it must reach 130. And when these are interrupted by gelid blasts from gaping casino doorways, it's a little like wandering along the perimeter of the eighth and ninth circles of Hell—all of this, mind you, while trudging a block north to Paradise.

Sandy and Rick after hearing guilty verdicts (author in upper left background)

♣ ♥

ZOMBIES IS BAWTH OF 'EM

♦ ♠

Under the influence of uncontrollable ecstasy, the players
gambled their wives, their children and ultimately themselves
into captivity.
—TACITUS, *Germania*

It had been my intention to play all the positions—to get, as I
put it to myself, a more "rounded" perspective of the game.
—GEORGE PLIMPTON, *Paper Lion*

No longer in training, I've treated myself to a cheeseburger and
two Coronas at the counter in the Horseshoe's race book. The room is
basically a medium-sized auditorium with a snack bar attached; instead
of a stage, it has twenty-five monitors, all of them tuned on most days
to various racetracks and stadia. Right now at least three are showing
verdict postmortems: Becky exiting the courthouse, Tabish's parents
avoiding the cameras, then Murphy's, Palazzo pointing fingers and
bloviating.

I can still make the 12:05 flight. If wrapping things up runs too late,
there's another at six in the morning. I'd have to fly standby on that
one, though I'm guessing a seat would be open. I could also keep my
room through tomorrow.

The Behnens show up right on schedule. Two dozen reporters and
several minicam crews were waiting in front of where Becky now sits
with a small margarita. She waves; I wave back. She certainly looks

more relaxed, even forced, as she is, to field the same questions again and again. How do you feel? Did you expect the jury to find them guilty? What would Ted make of the verdicts? "I'm sure he'd have something funny to say," she replies. "I don't know." When a reporter points out that she, Becky, was the first person to demand a review of the coroner's initial report, Becky shrugs. "It's nice to be right."

I've taken a seat beside Nick at one of the two-dollar slots and brought out a notepad. I've heard that he doesn't much cotton to poker players, preferring the fish who throw dice or feed these machines, but he seems to be okay with this one. He tells me that his father, an Austrian Greek, served in the OSS during World War II before moving his family to America. Nick met Becky in 1964, when they were both nineteen. He went into oil and real estate. These days, besides "several business interests," he is working with a cowriter on a biography of his father-in-law.

I ask him whether it will include the murder of Benny's son and the trial.

"We haven't decided that yet."

The next one is harder to ask. "Does Becky believe the rumor that Ted put out a contract on her?"

"She believes it because it's true, Jim."

"Then why—"

"He rescinded the order when the FBI moved in on him. All that surveillance, too chancy. I also think Teddy, well, he just changed his mind." After answering another reporter's question about Murphy, he asks me, "You know the strangest thing she did?" I do not. "Three or four years ago it was, she told me, 'I'm gonna make this family famous again. I just don't know how I'm going to do it.' Joking, I told her, 'I'll bet you'll do it by killing the SOB.' And she laughed.

"Teddy told me, 'I know she's not worth eight eggs.' He told me this a number of times. Told me, 'It's lonely around the house. I just have her around for some excitement.' "

For the third or fourth time, Becky is asked what Ted would have thought of the verdicts. Tequila must make her jangly, because this time she contends, " 'The bitch got what she deserved,' is what he'd be saying. 'She's the most evil, the most devious person I've ever met.' "

Asked to describe Murphy herself, Becky pauses to measure her tone. "She's a young girl who was using her youth, her looks, and her body to get what she wanted, and she finally found herself in a situation with the jury where that no longer worked. I couldn't even look at her, you know, while we were waiting for the verdict. I thought of Ted lying in that coffin and the pictures of him in that body bag. My thoughts were more on my brother than any kind of animosity toward them." She interrupts the next question to add: "What really stays with me is what the end for him must have been like, the terror of being handcuffed and knowing you're going to die . . ."

But didn't he physically abuse Murphy before that?

"The only abuse she ever took was having hundred-dollar bills being thrown at her." On a softer note, Becky admits having sympathy for Tabish's wife and young children, then tosses this out: "Sandy doesn't have the temperament to do well in the penitentiary." This elicits whoops and applause from several nonreporters who've gathered, plus a couple of hearty guffaws. I've been trying to picture that, too.

In the meantime, Nick tells me how proud Becky is of Jack—their younger son, that is, not her brother. Nick gives her and Benny most of the credit for helping Jack get to the good place he's in. The four of them have started playing no-limit hold'em at home, starting with sixty chips each. "Jack's won his fair share of pots," his proud father wants me to know.

Another reporter asks whether Becky thinks it was Murphy's or Tabish's idea to kill Ted. Becky sips her drink, shrugs her shoulders. No answer. One row behind me, a slot machine dings and spits metal.

"Remember that business," Nick asks me, "all that stuff about Sandy proving her love by cleaning up after Ted's binges?"

" 'The only one who really loved him,' " I say, quoting Momot.

"Well, she did that exactly once—right after she killed him. That's what happens when you've got that much liquid heroin in your digestive tract. Teddy shit himself, and she had to clean it up to avoid getting caught, and she practically admitted all that to the real estate agent. *That's* what she was talking about."

"More raw material for concocting a plausible story . . ."

"You got it."

We shake our heads at the gall of her.

"Let me tell you something about Teddy," says Nick. "He sat me down once on the curb across the street from the church in a little town in eastern Montana. Seven o'clock Sunday morning, we've been drinking all night—this was in our younger days, mind you—and now Teddy brings out a paper bag holding our bottle of cheap red wine. He pretends he's taking a swig then passes it over to me, all of these churchgoers staring at us with contempt. He says to me, 'Isn't that a kick? Look at how they stare, just like *we* would. But when you look at it from the curb up, everything's different.' "

As I furiously scribble, an arm bumps my elbow, so *curb* looks like *cur* with a flourish above and behind it. It's Benny.

"Hey."

"Hey. Where's Andrea?" I ask.

"She had to go back to work."

"Speaking of which, I've been trying to get Benny to try real estate," says Nick, evidently following through on a previous conversation with his son, "but he seems to prefer the casino business."

"I can see that," I say. "He's a natural."

"Don't say that," says Nick, though it's clear he is pleased by the way Benny Behnen has handled the host job. He excuses himself to answer a TV crew's questions.

Says Benny, "You wanna get outta this place, get a drink?"

Cruising south in Benny's red Jaguar, I'm struck by how much he cultivates the outlaw personae of his Uncle Ted and eponymous grandfather, even down to the angle of the Marlboro Red in his lips. Smoking one myself, I ask him, "Not really cut out for the real estate?"

"Naw." A big smile. "I feel more at home at the Horseshoe. Pretty soon, down the road, I'll have to start running the tournament."

"No doubt about it."

Getting more used to the notion, he steps on the gas, changes lanes. We're headed for the Spearmint Rhino, and that's fine with me. Interviewing people about Ted and Sandy's cute meet at Cheetahs five years ago, I've been told more than once that "the Rhino is the new bomb" in Vegas; that if Murphy arrived here today, that's where she'd wind up dancing, and where Ted would most likely be cruising.

When I bring up his father's biographical project, Benny shakes his head, winces. "That kinda family stuff shouldn't be written about. Not by your own, you know, family."

I recall Peter Alson saying in *Playboy* that in the months before he died, Ted often spoke of writing a book about his father. When I ask Benny about this, he shrugs. "Who knows with Teddy, you know?" A manuscript has yet to turn up.

What Benny wants to talk about is poker. He's been playing tournaments at the Mirage, the Orleans, and out in LA at the Bike and the Commerce, developing his no-limit skills the way a pilot logs hours in the cockpit. Next year he'll play in the Big One, for the first and perhaps the last time. "I wish I could play *and* direct, but no way you could do that." In the meantime, he's pleased with the turnout for the 2000 Series. "Keep breakin' our own record each year." He's also impressed by the way I called T.J. down with no pair. Mimicking Slim's Texas drawl, he repeats the "heart of a cliff divah" line.

"That made my whole tournament, man, just hearing him say that. Wish you could've stopped it right there."

"Yeah, just gave you the money and the bracelet . . ."

Even though the idea makes absolute sense to me, we both have to laugh. What a week! Twenty blocks south of downtown, I've arrived once again in the Naked City, aka Silicone Valley. Warehouses, tool and die shops, cabarets, tiny factories sandwiched between vast used car lots, viaducts under the freeway. Hot pavement simmers in three hundred sixty directions.

"I heard that you got to know Murphy and Tabish, that you—"

"Oh, *real* well," he says. "Both of them. We used to hang out all the time."

"What about, you know, at Cheetahs?"

He nods twice but doesn't elaborate. Too young to get in when Murphy was dancing there, he probably couldn't add much to that part of the story.

"That place is still pretty good," he says, pulling the Jag up to the canopied front of an otherwise nondescript one-story edifice. Three strapping bouncers approach. The stucco exterior is decked out with mint-colored neon rhinoceri. "We could go on down there later, you want to. This place is better."

A bouncer in bow tie and vest holds the door for me. "Evening, sir." We shake hands all around. "Gettin' warm again," the biggest guy tells us as Benny slips him a bill. "Yeah, no shit."

Standing around on the asphalt, it must be 120, but inside the AC is *pumping*. Paying the ten-dollar cover, I hear "Janie's Gotta Gun" thunder from a room on the right, where the stages must be. Benny leads the way to the left, sidling up to the long, swank zinc bar. I take the stool on his right. He orders a Ketel martini, two olives. "Two," I say, peeling a leaf off my bankroll. My young friend waves it away. "I got it, I got it."

One TV above the bar is tuned to ESPN, the other to a closed-circuit shot of a stage lit with multicolored spots. The picture isn't clear enough to tell whether it's a girl or a boy grinding its booty to Aerosmith, but it must be the former, *n'est-ce pas?* The red-haired bartender flirtatiously informs Benny that "Petra's here" as she pours our martinis.

"She is," he says, cool but still interested.

"Yeah, well, she *was* . . ."

I sip, sip again. Mmm-mmm good. But whether this Petra is here appears to depend on what your definition of "was" is.

Benny thanks the bartender, adds, "I'll take care of you."

"I'll have Jill go and see."

Longer swallow. After six days of near-abstinence, the Ketel swats me upside my head. And it turns out I'm drinking it with a local celebrity. The bartender and cocktail waitresses, if not Petra (yet), are all over Benny, as are several patrons, among them the slick young player on the stool to Benny's left. Benny introduces him to me as Robert Baretta. Eavesdropping, I've already gathered that Robert's grandfather is "doing ninety-nine years," which for some reason strikes his companions as downright hilarious.

"For what?" I ask, tempted to take out a Post-it.

"Manslaughter," he shouts proudly across Benny's chin, this as "No

Sleep Till Brooklyn" erupts from the stage room. "He's out in a couple of months."

I shoot back my most impressed nod but decide not to take any notes.

While Benny holds court among the junior Moltisantis and the bartender tracks down Petra, I excuse myself, slide off the stool. The vodka is bringing some things into focus, thank God. Benny's affinity with Tabish and Murphy, for one. Manslaughter, murder, man's laughter; players and killers and dancers. Benny's namesake is the godfather of no-limit tournament poker and 100X odds on the craps tables, a Vegas prime mover and shaker; he didn't establish his rep hosting cotillions or soup kitchens, or staying home with his wife of an evening. He was respected as a player, a man who'd done time, and feared as an enforcer. Uncle Ted, in his turn, took a shine to Rick Tabish in part because Tabish had done time for assault, smuggling cocaine, and boosting a $600,000 painting from his parents' friends' living room. Ted's code of honor among felons made it seem like a good idea to hire this guy to bury his silver and chips, introduce him to his nephew and girlfriend, let him hang at his house, paint the town with him. Benny is following suit. And modeling himself after *his* maternal uncle and grandfather is exactly what Bad Jim is doing.

Keeping the martini glass level, I drift past the bar and into the bottlenecked powwow of dancers and customers, making my way around the corner and into the stage room. (Picture Christopher Walken as the Continental, at large in a crowd of his cultural inferiors.) Much like *moi*, the Spearmint Rhino is suaver, less "horny" than Cheetahs: higher ceiling, fewer mirrors, appointed with darker wood and subtler upholstery, more expensive tailoring on most of the patrons. Cheetahs has five or six stages, depending on how small a platform you're willing to count; here the girls dance in the round on a single oak platform. Take Darla, for instance. In a move requiring gymnast-caliber muscle tone and coordination, she hoists herself laterally by her own . . . petard, splayed legs perpendicular to both the shiny brass pole and each other. My word! Where's a point set topologist when you finally need one? As I sit down to watch her, Darla reverses direction, catching the pole in another flying crotch-lock; then, pouting sultrily, she plummets the length of it, touching down in a maculate splits timed to the final note of our bludgeoning by the Beasties, followed by the sound of two hands applauding. *Zen and the Art of the Solo Pole Tango*, by Darla "The Dervish" Derlinski: the workout video, the inquiry into values, the major motion picture, the sound track.

As I swallow the last of the Ketel, a duo of other-planetary women saunters up to my table. Hi, hi; hi, hi. "May we sit dawn?" says the blond one. I blink. "Mother, may we?" says the jet black one towering above me. Picture Michael Jordan as a twentyish party girl in eight-inch lucite platforms, wavy black hair to her collarbone. Add acres of décolletage, subtract veins and soul patch. Gulp.

"Yes, you may."

Taking chairs to either side of their quarry, they tidily cantilever yard-long shins beneath bony knees, limber thighs, and exquisite Corinthian leathers, much in the manner of upside-down German convertibles. *Whrrrrr*. Hands on my forearms and shoulders, each of them cozies right up. What's your name? Where you from? What's *your* name? Where *you* from? Bunny, the blonde, is from Duluth, Minnesota, whence the tilt of her vowels. She's the sort of Nordic goddess even the most optimistic among us always pray without hope we will meet on a hayride one brisk upper-midwestern autumn—or, better, here in the desert on the nineteenth of May, with AC. Sipping from a bottle of Evian, she tells me she's studying computer science at UNLV, so I give her my most impressed nod. I cannot help picturing Coach Tarkanian sucking on a big white terrycloth towel as the Runnin' Rebels nurse a late one-point lead. This usually happens when someone, even a woman like Bunny decked out in black patent leather, mentions UNLV, but the fact is, I could use a white towel myself. To surrender.

Anna, on my right, works for a "web site place" in Seattle. When I give her the Nod, she proceeds to volunteer that she only flies into Las Vegas every third weekend to dance.

"Why not more often?"

"That is ex-act-ly e-nough," she enunciates, all lips and white teeth.

"Plus, you know, the advance-purchase requirements." She dings my empty glass with a fingernail. "Thirsty?"

"Discounts for every third weekend these days?"

Puzzled by my question apparently, Anna smiles, nods, then asks me again if I'm thirsty. Bunny stares into the smoky near distance, says, "*I* am." As far as I can tell, which is far, neither Anna nor Bunny has mutilated herself with silicone implants, which becomes one of several determining factors as they press me to order three zombies. "Let's party, Jim. Whuddaya say?"

"I say, *garçonne!*"

As soon as a saucily microskirted valkyrie has taken the order, Anna fixes me with a meaningful hazel gaze in order to pop the question: "Would you like a private dance, Jim?"

"From both of you?"

Says Bunny, "Uh, yup?"

"What's the difference," I ask, "between a dance and a private dance?"

Their tag-team reply runs as follows: a dance they do here; for a private dance we'd retire to the executive area, where dances are "three for a hundred, apiece." What about two private dances? Not possible. One? "Oh c'mon, Jim," chides Bunny. "It makes the same difference." The same in what sense? Please explain your position in a ten- to fifteen-page essay, comparing and contrasting Option A with Option B. Include as many vivid supporting details as possible and follow the MLA Manual of Style for your footnotes. And don't forget to double-space! "Yeah, c'mon," Anna says, unfolding her thoroughbred gams while tugging my forearm. "We'll just have to *show* you . . ."

In see-through high heels, Anna must be seven feet tall, Bunny a more petite six three and a half. Together now, hands on my elbows, they escort their teetering five-nine homunculus past the stage and into a warren of writhingly occupied cubicles. "Ew," comments Bunny, passing a couple to whom with a vengeance I am keeping my back. "Later, Zoey." For extra semi-privacy, Anna commandeers the booth farthest back, marginally larger and darker than those we have passed through. With a comparatively platonic couple on our left and a wall on our right, our voodoo love lounge comes to the size and shape of a second-class train compartment cut lengthwise in half, furnished with a table barely wide enough for a couple of drinks and an ashtray. The bottom third of the front wall is solid black wood, topped by a frosted-glass panel with the silhouette of a woman etched from the frosting. The panel, because of the woman, is easily seen through (to satisfy some local ordinance, I gather), but the spearminty no-peeping ambience seems to rule out that anyone would bother.

Having comfortably settled in, we enter into an oral contract for matching sets of three semi-private dances, said sets to be concurrently performed, this in exchange for two hundred dollars. "Plus tip," appends the businesslike Minnesotan. "If you like us, Jim, you'll want to shaw us you like us."

"This boy *better* like us!" says Anna, scowling black-humorously.

To that end, Def Leppard's magisterial "Pour Some Sugar on Me" sets them a-grinding and a-bumping, against me and each other, taking turns gliding their endless limbs along the insides of my thighs, strategically noodging me with flesh-colored cattle prods. In all my born days I have never felt anything like it. "Don't ever come home, then, you born-again loser," barks Jennifer's apple-cheeked countenance, and my quandary corkscrews deeper into my limbic and dopamine systems. Because even if I wanted to, I hear myself telling myself, there's no turning back at this point. Yet how would I like it if my wife or one of my daughters worked here? Am I not ipso facto sanctioning the defilement of other men's daughters by paying these girls to assault me? There's also a writerly problem: no words, no thoughts even, could capture the two thirds or so of Bunny's and Anna's derrieres now on view—nates, tensor fasciae latae, and gluteal folds—combined with their untrammeled freedom of artistic expression, no matter how many Post-its I spent. And that's just for starters.

As Bunny gets busy with the snaps on Anna's top, the waitress arrives with our zombies. "Found you!" she chirps. "Hope you guys're thirsty!" Handing around the generous tumblers, she compliments Bunny's unbroken tan and puts down three coasters before buoyantly announcing, "That'll be nineteen-fifty, young man." I have no tens or twenties on me, just a couple of fives and a single, and I sense that this might be a problem. I could charge them, of course, but how's that gonna look? Three-stone platinum anniversary ring from Neiman Marcus, $2,600. Three zombies plus tip from Spearmint Rhino, $24.50. Look on your face when your wife asks for the third time, "What's Spearmint Rhino?" Priceless. When I peel off a C-note, exposing my wad for a brief extra moment, Anna ejaculates, "Dude! And, honey, but what about *my* tan?"

"Shonge," I insist, too loudly perhaps, to the waitress, *"s'il vous plaît, Ma'moiselle,"* since I tend to speak French when I'm nervous. I tend to speak Up when I'm hammered.

"Oui oui, monsieur."

But how do you say, Why not join us?

"I mean it," says Jennifer, softly. She's holding our beautiful girls— not as hostages, not to threaten me, simply to remind me how much I love them. "So, do you?" Of course I do, damn it! I've already been through one divorce, and neither of my first two children have ever gotten over it. "Good girl, Dat!" cheers Beatrice, encouraging this line of argument. Gracie just gurgles and mewls, looking cute but now terribly vulnerable, her whole life ahead of her with me as her father, as the three of them fade out like heat waves.

I sit up, clear my throat. I'm afraid . . .

"I'm afraid . . ."

"Awnly two things I'ze afraid of," says Bunny, now that the three of us are alone together again, "and zombies is bawth of 'em." This is a quote from a movie the title of which now escapes me, though I'm pretty sure the words "bawth" and "zombies" don't occur in it.

Bunny sets her glass on a napkin without having taken a sip, and I mean to protest. THOU SHALT NOT QUESTION BUNNY, thunders some bent gene or deity. THOU *SHALT* COVET ANNA *AND* BUNNY! Whereas Anna, bless her heart, takes a long, healthy swallow of hers. As do I. Just in time, too, to better appreciate Keith Richards viciously ripping the opening bends and two-note chords of "Can't You Hear Me Knocking?" If he didn't use open-G tuning (as my son, James, recently explained to me), he couldn't have played them so aggressively, and there must be a lesson in that. A commandment. I also assume the DJ is spinning the short version, minus the saxophone solo, for the sake of lap-dancer economy. To affirm these deductions, Anna and I clink our glasses together, slurp zombie. S*crum*pdiddleyumptious! Rum-yummy! If this were a '91 cabernet and Beethoven's sixteenth string quartet were playing (as recorded by the Alban Berg Quartet, or even the sprightlier Juilliard), I might be better able to get up, pay them off, and walk out. But they're not. So if this is to be the first and final lap dance of my life, I may as well sit back and enjoy it.

Sitting back happens to be the only permissible posture while getting lap-danced upon, so back do I sit, squinting and sipping and craning my neck as Bunny undoes Anna's top. There they are, then: a couple of certified members of America's Millennial Nubility, stripped to their G-strings and grating against one another. And me. And it *hurts*! And if Dante chastised adulterers by lashing them with hurricane winds, this wouldn't seem out of line now, even as Jennifer's specter reminds me that betrayers of family spend eternity frozen chin-deep in ice, gnawing their torturer's brain while taunted by babbling giants. Yet that's nothing but a *poem*, for Christ's sake. Plus there's no way on earth for Dante or Virgil or Grandma Grace or Jennifer or any of my daughters to find out where I am, so I'm safe. I am perfectly safe . . .

Eyeing Bunny's forsaken zombie, I knock back the rest of my own. Glug-glug-glug-glug. Put down glass, swipe mouth with sleeve while belching up flavor of cheeseburger, grab zombie *deux*. Paid for it, didn't I? When I'm finished with this one, please bring Anna and me one Atomic Cocktail apiece. Roger that, valkyries? In fact, make 'em doubles! Better yet, fetch the cylinder and hose a quart right down my gullet!

I squint at the duet in front of me, focus on dimples and goosebumps, on freckles, pale scars, tiny veins, shut my eyes—the better to steady myself, the better to let all this register then wipe it all out, the better to listen for Mick Taylor's wah-wah funk rhythm to chime behind Keith's nasty licks. And the cubicle doesn't start spinning. We're at the still point of the universe all of a sudden, this Bunny and Anna and I. If syringefuls of speedball were available now to be injected simultaneously by these shimmying nurses into my temple and coccyx, I wouldn't hesitate for a second. Fire me up, pretty please! You can certainly have all my money and love and attention so long as this dance, this whole album, goes on forever and ever. Because research is research, *n'est-ce pas*? I mean, right? The answer arrives with Charlie's first rim shot, after which Jagger starts yowling. Morrison shmorrison, girl. That's all *I* know. Because as Bunny or Anna knees my raw, married penis through denim and the other one mounts my chest upside down backwards, I decide there's no way in the world that *Sticky Fingers* wouldn't have been, wouldn't *be*, Ted's favorite album as well.

Judge Bonaventure

♣ ♥
TONS AND TONS OF LUCK
♦ ♠

Who is weak, and I am not weak?
— PAUL, 2 Corinthians

DON: And what makes you such an authority on life
all of a sudden?
TEACH: My life, Jim. And the way I've lived it.
— DAVID MAMET, *American Buffalo*

A tornado touched down, splintering trees and tearing off sections of roofs, not five blocks from our house Thursday evening, while I was breaking bread with the Ferguson crew. A willow sheared from its roots crashed through a wall of our friends' house on Picardy Drive, demolishing their dining room, kitchen, and one upstairs bedroom. A thirty-foot limb snapped from an elm along Lake Avenue and speared a car's windshield, killing the grandfather of six who was driving.

"Can't You Hear Me Knocking" ended abruptly on Friday, minus the saxophone solo. The next and last song of my evening was "1999," that cheesily futuristic party-boy ditty by ♣, perfect accompaniment to my feckless and weak-willed debauchery. As ♣ squealed and grunted, Jennifer and June and the girls were completing the last leg of their trip back through Illinois, serenaded for the most part by Bob and Lucinda and Bruce. Three hundred twenty-eight miles, three diaper-

change stops, seven hours of soybeans and silos and corn, not one fun-
nel cloud; the weather forecast had been accurate. When they got
within a few miles of our house, the moist white meat of overturned
trees littered sidewalks and lawns. Viaducts flooded, police cars and
Commonwealth Edison trucks parked every which way, block after
block without street or traffic lights. By this point, both girls were
asleep. Bidding adieux to my dancers, I looked around for Benny by
the stage, at the bar, in the men's room. When a bouncer informed me
that "Benny and a friend" had left a few minutes earlier, I took a cab
over to the Bellagio and sat down, feeling good, in the $80-$160
hold'em game. Arriving home safely, Jennifer discovered a small package from Neiman Marcus left inside our screen door by the UPS
driver, still damp from Thursday night's storm. Noting that it had
been addressed to her husband from a luxury store in Las Vegas, Jennifer decided to open it.

I fly home on Saturday morning. The main issue, as I see it, is whether
the lap artistry I endured can appear in the article. Reviewing ten days
of notes and behavior, my encounter with Anna and Bunny seems to
shed light on what happened with Tabish and Binion and Murphy, or
at least on my empathy with the guy at the apex of the triangle. What
better way, then, to wind up my account of the murder convictions?
And yet if I decide to go with what actually happened, I have little
choice but to tell Jennifer about A and B the minute I get off the
plane, since I could hardly let her find out while helping me revise the
first draft. The longer I put off confessing, the more pungently those
catfish would reek when I finally had to unwrap them.

Or not.

My calculus of utility runs roughly as follows: the obvious pluses of
not telling Jennifer would cost me terrific material about the ongoing
cycle of Binion men at strip joints, not to mention the beauty of celebrating Murphy's conviction with Benny at one of those places, assuming that's what we were doing. So I have to consider finessing it,
letting a "composite character" get a two-on-one lap dance while
Good Jim semi-innocently watches, has a drink, talks to Benny; "Can't
You Hear Me Knocking" comes on, Ted is brought back into context,

the end. However effective the factual version might be, admitting my dalliance would ruin the trust I had earned with Jennifer since 1989. Even though neither of our chest-waist-hips ratios is what it used to be—mainly, in her case, because she has borne and suckled our two children—our emotional and erotic intimacy makes up for the fact that our skin fits more loosely these days. Trust involves telling the truth, I've been told, so admitting to your wife that you've harbored a quark of desire for another woman may seem like the ethical course. The problem occurs when you don't have permission to *have* these aspirations, let alone to act on one; doing so in the cover story of a national magazine would be worse by six orders of magnitude. The point is, I shouldn't have done it in public *or* private, and nothing could be any more clear. On the other hand, this is the first long-term or marital relationship to which I've been a hundred percent faithful and I consider that record intact, though I don't know that Jennifer would. Bottom line? Having as my wife a beautiful human who loves me, who is the mother of our girls and who may want to have another child with me—I cannot risk mucking this up.

Jennifer and the girls see Gaga off on the TWA concourse then hustle over to H26, where AA2458 (top pair, belly draw to a wheel) arrives at 2:46, right on time. I'm the first coach passenger out through the jetway. "Su-prise!" Bea sports the first modest tan of her life, which for some reason makes her seem twice as big, twice as *heavy*, as she was eleven days ago; and the post-tornado humidity has given her shoulder-length hair extra curl. Grace looks exactly the same. As I take her from Jennifer and hold on to both of them, their little hands fondle my face.

Accepting a nip on her chapped lower lip, Jennifer tells me that Grace started crawling this morning, then shows me she's wearing the ring.

"You were going on a trip, Dat?" says Bea.

"I was, but I'm back now. I'm home."

"You were working?"

"I was. But I missed you and Grace, and I really missed Mama. Wow did I miss her . . ." We kiss.

Once we drive home and the girls have gone to sleep, we order in Thai food and Singha beer, toast the big check, make love on the living-room carpet. We finish eating dinner and replay a few more hands before going to sleep in our sleigh bed. I have waited in vain, though, for the subject of lap dances to naturally come into context.

In the morning, unpacking, I finally confess and apologize. Jennifer's cheeks and the patch on her throat flush bright pink; with her wide, green, Mesopotamian eyes, it's impossible not to think of a Macintosh apple with smoke coming out of its ears.

"Are you serious?"

When I tell her I am, she needs a long moment to gather her thoughts, during which I keep my mouth shut.

"I guess I thought we had . . . that you had more class than that."

Unable to take this as a compliment, I proceed to get technical if not altogether more truthful, another thing I do when I'm nervous. "Just one, though. Just once." I do not say two dancers. I do not say two hundred and eighty dollars; I say twenty. I do not ask for help in recalling the title of the movie that Bunny had quoted from; I do not mention Bunny at all. I say, "Benny took me down there right after the—"

"Why?"

My short answer is, "I don't know." The long one involves terms like "natural curiosity," "one-shot deal," "journalistic verisimilitude," "just a Vegas thing." I even suggest that risk-taking behavior like Ted's "comes from the same psychological crannies that generate poker success," that is, my own. I decide that no good can emerge from admitting that I find Murphy's body attractive, let alone Anna's (or Anya's) or Bunny's. "So I really don't know, but I want you to know, I apologize."

She actually laughs at me.

"What?"

She heads toward the kitchen, where Bea has been pleading for, and charmingly mispronouncing, Spaghetti-O's. Couldn't we laugh about *that?*

We cannot.

"Any other assholerics you want to confess?"

There are not.

Within five or six weeks I'm forgiven, it seems. At least we have re-resumed conjugal visits, although not, thank God, on what Daphne Merkin would call "a mature and responsible level." If anything, our sex life has gotten smokier. My Polish-Sicilian consort has become even more—not hostile, exactly. Assertive, I guess, is the word. We manage to refrain, however, from reenacting either the scene at Spearmint Rhino or the one in which Sandy and her studly young boyfriend handcuff Ted, tranquilize him, taunt him, and strangle him. Sort of. But the key remains how long we talk and touch afterwards, usually until one or both of the girls calls a halt to our amorous languor.

Jennifer does hire an absurdly handsome Italian contractor to build us a fence and a fancy brick patio, leaving four shirtless laborers at large in our yard for nine days. She puts aside enough money to buy Bridget a Beetle when she graduates at the end of the summer, and a Telecaster for James right away. She comes up with a plan which, after paying the taxes, will reduce our mortgage period from twenty-four years to nine. There are even a few bucks left over for "gambling." (I don't know about gambling, but I've already reserved Room 1016 during next year's World Series of Poker.) In the meantime, I've promised her several more times never to get another lap dance, and each time I've meant it. Both of us know she can read me "like a dog," as she puts it, as to whether or not I'm sincere.

"You actually have tells from here to Las Vegas."

"I know."

In July my bicycle is stolen from our garage. "Landscapers with cell phones" is the cop's explanation. I don't have the serial number, of course, but since I rode that old Trek from Chicago to western Canada while researching my novel *Going to the Sun*, I still want the goddamn thing back. "We'll put it in the computer," the cop says. "I wouldn't save your breath."

After the deductible, our insurance covers $500 toward a replacement. Shopping around for a couple of days, I finally upgrade to a Trek X10 Alpha XL, a $1,100 cross-trainer with an alpha, a ten, and two, count 'em, exes in its model number. Another reason I choose it is the metallic saffron paint job, which normally I would have detested. Now I decide that it's actually Horseshoe Gold, my new favorite color.

Also in July, I make what I believe is my first appearance within heroic couplets, this in Peter Costa's 140-line poem, "The Big One," on PokerPages.com.

> *The final six now take the table*
> *Each has shown that they are able*
> *In seat one there is "Jesus" Chris*
> *Who must have dreamed of a day like this*
>
> *In seat two, there is Hasan Habib*
> *Learned to play the game from his crib*
> *Next to him is Jim McManus*
> *A great poker brain with great poker manners*
>
> *In seat four it's T.J. Cloutier*
> *Lowest stack but always there*
> *In seat five there's Roman Abinsay*
> *Who hopes that this may be his day*
>
> *Finally, Steve Kaufman from Ohio*
> *All six are seated; let's start the show*
> *Good luck to each one and all*
> *Deal the cards let's have a ball*
>
> *"Jesus," with help from above*
> *Is in a position that we would love*
> *He's stacked high, the others low*
> *He sits there while out they go*
>
> *One by one they drop away*
> *On this crucial final day*
> *First to go was Abinsay*
> *His ace and queen did not play*
>
> *The first bad beat of the final day*
> *Helped send McManus on his way*
> *He was there to write a book*
> *As fifth place he proudly took . . .*

Dum de dum de dum. Eccentric punctuation aside, I doubt that either Alexander Pope or George Gordon, Lord Byron, could have rhymed those last names more adroitly.

In August I get a sneak preview of Dan Abrams' documentary, to be aired in October. Dan has deployed a host of swanky graphics to show the viewer how no-limit hold'em is played; he also gives card-by-card odds as the hands are played out. In one of his at-home cutaways, Jennifer is able to articulate how much the $4,000 meant to us, as well as why she had faith in me. The only downside is that the look on my face when Hasan's four hits the table detonates any pretensions I may have harbored about looking steely or cool on TV. While we all know that cameras put ten pounds on a person, the question among my students and poker-playing buddies quickly becomes, "How many cameras were *on* you?"

Checking facts for my article, I find out that T.J. quit smoking cold-turkey as soon as the Series was over. On June 16 (Bloomsday), Annie Duke gave birth at home in Montana to Lucy, a healthy eight-pound girl. Katy Lederer got a contract for her marvelously erotic first book of poems, *Winter Sex*, and another to write a memoir about growing up in her family, called *Poker Face*. Kathy Liebert and Tom McEvoy broke up again, but still remain friends; and Kathy went on to become the first woman to win a seven-figure first prize, in the inaugural Party Poker Million, held on a cruise ship off the Pacific coast of Mexico. Steve Kaufman used part of what should have been *my* $570,500 to purchase a condo in Las Vegas, where presumably he's better able to decipher the syntax of Linear B than he is in Cincinnati. Hasan bought a maroon CLK convertible and put a down payment on a house in Los Angeles. He also wrote a letter to *Card Player* responding to Nolan Dalla's criticism, which the magazine printed on August 18.

"With all due respect, I have been fortunate enough to make seven major tournament no-limit hold'em final tables in the past six months without the benefit of advice from any one person in particular. Although Tony's advice on a hand would be helpful, it would hardly be important enough to risk breaking any rules. . . . Mr. Dalla, whether you believe me or not, you must consider the possibility that the hand in question was in fact not discussed. I was particularly taken aback when the column stated it as a *fact* that I 'had already benefitted from the advice' of Tony Ma regarding that particular hand. And then it went on to compare me to someone who has stolen money from a bank!

"I know Mr. Dalla understands well how hard it is to make it in this business. Many have tried and continue to try, with little or no recourse. Whether I will make it in this great but often punishing profession remains to be seen. It will take immense discipline, a lot of courage to play well, and tons and tons of luck. But along the way, I can only hope that I am represented fairly and seen for who I really am."

Dalla's response appears in the following issue: "My report of the incident was meant to illustrate a growing problem at many tournaments, which is the ever increasing influence of nonparticipants on the proceedings. What should be avoided is the prospect that any future 'champion' will ever be tainted by the inevitable suspicions that are raised when discussions (between players themselves or involving a player and a spectator) are not completely out in the open. If you did not discuss a strategy with Mr. Ma during the hand, you did nothing wrong, 'technically' speaking. However, observers did not have the benefit of that knowledge and were left to draw their own conclusions. My column was a call for stricter enforcement of the rules that govern player behavior, with commentary as to why implementation of rules that will address this issue in the future are essential."

Two issues later, Dalla graciously follows up: "I wrote that Habib 'benefitted from the advice' of the outsider during a hand—when, in fact, there was no proof that Habib actually had been given advice by the outsider." This fudges the question of what other observers might reasonably infer, though it's also consistent with my own sense of Hasan's integrity. Dalla reports that some of his readers "were outraged that I used my column to single out Habib for his actions." After summarizing Hasan's letter and his own initial response, Dalla writes: "I thought that would be the end of the controversy, since both sides were given an opportunity to defend themselves and clarify their positions—but it did not. Habib remained upset, and has protested ever since against the lingering suspicions about his behavior—I might add, in a manner that consistently has been courteous, professional, and appropriate given the degree of defamation to his character." He notes that other readers have testified to Hasan's integrity, and that, since the incident in May, Hasan's tremendous success in other events—in late July he made the final table in the Tournament of Champions, for example—has helped to reestablish his reputation as an excellent player and honorable tournament competitor. Dalla concludes: "I hereby apologize to Hasan Habib for any misunderstanding and damage that may have occurred as a result of my column."

Watching the sentencing hearing on Court TV, Jennifer and I see David Roger introduce a ninja fighting knife that Ted asked his friend Joe Gonzaque to safeguard for him in July of '97. Ted told Gonzaque that Murphy had pulled the knife on him the night before and he wanted it out of the house. Over a foot long, the bottom part resembles brass knuckles festooned with eight inch-long spikes, and the top is an ax head. When Ving Rhames tells the man who just sodomized him in *Pulp Fiction*, once the tables are turned, "Now I'm gone get medieval on yo' ass," this was probably the sort of instrument he had in mind, though the dungeon they're in gives him plenty from which to choose.

Weeping uncontrollably, Murphy's stepmother begs the jurors and judge to be lenient. A neighbor recalls that Murphy had been a Campfire Girl and a terrific athlete. Another testifies that a sixteen-year-old Murphy had saved her from drowning.

When it's her turn to speak, Murphy claims to be sorry . . . that she never took the witness stand. "I believe I was wrongly convicted," she moans, puffy and wet-eyed. "It's hard to look guilty when you're innocent." She nonetheless apologizes, in a way, to Ted's family. "I'm sorry that I walked out the door on September 17, 1998, and left him alone . . . when Teddy needed me most. I loved Teddy with all my heart, and I know he loved me just as much." She says this while looking at Bonnie, who responds with an icy, unwavering glare. Murphy turns back to the jury. "You may have taken away my freedom, but you can never take away the love we had for each other. I am so sad for all my hopes and dreams, for the family I will never have, the wedding that will never be, and my children that will never come." David Wall immediately calls her performance "a cheap shot," and Bonaventure admonishes the jury to disregard her protestations of innocence.

In pleading for leniency, John Momot invokes Dante's definition of Hell as "the loss of all hope," suggesting this would be too harsh a punishment for his client. He's referring, I gather, to the inscription above the portal: ABANDON ALL HOPE, YOU WHO ENTER HERE. He might have mentioned as well that Dante punishes lustful adulterers in the relatively balmy second circle, where, in Robert Pinsky's translation:

> All light is mute, with a bellowing like the ocean
> Turbulent in a storm of warring winds,
> The hurricane of Hell in perpetual motion
>
> Sweeping the ravaged spirits as it rends,
> Twists, and torments them.

As with all Dante's punishments, this fits the crime to a T. According to the moral and theological judo he calls *contrapasso*, those who cannot control their bodily urges while alive get paid back in spades when they die. (That will be my fate as well—unless I confess, say my penance, and make a good act of contrition.) But for those like Murphy and Tabish who coolly betray their benefactors on top of it, Dante reserves the lowest, most cryogenic circle of the Inferno, where shades are suspended in ice alongside the likes of Brutus and Judas, who is being eaten alive by three-headed Lucifer himself. For them and their ilk, it's a cold day in Hell for eternity.

Without mentioning Kathy Kolberg, Mary Jo Tabish recounts her courtship by Rick, as well as the early days of their marriage: what a good father he was, what a good provider, etc. For the last two years, however, she has been forced to shield their children from the real reason Dad cannot see them, and she begins to weep as she describes breaking the news of the guilty verdicts to their daughter, Amanda. "I had to tell her that her father was in jail. That her father had been accused of doing these things that he didn't do, and he couldn't leave there until he convinced people that he didn't do these things. She cried herself to sleep." Taking a while to compose herself, Mary Jo finally goes on. "He calls, and she puts the phone next to the piano, and she plays her little recital pieces."

"My God," whispers Jennifer. She closes her eyes, shakes her head. "How could a guy ever handle that?"

He couldn't, say Jennifer's nuanced exhalations, but only *guys* ever would have to.

After Lani Tabish requests that the judge take away her own freedom instead of her son's, even Rick starts to weep. "Your mother is always the one who gets to you," he tells jurors when he gets to the stand. "It's hard. It's hard on everybody. There's so many things that needed to come out, and I just can't talk. My heart's out to the Binion family, I mean that sincerely. I can look everybody in that front row in the eye and tell you I'm sorry. And please take that from my heart because that's where it's coming from." A camera zooms in on Jack Binion, who appears vaguely sickened and unvaguely wrathful. Tabish keeps talking. "I hope someday something can get rectified. The prosecution did their job. They put on a case. I'm not supposed to talk about the case so I won't go there. I know you guys had a big burden, and you did what you had to do based on the evidence presented to you, and I applaud you." Who coached him, I wonder, on that slice of blague? Tom Palazzo? "Let's talk about who Rick Tabish *is*," he continues. "Twenty months have gone by. There's been a lot about Rick Tabish. Let me tell you who I am. I'm *proud* of who I am . . ."

Jennifer's gloss consists mostly of snorts and vomitory noises, though she does run some real words together. "Oh, please," for example. And "This guy's the ultimate tool." Tabish's state of denial turns out to be so profound that Bonaventure is forced to remove the jury before instructing the convicted murderer to cease protesting his innocence.

"I'm not perfect by all means," Tabish resumes after the jury has returned. "I have no real regrets about anything I did except getting involved in this situation."

"By all means," says Jennifer.

In more neutral tones, David Roger urges jurors not to be persuaded by Murphy's and Tabish's requests to be reunited with their loved ones eventually, noting that Ted wouldn't be around for the milestones in Bonnie's future. "What would Ted Binion give to walk Bonnie down the aisle? He can't, because he died at the hands of two killers."

Bonnie takes the stand the next day to describe how her father took care of her when she was sick, how he taught her to play poker and fish, and how much he loved her. "Most kids get a kiss when they leave for school in the morning," she says, bursting into tears. "But I couldn't leave without a *hug* and a kiss." After showing jurors photographs of herself with her dad, she tells them he used to recite from memory Edgar Allan Poe's "Annabel Lee" when tucking her in for the night. An odd choice, I have to say, for a spoken-word lullaby; but then, Ted was Ted. The final stanza must have mesmerized his young daughter, burning into her fall-asleep reveries in ways he cannot have accounted for.

> *For the moon never beams, without bringing me dreams*
> *Of the beautiful Annabel Lee;*
> *And the stars never rise, but I feel the bright eyes*
> *Of the beautiful Annabel Lee;*
> *And so, all the night-tide, I lie down by the side*
> *Of my darling—my darling—my life and my bride,*
> *In the sepulchre there by the sea,*
> *In her tomb by the sounding sea.*

It is also revealed that Oscar Goodman's $125,000 fee was paid by Bill Fuller, who testifies that he "loaned" Murphy the money to pay Goodman. When records of his fees are subpoenaed, Oscar declines to entertain questions from the press, saying only, "I'm the mayor, and I had nothing to do with the case." After a few more months in office, however, he is willing to admit: "Las Vegas is either the most unreal place in the world or the most real place. I've lived here thirty-seven years, and I've yet to figure out which it is." He has nonetheless persuaded the FBI to keep its regional headquarters there, instead of moving it ten miles southeast, to Henderson. This latest political triumph brings a sardonic letter from the bureau to the star of *Mob Law*, wondering if he would still prefer his daughter to date a hit man before an FBI agent. "I'm reconsidering," says Oscar.

"Here it is," says Judge Bonaventure on September 15, 2000, "almost two years to the day of Mr. Binion's murder, and we all wish we were not here today. Unfortunately, due to the cowardly acts of the two defendants, we are. The many lives they have ruined will never be the same." He ticks off the letters he has received from people asking for justice—from the victim's brother, his daughter, and several others—before continuing: "It is clear that Mr. Binion was truly in love with the defendant Ms. Murphy. What a horrendous image this court envisions when it conjures up the picture of a man who so completely entrusts his confidences to his loved one, only to be a victim of her ultimate betrayal." Jennifer shoots me a glance that gently but firmly conflates Murphy's betrayal of Ted with my dalliance at the Spearmint Rhino—*my now ancient dalliance*, as I've come to think of it. My return glance does not disagree with her but quickly returns to the image on-screen. I struggle to not clear my throat. "It is the sad irony of Ted Binion's life that whatever caused him to devote his love to Ms. Murphy also started the spiral of his demise. The disdain that our society has for individuals who gain the trust of others only to cause them harm is far greater than the aversion we have for criminals who carry out their crimes upon complete strangers."

Says Beatrice, "That man is sad."

"Yes he is, Bea," says Jennifer, offering no explanation—most unlike her, as Bea's face is registering.

The judge reminds Tabish that he'd made "a decent, fair, and honest living, one which most people would be content with having. It was a life that you decided to give up to satisfy the most primal of your desires." Speaking directly to his face, Bonaventure calls him "an individual who is friendly and personable towards others. This is not surprising to this court as you are a con man, one who gains the trust of others only to then betray them for your own personal gain."

Poker, of course, is a parallel arena in which similar conduct is lionized. Whether at Binion's World Series or played for pennies around the kitchen table, poker makes con jobs not only legal, but lucrative;

laurels are placed on the brow of the most notably duplicitous players. Even away from the poker table, misleading half-truths like the ones I delivered to Jennifer can help to make harsh facts more palatable, though we don't hand out laurels for that, last I heard.

Turning to Murphy, Bonaventure says her behavior is "horrific and strikes at the very core of trust between significant others. Through your greed and betrayal, you plotted an elaborate scheme to kill Mr. Binion and steal his money, as well as swap him for a younger boyfriend. You presented yourself as a caring and loving girlfriend only to lure your victim into a trap . . ."

While Gracie continues to nap, Bea has pulled the cushions off our couch and is using the springs underneath as a trampoline. I love to watch her budding athleticism, but her possible headfirst landing places are making me cringe as I try to take notes, even though we have rubber cushions attached to the corners of the coffee table. I picture a gash, a snapped neck . . .

"Be careful now, sweetie," says Jennifer.

"Look it me shumping!" says Bea, not being careful at all.

"Please sit with Daddy, okay?"

"The public must be protected," Bonaventure tells Murphy, "from individuals like yourself, for you do not display the telltale signs of a criminal actor. You chose to betray and kill your lover, and now you must live with the consequences. It is this court's hope that after your period of incarceration you will have awaked from the Alice in Wonderland dreamlike state you have attempted to portray . . ."

"Are you going on a trip, Dat?" calls Bea from the couch, part of her once-a-day ritual.

"No, Sweet. I'm staying right here with you, watching TV. C'mon over and sit with me."

"Are you working?"

"I am. But next time we *all* can go, right?"

"On a *trip*?"

"On a really really really fun trip."

While Bea nods and jumps, Bonaventure sentences Tabish to a term that will keep him in prison for a minimum of twenty-five years, until he's at least sixty-one. Murphy will serve a minimum of twenty-two years, with zero credit for her eight months of house arrest. She will thus be ineligible for parole until she is just shy of her forty-ninth birthday, or my age. Under the provisions of the final codicil of Ted's will, she was to receive the Palomino Lane house and its contents, plus $300,000 in cash, but a first-degree murder conviction precludes inheriting any part of the victim's estate. The estate, in fact, is now pursuing a wrongful death suit against Tabish and Murphy. Her $2 million palimony suit has also been dismissed, of which Dante would surely approve. She may have to start gnawing brain.

Murphy will serve her time here on earth at the Southern Nevada Women's Correctional Facility in North Las Vegas, Tabish at the High Desert State Prison at Indian Springs. Both have been branded "high-maintenance inmates" by the director of the Metro Detention Services Division. "Gave us nothing but grief." Among other foul deeds, Tabish tampered with witnesses, and Murphy had to be removed from a cell she was sharing with Margaret Rudin (who murdered her husband) and Jessica Williams (a topless dancer who killed six teenagers by plowing into them with her car) when Rudin complained that Murphy was carrying on an intimate relationship with Williams in exchange for money and contraband. Tabish has already lined up the inevitable Alan Dershowitz to help appeal the convictions—on the grounds, among others, that Palazzo gave poor legal advice by not calling Rick to the stand.

Speaking of not calling Rick, Mary Jo Rebhein's divorce was finalized July 17. In public she'd stood by the father of her children during the trial, and he begged her not to divorce him before his appeals were exhausted, but this time he'd asked for too much.

The defendants don't look at each other as Bonaventure continues: "It is the court's desire that the victims and the families of the victims will also find some closure. Hopefully they will be able to resume some semblance of normalcy as they move forward in their lives." Shots of the various family members make this appear highly doubtful. But as the camera lingers on Murphy and Tabish, what strikes me is not how recalcitrant and miserable they seem, but how *alive*. Ted is dead. Gracie in the meantime has woken up from her nap with her usual squawking for "Binky Red," and Jennifer gets up to change her "so Daddy can finish his 'research.' " I thank her.

"You're welcome, Braino," she calls from the hallway. " 'Because research is research, *n'est-ce pas?'* Haven't I read that somewhere?"

"I'll get her the next time. I promise."

Tired of bouncing, Bea has climbed into my lap. "Can we go to the park, Dat? Can I go on your shoters?"

"Justice," says Bonaventure, "though due the accused, is due the accuser also. Justice has been served." He brings down the gavel. "Case closed."

"Of course," I say, getting out of the La-Z-Boy and stretching my tendons. Next spring I'll be fifty. When Bea and Grace are Murphy's age, I'll be seventy-something. That is, I would be. To make it I'll need to speed up, to slow down, to take better care of myself. And some luck. With time off—no, with time *added*—for good behavior . . .

"I can?" says Bea again, louder, interrupting my reverie.

"Sure!"

Up she goes. The slide, the new swing, the ride on my shoulders both ways are three of her favorite things at this stage of her life. I let her Mom know where we're going and head out into bright autumn midwestern sun with Bea's chubby legs on my neck, the backs of her flip-flops bouncing against my chest. "Go dat way, Dat. *Dat* way." Her hands brush my ears, tug my hair. As we round the corner toward what she calls Bea's Park, I can't shake the recent news from Frank and Lani Tabish (in the *Missoula Independent*) that their son has refused to accept visits from Amanda and Kyle. "He doesn't want them to see him in jail," Frank explains. "He doesn't want them to have childhood memories of seeing their daddy behind bars." The report says Rick does take their phone calls, but I can't imagine what he would say to them. Just a Vegas thing? I had nothing to do with the case? Some bad, bad men made a mistake, but Daddy'll be home real soon? Once their schoolmates and the newspapers and the folks on TV begin to say differently, how long will Dad's version hold up?

And what about *my* protestations?

In a letter last fall to Judge Bonaventure asking him to release her husband on bail, Mary Jo Tabish wrote: "To the children (Amanda— age five, Kyle—age two) Rick is everything. He was there when they took their first breath of life, he changed their first diaper, he gave them their first bath and . . . a day does not go by without them asking when he will be home. Rick needs them, too. He calls and talks to them, but it is hard for him to hear what they are doing because he re- alizes how much he is missing. On October 10th Amanda had her 5th birthday and both my family and Rick's family were there to help her celebrate. The only thing missing was Rick, and she knew it."

Beatrice was two a few weeks ago, and Grace will be one in No- vember. At her party, Bea told me, "Don't blow my candles out, Dat, 'cause *I'm* gonna do it." Counting "gonna" as "going to," that's a twelve-word grammatical sentence, the very equipment she'll need to develop a moral sense of the world. She already understands what "good" and "bad" mean, though I don't think she gets things like "soon," let alone twenty-five years. But she *knows* when I'm doing her wrong.

Certainly, going on six, Amanda knows, too. Certainly once she's done playing "Hot Cross Buns" or Bach's Minuet in G or the opening of "Für Elise," she's telling her dad what she thinks about stuff. Cer- tainly she tells him she loves him, and he says the same. Unable to kiss, touch, or see one another, they both say "I miss you" and mean it with scalding ferocity. Telephone time will be short, in Rick's case, but there must be long moments of silence.

And here we are now at Bea's Park.

"Daddy?"

"What, sweetheart?"

According to her grandfather, Amanda puts the mouthpiece against her cheek and whispers, "Daddy, I don't want you to *ever* go to Las Vegas again."

POKER TERMINOLOGY

BIBLIOGRAPHY

ACKNOWLEDGMENTS

INDEX

POKER TERMINOLOGY

ABC player: one who plays by the book or wagers in predictable patterns.

Aces up: a pair of aces plus any other pair. Similarly, *kings up, queens up,* etc.

Action: whose turn it is to check, bet, or fold. "The *action*'s on you, sir." Can also refer to the level of stakes or betting aggression. "She dominates the white-chip *action* at the Bellagio."

Advertise: to turn over hole cards to show how loose or tight you are playing, ideally to be used to your advantage later on, when you'll play in the opposite fashion.

Ajax: A-J in the hole.

All blue: a club flush.

All-in: having all your chips in the pot. "He went *all-in* holding ace-queen."

American Airlines: A-A in the hole.

Angle shooter: player attempting to win extra money with tactics of dubious legitimacy.

Ante: small compulsory bet that all players must post before the hand starts. Usually comes into effect during the later stages of a hold'em tournament.

Baby: small card, usually eight or lower.

Backdoor: to make a big hand you weren't expecting, by hitting two lucky cards in a row. "Drawing to a straight, he *backdoored* a flush."

Bad beat: having a big hand overcome on the last card by someone playing a long-shot draw. To take one is to have been *sucked out on*, to have lost to a lucky maniac.

Bad game: one in which you're in over your head.

Belly-buster, or **belly:** straight draw that lacks one inside card, such as 7-8-10-J. Also called a *gutshot draw* or an *inside straight draw*.

Best of it: having the odds in your favor.

Bet: to put money in the pot, hoping to either increase its size (called a *value bet*) or win it right there (often with a weak hand, as a *bluff*).

Bet into: to aggressively wager against a player who has represented a very strong hand by her earlier action.

Bet on the come: to bet and raise before your hand is made. See also *semibluff*.

Big-bet poker: all games with no-limit or pot-limit structure, usually hold'em and Omaha.

Big blind: mandatory bet made, or posted, by the player two to the left of the dealer. (The *small blind* sits to the left of the dealer and is forced to post half of the *big blind*.)

Big Slick: A-K in the hole.

Blank: see *rag*.

Blinds: in hold'em, the mandatory bets posted by the player to the left of the dealer (the *small blind*) and two to the left (the *big blind*, usually twice the size of the small).

Bluff: to bet with a weak hand, thus representing a strong one.

Board: the community cards dealt faceup in the middle of the table; the first three are dealt simultaneously (called the *flop*), then a fourth, then a fifth.

Boat, or **full boat:** full house. Three cards of one rank, two of another.

Boss trips: highest possible three of a kind, which you hope becomes the *boss full*, the highest possible full house.

Bring it in: to make the first optional bet.

Broadway: ace-high straight.

Bully: to use a big stack of chips (instead of strong cards) to intimidate opponents.

Burn and turn: what the dealer does before revealing the flop, fourth street, and fifth street.

Burn card: card from the top of the deck discarded by the dealer before he turns over the board cards.

Busted hand: four-card straight or flush that fails to get completed. Can also mean two pairs or three of a kind that fails to become a full house.

Button: disk that rotates clockwise and indicates which player is the dealer; in games with nonplaying dealers, the *button* indicates which player acts last.

Buy-in: amount of money required to sit in a game or enter a tournament; literally, the chips you buy to put into action.

Call: to match an opponent's bet but not raise.

Calling station: weak player who calls far too often and is therefore almost impossible to bluff.

Case card: the fourth or last card of that rank. "She hit the *case* nine to beat me."

Catch: to receive a card you need to make your hand.

Catch perfect: to receive *exactly* the card you need, such as the four of diamonds to make a straight flush.

Change gears: to suddenly play much less, or much more, aggressively.

Chase: call bets with draws instead of made hands, an especially dangerous tactic in no-limit hold'em.

Check: declining to bet when the action gets to you. (Can only be done when no bets have been made earlier in that round.)

Checkraise: to check when it's your turn to bet, then raise after someone else bets. (A "sneaky" tactic sometimes banned in too-friendly home games.)

Checks: chips, usually the higher denominations.

Chips: clay or plastic disks representing money.

Coffeehousing: table talk, often designed to distract opponents. "Slim *coffeehoused* his way through most of the final table."

Cold: a run of bad cards and losing hands.

Cold-call: to call a raise without having made a bet.

Cold deck: cards presequenced by a cheat to give you the second-best hand.

Come over the top: to reraise, usually with a dramatic number of chips. Also called *playing back* or, simply, *coming*. (Not to be confused with *betting on the come*.)

Connectors: cards of consecutive order, such as 4-5, 5-6, etc.

Court cards: jacks, queens, and kings.

Cowboys: kings.

Crying call: a call with a hand you think has a small chance of winning, or when long pot odds mathematically "force" you to call, especially if you complain while doing so.

Dead card: one no longer in play because of a misdeal or other irregularity.

Dead hand: one no longer in play because you have mucked it, or exposed it too soon, often by accident.

Dead man's hand: aces and eights, named after "Wild Bill" Hickok, who was gunned down from behind on August 2, 1876, while holding it.

Dead money: buy-ins of players with no chance of winning prize money.

Deuce: a two. "The *deuce* of clubs gave me a wheel."

Double belly-buster: a string of five cards, such as 4-6-7-8-10, with two "gaps," either of which can be filled to make a straight. (Gives you the same eight *outs* as an open-ended straight draw but is more easily disguised.)

Doyle Brunson: 10-2 as hole cards. Also, the author of *Super/System* and two-time World Champion, who won both times while holding those cards.

Draw: to have four cards to a straight or a flush, with one or two community cards still to be revealed. "I knew he was on a *draw*, so I reraised all-in with my pair."

Draw dead: to have no chance to make the best hand, even with cards still to come; to draw to a straight, for example, when someone else has already made a full house.

Draw fat: to have many cards still in the deck that would win you the pot; when you have, for example, top pair and both a straight draw and a flush draw, and all you need to beat is two pairs.

Draw out on: to make a big hand on fifth street, defeating a hand that was leading until that point. See *bad beat*; *suck out*.

Draw poker: version of the game in which players are dealt five cards facedown and have the option of replacing up to four of them to make a stronger hand.

Draw thin: to have only one or two cards that would win you the pot.

Ducks: deuces; twos. "With *ducks* on the pond, and two in my hand, I checked."

Family pot: one with several players seeing the flop. Also called *multiway action*. (Much more rare in no-limit than in limit hold'em.)

Fifth street: fifth and final community card. Also known as the *river*.

Fish: weak, often well-funded player; a sucker. If you don't know who it is . . .

Flat-call: to call when a raise is expected. See *slow-play*.

Floorperson: card room official who enforces rules and settles disputes.

Flop: first three community cards, exposed simultaneously. As a verb, to make a strong hand by combining these cards with your pocket cards. "He *flopped* a set of jacks."

Flush: five cards of the same suit.

Fold: to decline to call a bet. Requires that you push your cards into the muck, thereby relinquishing any chance to win (or split) the pot.

Fourth street: fourth community card. Also known as the *turn*.

Four tits: two queens.

Free card: board card you didn't have to call a bet to see. "We'd all checked the flop, so he turned that third seven for *free*."

Freeroll: to compete with other people's money. "After winning a super-satellite, she was *freerolling* in the Big One." Also, when two players have tied hands, such as K-K v. K-K, but a flush draw on the board gives the *freerolling* player with the king of that suit a chance to win the pot. If neither makes a flush, the pot will be split.

Freezeout: tournament without rebuys played until one contestant has all the chips.

Full house: three cards of one rank, two of another.

Get there: to make your hand. "I needed a club on the river to make the nut flush, and I *got there*."

Give action: to call bets against aggressive player(s) with a hand that is not (yet) very strong.

Good game: one that features bad players.

Handcuff: to bet an amount equal to roughly two thirds of your opponent's stack, thus making it impossible for her to make a significant raise.

Heads up: when the action gets down to two players.

Hold'em: poker game in which each player receives two cards facedown, to be combined with five community cards to make the best five-card hand.

Hole cards: your two pocket cards dealt facedown after the blinds have been posted.

Hooks: jacks.

Ignorant end: low end of a straight, often beaten by a higher straight.

Implied pot odds: ratio of the amount of money you expect to win if you make your hand to the size of the bet you must call to continue drawing to it. Can be much larger in no-limit than in limit action.

Inside straight draw: sequence of four connecting cards with a gap in it, such as 8-9-J-Q, which requires a 10 to make a straight. Also called a *belly draw* or *belly-buster draw*.

Jesse James: 4-5 as hole cards, after his Colt .45 sidearm.

Johnnies: jacks.

Kicker: highest side card accompanying a pair, two pairs, or three of a kind; often determines who wins a big pot.

Lay down: to fold a strong hand. "With a four-flush on board, she *laid down* her straight."

Limp: to enter the pot by calling the big blind, not raising. "Four *limpers* got to see the flop."

Little Slick: K-Q suited as hole cards.

Live action: game at a single table played without escalating blinds, as opposed to tournament action. Also called *side action*.

Live one: a weak but well-funded opponent.

Made hand: strong hand, such as a straight or a flush, no longer requiring a card to complete it.

Move: a large bet without a strong hand. "I sensed she was putting a *move* on me, so I reraised all-in. I was wrong."

Move in: to bet all one's chips, usually as a raise or a reraise.

Muck: the scattered pile of previously folded cards facedown in front of the dealer. (Cards touching any part of this pile are *dead*.) As a verb: to push your cards into this pile.

Nit: neurotically conservative or unsociable player; someone who wins a few dollars early and immediately gets up from the table.

No-limit: variety of poker in which players can wager up to all the chips they have in front of them.

Nut, or **the nuts:** highest possible hand given the community cards. If neither a pair nor three-of-a-suit appear on the board, the highest possible straight is *the nuts*. Also known as a *lock* or a *cinch*, or as the *mortal nuts* or *stone cold nuts*.

Off-suit: pocket cards of different suits. Also called *unsuited*.

Off the money: to be eliminated in the last place that does not receive prize money.

Omaha: variety of poker in which players receive four cards facedown, to be combined with five community cards; often played "high-low," in which the high and low hands split the pot.

On the bubble: to be low on chips in one of the last few places before prize money is awarded.

On the come: betting aggressively before your hand is made.

Outs: unseen cards that would complete a winning hand. If you hold four diamonds, for example, the nine other diamonds give you nine *outs* to a flush. "The idiot with two *outs* calls me all-in and knocks me out of the tournament! If he goes on to win it, I'll shave my head!"

Overcard: any card higher than the highest card on the board; or any card on the board higher than the pair in your hand.

Overpair: pocket pair higher than any card on the board.

Over-under: dividing line for bettors, who must choose whether the outcome will exceed or fall short of it. "The *over-under* for the winner's age was forty-nine."

Pip: number or letter on a card, indicating its rank. Also, 3-3 in the hole, after Scottie Pippen, who wore No. 33 for the Chicago Bulls.

Play back: to raise or, especially, reraise.

Play the board: to show down a hand that doesn't improve on the five community cards.

Pocket rockets: A-A in the hole. Also known as *American Airlines, asses, bullets, Fric and Frac, steeples,* and other affectionate monikers.

Position: your place in the clockwise rotation with respect to the dealer. Those first to act are in *early position;* those who act from *later position* have the advantage of knowing whether and how much you've bet. "He had *position* on me, so I folded."

Post: to put your small or large blind (and/or your ante) into the pot before any cards are dealt.

Pot: chips at stake in the center of the table.

Pot limit: structure that prohibits bets larger than the current size of the pot but makes possible very large bets on the later streets. Usually the second-favorite game of no-limit players.

Pot odds: the ratio of the money in the pot to the amount you must put in to remain in the hand.

Put on: to make an educated guess about an opponent's hand. "I'd *put him on* ace-king, so when the flop came with babies, I bet."

Quads: four of a kind. Can only be beaten by higher *quads* or a straight flush.

Rag: small card not helpful to your hand. Also known as a *blank.*

Railbird: chattering spectator.

Rainbow: flop with three different suits.

Raise: to not only match an opponent's bet but increase it by at least 100 percent.

Rake: percentage of each pot or tournament buy-in removed by the house to cover the cost of dealers, chips, food service, security, etc.

Read: to study body language, eyes, or betting patterns to determine the strength of an opponent's hand.

Rebuy: to purchase another set of chips, assuming the tournament's format permits it.

Represent: to pretend with bets and body language to have a particular hand: a flush with three or four hearts on the board, for example.

Reraise: to raise a player who has already raised on that round of betting.

Reverse implied pot odds: ratio of the amount of money you might lose if you don't make your hand to the size of the bet you must call to continue drawing to it.

Ring game: nontournament poker played at one table. Also called *live action*.

River: final community card, also known as *fifth street*. As a verb, to make your hand on that card. "She *rivered* a flush to beat my set of queens." A *river rat* is a player who does this too often, or else a bad card that jumps up and bites you.

Rock: solid, usually conservative player who seldom enters pots with less than A-K or a big pocket pair.

Rounder: professional who plays for high stakes, often traveling widely to find the best games.

Royal: ace-high straight flush, the highest possible hand.

Runner-runner: two consecutive lucky cards on fourth street and fifth street that make someone's hand.

Sandbag: see *slow-play*.

Scare card: a third jack or fourth club on the board, for example, making it much more likely that someone has a very big hand. Often used by bluffers to *represent* a big hand.

See: to call a bet; or to still be in the pot when the *flop*, or *fourth street*, or *fifth street*, is revealed.

Semibluff: to bet or raise with a hand you don't think is the best one at the moment but which has a reasonable chance of improving to the best hand. Also called *bluffing with outs*.

Set: pocket pair that combines with the board to make three of a kind. (Note that a pair on the board matching a third card in your hand is called *trips*. Because only one card of three appears on the board, a *set* is more easily disguised.)

Set in: to bet as much as your opponent has in front of him; to put him all-in.

Set over set: when one set beats a lower set.

Show down: to turn over your pocket cards to compare the strength of your hand with the hands of other players still in the pot. At the *showdown*, after all bets are completed, the best five-card poker hand wins.

Shut out: to force an opponent out of a pot (or "off their hand") with a very large bet.

Side action: nontournament poker. Also called *live action*.

Siegfried and Roy: a pair of queens.

Slow-play: to check or only call an opponent's bet while holding a strong hand, in hopes of winning more money from him on later betting rounds. Also called *sandbagging*.

Small blind: sits one to the left of the dealer and is forced to bet, or post, half of the *big blind*.

Smooth call: a call when a raise is expected. See *slow-play*.

Snap off: to reraise a bluffer.

Spike: to appear unexpectedly on the board, usually making a big hand for your opponent.

Steal: to bet enough chips to cause opponents to fold when your own hand is weak. "She's been *stealing* blinds all afternoon."

Steal-raise: to raise with a weak hand before the flop, hoping to win the antes and blinds.

Steam: to play too aggressively because you are angry. See *tilt*.

Steel wheel: five-high straight flush.

String bet: illegal action that involves going back to your stack in midbet for additional chips. Can be easily avoided by verbally declaring the size of your bet before your hand moves forward.

Stuck: losing money.

Stud: older form of poker played without community cards. In the commonest version, each player receives two cards facedown, four cards faceup, and the final card facedown (called *seven-card stud*). Allows for fewer players than hold'em, and requires a better short-term memory. In *five-card stud*, each player receives one card facedown, four cards faceup.

Suck out: to complete a lucky draw on *fifth street*, especially with a hand you should have folded earlier.

Suited: hole cards of the same suit. Weak players tend to overestimate their added value in no-limit hold'em.

Sweat: to watch a friend play, usually from close behind his shoulder.

Take a card off: to call a bet on the flop, usually with a mediocre hand, hoping to improve on *fourth street*.

Tell: nervous tic or habit that helps opponents read the strength of your hand.

Throw a party: to lose a lot of money, often because of a *tell*.

Tilt, or on tilt: to play badly because you are angry or frustrated. Also called *steaming*.

T.J. Cloutier: the 9-J (not 10-J) of clubs in the hole; author (with Tom McEvoy) of *Championship No-Limit and Pot-Limit Hold'em*.

Torture: to make big bets against an opponent whose hand is clearly beaten, even if it's not clear to him.

Trey: a three.

Trips: three of a kind with one in your hand, two on the board.

Turn: fourth community card, also known as *fourth street*. As a verb, to make one's hand with that card. "He *turned* a set of treys to crush my top two pairs."

Underpair: any pair smaller than at least one card on the board; assumes that someone else has (or may have) paired the higher card.

Under the gun: the player forced to act first; the one sitting to the left of the *big blind* before the flop, to the left of the dealer thereafter.

Up: word following the larger of two pairs when declaring your hand. A player with two kings and two nines has *kings up*. See *aces up*.

Value bet: wager made while holding a strong hand, in hopes of increasing the size of the pot you will win.

Wheel: five-high straight, called a *steel wheel* when all five cards are of the same suit.

Wired: pocket cards of matching rank. "With *wired* cowboys, I came back over the top of her."

Worst of it: having the odds against you. "With only three outs, I was *taking the worst of it*."

BIBLIOGRAPHY

Alson, Peter. "Love and Death in the Desert." *Playboy*, March 2000.

———. *Confessions of an Ivy League Bookmaker.* New York: Crown, 1999.

Alvarez, A. *The Biggest Game in Town.* New York: Houghton Mifflin, 1983.

———. *Poker: Bets, Bluffs, and Bad Beats.* San Francisco: Chronicle, 2001.

———. *The Savage God: A Study of Suicide.* London: Weidenfeld and Nicholson, 1971.

———. *Where Did It All Go Right?* New York: Morrow, 1999.

Auster, Paul. *The Music of Chance.* New York: Viking, 1990.

Baden, Michael, M.D., with Marion Roach. *Dead Reckoning: The New Science of Catching Killers.* New York: Simon and Schuster, 2001.

Baldwin, Bobby. *Tales Out of Tulsa.* New York: Lyle Stuart, 1984.

Berger, Jamie. "Annie Duke, Poker Pro." *Columbia*, Spring 2002.

Bergler, Edmund. *The Psychology of Gambling.* London: [publisher unknown], 1957.

Berlinsky, David. "Iterations of Immortality." *Harper's*, January 2000.

Binion, Benny, and Mary Ellen Glass. *Lester Ben "Benny" Binion: Some Recollections of a Texas and Las Vegas Gaming Operator.* Reno, Nev.: University of Nevada Oral History Program, 1976.

Breger, Louis. *Dostoevsky: The Author as Psychoanalyst.* New York: New York University Press, 1989.

Bruck, Connie. "They Love Me," a profile of Oscar Goodman. *New Yorker,* August 16, 1999.

Brunson, Doyle, with Bobby Baldwin, Mike Caro, Joey Hawthorne, Chip Reese, and David Sklansky. *Super/System: A Course in Power Poker.* Las Vegas, Nev.: B&G, 1978.

Buford, Bill. *Among the Thugs.* New York: Vintage, 1993.

Campbell, Jeremy. *Grammatical Man: Information, Entropy, Language, and Life.* New York: Simon and Schuster, 1982.

Cartwright, Gary. *Dirty Dealing.* New York: Atheneum, 1984.

Clarke, Norm. Various columns in *Las Vegas Review-Journal.*

Clausewitz, Carl von. *On War.* Edited by Anatol Rapoport. London: Penguin, 1968.

Cloutier, T.J. "Tales from T.J." In various issues of *Card Player.*

Cloutier, T.J., with Tom McEvoy and Dana Smith. *Championship Pot-Limit and No-Limit Poker: On the Road to the World Series of Poker.* Las Vegas, Nev.: Cardsmith, 1997.

Costa, Peter. "The Big One," poem in *Poker Pages,* May 20, 2000.

Dabbs, James MacBride, with Mary Godwin Dabbs. *Heroes, Rogues and Lovers: Testosterone and Behavior.* New York: McGraw-Hill, 2000.

Dalla, Nolan. Various columns in *Card Player* and *Poker Digest.*

Dante. *The Inferno.* Translated by Robert Pinsky. New York: Farrar, Straus and Giroux, 1994.

Denton, Sally, and Roger Morris. *The Money and the Power: The Making of Las Vegas and Its Hold on America, 1947–2000.* New York: Knopf, 2001.

Diamond, Jared. *Guns, Germs, and Steel.* New York: Norton, 1997.

———. *Why Is Sex Fun?* New York: Basic Books, 1997.

Doniger, Wendy. *The Bed Trick: Tales of Sex and Masquerade.* Chicago: University of Chicago Press, 2000.

Dostoevsky, Feodor. *Crime and Punishment.* Translated by Richard Pevear and Larissa Volokhonsky. New York: Knopf, 1992.

———. *The Gambler.* Translated by Victor Terras. Chicago: University of Chicago Press, 1972.

———. *Notes from Underground.* Translated by Pevear and Volokhonsky. New York: Knopf, 1993.

Dunn, Stephen. *Riffs and Reciprocities.* New York: Norton, 1998.

———. *Walking Light.* Rochester, N.Y.: BOA Editions, 2001.

Frank, Joseph. *Dostoyevsky: The Miraculous Years, 1865–1871.* Princeton, N.J.: Princeton University Press, 1995.

Garrison, Deborah. Review of *Vox,* by Nicholson Baker. *The New Yorker,* March 9, 1992.

German, Jeff. *Murder in Sin City*. New York: Avon, 2001.

Glazer, Andrew N. S. *Casino Gambling the Smart Way*. Franklin Lakes, N.J.: Career Press, 1999.

———. *Poker Brat*. (In progress.)

———. Various reports in "Wednesday Night Poker" e-newsletter, as well as in *Card Player* and *Poker Digest*.

Goulish, Matthew. *39 Microlectures: In Proximity of Performance*. London: Routledge, 2000.

Hale, Johnny. *Gentleman Gambler: The Life and Times of 'Oklahoma Johnny' Hale on Poker and Las Vegas*. Las Vegas, Nev.: Poker Plus, 1999.

Heims, Steve J. *John von Neumann and Norbert Weiner: From Mathematics to the Technologies of Life and Death*. Cambridge, Mass.: MIT Press, 1981.

Hellmuth, Phil. Various columns in *Card Player* and on philhellmuth.com.

Hemingway, Ernest. *Death in the Afternoon*. New York: Scribners, 1932.

Herrick, Richard, and Lou Krieger. *Poker for Dummies*. Foster City, Calif.: IDG Books, 2000.

Hirsch, Edward. *The Demon and the Angel: Searching for the Source of Artistic Inspiration*. New York: Harcourt, 2002.

Holden, Anthony. *Big Deal: A Year as a Professional Poker Player*. Toronto: McClelland & Stewart, 1990.

Jenkins, Don. *Johnny Moss: Poker's Finest Champion of Champions*. Las Vegas, Nev.: JM Press, 1981.

Johnson, Linda. Various columns in *Card Player*.

Johnson, Linda, with Max Stern, M.D., and Tom McEvoy. *Championship Stud*. Las Vegas, Nev.: Cardsmith, 1998.

Juipe, Dean. Various articles in *Las Vegas Sun*.

Kawabata, Yasunari. *The Master of Go*. Translated by Edward G. Seidensticker. New York: Knopf, 1972.

Koestenbaum, Wayne. *Cleavage: Essays on Sex, Stars, and Aesthetics*. New York: Ballantine, 2000.

Koller, Daphne, and A. J. Pfeffer. "Representations and Solutions for Game-Theoretic Problems." *Artificial Intelligence*, July 1997, 167–215.

Konik, Michael. *The Man with the $100,000 Breasts and Other Gambling Stories*. Las Vegas, Nev.: Huntington Press, 1997.

Krieger, Lou. Various columns in *Poker Digest*.

Land, Barbara, and Myrick Land. *A Short History of Las Vegas*. Reno, Nev.: University of Nevada Press, 1999.

Liebert, Kathy. Various "Techniques for Women" columns on poker pages.com.

Livingston, A. D. *Poker Strategy.* New York: Lyons Press, 1971.

Lukacs, John. "Poker and the American Character," [periodical un-known], 1963.

Malmuth, Mason. *Poker Essays.* Henderson, Nev.: Two Plus Two, 1996.

———. *Gambling Theory.* Henderson, Nev.: Two Plus Two, 1999.

Malmuth, Mason, and David Sklansky. *Hold'em Poker for Advanced Players.* Henderson, Nev.: Two Plus Two, 1999.

Mamet, David. *American Buffalo.* New York: Grove Press, 1977.

———. *Writing in Restaurants.* New York: Viking, 1986.

May, Jesse. *Shut Up and Deal.* New York: Anchor, 1998.

McEvoy, Tom. *Tournament Poker.* Las Vegas, Nev.: Cardsmith, 1995.

Merkin, Daphne. "The Last Taboo." *New York Times Magazine*, December 3, 2000.

Mochulsky, Constantin. *Dostoevsky: His Life and Work.* Translated by Michael A. Minihan. Princeton, N.J.: Princeton University Press, 1967.

Moore, Susanna. *In the Cut.* New York: Knopf, 1995.

Muldoon, Paul. *Hay.* New York: Farrar, Straus and Giroux, 1998.

Murray, Les. *Subhuman Redneck Poems.* New York: Farrar, Straus and Giroux, 1997.

Negreanu, Daniel. Various columns in *Card Player.*

Nichols, George Ward. "Wild Bill." *Harper's*, February 1867.

Nixon, Richard. *RN.* New York: Touchstone, 1990.

Olds, Bruce. *Bucking the Tiger.* New York: Farrar, Straus and Giroux, 2001.

Paulle, Mike. "Snow White Fends Off Seven Dwarves" and other reports on the Binion's home page.

Phillips, Larry W. *Zen and the Art of Poker.* New York: Penguin, 1999.

Pinker, Stephen. *How the Mind Works.* New York: Norton, 1997.

Plath, Sylvia. *Ariel.* New York: Harper & Row, 1965.

Plimpton, George. *Paper Lion.* New York: Harper & Row, 1966.

Preston, Thomas "Amarillo Slim," with Bill G. Cox. *Maverick Poker.* New York: Grosset and Dunlap, 1973.

Rhodes, Richard. *The Making of the Atomic Bomb.* New York: Touchstone, 1995.

Rodrick, Stephen. "Snake Eyes." *GQ*, December 1999.

Rosenthal, Margaret F. *The Honest Courtesan: Veronica Franco, Citizen and Writer in Sixteenth-Century Venice.* Chicago: University of Chicago Press, 1992.

Ruchman, Peter. Various issues of *Gamblers Book Club Digest.*

———. *After the Gold Rush.* (In progress.)

Scott, Cathy. *Death in the Desert: The Ted Binion Homicide Case*. Las Vegas, Nev.: First Books, 2000.

Sedaris, David. *Do You Know What Time It Is?* (Artist book, 1986).

———. *Me Talk Pretty One Day*. New York: Little, Brown, 2000.

Sexton, Mike. Various columns in *Card Player*.

Sklansky, David. *Hold'em Poker*. Henderson, Nev.: Two Plus Two, 1976.

———. *Poker, Gaming & Life*. Henderson, Nev.: Two Plus Two, 1997.

———. *The Theory of Poker*. Henderson, Nev.: Two Plus Two, 1994.

———. *Tournament Poker for Advanced Players*. Henderson, Nev.: Two Plus Two, 2002.

Sklansky, David, and Mason Malmuth. *Hold'em Poker for Advanced Players*. Henderson, Nev.: Two Plus Two, 1999.

Smith, Dana. Interview with "Amarillo Slim" Preston. *Card Player*, December 21, 2000.

Smith, John L. *Quicksilver: The Ted Binion Murder Case*. With photographs by Jeff Scheid. Las Vegas, Nev.: Huntington Press, 2001.

Spanier, David. *Total Poker*. London: Secker and Warburg, 1977.

———. *The Little Book of Poker*. Las Vegas, Nev.: Huntington Press, 2000.

Stimson, Henry. "The Decision to Use the Atomic Bomb." *Harper's*, February 1947.

Sun Tzu. *The Art of War*. Translated by Thomas Cleary. Boston and London: Shambhala, 1998.

Thompson, Hunter S. *Fear and Loathing in Las Vegas*. New York: Random House, 1971.

Wheeler, Susan. *Smokes*. Marshfield, Mass.: Four Way Books, 1998.

Willis, Stacy. Various articles in *Las Vegas Sun*.

Wills, Garry. *Saint Augustine*. New York: Viking, 1999.

Wilson, A. N. *Tolstoy: A Biography*. New York: Norton, 1988.

Wilson, Edward O. *Consilience*. New York: Knopf, 1998.

———. *On Human Nature*. Cambridge, Mass.: Harvard University Press, 1978.

———. *Sociobiology: The New Synthesis*. Cambridge, Mass.: Harvard University Press, 1975 and 2000.

Yardley, Herbert O. *The Education of a Poker Player*. Athens, Ga.: Orloff Press, 1957.

♣ ♥

ACKNOWLEDGMENTS

♦ ♠

Lewis Lapham, Ben Metcalf, and Ann Kyle Gollin got this project off the ground, changing my life even more than their other encouragements have. Colin Harrison muscled the *Harper's* article into shape and helped me think more clearly about larger erotic concerns. My agent, Sloan Harris, chopped, channeled, chiseled, and cheered it along from the outset, as did his assistants Teri Steinberg and Katharine Cluverius. Jonathan Galassi, James Wilson, Susan Mitchell, and Anne Nolan at Farrar, Straus and Giroux have made the book better in hundreds of ways, large and small. For their insight on individual chapters, I also thank Alison True at *The Reader*, Jennifer Schuessler at the *Boston Globe*, and David Bonanno and Elizabeth Scanlon at *American Poetry Review*.

Paul Ashley, Carol Becker, Beth Wright, and Jana Wright, my bosses at SAIC, provided me with an early sabbatical to finish the project; Beth Nugent, my fifth boss, also threw in a lucky penny. Paul Ashley, Peter Brown, Linda Johnson, Katy Lederer, Ellen McManus, George Roeder, and Scott Turow read early drafts and made some enormously helpful suggestions.

Melissa Hayden provided deep poker insight and high Vegas art. Tom Sexton's wonderful photographs helped me write the first draft and fact-check the final one. Other folks from the tournament circuit who've provided good counsel and camaraderie—there are simply too many to name.

Among them, however, are Peter Alson, Benny and Jack and Nick and Becky Behnen, Chris Bigler, Humberto Brenes, Joy and T.J. Cloutier, Nolan Dalla, Bob and Maureen Feduniak, Chris Ferguson, Ken Flaton, Jack Fox, Andy Glazer, Hasan Habib, Jennifer Harman and Marco Traniello, Dan Harrington, Ken and Tom Jacobs, "Rockford Jim" Kasputis, Rabbi Steve Kaufman, Kathy Liebert, Tony Ma, Mansour Matloubi, Jesse May, Jack McClelland, Tom McEvoy, Mark and Tina Napolitano, Daniel Negreanu, Padraig Parkinson, David Plastik, Slim Preston, Q, Erik Seidel, Mike Sexton, Barry and Jeff Shulman, David Sklansky, Richard Tatalovich, Harry and Jerri Thomas, Amir Vahedi, Jason Viriyayuthakorn, and Dewey Weum. I've also learned plenty from my friends and opponents in the Thursday night game: Andrew, Bea, Hank, Kenilworth Ken, K-Rex, Mel, Molly, Norm, and the pilots.

And, always, Jennifer.

INDEX

Page references in *italics* refer to illustrations.